GRADE 5

Scaffolded Strategies
HANDBOOK

Glenview, Illinois • Boston, Massachusetts • Chandler, Arizona • Upper Saddle River, New Jersey

Table of Contents

Part 1 Unlock the Text

Table of Contents

Part 2 Unlock the Writing

Scaffolded Lessons for the Performance-Based Assessments

Scaffolded Lessons for the Writing Types

Part 3 Routines and Activities

Reading Routines

Writing Routines

Table of Contents

Part 4 Unlock Language Learning

Anchor Text, Supporting Text, and Writing

Language Routines and Resources

Acknowledgments

About This Book

What is the Scaffolded Strategies Handbook?

The *Scaffolded Strategies Handbook* is a valuable resource that provides support at the module level for all learners. As part of an integrated reading and writing program, this handbook works in tandem with each unit of the *ReadyGEN™ Teacher's Guide* to help you guide students as they read and write about the texts within each module. It provides models of scaffolded instruction, useful strategies, and practical routines that you can employ during reading and writing to support

- English language learners
- struggling readers
- students with disabilities
- accelerated learners

It is intended that these lessons be used during small-group time with students that you determine need additional scaffolded instruction for any of the ReadyGEN texts or writing activities. Refer to this handbook during planning to determine which lessons will provide the most focused scaffolds for your students. You may use any or all of the lessons or lesson parts as dictated by the needs of your students. Keep in mind that this handbook is meant not only for the classroom teacher, but can be used by any support person working with the diverse student population in your school.

Using the Scaffolded Strategies Handbook

Part 1 Unlock the Text

Within Part 1 of this handbook, titled Unlock the Text, every anchor and supporting text in the ReadyGEN program is supported by research-proven scaffolds and strategies. Each lesson is divided into three parts:

- **Prepare to Read** This portion of the lesson provides more intensive readiness before reading. Students preview the text, activate background knowledge, and are introduced to troublesome vocabulary.

- **Interact with Text** Here, students do close reading and focus on stumbling blocks in the text.

- **Express and Extend** This section allows students to react to the text by discussing and writing about their ideas.

With every student text, qualitative measures of text complexity, such as those determined by the Common Core Learning Standards, are identified:

- Levels of Meaning
- Structure
- Language Conventionality and Clarity
- Knowledge Demands

Each of the three lesson parts is divided to address all of these qualitative measures. These become customized access points for your specific student populations, allowing all students to access and make sense of complex texts.

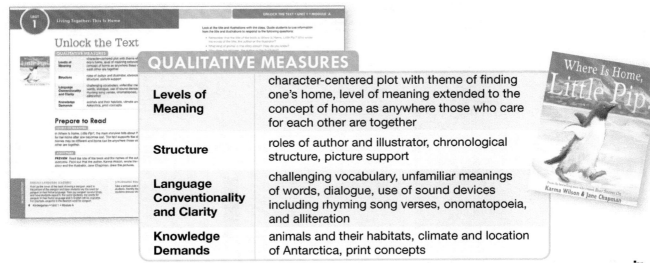

QUALITATIVE MEASURES

Levels of Meaning	character-centered plot with theme of finding one's home, level of meaning extended to the concept of home as anywhere those who care for each other are together
Structure	roles of author and illustrator, chronological structure, picture support
Language Conventionality and Clarity	challenging vocabulary, unfamiliar meanings of words, dialogue, use of sound devices including rhyming song verses, onomatopoeia, and alliteration
Knowledge Demands	animals and their habitats, climate and location of Antarctica, print concepts

Part 2 Unlock the Writing

Part 2 of this handbook, titled Unlock the Writing, features two types of scaffolded writing lessons.

First, there are scaffolded lessons for each of the module-level Performance-Based Assessments in the core Teacher's Guide. Each lesson in the handbook walks students through the Performance-Based Assessment for that module, providing guidance with unlocking the task, breaking it apart, thinking through the process, and then evaluating their writing.

Next, there are scaffolded writing lessons that provide grade-appropriate support and guidelines for teaching each of the writing types required by the Common Core Learning Standards:

- Opinion Writing
- Informative/Explanatory Writing
- Narrative Writing

Each of these three lessons is divided into the tasks specific to the writing type. Instructional support is provided to help you introduce and model each task so that students will better understand the writing type and how to become proficient writers of each. There are ample opportunities for practice, including robust Deeper Practice activities.

As in Part 1, Unlock the Text lessons, the Unlock the Writing lessons provide specific scaffolded "notes" to support English language learners as well as both struggling and accelerated writers.

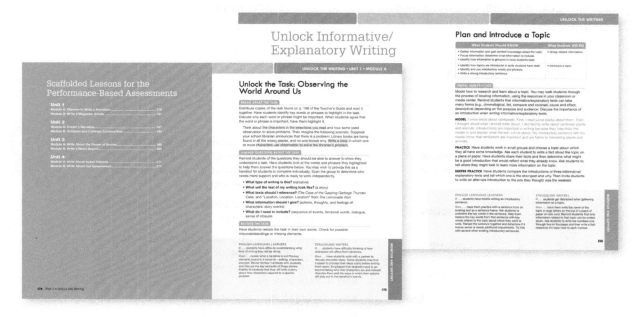

Part 3 Routines and Activities

Part 3 of the *Scaffolded Strategies Handbook* is a collection of routines and reproducible graphic organizers as well as engaging activities that you can use for support as you teach English Language Arts skills and address the Common Core Learning Standards. When appropriate, specific routines and activities are suggested and referred to in the lessons in Part 1 of this handbook.

You will find routines, many with accompanying graphic organizers, for teaching skills in

- Reading
- Writing
- Listening and Speaking
- Language, including Vocabulary and Conventions

Part 3 also contains a variety of activities that provide extra scaffolded practice and instruction for language skills and vocabulary development, such as

- Noun and Pronoun Activities
- Verb Activities
- Adjective and Adverb Activities
- Sentence Activities
- Punctuation Activities
- Word Study Activities
- Vocabulary Activities and Games

This section of the handbook will be useful at any time during your teaching day. As you become familiar with the routines, graphic organizers, and activities, feel free to use them whenever they fit the needs of your students. Think of this section as a toolbox of ideas and suggestions to use with your struggling readers and writers. Turn to it often.

Part 4 Unlock Language Learning

Part 4 of the *Scaffolded Strategies Handbook* provides additional instruction for each Anchor Text selection and for each Supporting Text selection in the ReadyGEN program. Use these lessons to help English language learners construct meaning in the selections and explore vocabulary in order to develop mastery of reading, writing, and speaking.

Part 4 scaffolded support includes:

- **Build Background** Students explore important information needed to comprehend and enjoy each selection. Student pages provide practice and stimulate conversation.

- **Talk About Sentences** Students discover how good sentences are constructed. They learn to access key ideas by understanding the relationships between words and phrases in sentences.

- **Speak and Write About the Text** Students build academic language skills by asking and answering critical questions. Writing frames support students' development as they express ideas in specific writing modes.

- **Expand Understanding of Vocabulary** Students discover the generative nature of vocabulary and develop a curiosity about language as they gain an understanding of how words function in sentences.

- **Writing** Students benefit from extra scaffolding, including a student model, as they work toward addressing the Performance-Based Assessment writing prompt.

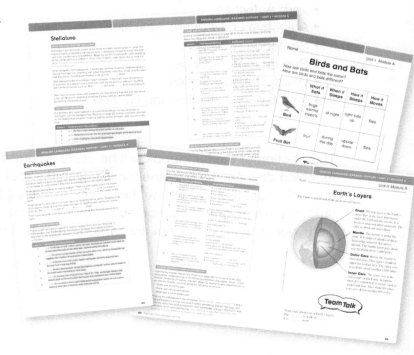

The following **Part 4** Routines provide English language learners with additional scaffolded instruction in reading, speaking, and listening.

- Dig Deeper Vocabulary
- Sentence Talk
- Clarifying Key Details
- Clarifying Information
- Have a Discussion
- Reach a Consensus
- Text-Based Writing

PART 1

Unlock the Text

Depending on Each Other

TEXT SET

ANCHOR TEXT
Night of the Spadefoot
Toads

SUPPORTING TEXT
Shells

SUPPORTING TEXT
Hatchet

TEXT SET

ANCHOR TEXT
Washed Up!

SUPPORTING TEXT
Rain Forest Food
Chains

SUPPORTING TEXT
Pale Male: Citizen Hawk
of New York City

Cognates

Cognates are words that have similar spellings and meanings in two or more languages. Many words in English and Spanish share Greek or Latin roots, and many words in English came from French, which is closely connected to Spanish (and to Portuguese, Italian, and Romanian). Because of this, many literary, content, and academic process words in English (e.g., *gracious/gracioso; volcano/volcán; compare/comparar*) have recognizable Spanish cognates.

Making the connection to cognates permits students who are native Spanish speakers to understand the strong foundation they have in academic and literary English. These links between English and Spanish are also useful for native speakers of English and other languages because they help uncover basic underlying features of our language.

ANCHOR TEXT Night of the Spadefoot Toads

ENGLISH	SPANISH	ENGLISH	SPANISH
amphibians	anfibios	information	información
appreciate	apreciar	insignia	insignia
attention	atención	interested	interesado
bandit	bandido	interrupt	interrumpir
biology	biología	invitation	invitación
class	clase	methodically	metódicamente
complicated	complicado	minute	minuto
conversation	conversación	moment	momento
creature	criatura	nervous	nervioso
desert	desierto	nocturnal	nocturno
difference	diferencia	papers	papeles
disappear	desaparecer	particular	particular
emergency	emergencia	person	persona
encounter	encuentro	progress	progreso
exhale	exhalar	pronounce	pronunciar
expedition	expedición	property	propiedad
experiment	experimento	rare	raro
explore	explorar	science	ciencia
frantic	frenético	secret	secreto
garage	garaje	sound	sonido
geography	geografía	species	especies
hysterical	histérico	specimen	espécimen
idea	idea	stomach	estómago
illegal	ilegal	terrarium	terrario
important	importante	toxic	tóxico
impress	impresionar	vigorous	vigoroso

SUPPORTING TEXT Shells

ENGLISH	SPANISH	ENGLISH	SPANISH
attraction	atracción	loyal	leal
condominium	condominio	perfectly	perfectamente
different	diferente	phenomenon	fenómeno
distinguish	distinguir	residents	residentes
dramatic	dramático	tank	tanque
family	familia		

SUPPORTING TEXT Hatchet

ENGLISH	SPANISH	ENGLISH	SPANISH
animal	animal	granite	granito
breeze	brisa	immediately	inmediatamente
brilliant	brillante	intense	intenso
cave	cueva	muscles	músculos
depression	depresión	oxygen	oxígeno
dozens	docenas	rocks	rocas
fluid	fluido	terror	terror
frustration	frustración		

These lists contain many, but not all, Spanish cognates from these selections.

Unlock the Text

QUALITATIVE MEASURES

Levels of Meaning	realistic fiction; relationships and friendship; new experiences; changes
Structure	straightforward chronological structure; foreshadowing and building suspense; chapters divided into sections; change in text font to represent thought and spoken dialogue
Language Conventionality and Clarity	informal language in dialogue between characters; idioms; scientific and technical vocabulary
Knowledge Demands	ecology and environmental science; adaptation; habitat preservation

Prepare to Read

LEVELS OF MEANING

In *Night of the Spadefoot Toads*, there are two levels of meaning. One purpose of the text is to tell an explicit story about a child discovering and protecting a habitat, and the other is to explore themes about relationships, friendship, loneliness, and honesty.

STRUCTURE

PREVIEW Form small groups, and have students look through the book to get an idea of the structure. Ask questions such as:

- How is the book divided? (It is divided into chapters; chapters are divided into sections separated by frog icons. There are no specific chapter titles.)

ENGLISH LANGUAGE LEARNERS

Help students expand their understanding of critical vocabulary by sharing sentences, definitions, and pictures that demonstrate their meanings. Use the Act Out or Draw Meaning Routine in Part 3 for ideas to provide more visual support for the scientific and technical vocabulary.

STRUGGLING READERS

To reinforce learning, have students define vocabulary words in their own words, and then create a sentence using the word to demonstrate understanding.

MORE SUPPORT

- Read the italicized text on page 14. What information about the story does the text give you? Why is the information in italics? (The characters will be studying the environment, a habitat, and an animal or animals. The information is in italics because it is an assignment sheet from the teacher.)
- Read the book title, and look at the cover illustration. Read the back of the book. What do you think the book will be about? (A child discovers a toad and has outdoor adventures.)

LANGUAGE CONVENTIONALITY AND CLARITY

PREVIEW VOCABULARY Use the Preview and Review Vocabulary Routine in Part 3 to assess what students know about terms such as *habitat, vernal pool, spadefoot toads, ecosystem, spring peeper, species, camouflaged, salamanders, herpetologist, amphibians, warm-blooded, cold-blooded, terrarium,* and *endangered.*

COGNATES Use the Analyze Cognates Routine and Graphic Organizer in Part 3 to teach students how to recognize cognates and to use their knowledge of cognates to understand new words. For your Spanish-speaking students, use the list of Spanish cognates for each selection at the beginning of this module as a reference.

KNOWLEDGE DEMANDS

ACTIVATE BACKGROUND KNOWLEDGE Use the Quick Write and Share Routine in Part 3 to assess what students already know about adapting. Ask questions such as: What does it mean to adapt? How do animals adapt to a new environment? How do people adapt?

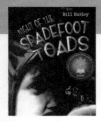

Interact with Text

As you read *Night of the Spadefoot Toads,* periodically stop to assess students' level of understanding of the characters and their relationships with each other.

If . . . students have difficulty keeping track of the characters in the first few chapters,

then . . . have students use the Web Graphic Organizer in Part 3. Put Ben's name in the middle circle, since he is the main character. Students can write other character names in each outer circle. Along the line of each spoke, students can write how that character is related to Ben (is his science teacher, is a classmate who teases him, is a possible new friend, and so on).

Point out that characters go by different names. For example, in Chapter 1, Tommy Miller and Dennis Dimeo are alternately called by their full names and their first names.

STRUCTURE

As students read, periodically stop to assess their understanding of how spoken and thought dialogue are differentiated in the text.

If . . . students have difficulty differentiating dialogue from the main character's thoughts,

then . . . point out to students that dialogue between characters is surrounded by quotation marks, while Ben's internal thoughts are shown in the text or in italics.

For example, have students read p. 9. Have them find an example of Ben's thoughts being described without italics. (He wonders if Mrs. Tibbets walked to school.) Then have them find an example of Ben's thoughts being described in italics on the same page. ("Mrs. Kutchner has fingernail polish on her fingernails.")

ENGLISH LANGUAGE LEARNERS

Encourage students to ask clarifying questions when they do not understand something. Display a list of question starters such as: I don't understand ___. Why did ___happen? What does ___ mean?

STRUGGLING READERS

Repeated readings make it significantly easier for students to understand key events. Have students work in pairs. As one student reads, the other student writes a question about the text. Then have students switch roles. Discuss questions as a class.

LANGUAGE CONVENTIONALITY AND CLARITY

While the language of the story is direct and can be understood on a literal level, much of the dialogue uses idioms, expressions, and phrasal verbs. Assess students' level of understanding of figurative language by asking them to restate the expressions in their own words.

If . . . students have difficulty with a term containing idioms, expressions, or phrasal verbs,

then . . . define the term for students by relating it to something they may be familiar with or by acting it out.

Point out the following example of figurative language on p. 12: "[the rain is] making the puddles on the playground dance," Show students a shallow bowl of water. Add drops of water to the bowl and have students describe what happens to the water in the bowl. Point out that the water moves. Discuss how the moving water resembles dance movements.

Use the Analyze Idioms and Expressions Routine in Part 3 for other phrases that may be difficult for students, such as *a human noise machine, to drive crazy, patrols the aisles* (Chapter 1); *buried in a book, a book sponge* (Chapter 2); *wolfs it down, jumps out of his skin* (Chapter 3); *in hot water, dies down* (Chapter 4).

KNOWLEDGE DEMANDS

Engage students in a discussion about habitat preservation. Ask: Why do you think the characters in this book want to save the spadefoot toads' habitat? (They want to protect the toads' home because without a home, the toads may have to go somewhere else or could even die. The characters think the toads are special and they want to save them.) Ask: Why is Tabitha Turner's property so important for the spadefoot toads? (The vernal pools located on her land are the habitat for the spadefoot toads.)

If . . . students have difficulty understanding why Tabitha Turner's property is so important for the spadefoot toads,

then . . . use the Cause and Effect Routine and Graphic Organizer in Part 3 to demonstrate what could happen to the spadefoot toads if the land is sold.

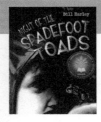

Express and Extend

EXPRESS Have pairs of students work together to show their understanding of the central themes of friendship and relationships. Have them tell how Ben changes over the course of the story from having a close friendship with Toby to developing friendships with Ryan, Jenny, and Mrs. Tibbets. (At first he calls and e-mails Toby often and is not interested in making new friends in Massachusetts, but later he becomes close friends with Ryan, Jenny, and Mrs. Tibbets.)

If . . . students have difficulty summarizing the story,

then . . . use the Retell or Summarize Routine and Graphic Organizer in Part 3.

EXTEND Have students pretend they are Ben, and have them write an e-mail to Toby describing Mrs. Tibbets, Ryan, or Jenny. In the e-mail, have students tell how they met their new friend and what activities they do together.

EXPRESS Have small groups discuss how the author uses suspense to make students wonder how the story ends. Have them create a short list of questions that they had.

If . . . students have difficulty generating questions about the story,

then . . . display sentence frames to guide questions. For example: After I read Chapter ___, I wondered if ___. Would Mrs. Tibbets ___? Would Ben ___? What would ___ do about ___?

EXTEND Have small groups prepare posters that summarize the suspenseful points and include answers to their questions. Encourage students to use vocabulary words from the story in their posters.

MORE SUPPORT

ENGLISH LANGUAGE LEARNERS

When reading fiction, students can draw pictures of characters with thought bubbles to keep track of how the characters' feelings change. For instance, a picture of Ben from Chapter 1 might have a thought bubble that reads, "I feel angry because I did not want to move."

STRUGGLING READERS

If students have difficulty completing an activity, then model breaking down the steps. For example, model finding the most important event from the first six chapters, then from the next six chapters, and finally from the last six chapters.

EXPRESS Talk about Sentences and Words

Display the following passage from *Night of the Spadefoot Toads*. Read it aloud with students, and discuss the sentences.

> Ryan lifts it [a mouse] up in the air like it's a trophy or something. "I've got it!" he shrieks. "It's squirmy!"
> "Well, duh," Frankie sneers.
> "Well, duh," three other boys echo.

Ask: What is going on in this scene? What does the word *squirmy* mean? How is the mouse like a trophy? What informal phrases are used in the dialogue? Why does the author use informal language?

TEAM TALK The author writes in a way similar to how schoolchildren talk. Have partners add the next few lines of dialogue, keeping the same tone and use of informal language.

> If . . . students need more support with understanding verb tenses,
> then . . . use the Verbs in Present Tense Activity in Part 3.

EXTEND Have students use dialogue, slang, and present verb tense to write a description of an event in their own classroom.

KNOWLEDGE DEMANDS

EXPRESS Have students write a one-paragraph description of a vernal pool using their five senses (sight, sound, smell, touch, taste).

> If . . . students have difficulty writing a descriptive paragraph,
> then . . . use the Description: Sensory Details Routine and Graphic Organizer in Part 3.

EXTEND Give students an example of a local environmental issue, and have them write a letter to the local government, telling why this problem needs to be solved. Have students use sensory details in their letter.

ACCELERATED LEARNERS

Have small groups of students use the resources referenced in the Author's Note to research vernal pools. Have them prepare a public service announcement that shares the information they learned and explains how people can help.

MORE SUPPORT

Unlock the Text

QUALITATIVE MEASURES

Levels of Meaning	coping with loss; comparison between animals and people
Structure	chronological structure; dialogue; illustrations; text treatment
Language Conventionality and Clarity	imagery; informal language; comparisons
Knowledge Demands	character details and interactions; making predictions and inferences

Shells, pp. 4–11

Prepare to Read

LEVELS OF MEANING

The explicit purpose of "Shells" is to show how a boy and his aunt learn to live with each other after the death of the boy's parents. The text also has implicit concepts such as comparisons between animals and people, and it includes inference-heavy text.

STRUCTURE

PREVIEW Form small groups and have students read the book title, view the picture on p. 4, and then read the text on the page. Afterward, have students discuss the following questions. Make sure students refer to the text and illustrations when answering the questions.

MORE SUPPORT

ENGLISH LANGUAGE LEARNERS

Students may need help understanding expressions such as *scrape a chair* and *slam a glass* or why a person *could not imagine* something. Help students understand by showing differences between the literal and figurative word meanings.

STRUGGLING READERS

Give small groups of students a vocabulary word. Then, assign a job to each member in the group. Students can choose to create a word web, draw a picture of the word, or write three synonyms or antonyms for the word. Have groups share their work with the class.

- Where does the first scene take place? How do you know? (It takes place in a kitchen; Michael is sitting at a table drinking milk and Aunt Esther is washing dishes. The illustration shows a boy and a woman in a kitchen.)
- On the first page, notice that the words *hate* and *you* are in italics. Why do you think the author wrote these words this way? (The author wants to show that the character is emphasizing those words or saying them with more emotion.)
- This story is called "Shells." What kinds of shells do you think this story will be about? (the shells of sea creatures; shells, in a figurative sense, as in "coming out of your shell" or a literal sense as in "a place to hide")

LANGUAGE CONVENTIONALITY AND CLARITY

PREVIEW VOCABULARY Use the Preview and Review Vocabulary Routine in Part 3 to assess what students know about the following words: *gawked, condominium, residents, talc, prejudiced, distinguished, peering, attraction, intrude, craned, inherit, stupor,* and *Founding Father.*

COGNATES Use the list of Spanish cognates at the beginning of this module to guide your Spanish-speaking students as they read the selection.

KNOWLEDGE DEMANDS

ACTIVATE BACKGROUND KNOWLEDGE Give each student a slip of paper with one of the following sentences:

- "He slammed down the glass, scraped his chair back from the table and ran out the door."
- "Michael's other relatives could not imagine dealing with a fourteen-year-old boy. They wanted peaceful lives."

Ask students to think about the literal meaning of their sentence and then make an inference about it. Then have students walk around the room and find a student who has a paper with the other sentence. When students meet, they should each read aloud the sentence on their paper, share what they think it means, and discuss how the two sentences might work together in the story. Afterward, display the sentences, and have students work in groups to predict what the story is about. Use the Story Prediction Routine and Graphic Organizer in Part 3 to help students record predictions.

STRUGGLING READERS

Students may have trouble making inferences about text they are struggling to understand. Provide them with thought starters to help with making inferences. For example, you might ask: Based on the words *slammed, scraped,* and *ran,* how do you think Michael feels? Why would he feel that way? How do you think Michael's feelings will affect the story's events?

Interact with Text

LEVELS OF MEANING

As you read "Shells," periodically stop to assess students' level of understanding of the relationships between characters in the story. Have them compare the characters of Michael and Aunt Esther, and then compare Michael and Sluggo.

> If . . . students have difficulty understanding why Michael and Aunt Esther have a difficult relationship at the beginning of the story,
>
> then . . . use the Venn Diagram Routine and Graphic Organizer in Part 3 to compare and contrast the two characters.

Have students reread the text to find differences. For example, point out that Michael is fourteen, while Aunt Esther is much older. Michael also dislikes that Aunt Esther is very different from his parents.

> If . . . students have difficulty understanding the comparison between the hermit crab and Michael,
>
> then . . . have students use a T-chart to compare how Michael and Sluggo react to Aunt Esther. They should list specific behaviors of Michael and Sluggo and then see if there are any similarities in their behavior.

STRUCTURE

As students read, periodically stop to assess their understanding of the story's plot. Ask students what happens in the beginning, middle, and end of the story.

> If . . . students have difficulty with the story's sequence of events,
>
> then . . . use the Sequence of Events Routine and Graphic Organizer in Part 3 to help students determine the order in which the story events take place.

Ask students to describe how the illustrations contribute to their understanding of what's going on in the story. (The illustrations help to show plot events, and the images of Michael give me an idea of how he is feeling.) Have students use evidence from the text to provide an example.

ENGLISH LANGUAGE LEARNERS

To help students make comparisons between characters in "Shells," provide phrases students can use when making comparisons, such as *like, similar to, same as,* or *different from.*

STRUGGLING READERS

Have students strengthen their understanding and fluency through repeated readings of a passage. Have pairs work together to practice reading dialogue. Have students take turns acting and speaking the roles.

LANGUAGE CONVENTIONALITY AND CLARITY

While the use of descriptive imagery and figurative language in "Shells" makes it interesting to read, it can confuse the meaning of the story for some students. Assess students' level of understanding of imagery and figurative language by asking them to restate the expressions in their own words.

If . . . students have difficulty with imagery or figurative language,

then . . . reread the passage and ask students to think about the feelings and ideas specific imagery evokes. For sentences using figurative language, use the Analyze Idioms and Expressions Routine in Part 3 to provide additional support.

Read the following excerpt from the story and ask students to think of a word to describe the way Esther dresses. Then, reread the text, and ask students why these things might embarrass Michael: Esther was so dramatic. . . her bangle bracelets clanking, earrings swinging, red pumps clicking on the linoleum—that she attracted the attention of everyone in the store.

Other descriptions that may be difficult for students are: "He said it dully, sliding his milk glass back and forth on the table" and "Esther grabbed the rim of the tank and craned her neck over the side."

KNOWLEDGE DEMANDS

Ask students how Michael and Aunt Esther's relationship changes over the course of the story.

If . . . students have difficulty understanding the evolving relationship between Esther and Michael,

then . . . have students reread key passages that show how their interactions change.

For example, they could read p. 4, p. 6 (the last paragraph), p. 8 (the dialogue in Michael's bedroom), or pp. 9–10. For each page or passage, have students write a sentence to describe the relationship between Michael and Aunt Esther. They should choose one phrase or sentence to support their response. If reviewing the entire story, have students describe how the characters' relationship differs from one part of the story to the next.

Discuss with students why they think Michael and Aunt Esther are having a hard time living together. Lead them to understand that Michael is going through a difficult time because of the loss of his parents, and he is taking out his sad feelings on Aunt Esther.

ENGLISH LANGUAGE LEARNERS

Help students engage with the text by stopping at certain pivotal points in the story to make predictions. For example, after reading "One day after school Michael came home with a hermit crab," stop and ask questions such as: What will Michael do with a hermit crab? How will having a pet change the way Michael acts? How will it affect his relationship with Aunt Esther?

MORE SUPPORT

Express and Extend

EXPRESS Have students work in pairs. Have one student select parts in the text that show how Michael changes, while the other student chooses parts in the text that show how Sluggo changes. Afterward, have them work together to write a paragraph showing how Michael's transformation is similar to Sluggo's transformation.

> If . . . students have difficulty writing about how Michael and Sluggo changed,
>
> then . . . have them use a T-chart to organize examples from the text. One column should be labeled *How Sluggo Changes,* and the other *How Michael Changes*.

EXTEND Have pairs choose scenes in "Shells" to show their understanding of the relationship between Michael and Aunt Esther. Tell them to choose scenes that represent the difficult relationship the characters have, the moment when they begin to open up to each other, and the moment when they finally accept one another. Have them then share the scenes they chose with the class and explain why they chose the three scenes. Have students cite evidence from the text to support their choices.

EXPRESS Have pairs of students use the Retell or Summarize Graphic Organizer in Part 3 to help them summarize in their own words or to help them verbally retell the story.

> If . . . students have difficulty summarizing the story,
>
> then . . . use the Sequence of Events Routine and Graphic Organizer in Part 3 to help students summarize using the most important details from the story.

EXTEND Have small groups write their own story with a plot that is similar to "Shells." Provide students with prompts (for example, two people who don't like each other must work together to finish a project) to help them get started. Encourage students to use vocabulary words from "Shells" in their stories.

ENGLISH LANGUAGE LEARNERS

Have students create visual representations of Michael and Aunt Esther's relationship or the transformation of Michael and Sluggo as part of the Express activities or discussion. Their pictures can serve as an aid as they work.

STRUGGLING READERS

Keep copies of commonly used graphic organizers in a visible area of the classroom, and encourage students to use them when they have difficulty comprehending the text. This will help students support their own learning.

LANGUAGE CONVENTIONALITY AND CLARITY

EXPRESS Talk about Sentences and Words

Display the following sentence from "Shells." Read it aloud with students, and discuss the sentence.

> Michael, in a stupor over his Aunt Esther and the phenomenon of twenty-one hermit crabs, wiped out the tank, arranged it with gravel and sticks (as well as the plastic scuba diver Aunt Esther insisted on buying) and assisted her in loading it up, one by one, with the new residents.

Ask: What is being described? (Michael's process of setting up a new tank for his hermit crabs) What does it mean to be *in a stupor*? (Michael doesn't feel awake; he doesn't fully understand what is going on.) What other words could the author have used? (*in a daze, half asleep*) What is a *phenomenon*? Why does the narrator consider this situation a *phenomenon*? (A phenomenon can be a rare event, such as the situation Michael finds himself in.)

TEAM TALK Have students turn to a partner and rewrite the sentence using new words but keeping the same meaning.

Michael, ___ over his Aunt Esther and the ___ of twenty-one hermit crabs . . .

If . . . students need more support with understanding the language,

then . . . have them define a term in their own words and create a word web. If students have access to a thesaurus, they can use that as a resource as long as they can say what their chosen word means.

EXTEND Have students use descriptive language to describe another scene in the story, using their own words.

KNOWLEDGE DEMANDS

EXPRESS Have small groups make a word web for Michael and Aunt Esther. To create the web, they should go through the text and select words and phrases that best describe each character. Afterward, have them write a paragraph to describe the characters. Offer sentence starters to students who struggle with writing.

EXTEND Have the same small groups each act out a scene they think best demonstrates the traits or behavior of each character.

ACCELERATED LEARNERS

Have students write an afterword that describes what Michael's life is like a month after the end of the story. In the paragraph, students should address either how Michael is changing to fit his new home or how he and Aunt Esther are getting along.

MORE SUPPORT

Unlock the Text

QUALITATIVE MEASURES

Levels of Meaning	understanding realistic fiction; survival stories; character development and traits; summarizing
Structure	introductory note; conventional structure; text features; sequence of events; character motivation
Language Conventionality and Clarity	use of enlarged text for emphasis; figurative language; determining sentence meaning
Knowledge Demands	the idea of the wilderness; building a fire; finding solutions to problems

Hatchet, pp. 12–25

Prepare to Read

LEVELS OF MEANING

One purpose of *Hatchet* is to tell a fictional story about a boy who is trying to survive alone in the wilderness with only a hatchet. The other is to illustrate the boy's character and show traits that will help him survive.

STRUCTURE

PREVIEW Form small groups, and have students read the title page and the headnote on p. 14, look at the photographs, read the enlarged text, and try to predict what challenges Brian will face. Ask:

- What is the purpose of the headnote? (It explains what happened previously in this novel. This selection is one chapter of the novel.)

MORE SUPPORT

ENGLISH LANGUAGE LEARNERS

The concept of wilderness may be difficult for ELL students. Explain the term and show pictures of wilderness areas. Ask: What do you know about camping or hiking in the wilderness? What supplies would you need?

STRUGGLING READERS

When discussing new vocabulary, be sure to include practice with pronunciation. Point out to students which syllables are stressed in a word. Have them gently tap the syllables of the word on their desk as they say it, tapping louder for stressed syllables.

- Notice that some of the text is larger and looks like handwriting. What purpose do you think this text might have? (Possible responses: It will summarize important parts; It may be reprinted text, so it will draw my attention back to a certain part of the story.)
- The pages this story is printed on are made to look like burnt paper. What might this lend to the story? (Possible responses: It tells you that the character's things got burnt; It makes the story seem like a journal entry.)
- What information do the photographs and illustrations give you? (They illustrate the setting of the story, and they show different things that are crucial to the events of the plot.)

LANGUAGE CONVENTIONALITY AND CLARITY

PREVIEW VOCABULARY Use the Preview and Review Vocabulary Routine in Part 3 to assess what students know about the following words: *gestures, wincing, ignite, exasperation, depression, hatchet, cave, porcupine, quills, sparks,* and *bark.* Clarify understanding with photographs and gestures to explain new words.

COGNATES Use the list of Spanish cognates at the beginning of this module to guide your Spanish-speaking students as they read the selection.

KNOWLEDGE DEMANDS

ACTIVATE BACKGROUND KNOWLEDGE Use the Quick Write and Share Routine in Part 3 to activate students' background knowledge. Ask students to share with a partner what they know about surviving in the wilderness.

Before students get started, model what you know about wilderness camping. For example: I know that everybody needs food, water, and shelter to live. If I were alone in the wilderness, I'd first see what supplies I had to last me until I found my way back to civilization. Then I'd have to figure out how to get the things I needed that I didn't have.

STRUGGLING READERS

Brian is never pictured in the selection. When students encounter stories that contain no illustrations or none that show characters and specific plot events, encourage them to use clues from the text to draw their own illustrations showing characters, setting, and the events of the story.

MORE SUPPORT

Interact with Text

LEVELS OF MEANING

Discuss the story's genre. Point out that *Hatchet* is an example of realistic fiction that focuses on survival. Ask: What other survival stories have you read and how were they similar to and different from this story? (Answers will vary, but students may note other stories where young people are alone in the wilderness and have to overcome obstacles to survive.)

> If . . . students have difficulty comparing two examples of realistic fiction,
>
> then . . . use the Story Comparison Routine and Graphic Organizer from Part 3 to help students visualize the similarities and differences.

STRUCTURE

As students read, periodically stop to assess their understanding of the story's structure. Have them describe what has happened in the story so far.

> If . . . students have difficulty following the sequence of the story,
>
> then . . . have them estimate what time of day each event happens and find evidence to support their estimates.

For example, the porcupine enters the cave in *the middle of the night,* and the dreams that Brian has happen *in the last doze period before daylight.*

> If . . . students have difficulty understanding the sequence of events in the story,
>
> then . . . use the Sequence of Events Routine and Graphic Organizer from Part 3 to keep track of the events. Have students fill in their own graphic organizer with the events up to that point and continue to fill out the chart as they read the story.

For example, point out to students the phrase *Then he heard the slithering* to indicate a change in the sequence of events. Have students use this phrase to record the first main event in the Sequence of Events Graphic Organizer. Then have students work in groups to complete the chart.

MORE SUPPORT

ENGLISH LANGUAGE LEARNERS

Read aloud the second and third paragraphs on p. 19. Point out the word *nick*. Point out the phrase a *chip in the top of the head* (of the hatchet), which defines *nick*. Then have students read on and figure out the meanings of *staff* and *lance*.

STRUGGLING READERS

Encourage students to use sticky notes as they read texts. They can use them to write questions, mark important parts, or take notes and stick them next to the part of the text the note refers to.

LANGUAGE CONVENTIONALITY AND CLARITY

While the language of the story can be understood on a literal level, some of the story contains figurative language and potentially unfamiliar expressions.

If . . . students have difficulty understanding figurative language and expressions,

then . . . define the expression for students by relating it to something with which they may be familiar.

For example, say: The author wrote "He had to feed the flames," and "feed the hungry flames." Flames don't really eat. The author compared putting fuel on a fire to eating when we are hungry.

Other phrases that may be difficult for students are: *hit with a smell, sailed into the wall, shower of sparks, catch his breath,* and *caught his eye.* Have pairs draw the literal meaning of the expression and describe the figurative meaning.

KNOWLEDGE DEMANDS

Have students work with a partner to use the story to retell the steps required for building a fire.

If . . . students have difficulty understanding the process of starting a fire,

then . . . have students review pp. 21–25 and list the various methods Brian used before he was successful at starting a fire. Provide students with sentence stems such as: First, Brian ___. Next, Brian ___. Then, Brian ___. Finally, Brian___.

For example, "First, Brian tried to use dried grass as fuel for the sparks."

STRUGGLING READERS

Students may lack background knowledge of or familiarity with vocabulary related to topics covered in texts. Share short videos and pictures whenever possible to help clarify ideas. For example, in this excerpt from *Hatchet,* consider sharing a short video of a porcupine that shows how they use quills to protect themselves and how people can use sparks to start a fire.

Express and Extend

EXPRESS Have small groups select one of Brian's unsuccessful attempts to start a fire and write a paragraph about how and why it failed.

If . . . students have difficulty writing about one of Brian's failed attempts to start a fire,

then . . . have pairs take turns rereading pp. 21–25. Have them record details of Brian's unsuccessful attempts in the Cause and Effect Graphic Organizer in Part 3. Then have students use the graphic organizer to guide their writing.

EXTEND Have small groups focus on the last few paragraphs of the story. Ask: Why was the fire so important to Brian? (Fire would allow him to stay warm, cook food, and scare away animals; it meant he could survive.) Why is *Hatchet* a good title for this story? (The hatchet helps him make fire and survive; it will probably help him do other things later in the story such as build a shelter or hunt.)

EXPRESS Place students into small groups. Have them discuss how Brian's dream affected his actions when he woke up.

If . . . students have difficulty understanding how the dream affected his actions,

then . . . have them reread the parts of the text that describe Brian's dream on pp. 17–18. Have students record the events of Brian's dream in the Sequence of Events Graphic Organizer in Part 3. Then have students refer to the graphic organizer as textual evidence to guide their group's discussion regarding Brian's next actions. If necessary, have students complete a second graphic organizer to record the events that happened once Brian woke up from his dream. Then have students compare the events in the two graphic organizers.

EXTEND Review group responses regarding how Brian's dream motivated his actions once he woke up. Then have groups locate other events in the story to determine how they, too, motivated Brian's actions. Lead students to see how the conventional structure of the story is set up in a cause and effect manner, beginning from an initial event in the beginning of the selection and culminating in a final outcome.

MORE SUPPORT

ENGLISH LANGUAGE LEARNERS

Explain to students that creating pictures in their minds as they read can help them better understand the story. Read aloud the last paragraph on p. 24 and the first paragraph on p. 25. Ask students to list the details that help them visualize the sparks turning into flames.

STRUGGLING READERS

Always encourage students to connect the experiences of a character to their own or to those of other characters they know. For example, ask students to share an experience in which they had to try over and over again to overcome a challenge like Brian did.

EXPRESS Talk about Sentences and Words

Display the following sentence from *Hatchet*. Read it aloud with students, and discuss how the meaning unfolds. Clarify any misunderstandings.

> He did not know how long it took, but later he looked back on this time of crying in the corner of the dark cave and thought of it as when he learned the most important rule of survival, which was that feeling sorry for yourself didn't work.

Ask: What does this sentence mean? What is the author trying to tell you? (Brian learned something to help him survive—feeling sorry for himself will do no good.) What words give you a clue that he came to this realization? (*but later he looked back*; The word *later* tells that he didn't realize it until after this experience.)

TEAM TALK Have partners reread the sentence and then reorganize the sentence while keeping the same meaning.

If . . . students have difficulty reorganizing the sentence,

then . . . provide sentence frames for guidance. Example: At first, Brian ___. But then he realized that ___. That was the ___.

EXTEND Have students find other sentences that show how Brian came to another realization. Have them discuss clue words that indicate this realization.

EXPRESS Have small groups express their understanding of Brian's situation in the wilderness. Use the Problem and Solution Routine and Graphic Organizer in Part 3 to guide students.

If . . . students have difficulty identifying problems and solutions in the story,

then . . . model finding a problem and a solution. Example: The porcupine entering the cave was a problem. The solution is that Brian threw the hatchet to scare it away.

EXTEND Have small groups break down Brian's efforts to start the fire into a series of problems and solutions. They can make an extended problem-solution chart showing the chain of his efforts.

ACCELERATED LEARNERS

Provide access to reference materials, the library, or the Internet. Have pairs of students research a real-life story of survival and prepare a presentation for the class.

MORE SUPPORT

Cognates

Cognates are words that have similar spellings and meanings in two or more languages. Many words in English and Spanish share Greek or Latin roots, and many words in English came from French, which is closely connected to Spanish (and to Portuguese, Italian, and Romanian). Because of this, many literary, content, and academic process words in English (e.g., *gracious/gracioso; volcano/volcán; compare/comparar*) have recognizable Spanish cognates.

Making the connection to cognates permits students who are native Spanish speakers to understand the strong foundation they have in academic and literary English. These links between English and Spanish are also useful for native speakers of English and other languages because they help uncover basic underlying features of our language.

ANCHOR TEXT Washed Up!

ENGLISH	SPANISH	ENGLISH	SPANISH
adapt	adaptar	labyrinth	laberinto
adventures	aventuras	miles	millas
camp	campamento	nymph	ninfa
civilization	civilización	ocean	océano
coconut	coco	palm	palmera
conclusions	conclusiones	paradise	paraíso
conversation	conversación	postponed	pospuesto
crocodiles	cocodrilos	predicted	predije
currents	corrientes	primates	primates
disappeared	desapareció	rations	raciones
dramatically	dramáticamente	rectangle	rectángulo
eruption	erupción	remote	remota
friction	fricción	resources	recursos
frugally	frugalmente	stomach	estómago
glamorous	glamorosa	survival	supervivencia
helicopter	helicóptero	suspended	suspendido
humanity	humanidad	tundra	tundra
hypothermia	hipotermia	turquoise	turquesa
ingenious	ingenioso		
jungle	jungla		

SUPPORTING TEXT Rain Forest Food Chains

ENGLISH	SPANISH	ENGLISH	SPANISH
adapt	adaptar	organism	organismo
cycle	ciclo	plant	planta
depend	depender	extinct	extinto
different	diferente	primary	primario
example	ejemplo	secondary	secundario
fruit	fruta	process	proceso
human	humano	vegetation	vegetación
lessons	lecciones	temperature	temperatura
omnivore	omnívoro	habitat	hábitat
herbivore	herbívoro	protect	proteger
carnivore	carnívoro	pollination	polinización
photosynthesis	fotosíntesis		

SUPPORTING TEXT Pale Male: Citizen Hawk of New York City

ENGLISH	SPANISH	ENGLISH	SPANISH
apartment	apartamento	organized	organizado
baseball	béisbol	ornate	ornamentado
celebrity	celebridad	park	parque
construction	construcción	permitted	permitido
days	días	preparation	preparación
destruction	destrucción	protection	protección
disorient	desorientar	publicity	publicidad
distinctive	distintivo	renovate	renovar
ecstatic	extático	residence	residencia
exclusive	exclusivo	spectacular	espectacular
observe	observar	telescope	telescopio
obvious	obvio		

These lists contain many, but not all, Spanish cognates from these selections.

Unlock the Text

QUALITATIVE MEASURES

WRITTEN BY PAYAL KAPADIA
ILLUSTRATED BY ROBIN BOYDEN

Washed Up!

Levels of Meaning	understanding realistic fiction; character interaction and motivation; themes about working together and maintaining humanity in the face of competition
Structure	chronological text structure; multiple alternating storylines
Language Conventionality and Clarity	figurative language; challenging vocabulary
Knowledge Demands	wilderness survival; adapting to an environment; understanding problems and solutions

Prepare to Read

LEVELS OF MEANING

Washed Up! is a realistic fictional story about three families who must compete to survive on a remote island. Each team must use wilderness survival techniques suited to a specific environment to survive. Another purpose of the story is to illustrate themes about how people act and interact during a challenging competition.

STRUCTURE

PREVIEW Have students read the title and study the illustrations in the text. Ask: How is the story organized? (It is divided into chapters, with separate sections within each chapter.) Ask: Based on the illustrations, can you predict what the story is about? (The story is about different families trying to survive in different settings on an island.) Ask: What

ENGLISH LANGUAGE LEARNERS

Help students recognize the figurative meanings of phrases such as *bit down hard on his tongue* (p. 5) and *bit his lip* (p. 19). Explain that these phrases mean that the children were stopping themselves from saying something that would not be appropriate in the situation.

STRUGGLING READERS

Illustrations can help students determine the meaning of an unfamiliar vocabulary word. For example, if students do not know what *mangroves* are, have them use the illustrations of the Garcias' storyline to describe their environment.

types of environments do you see in the illustrations? (mountains, mangroves, rain forest) Ask: How do you think these environments will be important to the story?

LANGUAGE CONVENTIONALITY AND CLARITY

PREVIEW VOCABULARY Use the Preview and Review Vocabulary Routine in Part 3 to assess what students know about the following words: *ultimate, reality, civilization, vied, rations, shelter, predicted, teeming, frugally, ingenious, windswept, yielded, murky, squelchy, comfort zones, conclusions, precisely, notoriously, gratefully,* and *dramatically.*

COGNATES Use the list of Spanish cognates at the beginning of this module to guide your Spanish-speaking students as they read the selection.

DOMAIN-SPECIFIC VOCABULARY Use the Vocabulary Activities in Part 3 to preteach the following domain-specific vocabulary: *environment, tide, swamp, canopy, jungle, inland, saltwater, tundra, freshwater,* and *lowlands.* Explain that students can use these words to talk about different settings in nature.

KNOWLEDGE DEMANDS

ACTIVATE BACKGROUND KNOWLEDGE Have students recall what they know about wilderness survival and consider which types of environments might be the most challenging for survival. Ask: What is very important to have when trying to survive in the wilderness? (water, food, shelter, fire) Ask: In what environments would it be difficult to survive? Why? Encourage students to give reasons for their answers based on what they know about the requirements for survival.

STRUGGLING READERS

When students struggle with a vocabulary word, encourage them to use context to say as much as they can about the word's meaning. For example, ask students to think about whether the word seems to have a positive or negative connotation, or whether the word is an adjective or verb.

Interact with Text

As they read, check students' understanding of the relationships and interactions within each family. Ask students to describe the relationships between Gabriela and her father, between Oliver and his parents, and between Shen and Mei and their parents.

If . . . students have difficulty identifying details that help define interactions,

then . . . have students focus on dialogue, actions, and attitudes to draw conclusions about character interactions.

For example, have students reread p. 16. Ask: Do Oliver and Mrs. Walpole feel the same way about the island? Use evidence from the text to defend your answer. (No. Oliver thinks the island is *suffocating* and sees the scorpions and other *nasties* in the forest. Oliver's mother calls the island *divine* and seems excited about the island.) Ask: What does Oliver's mother do with the fruit? How does Oliver react? (She pours water onto the fruit to wash it. Oliver is upset because his mother used half of their limited water supply.)

Check students' understanding of the four separate storylines within the text: the Walpoles, the Lius, the Garcias, and Berry Blue. Ask: Why do you think the author chose to switch between the four storylines instead of keeping them all separate? (The format allows the reader to see what is happening with each family and Berry Blue within the same time period even though they do not interact.)

If . . . students have difficulty keeping track of four separate storylines,

then . . . have students make a four-column chart with one column for each storyline. As they read, have students write key information and events in each column to organize the plots.

Point out that in Chapter 4, the storylines come together. Ask: How does the structure of the story change when the characters meet? (The chapter does not have separate sections for each family.)

ENGLISH LANGUAGE LEARNERS

Students may miss subtle cues in the text about emotions and attitudes. Read dialogue between the family members aloud, modeling emotions and attitudes as you read. Have students point out words and actions that indicate attitudes and emotions.

STRUGGLING READERS

If students struggle with the text's structure, point out words and phrases such as *meanwhile, closer to sea level,* and *many miles away* that indicate sequence and setting. For example, explain that the word *meanwhile* (p. 14) shows that the events with the Lius are taking place at the same time as the events with the Garcias on the previous page.

MORE SUPPORT

LANGUAGE CONVENTIONALITY AND CLARITY

Check students' understanding of figurative language used to describe the island environment. Explain that figurative language such as similes that compare two things can make descriptions more vivid and specific.

If . . . students have difficulty understanding similes, idioms, and other examples of figurative language,

then . . . talk through each example with students and discuss the effect of figurative language in context.

For example, point out the phrase *the jungle canopy, towering above them like a thirty-story building* on p. 20. Ask students to think about the difference between comparing the jungle to a thirty-story building and just saying that the trees were tall. Then point out the phrase *teeming with bugs* in the next sentence. Have students consider the effect of the word *teeming* compared with a phrase such as *full of*.

KNOWLEDGE DEMANDS

Students may have difficulty understanding the three families' choices for shelter due to challenging vocabulary in the text. Point out phrases such as *outcrop of three rocks, a narrow sill,* and *moored by rocks.* Direct students to the illustrations on pp. 26–27 to help them visualize the Lius' shelter. Then direct students to the phrases *palm fronds* and *insulate* on p. 23. Explain that Gabriela is using palm fronds, or branches from the trees, to create a layer between the ground and the Garcias as they sleep.

ENGLISH LANGUAGE LEARNERS

As they read, have students write down challenging phrases or descriptions. In small groups of students with mixed reading levels, have students share their questions and answer as many as they can as a group.

MORE SUPPORT

Express and Extend

EXPRESS Explain that environment affects each family's choices for survival strategies. Say: The Lius, Garcias, and Walpoles all choose different ways to survive because they are in different environments. In each setting on the island, there are different resources available and different challenges.

If . . . students have difficulty understanding the impact of environment on survival strategy,

then . . . have students work in small groups to identify unique problems associated with each environment. Then have students list the strategies each family used, and how each family used nature to help them survive.

EXTEND Have students imagine another setting on the island. For example, students may choose a beach setting or a cave setting. Then have students list the challenges of that environment and some ways that the setting could help provide elements necessary for survival.

EXPRESS Have students focus on the sections of the text with Berry Blue's dialogue. Ask: Who is Berry Blue speaking to? (television viewers) Ask: Why do you think Berry Blue speaks at the beginning of each chapter? (Berry Blue reminds readers that the families are involved in a reality television series, and she gives summaries of the competition's progress.) Ask: How is Berry Blue different from the families on the island? Choose specific words from the text to explain your answer. (Berry Blue is *radiant and rested* [p. 28] and is glamorous throughout the competition. She does not suffer and struggle on the island like the families do.)

EXTEND Have students write dialogue for Berry Blue for a scene taking place just after the Walpoles' experiences on pp. 28–31. Encourage students to include a summary of events in the dialogue. Remind students to address television viewers in Berry Blue's speech.

MORE SUPPORT

ENGLISH LANGUAGE LEARNERS

Help students gain familiarity with dialogue through repetition. In groups, have students alternate reading aloud sections with Berry Blue's dialogue. Encourage students to demonstrate Berry Blue's emotions and expressions.

STRUGGLING READERS

Provide additional structure for writing prompts if students have trouble. For example, to write a section of Berry Blue's storyline, have students begin by describing Berry Blue's clothing and appearance. Then, have students write dialogue to greet the audience. Have students complete the dialogue with a summary of what just happened with the Walpoles.

EXPRESS Talk About Sentences and Words

Explain that a writer's word choice can help create a tone or mood in a scene. Display and read aloud the following sentences from *Washed Up!*

> …as Shen **hurtled** down the zip line at more than thirty miles per hour, he wondered how this was going to end. He tried to touch the cable with his hand, but the friction **scorched** his skin.

Have students focus on the bold words above. Ask students to decide what *hurtled* means using context: for example, *more than thirty miles per hour*. (moving with uncontrolled, fast speed) For each bold word, have students find a synonym (such as *sped* and *burned*). Have students discuss how the bold words affect the meaning of the passage and set a mood.

TEAM TALK Have pairs choose a paragraph from the text to analyze. Have students note all of the verbs and descriptive words and phrases in the passage. Ask students to discuss the effectiveness of the author's word choice in setting a mood or tone.

EXTEND Have students write a paragraph about something they did today, including as many verbs as possible. Have students trade with a partner and replace the verbs in the story with more descriptive verbs that create a mood. Have students read aloud the new versions and discuss the differences in tone.

EXPRESS Have students consider the development of theme in the end of the text. Ask: What motivates the characters to work together in the end of the story? (Each has something that the other needs to survive. They realize it is more difficult for each family to survive on its own.) Ask: What message do you think the writer conveys with the ending of the story? Have students cite evidence from the text to support their answers.

> If . . . students have difficulty determining the themes and messages in the text,
>
> then . . . direct students to p. 56 and the lessons the children *taught the grown-ups.*

EXTEND Have students consider Berry Blue's comment on p. 48: "Maybe someone needs to tell these people that competitors can't be friends—there's only one prize, after all!" Ask students to write a paragraph agreeing or disagreeing with the statement, citing evidence from the text to support their answers. In pairs, have students share their reasoning.

ACCELERATED LEARNERS

Have students consider character motivation and the themes of the story to write a speech given by the Garcias on television stating why they chose to split their prize. Encourage students to incorporate dialogue between the Garcias and Berry Blue in the speech.

Unlock the Text

QUALITATIVE MEASURES	
Levels of Meaning	connections between animals in a rain forest; what different rain forests are like; how humans affect rain forests; summarizing
Structure	informational expository structure; glossary; index; table of contents; text boxes; captions; pictures; diagrams; cause-and-effect relationships
Language Conventionality and Clarity	structural analysis; domain-specific language; boldface text
Knowledge Demands	understanding a food chain, food web, and the connections between the parts

Prepare to Read

LEVELS OF MEANING

Rain Forest Food Chains demonstrates how organisms in a rain forest are connected and dependent upon one another. The final pages offer ways that humans can preserve the rain forest.

STRUCTURE

PREVIEW Form small groups, and have students read the section titles and captions, look at the photographs, and examine the diagrams in the book. Ask:

- How might the table of contents help readers? (It shows them what parts of the book they can use to answer specific questions.)

MORE SUPPORT

ENGLISH LANGUAGE LEARNERS

To help students understand the important ideas in the book, spend time discussing the graphics, such as the diagram on p. 16 that shows the levels of a food chain.

STRUGGLING READERS

Many of the words in this book are defined in a glossary, rather than in context. Make a photocopy of the glossary for students to have next to them as they read so they have easy access to definitions.

- How do glossaries and indices help readers? (A glossary defines difficult words, and an index shows where to find specific information.)
- Why are there green and blue boxes on each page? (The boxes have text captions, or more information about the pictures or text.)
- Why do some of the diagrams have arrows? (The arrows show the connections between different animals and plants in the pictures.)

LANGUAGE CONVENTIONALITY AND CLARITY

PREVIEW VOCABULARY Use the Preview and Review Vocabulary Routine in Part 3 to assess what students know about the following words: *omnivore, herbivore, carnivore, decomposer, consumer, adaptation, extinction, habitats, photosynthesis, endangered, extinction.* Preteach unfamiliar vocabulary by putting students in pairs and having them create 3–4 vocabulary cards that define each word, list each part of speech, and use each word in a sentence.

COGNATES Use the list of Spanish cognates at the beginning of this module to guide your Spanish-speaking students as they read the selection.

KNOWLEDGE DEMANDS

ACTIVATE BACKGROUND KNOWLEDGE Have students share with a partner what they already know about rain forests and food chains. Use the Quick Write and Share Routine in Part 3 and ask: What is a rain forest? What animals live in a rain forest? How can your actions affect rain forests?

Interact with Text

In the beginning of *Rain Forest Food Chains,* new domain-specific vocabulary may make it difficult for students to understand the concept of a food chain.

> **If . . .** students have difficulty understanding the different parts of the food chain *(producers, consumers [primary and secondary],* or *decomposers),*
>
> **then . . .** have them use the Three-Column Chart Graphic Organizer in Part 3 to keep track of new terms.

Label the three columns: *Definition, Other Names,* and *Examples.* Then put students in small groups to reread pp. 4–7. Assign one part of the food chain— producers, consumers (primary and secondary), or decomposers—to each group. On the first read, have students write a definition of their part of the food chain under *Definition.* On the second read, have students add other names for their group under *Other Names* and an example of an organism in that group under *Examples.* For example, another name for *secondary consumer* is *predator (Other Names),* and an example would be a jaguar *(Examples).*

As students read, periodically assess their understanding of the text's structure and features used in the text.

> **If . . .** students have difficulty understanding how pictures and sidebars relate to the text,
>
> **then . . .** have students use a T-chart with the headings *Description* and *Reasons* to explain how text boxes, captions, and pictures support information in the text.

For example, read aloud p. 23, and then display a T-chart and model the activity by looking at the picture and writing down what you see in the *Description* column. Next, write down reasons why the picture is used in the *Reasons* column. For example: The picture of the ocelot is used because ocelots are discussed in the "Top Rain Forest Predators" section. This section is right next to the picture. Have students work in pairs to complete a T-chart about the text boxes or captions.

MORE SUPPORT

ENGLISH LANGUAGE LEARNERS

Have students write down a question they have about *Rain Forest Food Chains* on an index card or sticky note. Without disclosing who wrote the question, share it with the class as a way to start a discussion for the day.

STRUGGLING READERS

Texts with a lot of information can be overwhelming for some readers. Have students work in pairs, reading one paragraph at a time. Have them work together to create a sentence summary of each paragraph before moving on.

LANGUAGE CONVENTIONALITY AND CLARITY

A variety of words in the text are in bold font. However, not all words are in bold font for the same reason.

If . . . students have trouble understanding why certain words appear in bold font,

then . . . have them reread parts of the text, identify the items in bold font, and explain the importance of those words.

For example, the boldfaced words are titles and glossary words. The author wants the reader to know they are important. Boldfaced words catch the readers' attention.

Discuss the structure of some of the vocabulary terms and how they can use related words to understand the meanings of these words better. For example, discuss the following words and relationships: *consumer, consume; producer, produce, production; secondary, second; endangered, danger; extinction, extinct.*

KNOWLEDGE DEMANDS

Engage students in a discussion about how something that has an impact on one organism in a food chain will eventually have an impact on the entire ecosystem.

If . . . students have trouble understanding what happens to a food chain when one link is endangered,

then . . . have students look at p. 6 and summarize each organism's role. Then, decide what would happen if that organism wasn't there.

Assign small groups a link in the food chain. Have them reread the introductory paragraph that corresponds with their link and create a summary. Have each group share and display their summary and, as a class, discuss what would happen if one of those links were taken away.

If . . . students have difficulty understanding how food chains and food webs are related,

then . . . have students review the food web diagram on p. 7 and discuss with a partner what the food web shows about how the organisms are related to each other. Have them also identify how food chains and food webs are alike and different.

Express and Extend

EXPRESS Have students create summaries about one of the rain forest habitats on pp. 28–33. The summary should include where the rain forest is located, what organisms live there, and a threat to the habitat.

If . . . students have difficulty creating their summaries,

then . . . provide students with the Three-Column Chart Graphic Organizer from Part 3 to organize their ideas. Label the chart with the headings *Location, Organisms,* and *Threat.*

EXTEND Assign students one of the threats to rain forest habitats from the text. Have them write a paragraph explaining how they could reduce the threat the section describes. Encourage students to include vocabulary from the selection in their paragraph.

STRUCTURE

EXPRESS Divide students into small groups, and assign a section from "How Are Humans Harming Rain Forest Food Chains?" Have groups write a paragraph describing the cause-and-effect relationship between human action and the decline of the rain forest.

If . . . students have difficulty writing a cause-and-effect paragraph,

then . . . provide a T-chart with the headings *Human Actions* and *Effects.* Have students reread their section twice, filling out column 1 after the first read and column 2 after the second read. They should draw arrows showing which actions in column 1 caused the effects in column 2.

EXTEND Have students write a short letter to the Kids Saving the Rain Forest conservation group. Their letter should discuss what they will personally do to help the rain forest based on what they have learned from the text.

ENGLISH LANGUAGE LEARNERS

Use visual representations of concepts from the text to support understanding. For example, provide pictures of the rain forest and label the different layers: *canopy, emergent layer, understory.*

STRUGGLING READERS

When small groups discuss complex sections of text, provide students with sentence frames and starters. This will allow them to focus more on the content of their responses rather than how to get started.

MORE SUPPORT

LANGUAGE CONVENTIONALITY AND CLARITY

EXPRESS Talk about Sentences and Words

Display and read aloud the following sentences from *Rain Forest Food Chains*.

> Some plants depend on the bat for **pollination** (fertilization). When a bat drinks **nectar** from a flower, it also **pollinates** the flower.

Ask: What does the phrase *some plants* suggest? (It suggests that not all plants are pollinated by bats.) Why are the words *pollination, nectar,* and *pollinates* in boldfaced font? (They are defined in the glossary; the author wants the reader to know the words are important.) Why is the word *fertilization* in parentheses? (It explains the word *pollination*.) How is the word *pollination* different from the word *pollinates*? (*Pollination* is a noun and *pollinates* is a verb.)

TEAM TALK Have students work in pairs to write sentences using the words *pollinate* and *pollination*.

> If . . . students have difficulty producing sentences with key vocabulary,
>
> then . . . provide sentence frames to help students properly use the words.

EXTEND Provide a T-chart with the words *pollinate, adapt, collect, protect, detect,* and *conserve* in column 1 and the words *pollination, adaptation, collection, protection, detection,* and *conservation* in column 2. Have students define the words as well as their part of speech.

KNOWLEDGE DEMANDS

EXPRESS Give students a word bank of the organisms from the text, such as *durian fruit, stinkwood leaves, black-and-white colobus monkey, fruit fly, chimpanzee, crowned hawk eagle, pitcher plant, fungus,* and *bacteria.* Have students categorize the organisms into *producers, primary consumers, secondary consumers,* and *decomposers.*

EXTEND Provide students with a list of organisms and materials to create a food chain. On each chain, students should write the name of the organism and how it is dependent on other links in the chain. For example, using the diagram on p. 6, the first link would be labeled *fig* and read *figs produce their own food, and sloths eat figs.* The next link would be labeled *sloth* and read *sloths eat figs, and jaguars eat sloths.*

ACCELERATED LEARNERS

Have students research a specific organization from the bibliography and create posters that briefly explain what the organization does and one way they will support it.

Unlock the Text

QUALITATIVE MEASURES

Levels of Meaning	informational text about a hawk living in New York City; connecting human behaviors with how they affect animals; summarizing
Structure	chronological narrative; illustrations on each page corresponding to narrative; using a time line
Language Conventionality and Clarity	prefixes and suffixes; idioms and expressions; comparing animals and humans
Knowledge Demands	preservation; ecology; human and animal cohabitation; protesting and debating

Pale Male, pp. 26–57

Prepare to Read

LEVELS OF MEANING

On the surface, *Pale Male* is an informational text about a red-tailed hawk living and becoming famous in New York City. Students should also glean the deeper meaning that humans and nature interact, which can cause conflicts.

STRUCTURE

PREVIEW Allow students to page through the selection and look at the title and illustrations. Ask: What do you think this selection will be about? (a hawk in a big city) What clues did you use? (The pictures give clues.) What sorts of problems might a hawk have in New York City? (interacting with people, finding food.)

ENGLISH LANGUAGE LEARNERS

Help students unlock the meaning of compound words from the selection, such as *smokestacks, skyscrapers, birdwatchers, farmlands, oversized, hardworking,* and *songbird.* Have them identify the two words in each compound word. Discuss their meaning.

STRUGGLING READERS

If students need more support to understand prefixes and suffixes in this selection, use the Prefixes and Suffixes Activities in Part 3 to provide meaningful practice.

PREVIEW VOCABULARY Use the Preview and Review Vocabulary Routine in Part 3 to assess students' familiarity with the following words: *oasis, distinctive, disoriented, withstand, evicted, ecstatic, enthusiastic, fledgling, novice, nominated, protest, legacy*.

PREFIXES AND SUFFIXES Remind students that adding the prefix *un-* and *in-* to the beginning of a word changes its meaning to the opposite of the original word. Display the words *inexperienced* and *undaunted*. Underline each prefix and explain each root word. For example, explain that *experienced* means "knowing how to do something through practice." Then have students tell what they think *inexperienced* means ("not knowing how to do something"). Have students share other words that have the *in-* or *un-* prefix.

IDIOMS AND EXPRESSIONS *Pale Male* contains idioms and expressions that students may need support with, such as *did them in, sporting a flashy red tail, true-blue New Yorkers, protection from the elements,* and *in a flash*. Point out these examples during the read aloud, and have students guess the meanings. Clarify any misunderstandings. Use the Analyze Idioms and Expressions Routine in Part 3 for more ideas.

COGNATES Use the list of Spanish cognates at the beginning of this module to guide your Spanish-speaking students as they read the selection.

ACTIVATE BACKGROUND KNOWLEDGE Have students tell what they know about New York City. Ask: What kinds of wild animals live there? What types of buildings are in the city? Then, use the Quick Write and Share Routine in Part 3 to have students brainstorm what problems a wild animal might have in a large city.

MORE SUPPORT

Interact with Text

During your reading of *Pale Male,* periodically stop to assess students' level of understanding of the events described in the text. Ask: How is Pale Male surviving in New York City? How are humans helping or hurting his chance of survival? Begin a T-chart to record events of when people help Pale Male and when they hurt his chance of survival. Have students add to the chart as they read.

If . . . students have difficulty connecting the humans' actions to the hawk's life,

then . . . point out how the U.S Fish and Wildlife Service helped ensure the nest would not be moved by the apartment building owners. Ask: Why did the U.S. Fish and Wildlife Service do that? What were they trying to accomplish? What were the building owners trying to do?

Although *Pale Male* follows a straightforward chronological structure, it is a lengthy text that is not divided into sections. To help students split the text into more manageable chunks, model how to scan the text for clue words that indicate periods of time and how to use sticky notes to define the sections. Say: This text is quite long. At times I get confused because I can't keep the different sections organized. I will scan the text looking for clue words that tell me a new part of the text is starting. Then, I will use sticky notes so I can remember where these sections are. The first paragraph on page 29 begins with the phrase *On a crisp autumn day in 1991.* This tells me a time. I'll put a sticky note here so I know this is where the text begins. Later, on page 35, the first paragraph begins with the phrase *In March.* This tells me that a new part of the text is beginning. I'll put another sticky note here so I know a new section is beginning. **Model putting the sticky notes on the pages. Then, have students scan the text looking for other clue words that indicate where new sections begin.**

ENGLISH LANGUAGE LEARNERS

To support small-group discussions, provide exchange frames such as:

S1: I think that ___ got more from ___ because ___.

S2: I agree/disagree with you because ___.

STRUGGLING READERS

Encourage students to use the pictures to understand the action in the selection better. On the page with protesters, have students examine the pictures after reading the text to summarize in their own words what happened on that page.

LANGUAGE CONVENTIONALITY AND CLARITY

Some of the sentences in this selection are lengthy and complex. Have students identify complex sentences and rewrite them as simple sentences.

If . . . students have trouble finding and simplifying complex sentences,

then . . . help students by modeling how to simplify a complex sentence.

For example, display the following sentence: "Then, in 2003, during a time when many conservation and wildlife laws were being relaxed by President George W. Bush's administration, the Migratory Bird Treaty was changed." Explain that there are two events being talked about in the sentence—wildlife laws being relaxed and the Migratory Bird Treaty being changed. Rewrite the sentence as: In 2003, the Migratory Bird Treaty changed. Around that time, many conservation and wildlife laws were relaxed by George W. Bush's administration.

KNOWLEDGE DEMANDS

Lead a discussion about how important the citizens of New York were to the survival of Pale Male. Then, ask: What did Pale Male give back to the citizens of New York? Why were they so interested in the hawk? Have students break into small groups to have a conversation about whether the hawk got more from the city or the city got more from the hawk. Encourage them to take notes in order to report their findings to the class.

If . . . students have difficulty understanding the connections between the citizens and the hawk,

then . . . have them refer to the class T-chart about people helping and hurting the hawk.

Express and Extend

LEVELS OF MEANING

EXPRESS Have pairs identify the main idea of *Pale Male*. Have students provide evidence from the text to support their ideas. (Humans and animals interact, but sometimes their interests clash in big cities.)

If . . . students have difficulty identifying the main idea of the text,

then . . . use the Main Idea and Details Routine and Graphic Organizer from Part 3 to guide students in completing the task.

EXTEND Brainstorm other ways people in cities interact with animals. Examples could include visiting a zoo, having pets, feeding birds at a park, or working at a rescue shelter. Then, have students discuss whether the interactions are more beneficial for the humans or the animals. Stress that there are no right and wrong answers because these are personal opinions.

STRUCTURE

EXPRESS Use the Time Line Routine and Graphic Organizer in Part 3 with students to create a time line of Pale Male's experiences in New York City from 1991 until spring 2005.

If . . . students have difficulty identifying key events in the text,

then . . . model how to break the activity into smaller parts. For example, first, have students skim the story and write down dates they find in the text. Then, students can create the time line with those dates and insert events from the text that match the dates.

EXTEND Have small groups compare time lines and fill in any gaps they may have. Then facilitate a discussion about how each event in the time lines led to the next. For example, Pale Male's eviction from the apartment building directly led to people protesting at the apartment building.

ENGLISH LANGUAGE LEARNERS

Students may require help understanding how one event causes another event to occur. Provide the following sentence frames for guidance: ___ happened because ___ happened first. I know this because ___.

STRUGGLING READERS

If students do not have much background knowledge about people and animal interactions, provide photographs and video clips of people with pets, working at shelters, and feeding birds at a park.

MORE SUPPORT

EXPRESS Talk about Sentences and Words

Display the following sentences from *Pale Male*. Read them aloud with students, and discuss the sentences. Clarify any misunderstandings.

> Pale Male hung around the park the way a teenager hangs out at a mall. He dive-bombed tasty pigeons and rats at their litter-can snack bars. He chased after ducks and was spotted terrorizing squirrels, seemingly just for the fun of it. As red-tailed hawks go, he *was* a teenager.

Ask: How does the author compare Pale Male to a teenager at a mall? Why do you think the author chose to do this? (The author uses this example because it helps the reader to visualize and connect the animal behaviors with things that people do.) What does the phrase *as red-tailed hawks go* mean? (The author is explaining that when red-tailed hawks are two years old, they are between the child and adult phases of life.)

TEAM TALK Have partners reread the above sentences and then compare the phases of a human's life to a bird's life. Then, have them share one similarity and one difference between the two with the class.

EXTEND Have students get into small groups and complete the Act Out or Draw Meaning Graphic Organizer from Part 3. Allow groups to perform the above passage to the class. Point out any similarities or differences in the performances.

EXPRESS Have small groups use evidence from the text to explain why people protested in favor of Pale Male living on top of the apartment building.

> If . . . students have difficulty understanding the motivation for people's actions,
>
> then . . . give them the following sentence frames to spur discussion: I think people were upset because ___. If I lived in New York, I would be ___ about Pale Male, because ___.

EXTEND Divide the class in half, and have one half argue on behalf of the tenants and the other half debate on behalf of Pale Male and the environmental groups. After the discussion, have students vote on whether the class would evict Pale Male or allow him to stay.

ACCELERATED LEARNERS

Have students create a pamphlet for the apartment tenants from the point of view of the environmental groups. Tell students their goal is to convince the apartment tenants to allow Pale Male to stay. The pamphlet should include information from the text as well as personal opinions.

Finding Courage

"I still believe that we shall overcome"

TEXT SET

ANCHOR TEXT
The Road to Freedom

SUPPORTING TEXT
Operation Clean
Sweep

SUPPORTING TEXT
Cesar Chavez:
Champion of Workers

TEXT SET

ANCHOR TEXT
Real-Life Superheroes

SUPPORTING TEXT
The Great Migration

SUPPORTING TEXT
Angel Island

Cognates

Cognates are words that have similar spellings and meanings in two or more languages. Many words in English and Spanish share Greek or Latin roots, and many words in English came from French, which is closely connected to Spanish (and to Portuguese, Italian, and Romanian). Because of this, many literary, content, and academic process words in English (e.g., *gracious/gracioso; volcano/volcán; compare/comparar*) have recognizable Spanish cognates.

Making the connection to cognates permits students who are native Spanish speakers to understand the strong foundation they have in academic and literary English. These links between English and Spanish are also useful for native speakers of English and other languages because they help uncover basic underlying features of our language.

ANCHOR TEXT The Road to Freedom

ENGLISH	SPANISH	ENGLISH	SPANISH
abolish	abolir	north	norte
abolitionists	abolicionistas	number	número
attic	ático	operations	operaciones
boots	botas	passenger	pasajero
captured	capturado	patrolled	patrullaron
carriage	carruaje	pillars	pilares
celebrated	celebrado	references	referencias
chimney	chimenea	reins	riendas
codes	códigos	rock	roca
constellation	constelación	sack	saco
continued	continuó	salty	salado
count	contar	secret	secreto
crossed	cruzó	sound	sonido
elaborate	elaborado	south	sur
escaped	escapó	space	espacio
fictional	ficticio	spongy	esponjoso
finally	finalmente	station	estación
fugitive	fugitivo	stomach	estómago
group	grupo	symbol	símbolo
historians	historiadores	system	sistema
historical	histórico	territory	territorio
lantern	linterna	train	tren
market	mercado	tremendous	tremendo
methods	métodos	trunk	tronco
moved	movió	voices	voces

SUPPORTING TEXT Operation Clean Sweep

ENGLISH	SPANISH	ENGLISH	SPANISH
baseball	béisbol	nervous	nervioso
cemetery	cementerio	nomination	nominación
decorate	decorar	office	oficina
election	elección	operation	operación
electric	eléctrico	persuade	persuadir
government	gobierno	politics	política
gratitude	gratitud	represent	representar
history	historia	respect	respeto
immediately	inmediatamente	respectable	respetable
instrument	instrumento	responsibilities	responsabilidades
interesting	interesante	silence	silencio
minutes	minutos	suffrage	sufragio

SUPPORTING TEXT Cesar Chavez: Champion of Workers

ENGLISH	SPANISH	ENGLISH	SPANISH
abundance	abundancia	illegal	ilegal
association	asociación	legislature	legislatura
champion	campeón	messages	mensajes
condition	condición	migrant	migrante
cultivate	cultivar	organize	organizar
depression	depresión	patience	paciencia
election	elección	percent	por ciento
governor	gobernador	pesticides	pesticidas
graduate	graduarse	sacrifice	sacrificio
groups	grupos	union	unión
guarantee	garantizar	victory	victoria
hero	héroe	violence	violencia

These lists contain many, but not all,
Spanish cognates from these selections.

Unlock the Text

QUALITATIVE MEASURES

Levels of Meaning	narrative realistic fiction about a girl and her mother escaping slavery through the Underground Railroad; theme of taking risks to help others
Structure	chronological text structure; some use of flashback; epilogue; integration of a historical figure into a fictional text
Language Conventionality and Clarity	sensory detail; tone; some challenging academic vocabulary
Knowledge Demands	understanding about the history of slavery in the United States; Underground Railroad

Prepare to Read

LEVELS OF MEANING

The Road to Freedom is a fictional first-person account of a girl and her mother escaping slavery through the Underground Railroad. Emma's fictional journey mirrors those of many individuals escaping slavery in the 1800s. Along their journey Emma and her mother are aided by several individuals who take great risks to help bring them to freedom.

STRUCTURE

PREVIEW Have students preview the illustrations in the text. Ask: What do the illustrations tell you about Emma and her mother's journey? (The journey looks difficult; Emma and her mother had to travel alone through dangerous conditions.) Have students scan the dialogue and the narrative

---

MORE SUPPORT

ENGLISH LANGUAGE LEARNERS

As students read, have them use sticky notes to write short captions for the illustrations. This will help them summarize the information and events on each page.

STRUGGLING READERS

Before students read pages with challenging vocabulary, have them scan the page and write down unfamiliar words. As they read, have students try to use context to determine the words' meanings. After students finish reading, have them use a dictionary to check definitions.

text. Ask: Who is telling the story? (Emma) Point out the Epilogue at the end of the story. Explain that the epilogue is separate from the narrative text, and offers additional historical information about the events in the story.

LANGUAGE CONVENTIONALITY AND CLARITY

PREVIEW VOCABULARY Use the Preview and Review Vocabulary Routine in Part 3 to assess what students know about the following words: *debts, auction, master, stumble, plantation, patrolled, curled, screech, grumbled, shivering, scent, quilt, conductor, shuffling, slavery, tumbled, whinnied, stuttered, drifted, lantern, scattered, hunched, capturing, blisters, carriage, surrounded, pillars, territory, historical, abolish,* and *tremendous.*

COGNATES Use the list of Spanish cognates at the beginning of this module to guide your Spanish-speaking students as they read the selection.

DOMAIN-SPECIFIC VOCABULARY Use the Vocabulary Activities in Part 3 to preteach the following domain-specific vocabulary: *North Star, slave catchers, Quaker, enslave, Underground Railroad, Philadelphia, Buffalo, Niagara, constellation, abolitionists,* and *fugitives.* Explain that students can use these words to explain how enslaved people escaped to freedom in the North.

KNOWLEDGE DEMANDS

ACTIVATE BACKGROUND KNOWLEDGE Check students' knowledge of slavery and its history in the United States. Ask questions such as: What do you know about slavery in the United States? Where did enslaved people have to travel to escape slavery? What were the risks of trying to escape? Explain that enslaved people tried to escape to states where slavery was illegal, but it required a lot of risk for both the travelers and people trying to help them along the way.

STRUGGLING READERS

Many of the scenes in the narrative include fast-paced action. Have students act out dialogue and narration to aid comprehension as they read.

MORE SUPPORT

Interact with Text

As you read *The Road to Freedom,* check students' understanding of Emma and her mother's responses to events in the text. Ask students to consider why Emma and her mother had given up on running away, and why they reconsider escaping in the first chapter of the story.

If . . . students have difficulty identifying the motivation behind Emma and her mother's actions,

then . . . help them identify causes and effects.

For example, direct students to p. 6. Ask: What caused Emma and her mother to stop talking about running away? What caused Emma's mother to decide "we gotta run" on page 8?

STRUCTURE

Explain that most of the narrative is told in chronological order, although it incorporates some flashbacks to when Emma's father was still with them. Help students sequence the events in the story by first summarizing key events in each chapter. Then, have students plot key events on a timeline. Point out that Emma's father planned an escape two years before the narrative begins.

If . . . students have difficulty identifying key events in the story,

then . . . make a short list of key events and details from a chapter. Have students sort details from main ideas to summarize the events in the chapter.

Remind students that key events tell the most important things that happened in a chapter. Details include extra information such as what characters said or how they felt.

MORE SUPPORT

ENGLISH LANGUAGE LEARNERS

Dialect and slang words may be confusing for students. Point out the words '*longside* on p. 22 and '*long* and '*bout* on p. 34. Explain that the apostrophe takes the place of the letter *a* in these words. Explain that the writer does this to make the words sound more like natural speech.

STRUGGLING READERS

If students have trouble sequencing the flashback on pp. 5–6, point to key phrases such as *before he left, then one day,* and *but now* that indicate chronology.

LANGUAGE CONVENTIONALITY AND CLARITY

Explain that the writer chooses language to build suspense and set a tone in the narrative.

> If . . . students have difficulty understanding how the writer uses language to create tone,
>
> then . . . discuss several examples from the text as a class.

For example, point to the paragraph on p. 13 beginning "'Walk on your toes, Mama!'" Have students reread the passage. Ask: What is the mood, or tone of the passage? (suspenseful, urgent, fearful) Have students consider how the language the writer uses conveys this tone: for example, point to the phrase "I stopped breathing," the repetition of words, and the use of multiple verbs close together.

Have students find other parts of the narrative that build suspense and create a tone of fear and urgency, such as instances when Emma and her mother are close to being caught. Point out how language contributes to tone.

KNOWLEDGE DEMANDS

Check students' understanding of the Underground Railroad. Explain that the Underground Railroad was not a literal railroad, but it was a transportation system that used secret messages and signals to help enslaved people escape to freedom. Check students' understanding of the various pieces of the metaphor. Ask: What did a "conductor" on the Underground Railroad do? (helped guide runaways on their journeys) Who were the conductors on the Underground Railroad in the story? (the Quaker woman, the man with the wagon, Harriet Tubman, the man outside the train) Ask: What were "stations" on the Underground Railroad? (homes or safe places where people could hide)

ENGLISH LANGUAGE LEARNERS

Reading aloud multiple times will help students internalize vocabulary and practice pronunciation. Preview difficult pronunciation before beginning a scene. Then have students take turns reading dialogue and narration in groups, switching parts after each reading.

MORE SUPPORT

Express and Extend

EXPRESS Explain that taking risks for a cause a person believes in is one of the themes of this story. Say: Many of the characters in the story take risks, or put themselves in danger, to fight slavery. Emma and her mother put themselves in danger with the hope of becoming free. Many conductors on the Underground Railroad risked their safety to bring others to freedom.

If . . . students have difficulty understanding the risks associated with the Underground Railroad,

then . . . have groups choose one conductor from the text and find examples of dangers he or she faced. Have students discuss why these individuals might have risked their safety to help others escape slavery.

EXTEND Have students research Harriet Tubman or another historical figure who was involved with the Underground Railroad. Have students summarize the individual's role and use evidence from the text to explain the risks he or she took in helping people escape slavery.

EXPRESS Have students read the Epilogue. Ask: Why do you think the writer included the Epilogue? (It gives historical context to the story.) Have students connect key information in the Epilogue to events in the story. Ask: Where in the story do you hear about "the drinking gourd"? What does the "drinking gourd" mean? (It happens when Mama has a dream about how she and Emma will escape; it refers to the Big Dipper and using the North Star to navigate.) Ask: Who in the story do you think were abolitionists? (Harriet Tubman, the Quaker woman, and the other conductors) Ask: How did the Fugitive Slave Act affect Emma and her mother on their journey? (They had to keep moving to Canada because in free states in the North, they could still be captured and sent back to the South.)

EXTEND Explain that an epilogue sometimes includes more information about the characters in the story, after the story has ended. Have students add one paragraph to the Epilogue explaining what happened to Emma and her mother after they reached Canada.

ENGLISH LANGUAGE LEARNERS

Students may have difficulty with challenging vocabulary and sentence structure used in the Epilogue. Read the Epilogue aloud with students, pausing after each sentence to summarize and clarify information.

STRUGGLING READERS

Encourage students to use key domain-specific vocabulary in their discussion of the text. Discuss the role of Quakers and abolitionists and their beliefs. Then encourage students to use these terms to talk about why characters in the text took risks to help with the Underground Railroad.

LANGUAGE CONVENTIONALITY AND CLARITY

EXPRESS Talk about Sentences and Words

Display and read aloud the following sentences from *The Road to Freedom.*

> The road was **bumpy**. My **head banged** against the side of the wagon, and the burlap **tickled my nose**.

Point out that the passage uses language that appeals to the senses. Ask: What sense do the bold words and phrases discuss? (touch) Explain that the writer uses language to describe sight, sound, smell, touch, and even taste throughout the story. This allows the reader to better understand everything Emma feels and sees.

TEAM TALK   In pairs, have students find at least one example in the text of language that appeals to each sense. Have groups share their examples with the class.

EXTEND Have students practice using sensory language to describe a specific experience they had recently. Ask students to write a paragraph about the experience, incorporating details that appeal to each of the senses. Have students share with a partner and underline sensory words.

KNOWLEDGE DEMANDS

EXPRESS Help students recognize the clues and codes Emma and her mother used to know that they would be safe. Explain that the Underground Railroad relied on secret codes and signals to identify stations and conductors to keep runaways hidden from slave catchers.

> **If . . .** students have difficulty finding subtle clues associated with the Underground Railroad,
>
> **then . . .** direct students to each scene in which Emma and her mother meet someone for the first time. Have students identify key details associated with each meeting. Explain that songs, signs in a window, or even the quilt the Quaker woman hung on a fence could be signs of the Underground Railroad.

EXTEND Have students use information from the Epilogue and the rest of the text to create a secret guide to the codes and signals of the Underground Railroad. Explain that the guide should explain what an individual should look for to ensure a home or location is safe.

Have students choose one topic from the Epilogue that they would like to learn more about. Have students conduct research on the topic and write one paragraph summarizing their findings.

MORE SUPPORT

Unlock the Text

**Operation Clean Sweep,
pp. 67–77**

QUALITATIVE MEASURES

Levels of Meaning	explicit theme is never underestimate the power of a woman; underlying theme is women's rights
Structure	chronological first-person narrative by a young boy; dialogue
Language Conventionality and Clarity	clear writing style; compound sentences; slang, figurative language, and idioms
Knowledge Demands	history of women's suffrage; women's rights; running for office

Prepare to Read

LEVELS OF MEANING

In *Operation Clean Sweep*, there are two levels of meaning. One purpose of the text is to show that one should never underestimate the power of a woman. The other purpose is to show that giving women the right to vote also gave them power.

STRUCTURE

PREVIEW Form small groups, and have students discuss the organization of the book. Have students look at the cover illustration and read the title. Ask:

- What information is included before the main text? (An overview, or explanation, that describes Cornelius and Otis and what their lives are like.)

ENGLISH LANGUAGE LEARNERS

Explain that *clean sweep* is an expression. It does not mean literally "to sweep something clean." It means "the winning of all of something in a group." Have students use the phrase in a sentence. Follow the same procedure with other multiple-meaning words and phrases in the text.

STRUGGLING READERS

When students struggle with vocabulary, it interferes with their comprehension of a text. Read aloud passages that contain critical vocabulary terms, and then have students repeat the passages in their own words. Focus on learning terms such as *nominations* and *mayor*.

- Based on the illustrations, when and where do you think this story takes place? How can you tell? (The clothes the characters are wearing make me think it takes place in the past. The stars and stripes flags tell me it takes place somewhere in the United States.)
- Look at the illustration on page 76. What do you think is going on? (A woman is speaking about something she feels strongly about.)

LANGUAGE CONVENTIONALITY AND CLARITY

PREVIEW VOCABULARY Use the Preview and Review Vocabulary Routine in Part 3 to assess what students know about the following critical vocabulary words and phrases: *operation, nominations, election, politics, mayor, suffragists, vote, run for office, acceptance speech, term in office, equal rights,* and *voting booth*.

COGNATES Use the list of Spanish cognates at the beginning of this module to guide your Spanish-speaking students as they read the selection.

KNOWLEDGE DEMANDS

ACTIVATE BACKGROUND KNOWLEDGE Have students share what they know about voting with the whole group. Use the Quick Write and Share Routine in Part 3, and ask:

- What are some different things people vote for?
- Why is it important that everyone is allowed to vote?
- Was there ever a time when a group of people was not allowed to vote?

Have students share any questions they might still have about voting. Write the questions in a prominent place in the classroom, and return to them as they come up in the text.

Interact with Text

As you read *Operation Clean Sweep*, point out that Cornelius has a hard time believing his mother would like to become mayor of the town. When he overhears her saying she would like to be nominated for office, he says, "I stuck my fingers in both of my ears and wiggled them to make sure I was hearing okay. I was."

Have student pairs look for other places in the text where people in the story show disbelief at things we see as typical today, such as a woman running for office. Have them record what they find in a T-chart labeled *Action* and *Reaction.* Model how to fill out the chart by writing *Mother running for office* under the *Action* column and the sentence above in the *Reaction* column.

In order to understand the story, students need to be able to identify each event and how it leads to the next event. Start a discussion about the main events in the story and how each one leads to the next.

If . . . students have trouble understanding each event and how it relates to the next event,

then . . . use the Sequence of Events Routine and Graphic Organizer in Part 3 to outline a particular event in the story. Then, assign story events to student pairs and have them summarize the event in a few sentences. Afterward, have pairs share their summary with the class. Then, as a class, work to draw connections between each event summary.

MORE SUPPORT

ENGLISH LANGUAGE LEARNERS

Use question starters to encourage students to ask clarifying questions throughout reading. Write a list of question starters on the board that begin with *who, what, where, when,* and *why.* Then have students ask and answer questions with a partner about the story.

STRUGGLING READERS

Repeated readings make it easier for students to recall important passages and process information. Have one student at a time read aloud the first paragraph on p. 69 and then ask other students to summarize it.

LANGUAGE CONVENTIONALITY AND CLARITY

While the sentence structure of the story is literal and clear, some phrases are expressed in figurative language or slang. For example, "Dad had said that the ladies were making a mountain out of a molehill." To help students understand sentences with figurative language, use the Analyze Idioms and Expressions Routine in Part 3.

Other phrases that may be difficult for students are: *get us some chow, cold in my tracks, spread the word, laid to rest, had my eye on, run for office, crazier than bedbugs, gussied up, booted you out of.*

KNOWLEDGE DEMANDS

Have students create a T-chart in which they compare what the boy thinks about what women can do and what the women in the story know they can do. Have students write down the page in the book where they found their examples.

If . . . students have trouble comparing the narrator's opinion of women with what women are able to do,

then . . . focus on identifying the narrator's opinion first by selecting examples from the text that exemplify the way he thinks. Afterward, have students decide on three words that describe the narrator's opinion. Repeat the activity for the women in the story.

Lead students in a discussion about American society during the time the story takes place. Point out that women in the early 1900s rarely held office or positions of power and that women in Oregon only got the right to vote in 1912, just a few years before the story takes place. Encourage students to share their observations about how life for women has changed since then. They can then write a short paragraph expressing their ideas.

Express and Extend

LEVELS OF MEANING

EXPRESS Have pairs create a small comic strip that shows each of the steps the narrator's mother took to run for mayor. There should be at least four boxes in each comic strip.

If . . . students have difficulty identifying the steps in this process,

then . . . use the Steps in a Process Routine and Graphic Organizer in Part 3 prior to completing the activity.

EXTEND Form small groups. Have students write a short narrative of their experiences with making changes or standing up for something they believe in. Use the Narrative Paragraph Writing Routine and Graphic Organizer in Part 3 as needed to help students organize their writing.

STRUCTURE

EXPRESS Have small groups show how the author uses dialogue to keep the story moving. Remind students that dialogue provides clues to the characters' thoughts and personalities, which are not always explicitly stated in the story.

If . . . students have difficulty determining who is speaking,

then . . . have them go through the text line by line, keeping track of the characters' names and words.

EXTEND Have partners add to a scene from the story by writing some additional lines of dialogue. Remind students that the new dialogue should be logical, based on actual story events, and accurately reflect the personality and thoughts of the characters.

MORE SUPPORT

ENGLISH LANGUAGE LEARNERS

Students may need help understanding how one event causes another event to occur. Help students summarize events in their own words before moving on in the story. Have them write their summaries on note cards or sticky notes, so they can refer back to them as they continue to read.

STRUGGLING READERS

If students have difficulty understanding the themes of the story, point out the last paragraph in the text. Ask them how the final sentence in the story tells one of the themes. Have students make a list of details that support the theme.

EXPRESS **Talk about Sentences and Words**

Display the following sentence from *Operation Clean Sweep.* Read the sentence aloud with students, and gauge their understanding of sentence structure by asking the guiding questions listed below.

Bacon popped in the skillet, and water whistled in the kettle.

Ask: What do the words *popped* and *whistled* show? (They show the sounds that the bacon and water made.) What kind of sentence is this? (compound) How do you know? (The word *and* connects two complete sentences.) What are the two complete sentences in this compound sentence? (*Bacon popped in the skillet* and *water whistled in the kettle*.)

TEAM TALK   Have student pairs work together to discuss and use compound sentences to write about events in the story.

If . . . students need more support with compound sentences,

then . . . use the Simple and Compound Sentences and Combining Sentences Activities in Part 3.

EXTEND Have students identify other compound sentences in the story. Have students write down the part of the sentence that helped them identify it as a compound sentence and then rewrite it as two simple sentences.

EXPRESS Have small groups use evidence from the text to describe why it was unusual, at the time, that the boy's mother might choose to run for mayor.

EXTEND Have students research the steps someone might need to take in order to run for office today. Provide students with grade-appropriate websites and books to aid their search.

ACCELERATED LEARNERS

Provide students with a few names of famous women from the women's suffrage movement. Have them choose one woman and write two paragraphs about her. The first paragraph should include a few interesting facts about the woman, and the second paragraph should include how the woman is like a character from *Operation Clean Sweep.* Have students conduct additional research as necessary.

MORE SUPPORT

Unlock the Text

QUALITATIVE MEASURES

Levels of Meaning	biographical overview of Chavez's life
Structure	chronological narrative; headings connect sections; photographs with captions; sidebars
Language Conventionality and Clarity	mainly familiar vocabulary; varied sentence structure
Knowledge Demands	Great Depression; migrant workers; unions; protest movements; California Agricultural Labor Relations Act

Cesar Chavez: Champion of Workers, pp. 79–98

Prepare to Read

LEVELS OF MEANING

Cesar Chavez: Champion of Workers provides a broad overview of Cesar Chavez's life and the role he played in organizing migrant workers. There are descriptions of the hardships the farmworkers suffered and how Cesar Chavez helped them start a union to protect themselves.

STRUCTURE

PREVIEW Display the title page. Ask students to think about what the word *champion* means to them as they read the section headings and subheadings and look at the photos. Ask:

• What information do the pictures and captions give you? (The pictures show different aspects of Cesar Chavez's life and the lives of other farmworkers. The captions explain the pictures.)

MORE SUPPORT

ENGLISH LANGUAGE LEARNERS

Discuss the relationship between graphic features, such as photographs, and new, unfamiliar vocabulary terms. Have students refer to the pictures and captions to help support their understanding. Ask what similarities the pictures, captions, and text share.

STRUGGLING READERS

Allow students to read the text aloud to become familiar with difficult words and phrases. To aid in comprehension, connect the captions, boxed text, and photos to the main text.

- Why are the boxes throughout the text important? (The Fact! boxes provide additional information about Cesar Chavez and migrant farmers. The Quote boxes are important sayings by Chavez and other key figures.)
- Why do you think the subtitle of the selection is *Champion of Workers*? (Chavez worked hard to support farmworkers.)

LANGUAGE CONVENTIONALITY AND CLARITY

PREVIEW VOCABULARY Use the Preview and Review Vocabulary Routine in Part 3 to assess if these critical vocabulary words and phrases are familiar to students: *wages, union, workers' rights, strike, ironic, migrant worker, cultivate, organize, nonviolence, justice, equality*. Use the Vocabulary Activities in Part 3 to preteach the vocabulary, such as the following: *boycott, strike, pesticides, citizenship*.

COGNATES Use the list of Spanish cognates at the beginning of this module to guide your Spanish-speaking students as they read the selection.

KNOWLEDGE DEMANDS

ACTIVATE BACKGROUND KNOWLEDGE Complete the Quick Write and Share Routine in Part 3 using the following questions. Ask:

- What does a migrant worker do?
- How is a migrant worker different from a farmworker?

Have students share their answers with a partner and combine them to create one statement answering each question. Have each pair share their statements with the class. Clarify any misunderstandings.

Interact with Text

LEVELS OF MEANING

Point out that section headings and subheadings help guide students through Chavez's life, from his childhood helping his family work on the farms to his adulthood as a champion for farmworkers.

Use the Main Idea and Details Routine and Graphic Organizer in Part 3, and have students look at one of the main ideas presented in the story, such as Chavez's life, the poor treatment of farmworkers, or use of nonviolence to achieve one's goals.

STRUCTURE

Discuss how each event in the selection leads to the next, and ultimately the events lead Cesar Chavez to become the "champion of workers." Have students work in small groups to summarize each event before sharing with the class and discussing how the events relate to each other.

> If . . . students have difficulty summarizing a particular event,
>
> then . . . use the Retell or Summarize Routine and Graphic Organizer in Part 3 to help students give an overview of a particular event. Afterward, have students write one sentence saying why that event is important.

Have students choose one of the events described in the text and write a short, first-person account of the event from the perspective of Cesar Chavez. The account should describe Chavez's reasons for his actions and explain how he felt during that period.

MORE SUPPORT

ENGLISH LANGUAGE LEARNERS

Read aloud paragraphs from the "Farmworkers" section that have important information about Chavez's early life as a farmworker and how he met his wife. Ask students to take turns reading the same paragraphs aloud and then summarizing the paragraphs.

STRUGGLING READERS

To help students understand the impact of the Great Depression on Americans, have students verbalize what they see in the pictures on pp. 82 and 83. Bring in photographs or use the Internet to share Depression-era photos that depict the lines of people waiting for food or money.

LANGUAGE CONVENTIONALITY AND CLARITY

Some important words are not defined in the text, so model finding context in the surrounding words to help students understand the meanings. For example, the text says, "The union used this attention to ask Americans to boycott grapes. The boycott caused many owners to lose money . . . Farm owners were not happy that their grapes weren't being picked or sold." Explain how students can use clues, such as "weren't being picked or sold" to help them determine the meaning of *boycott.*

If . . . students have difficulty understanding how to use context clues to understand an unfamiliar word,

then . . . have students put the difficult term in a word web that includes its definition and other words that are similar to it. Afterward, have students use the term in a sentence of their own.

KNOWLEDGE DEMANDS

Point out that many events in U.S. history influenced the path that Chavez chose to take with his life. For example, when the Great Depression began in 1929, Chavez's family was forced to close their grocery store and begin their lives as migrant workers.

If . . . students have trouble understanding how different events influenced Cesar Chavez's life,

then . . . have students fill out a T-chart with the headings *Life Event* and *Impact.* Assign students a particular event to dissect.

STRUGGLING READERS

Some of the sentences in *Cesar Chavez: Champion of Workers* are complex, such as the sentence, "When his chores were finished, he went to school." Use the Complex Sentences and Independent and Dependent Clauses Activities in Part 3 to help students understand the complex sentence structure.

MORE SUPPORT

Text Collection

Express and Extend

LEVELS OF MEANING

EXPRESS Have pairs work together to discuss the reasons Chavez organized the farmworkers and what effects the unions had on workers and owners.

If . . . students have difficulty identifying causes and effects,

then . . . use the Cause and Effect Routine and Graphic Organizer in Part 3 to help them recognize relationships between events.

EXTEND Have partners identify the causes and effects related to the following events described the text: the Chavez family selling their farm and store and moving to California, Chavez starting a union of farmworkers, the grape strike and boycott, and the protest against pesticides.

STRUCTURE

EXPRESS To help students keep track of the important events in Chavez's life, have them record events on a time line that begins with his birth and ends with his death. Use the Time Line Routine and Graphic Organizer in Part 3.

If . . . the Fact! and Quote boxes and the captions interfere with students' comprehension of important events,

then . . . remind them to focus on the main part of the text that appears in the center of the page. They can disregard the boxed features and captions for this task and come back to them during a later reading.

EXTEND Have students write a paragraph that gives an overview of Cesar Chavez's accomplishments, highlighting how he helped others. Use the Informative/Explanatory Writing Routine and Graphic Organizer in Part 3 to help students organize their writing as needed.

MORE SUPPORT

ENGLISH LANGUAGE LEARNERS

If students have difficulty completing the time line, have them select one main event and list the important details.

STRUGGLING READERS

Have students read the Fact! box on p. 89. Discuss with them what *Si se puede* means in English. Ask students to talk about challenges in their own lives when they struggled to accomplish something.

LANGUAGE CONVENTIONALITY AND CLARITY

EXPRESS Talk about Sentences and Words

Display the following sentences, and read them aloud with students.

> During the 1980s, Chavez tried to change the use of pesticides on crops. These chemicals could make farmworkers sick.

Ask: What context clues help you understand the meaning of the word *pesticides?* (chemicals, sick) What does the phrase *could make* imply? (It shows there is a chance the chemicals will make the workers sick, but it is not for certain.)

TEAM TALK Have students work in pairs to talk about the word *pesticides,* giving an example of it.

> If . . . students have difficulty using the word *pesticides*,
> then . . . use the Related Words Activity in Part 3.

EXTEND Have groups discuss why pesticides are still used if they make people sick. Have students create a T-chart and list the pros and cons of using pesticides.

KNOWLEDGE DEMANDS

EXPRESS Have small groups use evidence from the text to articulate the steps Chavez used to advance the California Agricultural Labor Relations Act to protect the rights of farmworkers in unions.

> If . . . students have difficulty recognizing the actions that led to the passing of the act,
> then . . . summarize one event that led to the targeted event.

EXTEND Have the small groups research the California Agricultural Labor Relations Act and give a brief presentation in which they give three facts that were not discussed in the book.

ACCELERATED LEARNERS

Have students create a time line of their last year in school. The time line should include four important events. At the end, they should write a few sentences summarizing their year.

MORE SUPPORT

Cognates

Cognates are words that have similar spellings and meanings in two or more languages. Many words in English and Spanish share Greek or Latin roots, and many words in English came from French, which is closely connected to Spanish (and to Portuguese, Italian, and Romanian). Because of this, many literary, content, and academic process words in English (e.g., *gracious/gracioso; volcano/volcán; compare/comparar*) have recognizable Spanish cognates.

Making the connection to cognates permits students who are native Spanish speakers to understand the strong foundation they have in academic and literary English. These links between English and Spanish are also useful for native speakers of English and other languages because they help uncover basic underlying features of our language.

ANCHOR TEXT Real-Life Superheroes

ENGLISH	SPANISH	ENGLISH	SPANISH
accused	acusó	nationality	nacionalidad
approval	aprobación	nominated	nominado
architecture	arquitectura	orphanage	orfanato
arrested	arrestado	parliament	parlamento
attacked	atacado	persecution	persecución
boycott	boicot	persuade	persuadir
brilliant	brillante	prevention	prevención
campaign	campaña	privacy	privacidad
commander	comandante	protection	protección
cruelty	crueldad	racism	racismo
deliberately	deliberadamente	reactions	reacciones
deported	deportado	rescues	rescates
determination	determinación	respected	respetado
diplomat	diplomático	ridicule	ridículo
discrimination	discriminación	sacrifice	sacrificio
duel	duelo	sculpture	escultura
evangelical	evangélico	segregation	segregación
ghetto	gueto	soldiers	soldados
miraculously	milagrosamente	superhero	superhéroe
missionary	misionero	tragedy	tragedia
mistreat	maltratar		

SUPPORTING TEXT **The Great Migration**

ENGLISH	SPANISH	ENGLISH	SPANISH
abolish	abolir	immigrant	inmigrante
arrested	arrestado	industrial	industrial
communities	comunidades	industries	industrias
compete	competir	migration	migración
destroy	destruir	nature	naturaleza
disdain	desdén	opportunity	oportunidad
education	educación	population	población
exclusion	exclusión	resist	resistir
exodus	éxodo	segregation	segregación
guard	guardia		

SUPPORTING TEXT **Angel Island**

ENGLISH	SPANISH	ENGLISH	SPANISH
agents	agentes	generally	generalmente
area	área	historic	histórico
authorities	autoridades	humans	humanos
club	club	identify	identificar
completed	completado	miners	mineros
criminals	criminales	museum	museo
deported	deportado	park	parque
discrimination	discriminación	preserve	preservar
escape	escapar	region	región
exclusion	exclusión	sacrifices	sacrificios

These lists contains many, but not all,
Spanish cognates from these selections.

Unlock the Text

QUALITATIVE MEASURES

Levels of Meaning	informational text about four individuals from history who fought to improve society; themes of courage, determination, and personal sacrifice for a cause
Structure	multiple text features on a page; glossary; index
Language Conventionality and Clarity	challenging domain-specific and academic vocabulary; subordinate clauses; transitional phrases
Knowledge Demands	understanding historical events; making connections between individuals and events; WWII; civil rights movement

Prepare to Read

LEVELS OF MEANING

Real-Life Superheroes is an informational text about four individuals who took personal risks to make important changes in society. Have students consider the associations they make with the word *superhero*. As they read, have students consider how each individual in the text fits the description of a superhero to determine themes in the text about personal sacrifice, risk, and perseverance.

STRUCTURE

PREVIEW Have students identify the many organizational sections of the text. Ask: How is the main text divided as a whole? (into four large sections, each about one individual; then into smaller sections within each larger one) Point out that the bold names in the Table of Contents indicate

ENGLISH LANGUAGE LEARNERS

Help students with idioms such as *make a difference* and *looked up to*. Explain that these phrases mean that superheroes make positive changes in society, and other people respect what they do and want to follow their example. Encourage students to use these phrases to talk about superheroes' characteristics.

STRUGGLING READERS

Students may be overwhelmed by the layout of each page. Check that students can separate the main text from captions and additional text boxes. Encourage students to read all of the main text on a page first, and then look to the other elements of the text's structure for extra information and explanations.

the large sections of the text. Have students scan the section about Richard Martin. **Ask:** What do you see on the pages of the section in addition to the main text? (a "fact file" with a timeline; illustrations; photographs; captions; a cartoon with speech bubbles; a small box of text with a lightbulb; a small box of text with a clock)

LANGUAGE CONVENTIONALITY AND CLARITY

PREVIEW VOCABULARY Use the Preview and Review Vocabulary Routine in Part 3 to assess what students know about the following words: *superheroes, ridicule, welfare, entitled, inherited, tenants, mistreated, cruelty, missionary, poverty, destitute, affected, tragedy, foster, charity, diplomat, persecution, deported, authorities, convince, campaign, sacrifice, segregated, privacy, protest,* and *discrimination.*

COGNATES Use the list of Spanish cognates at the beginning of this module to guide your Spanish-speaking students as they read the selection.

DOMAIN-SPECIFIC VOCABULARY Use the Vocabulary Activities in Part 3 to pre-teach the following domain-specific vocabulary: *RSPCA, ragged school, Nazi, ghetto, Jim Crow Laws,* and *civil rights.* Explain that students can use these words to talk about historical events that affected the individuals in the text.

KNOWLEDGE DEMANDS

ACTIVATE BACKGROUND KNOWLEDGE Assess students' knowledge of the historical context associated with each individual's story. **Ask:** What do you know about World War II? What have you learned about the Nazis' treatment of Jewish people during that time? In pairs, have students make a list of what they know. Then ask: What do you know about the civil rights movement in the United States? How did society treat African Americans and white Americans differently? What challenges did African Americans face? After students make lists in pairs, create a class list of background knowledge on the board.

STRUGGLING READERS

Have students use the glossary to look up domain-specific vocabulary words in the text before they read. As students activate background knowledge about the civil rights movement and WWII, encourage them to use new vocabulary words to discuss historical events.

Interact with Text

As you read *Real-Life Superheroes,* help students identify individuals' personal qualities that contributed to their success. Discuss the idea of *inner strength* mentioned on p. 2 and ask students to consider how the phrase applies to each individual.

> If . . . students have difficulty identifying and explaining each individual's qualities,
>
> then . . . model using key details in the text as evidence supporting a trait.

Point to the writer's use of the word *brave* to describe Raoul Wallenberg on p. 21. Ask: What did Raoul do that supports the idea that he was brave? Have students find specific evidence from the text. For example, students may point to the sentence: "Despite the danger of being killed by Nazi guards, Raoul stopped several trains taking Jews to death camps."

STRUCTURE

Point out the text boxes with a clock icon within each section. Have students reread these boxes and then ask: What is the purpose of these text boxes? (They all give historical context; they point out people's beliefs at the time or explain more about the time period in which a "real-life superhero" lived.) Explain that the clock icon indicates that the box will give more information about the time period in which the individual lived.

> If . . . students have difficulty identifying the purpose of text features,
>
> then . . . reread each text box with a clock icon individually. Ask students to explain what it contributes or adds to the information on the page.

MORE SUPPORT

ENGLISH LANGUAGE LEARNERS

Pair students of different reading levels. After reading each page, have students take turns summarizing the information on the page. Encourage students to use their own words to define difficult vocabulary on the page and to describe the individuals and events in the text.

STRUGGLING READERS

Provide sentence frames for students to provide key details that support each individual's personality traits. For example: Richard Martin is ____ because he ____.

Some challenging vocabulary words are crucial to understanding ideas in the text. While some of these words are defined in the glossary, encourage students to first use context to determine words' meanings. Model using context to define *segregated* on p. 26. Say: The text says that "the black . . . and the white communities were segregated by law." I'll look for more information about black and white communities to decide what *segregated* means. The sentence before this one says that "black and white people lived almost separate lives." The caption below the paragraph says "black and white citizens were kept separate." So, I can conclude that *segregated* must mean "kept separate."

> If . . . students have difficulty using context to define words,
>
> then . . . have students create a word web with a challenging word at the center. Have students list clues from illustrations and surrounding sentences within the web to gather context.

KNOWLEDGE DEMANDS

Explain that "real-life superheroes" often fought against beliefs or attitudes held by many other people at the time. Have students identify text features that explain society's views toward animals during Richard Martin's life. For example, students may point out the text box with a clock icon on p. 7 and the illustration of bear-baiting on p. 8. Then have students look for key details in the main text that illustrate how Richard Martin's ideas about animals were different from society's ideas about animals. Explain that others in society believed that animals did not have feelings, while Richard believed that animals deserved to be treated kindly. To pass laws protecting animals, Richard had to convince many people to change their minds about whether animals had feelings and should be treated with kindness.

ENGLISH LANGUAGE LEARNERS

Have students draw pictures on note cards to reinforce new vocabulary. Encourage students to caption their drawings with key words and phrases to help them remember a word's meaning.

Express and Extend

EXPRESS Have students determine theme by making connections between the individuals in the text. Ask: What personality traits or characteristics do all of the individuals in the text share? Say: All of the "real-life superheroes" in the text used perseverance, bravery, and courage to change something in society. They all stood up for what they believed in, even when that meant that they had to sacrifice or put themselves in danger.

If . . . students have difficulty making connections between individuals in the text,

then . . . have students work in small groups to identify key details that show how each individual demonstrated courage and sacrificed for what he or she believed in.

EXTEND Have students create a Venn diagram to compare and contrast two individuals from the text. Encourage students to include key details such as the time period in which they lived, personality traits, beliefs, and ways they took action to change something in society.

STRUCTURE

EXPRESS Point out the "fact files" and timelines at the beginning of each section. Point out that they act as a summary of the person's life and accomplishments. Explain that the timelines also place each person's accomplishments in historical context, showing events from that time period on the same line. Have students reread each section of the text and create their own fact sheets summarizing each individual's life, personality traits, and accomplishments. Encourage students to include more details than those on the fact sheets in the text.

EXTEND Have students add historical events to the timelines given in the text for each individual. For example, students might add "Jim Crow Laws enacted" to the timeline with Rosa Parks. Have students conduct research as necessary to confirm dates.

ENGLISH LANGUAGE LEARNERS

In groups, have students act out scenes from each individual's life to aid comprehension. For example, pairs might act out the confrontation between Rosa Parks and the bus driver.

STRUGGLING READERS

Provide students with categories as needed to add to fact sheets for each individual. For example, categories might include *personality traits, ways we see his/her impact today,* and *beliefs.*

LANGUAGE CONVENTIONALITY AND CLARITY

EXPRESS Talk about Sentences and Words

Students may have difficulty with complex sentences that use subordinate clauses and transitional phrases. Display and read aloud the following sentences from *Real-Life Superheroes.*

> ***When he was just 22 years old,*** *Richard became an MP for the first time.* ***As an MP,*** *Richard was known for his great sense of humor, which often had the other MPs in fits of laughter.*

Point out the bolded phrases in the passage. Explain that they help orient the reader to the time period in which events took place. Point out that without the phrases, the sentences would grammatically make sense, but would lose important information.

TEAM TALK In pairs, have students reread pp. 6 and 7. Have students use transitional phrases that indicate time to place events from the text on a timeline.

EXTEND Have students write a short one- to two-paragraph autobiography about major events in their own lives. Ask students to use transitional phrases that indicate time to sequence events.

KNOWLEDGE DEMANDS

EXPRESS Help students understand the lasting effects of each individual's actions. Have students create a chart that lists each of the four individuals in the text and his contribution to society today. Encourage students to look for organizations that still exist today, and ways that the four individuals helped to change people's attitudes over time.

> **If . . .** students have difficulty determining effects of each individual's actions,
>
> **then . . .** begin by focusing on Richard Martin's lasting impact on society. Ask: Are animal rights protected today? What organizations exist today to protect animals? How is Richard Martin connected to those organizations?

EXTEND Have students research one of the modern organizations mentioned in the text: the RSPCA, Barnardo's, or the NAACP. Ask students to write one paragraph about the organization and its mission in society today.

ACCELERATED LEARNERS

Have students conduct research on a recipient of the Wallenberg Medal. Ask students to give a summary of why the person received the medal and explain how he or she showed courage or determination.

Unlock the Text

QUALITATIVE MEASURES

Levels of Meaning	post-World War I great migration; multiple explicit themes
Structure	third-person chronological narrative with cause-and-effect paragraphs; paintings tell story; concluding poem reiterates themes
Language Conventionality and Clarity	multiple-meaning words; figurative language
Knowledge Demands	African-American history; slavery; conditions in the North and South after the Civil War; segregation; World War I

Prepare to Read

LEVELS OF MEANING

The Great Migration is a story told through the art and words of a man whose parents and other relatives lived through a time of change and sacrifice in American history. It explicitly explores the events that led up to the great migration, the difficulties that African Americans faced before and during the migration, and what happened when they arrived in the North.

STRUCTURE

PREVIEW Review with students how visual elements contribute to the meaning and tone of a text. Before students read the story, have them skim the book and look only at the illustrations. Ask: What can you tell about the people in the illustrations? (There are many African-American

ENGLISH LANGUAGE LEARNERS

Remind students that different words may have similar or related meanings. For example, in *The Great Migration*, the author uses different words related to moving, such as *exodus, migration, left, journey, movement, walking, coming,* and *arrived.*

STRUGGLING READERS

Point out that a visual can either add to the meaning of a story or help demonstrate what the writer has written. Provide students with sentence starters, such as: I see ___ in the illustrations. The people in the illustrations look ___. This illustration makes me feel ___ because ___.

people. Many of the illustrations show African Americans travelling somewhere.) Tone is the attitude an author takes, or the type of voice he or she uses to tell a story. Based on the illustrations, what might the tone of this story be? (sad or serious)

LANGUAGE CONVENTIONALITY AND CLARITY

PREVIEW VOCABULARY Use the Preview and Review Vocabulary Routine in Part 3 to assess what students know about the following words: *exodus, migration, settled, slavery, abolished, segregation, migrants*. Ask students to use each word in a sentence.

MULTIPLE-MEANING WORDS Students may have trouble understanding sentences with words that can be used as multiple parts of speech. For example, *left, time, shift, part, wave,* and *work* can all be nouns or verbs. Write sentences for each multiple-meaning word to help students comprehend the meanings and relationships of the related words. Use the Analyze Multiple-Meaning Words Routine in Part 3 for further support.

COGNATES Use the list of Spanish cognates at the beginning of this module to guide your Spanish-speaking students as they read the selection.

KNOWLEDGE DEMANDS

ACTIVATE BACKGROUND KNOWLEDGE Have students share what they know about African American history with a partner. Use the Quick Write and Share Routine in Part 3, and ask: What do you know about slavery? How did slavery end in this country? (with the Emancipation Proclamation) Why did many African Americans want to leave the South? What did African Americans hope to find in the North? Give students time to share what they discussed with their partners with the rest of the class.

Interact with Text

LEVELS OF MEANING

Students may have difficulty identifying the main ideas of the text. Use the Main Idea and Details Routine and Graphic Organizer in Part 3 to help students list the main ideas and details presented through the text and illustrations. Students may need additional support to understand the relationships between events and how they contribute to the overall meaning and theme. Have them work in small groups to ask and answer questions using the words *when* and *why* to clarify.

If . . . students have difficulty discussing main ideas and details in the text,

then . . . have them choose an illustration that they think shows the main idea of the text. Have them explain why they think it shows the main idea. Then, have them choose several other illustrations from the text that show details that support the main idea.

STRUCTURE

Use the Cause and Effect Routine and Graphic Organizer in Part 3 to help students organize the information in the text. Have students list all the general conditions that caused the migrants to travel north. Also, have students list other contributing cause-and-effect relationships, such as the boll weevil killing the cotton crops.

For example, ask: Why did food prices double? Why did life get harder for the poor? (Food prices doubled because of the war. Life got harder for the poor because food prices doubled.)

If . . . students have difficulty identifying causes and effects,

then . . . allow them to use drawings with the graphic organizer to show relationships between events and conditions. Have students write captions for the drawings.

MORE SUPPORT

ENGLISH LANGUAGE LEARNERS

Reinforce cause-and-effect relationships by modeling a think aloud. Say: The text says Southern landowners felt angry with the labor agents and the migrants. They thought labor agents were encouraging migrants to abandon them, causing their businesses to fail.

STRUGGLING READERS

Help students identify relationships between events or concepts by pointing out the author's repetition of "And the migrants kept coming." Ask: Why does he repeat this phrase? (It helps the reader remember that everything connects back to the great migration.)

LANGUAGE CONVENTIONALITY AND CLARITY

This text includes content-area vocabulary that is not defined in context. Students may have difficulty defining unfamiliar words without context clues. Discuss some alternate strategies, including using a dictionary (print or online), to determine the meaning of those words.

For example, have students look at this sentence: "The migrants soon learned that segregation was not confined to the South." Have students explain how to use a dictionary to determine the meaning of the word *segregation*. Remind students that sometimes more than one definition may appear in the dictionary, but only one will really make sense in the context of the sentence.

KNOWLEDGE DEMANDS

Lead a discussion about slavery, the Civil War, the Emancipation Proclamation, and segregation. Demonstrate to students how this background knowledge can help them better understand the events described in this story.

Have students work with a partner to write about the conditions in the South that drew the migrant workers to the North. Have students draw upon information in this text as well as what they may already know about African-American history.

In order for students to be able to infer that segregation was prevalent in the South but also existed in the North, they must have an understanding of what segregation is and what it looked like in the South at that time, such as separate water fountains to drink from and separate counters to eat at in restaurants. These examples serve to enhance the reader's understanding of the conditions and treatment migrants found when they arrived in the North.

STRUGGLING READERS

If available, show videos or documentaries related to the topics covered in the text. The visual and aural components can supplement the text they are reading. They can also help students get a better idea of the "big picture."

MORE SUPPORT

Express and Extend

EXPRESS Read aloud the following sentence with students: And the migrants kept coming. Point out that it is a refrain meant to show triumph over adversity, which is a strong theme running through the events described and illustrated in the story.

> **If . . .** students have difficulty understanding how this sentence highlights the theme of the story,
>
> **then . . .** review the events and illustrations in the story. As you go through each, ask students to identify scenes or words that show triumph over adversity.

EXTEND Point out to students that the prose in *The Great Migration* is a form of poetry. Have students write a poem about this story, using the refrain "and the migrants kept coming" as the focus and details from the text and illustrations to flesh it out.

STRUCTURE

EXPRESS Lead a discussion with students regarding the author's use of the phrase *And the migrants kept coming* and its relationship with the sequence of events in the story. Guide students to see that the author uses this phrase to break the events in the story into sections.

EXTEND Using the phrase *And the migrants kept coming* as a guide, have students use the Cause and Effect Graphic Organizer in Part 3 to record evidence from the text that demonstrates why the migrants chose to move to locations such as Chicago or Pittsburgh.

MORE SUPPORT

ENGLISH LANGUAGE LEARNERS

If students have difficulty identifying text evidence to use in their poems, have them focus on telling what they see in the illustrations first and then look for language that supports what they are trying to describe.

STRUGGLING READERS

Some students may have difficulty with the concept of prose as poetry. Take some time to review what a poem is, and explain that not all poetry is written in stanzas that rhyme. Model a think aloud that explains how this story is a poem by reading from the text and emphasizing the rhythm and tone.

EXPRESS Talk about Sentences and Words

Read aloud the following sentence with students.

> If our story rings true for you today, then it must still strike a chord in our American experience.

Discuss the meaning of this sentence. Ask: What does the author mean by *rings true* and *strikes a chord?* What are the literal and figurative meanings of these expressions? Why does he use these descriptive expressions?

If . . . students have difficulty understanding the figurative meaning of these expressions,

then . . . differentiate between the literal and figurative meanings of these musical terms. Then, ask them to draw connections between this sentence and the author's story.

TEAM TALK Tell students that writers often create expressions that relate to one of the five senses. The two expressions above relate to sound. Have student pairs discuss other expressions or images that relate to the five senses.

EXTEND Have students start a guide to idioms and expressions. For each entry, they can illustrate the literal meaning, and then illustrate and/or define the figurative meaning and use it in a sentence.

EXPRESS Read aloud the following paragraph with students.

> This is the story of an exodus of African-Americans who left their homes and farms in the South around the time of World War I and traveled to northern industrial cities in search of better lives.

Have small groups find evidence in the text to answer the following questions: While so many Americans were fighting in Europe during World War I, what was the resulting effect on the jobs they left behind? How did soldiers at war get the weapons and other supplies they needed?

EXTEND Have students imagine they own a business in the United States during the great migration. If their business is in the South, how would they convince workers to stay? If their business is in the North, how would they persuade workers to move north to work for them? Students should write a paragraph detailing their imagined experience.

ACCELERATED LEARNERS

Challenge students to use the paragraph they have written to persuade workers in the Extend Activity as a base for writing the same experience as a worker. Encourage students to use descriptive language, including all five senses, to explain why they will remain in the South or move to the North.

MORE SUPPORT

Unlock the Text

Angel Island, pp. 99–121

QUALITATIVE MEASURES

Levels of Meaning	explicit description of Chinese immigration through the history of Angel Island; relationships between people, ideas, and events
Structure	sequence of events; chapter headings; graphics; captions; cause-and-effect relationships
Language Conventionality and Clarity	multiple-meaning words; content-specific vocabulary
Knowledge Demands	immigration; citizenship; migrations to the U.S.; preserving historic landmarks

Prepare to Read

LEVELS OF MEANING

Angel Island, an informational text about a historic landmark, has one main purpose: to provide information about the part it played in the history of Chinese immigration to the United States.

STRUCTURE

PREVIEW Review with students that a sequence of events is a list of actions in the order in which they happened. Point out to students that the language in this selection gives clues to time and order. Direct students to page through the selection and read the chapter headings and photo captions. Then ask: What do you think this text is going to be about? (Chinese people who immigrated to the U.S. but faced discrimination) What do you think Angel Island is? (a place that Chinese immigrants traveled through)

ENGLISH LANGUAGE LEARNERS

Choral reading sections of text can give students the chance to practice making the sounds and words that make up the English language. Read aloud a section to students, then read as a group. Finally, have volunteers read aloud parts of the section to the rest of the group.

STRUGGLING READERS

Encourage students to use section headings as places to monitor progress. Provide them with the following list of questions to ask themselves when they begin a new section: What was the last section about? What questions do you still have? What is the name of this section? What questions do you hope will get answered as you read this section?

PREVIEW VOCABULARY Use the Preview and Review Vocabulary Routine in Part 3 to assess what students already know about the following words: *detained, immigrants, discrimination, persecution, citizens*. Ask students to use the words in reference to world events. For example, students should have read about *discrimination* and *persecution* when learning about Dr. Martin Luther King Jr.; they may know about *immigrants* and *citizens* from their personal experience or other texts they have read; they may also know about how the police *detain* criminals. Ask them how they think those words and ideas could relate to the experiences of Chinese immigrants on Angel Island.

MULTIPLE-MEANING WORDS Students may have difficulty understanding sentences containing words that can be used as multiple parts of speech. For example, "The immigrants did not have the *comfort* of their families because their families were not there to *comfort* them." Write sentences for each multiple-meaning word that will help students understand the different ways in which the words can be used. Use the Analyze Multiple-Meaning Words Routine in Part 3 for additional support.

COGNATES Use the list of Spanish cognates at the beginning of this module to guide your Spanish-speaking students as they read the selection.

ACTIVATE BACKGROUND KNOWLEDGE Have students share with the whole group what they know about immigration and citizenship. Use the Quick Write and Share Routine in Part 3 and ask: What is a migration? Why would a large group of people leave their homes to live someplace new? How is that different from going somewhere temporarily, such as going on vacation?

If students need more support, model thinking aloud about a time you or someone you know had to move. For example, say: When I was in high school, my mother got a new job in a different state, and my family had to move. It was scary to go live someplace new, but it was okay because we were together. After college, I moved out of state for a job, but I had to go alone. That was much harder for me.

Interact with Text

LEVELS OF MEANING

As you read, have students organize important events in the history of Angel Island and Chinese immigration into a time line. Periodically, ask students to summarize what they have read so far. Keep a class time line that all students can refer to as they read.

If . . . students need additional support to understand the relationships between events,

then . . . have students work in small groups to ask and answer "when" and "why" questions while reading to clarify any confusion.

For example, from 1851–1864, Chinese laborers came to the United States to help build a railroad. When the railroad was complete, they took jobs on farms. Ask: What caused Chinese laborers to take jobs on farms? (Their work on the railroad was finished.) Why didn't they choose to return to China? (Possible answer: They felt they could make a better life for themselves and their families in the United States.)

STRUCTURE

Use the Cause and Effect Routine and Graphic Organizer in Part 3 to explain how one event leads to another. For example, the text shows a causal chain of events, in which one event causes another event, and that event causes a third event. Chinese laborers were welcomed at first, so they took jobs that nobody else wanted. Since they worked longer hours for less money, more businesses hired them. They were being offered jobs over other Americans. Since other Americans felt threatened and robbed of these opportunities, they became violent.

If . . . students need additional support describing cause-and-effect relationships in the text,

then . . . have students draw a comic strip that starts with the discovery of gold in California. Have students then draw four or five additional scenes depicting the chain of events that followed. If necessary, have them dictate to you or a more accelerated peer what is shown in each picture while you or the peer write their words onto a separate piece of paper. They can then copy the descriptions under their pictures.

MORE SUPPORT

ENGLISH LANGUAGE LEARNERS

Help students identify relationships between events or concepts in a text by giving them signal words to look for. For example, *because* shows cause and effect. *First, next,* and *then* show sequence. Make a signal words chart for students to reference as they read and write.

STRUGGLING READERS

Model a cause and effect think aloud by asking and answering questions about what happened first and what the effects of that event were. Ask: Why did American workers feel threatened by Chinese immigrants? (They felt the Chinese were taking away their jobs.)

LANGUAGE CONVENTIONALITY AND CLARITY

This informational text includes content-area vocabulary that is not defined in context. Help students use alternative strategies, including a dictionary (print or online), to determine the meaning of those words.

For example, look at this sentence: "But discrimination kept the Chinese from mining in areas where gold was plentiful, and taxes took money away from those who did well." Ask students to define *discrimination* based on its use in this sentence. If students are struggling to define it, explain that context clues don't always tell us the meaning of unfamiliar words. Allow them to look it up and then write a new sentence using the word.

KNOWLEDGE DEMANDS

Discuss with students the conditions in other countries that drove immigrants to the United States. Draw parallels between the Pilgrims, who fled religious persecution in England to settle here, and the Chinese, who fled war and poverty to settle here.

If . . . students have difficulty describing the relationship between the Pilgrims and the Chinese in this text,

then . . . have them use the Venn Diagram Graphic Organizer in Part 3 to organize details from the reading and their recollections that support these comparisons.

For example, the text says wars and poverty in China forced young men to *leave their homeland for a better life.* Ask students: Why did the Pilgrims leave England? (religious differences) Why did they come to this country? (the promise of freedom) Why did the Chinese leave China? (wars and poverty) Why did they come to this country? (the promise of peace and a better life)

Express and Extend

EXPRESS Have students work with a partner to write a paragraph about the relationship between the two central ideas in this text: the history of Angel Island and the experiences of Chinese immigrants in the nineteenth century.

EXTEND Challenge students to create an informational brochure for Chinese immigrants arriving at Angel Island. Explain the types of work available to them, any laws affecting them, and questions immigration authorities might ask upon their arrival.

EXPRESS Read aloud the following sentences with students:

> However, in 1906, an earthquake and fire destroyed parts of San Francisco, including the Hall of Records. This building held all the city's marriage, birth, and death certificates. After these papers were gone, many Chinese people began claiming that they had been born in the United States and were citizens.

Use the class time line to model for students how the sequence of these events also represents causes and effects. For example, say: Because the Hall of Records burned down, the Chinese immigrants could claim that they were born here.

EXTEND Have students write a short fictional narrative about a person immigrating to the United States. Encourage them to include why the person is moving, what he or she hopes to see in the United States, and any fears the person might have. Use the Narrative Essay Writing Routine and Graphic Organizer in Part 3 to help students organize their writing as needed.

ENGLISH LANGUAGE LEARNERS

If students have difficulty writing their narratives, display the following sentence frames to get them started: I want to move because ___. When I arrive in America, I hope to ___. I am afraid that ___.

STRUGGLING READERS

Some students may have difficulty with the language associated with causes and effects. Help them to find and use words and phrases like *so, since, because,* and *as a result.*

LANGUAGE CONVENTIONALITY AND CLARITY

EXPRESS Talk about Sentences and Words

Display the following sentence from *Angel Island*. Read it aloud with students.

> To keep the "paper families" out, authorities asked these immigrants questions that they thought only real family members would know.

Ask: What does the author mean by *paper families*? (people who may not be related to anyone in the United States but who have fake papers that say they are related to someone here) What does this sentence tell you about the relationship between the authorities and the immigrants? (Authorities did not trust immigrants.)

TEAM TALK Have students work in pairs to debate whether it was right or wrong for authorities to try to keep people with fake papers out of the United States. Assign a side to each student. Then have each student summarize for the class what their partner said about the issue.

EXTEND Have students write a short paragraph from the point of view of a Chinese immigrant waiting to be interviewed by authorities at Angel Island. Then allow students to share their paragraphs in small groups.

KNOWLEDGE DEMANDS

EXPRESS Read aloud the following paragraph with students:

> The Chinese-American community rallied together and raised money to save this historic landmark. In 1976, the state of California set aside money to preserve the barracks and the poems.

Ask students to brainstorm as a group and discuss why Chinese Americans would want to be reminded of the way Chinese immigrants were treated. Explain that even though their ancestors were not always treated with kindness, they want people to appreciate the sacrifices their ancestors made to come to and live in the United States.

EXTEND Have students imagine that they are a descendent of these Chinese immigrants. Have them write a letter to their ancestor showing appreciation for the life they now have as a result of their ancestor's sacrifices.

ACCELERATED LEARNERS

Challenge students to create a short play about a Chinese immigrant making the journey to the United States. One student should be the person immigrating, and the other students should play people that character interacts with, such as immigration authorities, American citizens, and other Chinese immigrants.

Angel Island **87**

MORE SUPPORT

Understanding the Universe

TEXT SET

ANCHOR TEXT
George's Secret Key
to the Universe

SUPPORTING TEXT
The Man Who Went to
the Far Side of the Moon

SUPPORTING TEXT
Mayday on Moon of
Jupiter

TEXT SET

ANCHOR TEXT
Jess and Layla's
Astronomical
Assignment

SUPPORTING TEXT
Our Mysterious Universe

SUPPORTING TEXT
A Black Hole Is NOT
a Hole

Cognates

Cognates are words that have similar spellings and meanings in two or more languages. Many words in English and Spanish share Greek or Latin roots, and many words in English came from French, which is closely connected to Spanish (and to Portuguese, Italian, and Romanian). Because of this, many literary, content, and academic process words in English (e.g., *gracious/gracioso; volcano/volcán; compare/comparar*) have recognizable Spanish cognates.

Making the connection to cognates permits students who are native Spanish speakers to understand the strong foundation they have in academic and literary English. These links between English and Spanish are also useful for native speakers of English and other languages because they help uncover basic underlying features of our language.

ANCHOR TEXT George's Secret Key to the Universe

ENGLISH	SPANISH	ENGLISH	SPANISH
absolutely	absolutamente	invisible	invisible
alternative	alternativo	laboratory	laboritorio
apologetically	apológeticamente	members	miembros
atmosphere	atmósfera	nuclear	nuclear
authorization	autorización	optical	óptico
crater	cráter	orbit	orbitar
comets	cometas	organic	orgánico
declare	declarar	ovation	ovación
destructive	destructivo	perspective	perspectiva
disobedience	desobediencia	physics	física
emergency	emergencia	portal	portal
enormous	enorme	prototype	prototipo
equations	ecuaciones	reactions	reacciones
eternal	eterno	rectangle	rectángulo
explosions	explosiones	Solar System	Sistema Solar
fundamental	fundamental	succession	sucesión
fusion	fusión	universe	universo
galaxies	galaxias	urgent	urgente
generator	generador	usual	usual
horizon	horizonte	vapor	vapor
humanity	humanidad	vegetarian	vegetariano
improvise	improvisar	vigorous	vigoroso
indignant	indignado	volume	volumen
intersection	intersección		

SUPPORTING TEXT The Man Who Went to the Far Side of the Moon

ENGLISH	SPANISH		ENGLISH	SPANISH
astronaut	astronauta		potentially	potencialmente
communication	comunicación		planet	planeta
different	diferente		practice	practicar
experiment	experimento		prepare	preparar
horizon	horizonte		radio	radio
imagine	imaginar		simulator	simulador
inject	inyectar		transmission	transmisión
meteor	meteoro		trap	atrapar
module	módulo			

SUPPORTING TEXT Mayday on Moon of Jupiter

ENGLISH	SPANISH		ENGLISH	SPANISH
captain	capitán		invention	invención
column	columna		Jupiter	Júpiter
consist	consistir		orbit	órbita
contact	contactar		oxygen	oxígeno
contents	contenido		pages	páginas
distance	distancia		potential	potencial
emergency	emergencia		radiation	radiación
energy	energía		repair	reparar
evaporate	evaporar		silicate	silicato
fusion	fusión		situation	situación
generate	generar			

These lists contain many, but not all, Spanish cognates from these selections.

Unlock the Text

QUALITATIVE MEASURES

Levels of Meaning	science fiction book with a mixture of narrative plot lines and scientific facts about the universe; families and characters with differing traits
Structure	cause-and-effect structure; illustrations; sidebars or informational pages
Language Conventionality and Clarity	scientific vocabulary about planets and the solar system; figurative language; parts of speech
Knowledge Demands	understanding of the solar system: its parts, how it was created, and how it affects humans; the science fiction genre; space travel

Prepare to Read

LEVELS OF MEANING

One purpose of *George's Secret Key to the Universe* is to take readers on a fantasy adventure of traveling through outer space. The second purpose is to provide scientific facts about the planets in our solar system.

STRUCTURE

PREVIEW Have students view the book's title, photographs, captions, illustrations, and informational pages or sidebars. Ask: Based on the illustrations and sidebars, what do you think the book will be about? (outer space) Who might the main characters be? (the boy on the cover, who is probably George; a girl; an evil-looking scientist) What might be explained in the information pages and sidebars? (planets and the universe)

ENGLISH LANGUAGE LEARNERS

Throughout the selection, characters go by different names. For example, George's teacher is called Dr. Reeper, Greeper, and Graham. As "new" names occur, check to see if students know whom the text refers to.

STRUGGLING READERS

Students can help each other learn, use, and remember scientific vocabulary by playing a vocabulary guessing game. Each student chooses a vocabulary word and makes up a clue. The rest of the class guesses the word from the context of the clues.

PREVIEW VOCABULARY Use the Preview and Review Vocabulary Routine in Part 3 to assess what students know about the following words: *environmental, mysterious, organic, telescope, humanity, future, planets, dangerous, habitable,* and *dilemma.*

DOMAIN-SPECIFIC VOCABULARY Use the Vocabulary Activities in Part 3 to teach domain-specific vocabulary words, such as *asteroid, comet, galaxy, black holes, supernovas, cosmologist, global warming, portal, physics, chemistry,* and *circumference.*

COGNATES Use the list of Spanish cognates at the beginning of this module to guide your Spanish-speaking students as they read the selection.

ACTIVATE BACKGROUND KNOWLEDGE Tell students that this book is written in a genre called science fiction. Use the Quick Write and Share Routine in Part 3 and ask the following questions: What are the characteristics of a fiction book? (The story includes characters and events that are made up by the author.) What are the differences and similarities between regular fiction and science fiction? (Unlike fiction, science fiction includes scientific facts and information that is true. Like fiction, science fiction can also include characters and events that are made up.)

> If . . . students have difficulties with comparing and contrasting regular fiction and science fiction,
>
> then . . . provide them with a Venn diagram with the headings *Fiction* and *Science Fiction.* This will help them organize their ideas prior to completing the activity above.

If needed, explain to students that a science fiction text is a made-up story (fiction) based on a science topic, such as exploring space. Give the following example: A book about an astronaut that fights aliens in space is a science fiction book. While the book might contain actual scientific facts, such as information about how astronauts launch into space and what the solar system is like, it would also contain some things that were made up. For example, while there is some evidence that might lead scientists to believe there is life on other planets, we do not actually know if aliens exist in outer space.

MORE SUPPORT

Interact with Text

At the beginning of *George's Secret Key to the Universe*, the reader meets George's family and Annie's family. Have students distinguish between the families by working in pairs or on their own to fill out a T-chart with information about each family. Have them use the headings *Annie's Family* and *George's Family.* Remind students that they need to cite evidence from the text to support what they record in the graphic organizer. Afterwards, have students share their descriptions and where they found them in the text.

If . . . students have difficulty comparing and contrasting,

then . . . have them record descriptions of either Annie's family or George's family. Afterwards, students should partner up with someone who recorded descriptions of the other family and work together to compare and contrast the descriptions.

The following are a few other comparisons students can make: George and Annie; Eric and Dr. Reeper; Dr. Reeper and Ringo's gang; or Eric and George. These comparisons can serve as a gateway to talk about the selection's themes.

STRUCTURE

Use the Cause and Effect Routine and Graphic Organizer in Part 3 to help students keep track of major decisions made by the main characters as the story develops. After reading the first six chapters, divide students into small groups and assign each group one of the following major events: George's decision to go Next Door, Eric's decision to show George how Cosmos works, or George's decision to tell Dr. Reeper about Cosmos. Students should write the events in the *Causes* boxes on the graphic organizer and the effects of each event in the *Effects* boxes. Afterwards, have students discuss what these decisions show about the characters that made them. As students continue to read, have them select the chapter's major events on their own and organize them, including causes and effects, into a new cause and effect graphic organizer.

MORE SUPPORT

ENGLISH LANGUAGE LEARNERS

Provide a demonstration to help students understand that causes occur before effects. Drop a pencil on the floor. Provide sentence frames: What happened first was ___, which is the cause. What happened next was ___, which is the effect.

STRUGGLING READERS

Provide extra practice with figurative language by using idioms to describe several pictures. Ask students to look at the pictures to help determine what the idiom means. For example, "under the weather" could be used to describe someone who is sick.

94 Grade 5 • Unit 3 • Module A

LANGUAGE CONVENTIONALITY AND CLARITY

Students may have difficulty with some of the idiomatic language in *George's Secret Key to the Universe*, such as *catch a glimpse, blood ran cold, heart of the matter, on his tail, bitter wind, butterflies in his stomach, whipped around,* and *red-handed.* To help students understand these phrases, use the Analyze Idioms and Expressions Routine in Part 3.

As students become familiar with the routine, ask them to find idioms and expressions in the text and create a glossary. The glossary should contain the idiom, its literal meaning, and its figurative meaning. Students can also draw a picture of the literal meaning. As a class game, students can show their drawings to the class, and see if others can guess which idiom is being represented by the drawing of the literal meaning.

KNOWLEDGE DEMANDS

To help students unlock complex information about the solar system, as discussed in the selection, have them complete the following activity.

Tell students: When I ask you how one piece of text supports another, I am asking how a particular piece of text helps you understand something else on the page or in the chapter. In this case, I want to know how the informational page or sidebar helps you understand what you read in the chapter. **Assign students an informational page or sidebar from a chapter to read and summarize with a partner. Afterward, have students write a paragraph that tells how the informational page or sidebar supports the text from the chapter.**

If . . . students have trouble summarizing information from an informational page or sidebar,

then . . . use the Retell or Summarize Routine and Graphic Organizer in Part 3. Remind students that summaries should include the most important details from the text and should be written in their own words.

STRUGGLING READERS

After finishing each chapter, allow students to review the main ideas and events from the chapter by writing a short summary or summarizing the main events in a partner discussion. The summaries should demonstrate what students comprehend from the chapter and whether there are any common misconceptions about the plot.

MORE SUPPORT

Express and Extend

EXPRESS As Dr. Greeper points out to Ringo's gang, there is a difference between science fact and science fiction. Have students differentiate between the two by filling out a T-chart with the headings *Fact* and *Fiction.* Assign pairs a chapter and have them find examples of each. For example, jumping onto a comet from an invisible door in the library is fiction, but the geological makeup of a comet is fact.

EXTEND Since science fiction books are based on scientific facts, have students take one of the facts from their T-chart and use it as the basis for their own science fiction paragraph. For example, students learn that Pluto isn't a planet because it hasn't cleared a path around the sun. A student could write a paragraph in which Pluto becomes a planet by fighting an army of aliens that stand in its path around the sun.

STRUCTURE

EXPRESS Assign students a character from the selection and have them write a short summary of three important decisions made by that character. Provide students the option of choosing between the Retell or Summarize Graphic Organizer or the Three-Column Chart Graphic Organizer in Part 3 to help organize their writing. Afterward, discuss how those decisions affected the story's plot.

If . . . students have difficulty picking three important decisions,

then . . . give students five decisions George made, and have them decide which three are most important. Guide students by asking: If (character) had decided to do something different than (given option), would it drastically change the story? (If the answer is "no," then the event is not important.)

EXTEND Have students select an event in the story they found interesting and write a paragraph explaining whether they would make the same choice as the character. Students should cite evidence from the text supporting how their choice would affect the story's outcome.

ENGLISH LANGUAGE LEARNERS

To provide guidance with writing summaries, use the Main Idea and Details Routine and Graphic Organizer in Part 3. The graphic organizer will help students identify important details to include in their summaries.

STRUGGLING READERS

To help students compose opinions, use the Express Opinions Routine in Part 3. Provide sentence frames such as: I believe the government should spend money on ___. I think this is the best use of money because ___.

LANGUAGE CONVENTIONALITY AND CLARITY

EXPRESS Talk about Sentences and Words

Display the following sentences from *George's Secret Key to the Universe*.
Read them aloud with students.

> I think Graham's punished himself quite enough already. Best leave him alone.
> I doubt our paths will cross again.

Ask: Who is Graham? (Dr. Reeper, George's teacher) What does it mean when the
text says, "Graham's punished himself?" (It means he has done something that
negatively affects him.) What does the word *already* imply? (that something has
happened in the past) What does the word *best* suggest in the second sentence?
(It suggests that the most appropriate decision is to leave Graham alone.) What
does it mean to cross paths with someone? (It means to meet with someone. In this
case, the speaker is saying that he doesn't think he and Graham will meet again.)

TEAM TALK Have students discuss other ways to say the phrase *to cross paths.*
Then, have them rewrite the passage using their own phrase. Remind students that
the meaning of the sentence should stay the same.

> If . . . students need help rewriting the passage,
>
> then . . . have them work in pairs to identify the different parts of each sentence. Have
> students identify the following: the subject and predicate in each complete sentence, the
> missing subject in the second sentence, the meaning of *Graham's,* and the meaning of
> any unfamiliar words. Use the Sentence Activities in Part 3 for additional support.

EXTEND Have students decide if they think Graham has been punished enough
for what he did to Eric and George. Afterward, they should write a paragraph giving
their opinion and supporting it with at least one example from the text.

KNOWLEDGE DEMANDS

EXPRESS Have students work in small groups to create a presentation about an
object in our solar system. Information should be based on scientific facts given in
the book and should include the object's name, which type of object it is, its size,
its weather patterns, and its distance from the sun.

EXTEND Use the Opinion Writing Routine and Graphic Organizer in Part 3 as a
guide for students to write a persuasive paragraph responding to the following
prompt: Space travel is very expensive, and some people believe that the money
our government spends on space travel and research would be better spent
helping people on Earth. Do you agree or disagree with this statement? Provide
support for your opinion.

ACCELERATED LEARNERS

Have students rewrite the end of the story as if George was not able to retrieve Cosmos
and save Eric. The ending should be at least a page long and explain what Dr. Greeper
will do once he has Cosmos. Students should also create an informational page or
illustration to go along with their new ending.

MORE SUPPORT

Unlock the Text

QUALITATIVE MEASURES

The Man Who Went to the Far Side of the Moon, pp. 5–17

Levels of Meaning	narrative description of the first spacecraft to land on the moon; main idea and key details; description of personal feelings
Structure	informative text detailing events in chronological order; tables; photographs; captions
Language Conventionality and Clarity	scientific vocabulary; compound words; multisyllabic words
Knowledge Demands	space exploration; numerical information such as time, temperature, distance, and weight

Prepare to Read

LEVELS OF MEANING

The Man Who Went to the Far Side of the Moon tells readers about the first moon landing and the three astronauts who went on the mission. It also takes a closer look at the personal feelings and experiences of astronaut Michael Collins, who orbited the moon alone.

STRUCTURE

PREVIEW Have students read the title and view the photographs and text features. Ask: Based on the pictures, what do you think the selection is about? (a mission to the moon) Who might the people in the photos be? (the astronauts who went to the moon) There are large, colored words on the top of some of the pages. What are they for? (They are quotes from

ENGLISH LANGUAGE LEARNERS

Students may not have much background knowledge of space exploration. Show photos of the moon's surface to help students understand how the moon differs from Earth. Discuss other past moon landings to help students realize that many people have traveled to the moon.

STRUGGLING READERS

Have students keep a running list of multiple-meaning words from the text. For each word, have students write all definitions and draw illustrations. Then have students use the list to determine which definition fits best with the text.

the mission.) What is the purpose of the small writing next to the pictures? (They are captions that explain the pictures.)

LANGUAGE CONVENTIONALITY AND CLARITY

PREVIEW VOCABULARY Use the Preview and Review Vocabulary Routine in Part 3 to assess what students know about the following words: *spacecraft, astronaut, module, horizon, solar, simulator, crater, atmosphere,* and *quarantine.* Use the Word Knowledge Strategy Routine in Part 3 to help students determine the definition of each word.

COGNATES Use the list of Spanish cognates at the beginning of this module to guide your Spanish-speaking students as they read the selection.

PRONUNCIATION OF MULTISYLLABIC WORDS Use the Multisyllabic Word Strategy Routine in Part 3 to help students correctly pronounce the following scientific words: *astronaut, simulator, atmosphere,* and *quarantine.*

KNOWLEDGE DEMANDS

ACTIVATE BACKGROUND KNOWLEDGE Have students share what they know about space travel by asking the following questions: How did astronauts in space communicate with people on Earth? (with radios) Why do astronauts eat food that is different from food on Earth? (Lack of gravity would cause food to float away if it didn't have special preparation or packaging.) What do astronauts wear to protect themselves in space? (space suits, helmets, oxygen tanks)

Use the KWLH Chart Routine and Graphic Organizer in Part 3 to record information on the topic of space travel. Have students record information in the *What Do I Know* and *What Do I Want to Learn?* sections of the graphic organizer. Model an example: I know that gravity is different on the moon than it is on Earth. I want to know how to calculate what my weight would be on the moon.

Interact with Text

LEVELS OF MEANING

The text discusses the duties of astronauts, as well as the fact that each astronaut has a unique set of duties. To help students understand this part of the text, use the Web Routine and Graphic Organizer in Part 3. In the center circle, have students write *Astronaut Duties,* and have them write these names in each of the outer circles: *Buzz Aldrin, Neil Armstrong, Michael Collins.* As the students read, have them record the duties of each astronaut in a circle extended from the respective astronaut's name. Later put students in pairs, and have them discuss how each person's set of duties is important to the success of the mission.

STRUCTURE

Draw students' attention to the various text features in the selection: large colored type, narrative text, photographs, captions, tables, and illustrations. Guide students to see how the text features supplement the main text to enhance the reader's understanding of the text.

> If . . . students have difficulty understanding how a text feature supports the main text,
>
> then . . . have students use the Venn Diagram Graphic Organizer in Part 3 with the headings *Text Feature* and *Text.*

Under the heading *Text Feature,* they should record facts from the various text features. Under the heading *Text,* they should record facts from the text. In the section where the circles overlap, students should write the information discussed in both the text and the text feature. Afterward, pairs should decide whether the text feature supported the information in the text and share their opinions with the class. Ask: What is the purpose of each text feature? Which text feature did you find most helpful? Explain your answer.

ENGLISH LANGUAGE LEARNERS

Demonstrate how to determine the meanings of compound words by identifying and defining the two smaller words that make up the compound word. Model an example from the text, such as *spacecraft.* Have students find other compound words in the text and use the same strategy to define them.

STRUGGLING READERS

To help students understand the importance of text features, have students analyze one individual text feature. Provide sentence frames: This text feature helps me understand ___. This text feature is important because ___.

MORE SUPPORT

LANGUAGE CONVENTIONALITY AND CLARITY

Display a compound word from the text and demonstrate how to define the word based on its parts. For example, *backpack* consists of the words *back,* meaning "the rear part of the body," and *pack,* meaning "a load arranged for carrying." Therefore, *backpack* means "a load carried on the rear part of the body." Next, break down compound words from the text into two smaller words, and give students a list of these smaller words. Then, have students write the full compound words using words from the list. Have students identify the word in the text. They should write down the compound word, its definition, the definition of its parts, and a sentence that includes the compound word.

KNOWLEDGE DEMANDS

The first two spreads of *The Man Who Went to the Far Side of the Moon* start with descriptions that contain many numbers for temperature, height, distance, and time. Have students discuss, in pairs, why the author chose to use all these numbers when describing the astronauts' mission on and around the moon.

If . . . students have trouble determining the importance of numerical information,

then . . . ask guiding questions, such as the following: What do these numbers describe? How do the numbers help you understand the astronauts' mission? How would the text be different if the author did not include numerical information?

MORE SUPPORT

Express and Extend

EXPRESS In addition to facts about the astronauts' mission, the author includes a description of the personal feelings of Michael Collins. Read p. 9 aloud and have students choose a word they think describes how Collins felt about his mission around the moon. Possible responses could be sad, happy, or frightened. Students should cite two examples from the text to support their decision.

If . . . students have difficulty selecting a word to describe how Michael Collins felt,

then . . . provide the following choices for them to select from: lonely, angry, happy, sad, and scared. Provide other choices if desired.

EXTEND Have students write one paragraph that begins: I am Michael Collins, and I experienced ___. The paragraph should be written as a journal entry describing how Collins might have felt when he was inside the *Columbia*.

EXPRESS Have students read the table "Michael Collins's Food Pack on the Fourth Day of the Trip," and decide whether the information helps them understand the text and tell why or why not. Students should write down their responses in a few sentences before sharing them with the class.

EXTEND Have students read the table "Left on the Moon" and repeat the above activity. Then have them write a paragraph defending the author's choice to include the information.

ENGLISH LANGUAGE LEARNERS

Help students understand shades of meaning for words that describe feelings. Provide a list of words that all mean similar things, such as *upset, furious,* and *perturbed.* Say each word aloud, and vary your voice to give clues to each word's meaning and level of intensity.

STRUGGLING READERS

When having students write their opinion, aid their writing by providing sentence frames, such as: I think the table is/is not helpful because ___. I believe the table does/does not support the text because ___. I believe the table that gives better information is ___.

LANGUAGE CONVENTIONALITY AND CLARITY

EXPRESS Talk about Sentences and Words

Display and read aloud the following sentences.

> He looks up at the yellow disk in the sky and thinks to himself: *I have been there. It was beautiful, but compared to Earth it was nothing.*

Ask: What does the phrase *yellow disk* refer to? **(the moon)** Why does the author use this phrase instead of calling the object by name? **(to use descriptive language that gives the reader a visual image)** What does the author mean when she says, "[he] thinks to himself?" **(He is thinking about something, but not saying it aloud.)** Why is the text in italics and not in quotes? **(Only words that are spoken aloud are in quotes. These words are being thought, not spoken.)**

TEAM TALK Have students look at the phrase *yellow disk in the sky* and then turn to a partner to discuss another descriptive phrase that could be used to characterize or identify the moon. Afterward, have students rewrite the sentence with their partner, using their new phrase, and share it with the class.

> If . . . students have difficulty replacing the phrase,
> then . . . have them list characteristics of the moon, such as size or color, and pick an object that has some of those characteristics.

EXTEND Have students rewrite the sentence "I carry it inside, like a treasure," without changing the meaning of the sentence.

KNOWLEDGE DEMANDS

EXPRESS Have students work in small groups to record facts they learned about space exploration to complete their KWLH Chart Graphic Organizers. Ask: Which of your questions were answered? Which were unanswered? How might you answer those questions? Students should write information in the *What Did I Learn?* and *How Did I Learn It?* sections of their graphic organizers.

EXTEND Have students work with a partner to find an answer for one of their questions that wasn't discussed in the selection. Guide students in selecting appropriate resources.

ACCELERATED LEARNERS

Based on the text, have students decide which role they would have liked to have had in the mission. Would they have wanted to be in the lunar or command module? Then have them write a paragraph response justifying their opinion. They should also tell how they would prepare for the mission based on what they know about space exploration.

Unlock the Text

QUALITATIVE MEASURES

Levels of Meaning	science fiction story about twins who travel in space; character traits and feelings
Structure	short chronological story; illustrations; cause and effect; suspense
Language Conventionality and Clarity	scientific terms; word stems; figurative language
Knowledge Demands	space flight and geological terms; finding solutions to a problem

Mayday on Moon of Jupiter, pp. 18–28

Prepare to Read

LEVELS OF MEANING

In the short story "Mayday on Moon of Jupiter," a brother-and-sister team travel into outer space but end up crash landing in the wrong location. The text demonstrates how the two overcome this obstacle through teamwork.

STRUCTURE

PREVIEW Have students read the title and look at the illustrations. Ask: What do you think the story will be about? (a boy and girl who go into space) Based on the characters' expressions from the first two pages, how do you think they feel? (scared, nervous, angry) How can you tell? (The boy's eyebrows are pointed down and his face is in a frown, which show he's angry. The girl's eyes are wide, which show she's nervous or scared.) Look at the next page. Why is the boy upset? (The spacecraft that he was driving just crashed.) What conclusion can you draw based on

ENGLISH LANGUAGE LEARNERS

When students have questions about the text, direct their attention to the illustrations on that spread. Have students describe what they see in the pictures. Tell students that illustrations often give visual depictions of what is being described or explained in the text.

STRUGGLING READERS

When students come upon a stumbling block, provide them with graphic organizers and strategies that might help them organize information. For example, a web can help students work independently to list details about one main topic.

the illustrations on these first four pages? What clues led you to this conclusion? (The boy and girl have never traveled in space before. The girl looks scared and is reading a map or blueprint. The characters might not know how to operate a spacecraft, which is why it crashed.)

LANGUAGE CONVENTIONALITY AND CLARITY

PREVIEW VOCABULARY Use the Preview and Review Vocabulary Routine in Part 3 to assess what students know about the following words: *Mayday, crash-land, manual, reactor, ice-crusted, radiate, fusion, glinted, silicate, glancing,* and *crevasse.*

Vary steps 3–4 of the Preview and Review Vocabulary Routine by assigning pairs three or four of the vocabulary words and having them work together to define the words using classroom resources. Afterward, have students share each word's definition and the strategies used to define it. Students should write down at least one of these strategies in a vocabulary notebook for later use.

COGNATES Use the list of Spanish cognates at the beginning of this module to guide your Spanish-speaking students as they read the selection.

KNOWLEDGE DEMANDS

ACTIVATE BACKGROUND KNOWLEDGE Use the Web Routine and Graphic Organizer in Part 3 to activate students' background knowledge. Have them label the center of their webs *Descriptive Details.* Tell students: This story focuses on the space travel of a brother and sister. As you read, there will be clues in the text that tell you what the brother and sister are like. Think about the different ways authors use descriptive details to show their readers what characters are like. Write those details in the bubbles on your web graphic organizer.

Interact with Text

LEVELS OF MEANING

Read aloud the first page and have students write down words that describe how Justin and Alicia react as the space pod is crashing. Afterward, pair up students and have them review the words they wrote. Next, have them write a few sentences describing each character, using evidence from the text. For example, students might write: Justin is a very intense person. I know this because he punches the pod's touch screen as the ship crashes.

If . . . students have trouble using descriptive language,

then . . . model the activity by doing a read aloud in which you write down the actions of one character. As you write words, make sure to explain your choices. You might say: I'm going to write the words *steering* and *hammering* because they show what Justin was doing. Afterward, demonstrate how your list of words will help you write about the character by writing an example.

STRUCTURE

Use the Sequence of Events Routine and Graphic Organizer in Part 3 to help students identify story elements and visualize the chronology of the story. After students identify the setting and characters, have them write down the events that occurred after the crash. Afterward, have students share the events they recorded. Then discuss how each event led to the next event.

If . . . students have trouble understanding how one event led to the next event,

then . . . ask them what might happen if one of the events didn't occur. For example, what would happen if Justin and Alicia didn't find the emergency kit?

ENGLISH LANGUAGE LEARNERS

While using the Sequence of Events Routine remind students to identify sequence words in the story, such as *then, finally,* and *later.* Provide sentence frames that include sequence words for students to describe the events in the story during the class discussion.

STRUGGLING READERS

Keep a list of commonly used stems and roots and their definitions in a visible place in the classroom. When students find a word they don't understand, show them how they can use the chart to help them define the word.

LANGUAGE CONVENTIONALITY AND CLARITY

Complete the Extend activity from the Analyze Cognates Routine in Part 3 to help students break down the following words based on their stems: *oxygenated, smoldering, fuselage, chemiluminesence, reactor, radiation, crevasse,* and *fusion.*

After students have defined each word, provide groups with poster paper with one of the words written on it. Have students underline the different word parts in different colors and write the definition of the stem and the whole word. Display the posters in a prominent place in the classroom as a reminder of how to break up and define words based on their stems.

KNOWLEDGE DEMANDS

Discuss why it was important for Justin and Alicia to make the fusion reactor work. Ask the following questions: What does the fusion reactor do? Why do the characters need the fusion reactor to work? What happens if they aren't able to get the fusion reactor to work? Remind students to support their answers with evidence from the text.

> If . . . students have trouble identifying the reasons the characters need the fusion reactor,
> then . . . give them a T-chart with the headings *Needs* and *Solutions.*

Read aloud pp. 23–24 beginning with "We need heat . . ." to ". . . the radiation shield," and ask: What do Justin and Alicia need? (heat, food, communication, radiation shield) Have students write their responses under the heading *Needs.* Then read aloud p. 26 from "The baseball-sized . . ." to ". . . get us heat," and ask: If Justin and Alicia get the fusion reactor to work, which of their needs will be met? (heat, communication, radiation shield) Students should write how the fusion reactor will meet those needs in the *Solutions* column. Lead a discussion by asking students to talk about how meeting a need can sometimes be similar to solving a problem.

Express and Extend

LEVELS OF MEANING

EXPRESS At various times in the story, the author shows that Justin feels guilty. Have students identify points in the story where Justin feels guilty, using evidence from the text to explain why he might feel that way.

If . . . students have difficulty identifying examples of guilt,

then . . . act out different parts of the text that demonstrate Justin feeling guilty, such as when he is staring at the ground on p. 21. Then ask students whether that action demonstrates guilt. Next, reread the surrounding text and ask students to identify a reason why Justin might act that way.

EXTEND Have students write a paragraph in which they pretend they are Justin. In the paragraph, they should explain how he feels after the crash happens. Tell students not to focus on the physical effects (headache or soreness) but on how he feels emotionally (sad, angry, frustrated). Use the Narrative Paragraph Writing Routine and Graphic Organizer in Part 3 to help students organize their writing as needed.

STRUCTURE

EXPRESS One aspect of the story that keeps readers interested is the author's use of suspense. Explain to students that suspense is created when readers do not know what will happen next. Have students find examples of suspense in the story. Then have them decide which example is the most suspenseful.

If . . . students have difficulty deciding what is suspenseful,

then . . . find an example of a suspenseful moment in the story, such as the moment when Justin and Alicia realize their emergency kit is empty. Read aloud the excerpt and have students decide if it is suspenseful. Guide their responses by asking: If you were reading this for the first time, would you know for certain what happens next?

EXTEND Have students chart suspenseful events from the story on the Cause and Effect Graphic Organizer in Part 3 to display what caused the suspense. Then have pairs use their graphic organizers as well as evidence from the text to discuss how the story would have been more or less enjoyable to read had the author not included such suspenseful events.

MORE SUPPORT

ENGLISH LANGUAGE LEARNERS

Help students understand why the author chose to use suspense. Ask: What would the story be like if you knew exactly what would happen next? How does the use of suspense keep the story interesting?

STRUGGLING READERS

Use the Analyze Idioms and Expressions Routine in Part 3 to give students additional practice using and understanding figurative language. Ask students to find additional examples of figurative language from the story or to come up with an idiom on their own.

EXPRESS Talk about Sentences and Words

Display the following sentences from "Mayday on Moon of Jupiter." Read them aloud with students.

> Alicia shot him a sideways look. She was already doing *something*. She was the one calling "Mayday" for help. "We have to eject," she told him.

Ask: Who do the pronouns *she* and *him* refer to? (Alicia and Justin) What does it mean when the author says "Alicia shot him a sideways look" in the first sentence? (She looked at Justin very quickly.) Why is the word *something* in italics? (It adds emphasis.) Why is the word *Mayday* in quotes? (It is being spoken.) In the context of this sentence, what does it mean to call Mayday? (It means to send a call from the spaceship for help. Alicia is not calling a person named Mayday.)

TEAM TALK Have partners rewrite the sentences so that the phrases *shot him a sideways look* and *calling "Mayday"* are more literal.

EXTEND Have students discuss why authors chose to use figurative language. Guide student responses by asking the following: Is it more interesting to read sentences with figurative language? Why or why not?

KNOWLEDGE DEMANDS

EXPRESS Have partners read aloud the dialogue of the two characters on the last page of the story. Then, have students explain why Alicia believed the mission was a success and Justin believed it was a failure.

If . . . students have troubling explaining the characters' feelings about the mission,

then . . . have them reread the text for evidence supporting why Justin and Alicia traveled into space. Lead students to understand that the goal of the Marsen 8 Mission was to search for evidence of early life forms. Ask: Knowing the mission's goal, why does Alicia determine the trip to be a success? (They find water on Europa, which is the first sign of potential life.)

EXTEND Have students write a paragraph explaining whether they think the presence of water means there are other life forms on Europa. To answer the question, they can refer to this selection or others they've read in the module.

ACCELERATED LEARNERS

All three selections in this module are about space exploration, but not all of them are written the same way. Have students write two paragraphs in which they discuss the similarities and differences in style and content among the three selections from this module.

MORE SUPPORT

Cognates

Cognates are words that have similar spellings and meanings in two or more languages. Many words in English and Spanish share Greek or Latin roots, and many words in English came from French, which is closely connected to Spanish (and to Portuguese, Italian, and Romanian). Because of this, many literary, content, and academic process words in English (e.g., *gracious/ gracioso; volcano/volcán; compare/comparar*) have recognizable Spanish cognates.

Making the connection to cognates permits students who are native Spanish speakers to understand the strong foundation they have in academic and literary English. These links between English and Spanish are also useful for native speakers of English and other languages because they help uncover basic underlying features of our language.

ANCHOR TEXT Jess and Layla's Astronomical Assignment

ENGLISH	SPANISH	ENGLISH	SPANISH
admirer	admirador	invented	inventó
air-conditioning	aire acondicionado	laboratory	laboratorio
angels	ángeles	marble	mármol
arrest	arresto	meteor	meteoro
asteroid	asteroide	meteorite	meteorito
astrology	astrología	object	objeto
astronomer	astrónomo	obviously	obviamente
astronomy	astronomía	passengers	pasajeros
atmosphere	atmósfera	pedal	pedal
button	botón	planet	planeta
center	centro	reclassified	reclasificado
circle	círculo	scientifically	científicamente
comet	cometa	scientist	científico
correct	correcto	sculpture	escultura
crystal	cristal	solar system	sistema solar
cylindrical	cilíndrica	space	espacio
digital	digital	sphere	esfera
excuse	excusa	stomach	estómago
experiment	experimento	suggested	sugirió
flexible	flexible	telescope	telescopio
history	historia	temples	templos
horizon	horizonte	theory	teoría
imagination	imaginación	unison	unísono
inspiration	inspiración	universe	universo
interactive	interactivo	zodiac signs	signos del zodíaco

SUPPORTING TEXT Our Mysterious Universe

ENGLISH	SPANISH	ENGLISH	SPANISH
atoms	átomos	fossilize	fosilizar
carbon	carbono	hydrogen	hidrógeno
catalog	catálogo	hypothesis	hipótesis
collapse	colapsar	luminous	luminoso
constellations	constelaciones	microorganisms	microorganismos
distances	distancia	nebula	nebulosa
elements	elementos	particles	partículas
elliptical	elíptico	pulse	pulsar
expand	expandir	Renaissance	Renacimiento
explore	explorar	supernova	supernova
extraterrestrial	extraterrestre	theories	teorías

SUPPORTING TEXT A Black Hole Is NOT a Hole

ENGLISH	SPANISH	ENGLISH	SPANISH
anatomy	anatomía	images	imágenes
astronomers	astrónomos	imagination	imaginación
collisions	colisiones	interfere	interferir
conclusions	conclusiones	intergalactic	intergaláctico
decades	décadas	moments	momentos
destination	destino	relatively	relativamente
effects	efectos	space	espacio
energy	energía	supernova	supernova
experiments	experimentos	symmetric	simétrico
extreme	extremo	zone	zona
galaxies	galaxias		

These lists contain many, but not all, Spanish cognates from these selections.

Unlock the Text

QUALITATIVE MEASURES

Levels of Meaning	science-fiction narrative about time travel and astronomy; scientific and historical facts about astronomers and theories; theme of scientific discovery
Structure	chapters; dialogue; distinguishing fact from fiction; non-linear chronology
Language Conventionality and Clarity	domain-specific and academic vocabulary, sometimes defined in context
Knowledge Demands	understanding basic astronomy facts; understanding changing theories about Earth and the Solar System

Prepare to Read

LEVELS OF MEANING

Jess and Layla's Astronomical Assignment is a science-fiction text about two girls who travel back in time to meet famous astronomers. While teaching the astronomers facts about the Solar System today, the two girls make their own discoveries about the past and how theories develop and change over time.

STRUCTURE

PREVIEW Have students scan the chapter titles and illustrations. Explain that the story takes place throughout different time periods. Ask: Based on the illustrations, what can you tell about the timeline of the story? (The story starts in present day in a classroom and in a girl's house; the next

---

MORE SUPPORT

ENGLISH LANGUAGE LEARNERS

Have students practice vocabulary by describing what they see in illustrations as they preview the story. Pair students of different vocabulary levels and encourage students to build on partners' descriptions of illustrations.

STRUGGLING READERS

Point out the double meaning of the word *astronomical* in the title. Explain that *astronomical* refers to both the subject of the girls' assignment (astronomy, or the study of space and the universe), and to an adjective used to describe something very large.

scene shows a room from an older time; the story ends in the same time period as the beginning of the story.) Point out the timeline at the end of the book. Explain that students can refer to the timeline to help track characters and time periods in the story.

LANGUAGE CONVENTIONALITY AND CLARITY

PREVIEW VOCABULARY Use the Preview and Review Vocabulary Routine in Part 3 to assess what students know about the following words: *embarrassing, stern, disbelief, skidded, hesitated, fizzing, shrieked, pompously, sarcastic, bickering, distraught, hurtled, investigated, gazed,* and *muttering*.

COGNATES Use the list of Spanish cognates at the beginning of this module to guide your Spanish-speaking students as they read the selection.

DOMAIN-SPECIFIC VOCABULARY Use the Vocabulary Activities in Part 3 to pre-teach the following domain-specific vocabulary: *astronomy, spheres, universe, meteor, atmosphere,* and *orbit*. Explain that students can use these words to talk about outer space and the Solar System.

KNOWLEDGE DEMANDS

ACTIVATE BACKGROUND KNOWLEDGE Have students think about famous astronomers and scientists from the past. Ask: What famous astronomers do you know? What do you know about how people used to think about Earth, the Sun, and the planets in the solar system? Did astronomers always agree about their theories? Have students explain their answers. Explain that in the past, astronomers did not have the technology we have today. They developed theories that scientists would later challenge as technology improved; for example, Galileo used the telescope to form new theories.

STRUGGLING READERS

If students have trouble activating background knowledge, ask more specific questions such as: What shape did people used to think Earth was? What do we now know about how Earth orbits the Sun? Did people always think this way? Have students view the timeline at the beginning of the story to review astronomers and their theories.

Interact with Text

Help students track, compare, and contrast characters as they are introduced in the story. Have students identify what Jess and Layla have in common, as well as details that distinguish the two girls. For example, students may point to details such as the fact that Layla is "allergic to Science" (p. 4) while Jess "loved Science facts" (p. 17).

> If . . . students have difficulty comparing and contrasting characters,
> then . . . have students use a Venn Diagram graphic organizer to list details from the text that show similarities and differences between characters.

Encourage students to use the same strategy as they encounter each astronomer in the text. Remind students to cite specific details from the text to make comparisons.

STRUCTURE

Explain that while many events in the story, such as time travel, are fiction, characters in the story reveal true scientific facts. Point out that many of these facts are introduced through dialogue. Ask: Which characters in the story explain facts through dialogue? (Dr. Goggles, Jess) Have students create a list of facts about the Solar System that are given through dialogue.

> If . . . students have difficulty identifying scientific facts in the text,
> then . . . remind students that facts might include numbers, statistics, and dates.

Point out that a fact is different from a theory. Many of the astronomers had theories that they believed were true at the time, but were not proven as facts.

MORE SUPPORT

ENGLISH LANGUAGE LEARNERS

In groups, have students act out dialogue to aid comprehension. Encourage students to incorporate emotion and attitude into dialogue, using cues and vocabulary from the text such as "in disappointment" and "dreamily."

STRUGGLING READERS

Provide students with categories as needed to help them compare and contrast characters. For example, ask students to compare and contrast Jess's and Layla's school interests, personalities, and physical characteristics.

LANGUAGE CONVENTIONALITY AND CLARITY

Unfamiliar vocabulary may limit students' understanding of the more subtle details of the text. Encourage students to use context to determine the meaning of words that reveal information about characters' personalities and conversations.

If . . . students have difficulty understanding vocabulary,

then . . . model using context to define each example on a case-by-case basis.

For example, point out the word *balderdash* on p. 37. Point out surrounding context clues such as *wrong, glaring, frowning,* and *"We don't like him."* Ask: Based on context, does the word *balderdash* suggest that Galileo feels positively or negatively about Pythagoras's model? **(negatively)** Explain that students can use context to decide that *balderdash* means something that does not make sense, or is untrue. Repeat this process for the words *bickering* (p. 42), *pompously* (p. 41), and *distraught* (p. 47).

KNOWLEDGE DEMANDS

Students may have trouble tracking each astronomer's theories. To help students understand the fast-paced dialogue and dynamics between the astronomers, check their understanding of sources of agreement and disagreement. Make a list of the astronomers on the board. Have students use the timeline and text as necessary to discuss how each pair of astronomers might agree and disagree. For example, point to Aristotle and Aristarchus. Ask: How would these two astronomers agree? **(They both think Earth is round.)** Ask: How would they disagree? **(They disagreed about whether Earth or the Sun orbits the other.)**

ENGLISH LANGUAGE LEARNERS

Bring in objects to demonstrate each astronomer's theory. For example, use a plate and can of beans to demonstrate Thales's and Anaximander's respective theories about Earth's shape. Ask students to use the objects to demonstrate the orbits described by astronomers and to compare and contrast theories.

Express and Extend

EXPRESS Have students consider Jess and Layla's changing attitudes toward influencing history. Direct students to p. 28. Ask: Why does Jess want to find Galileo? (to "prove his theory was correct and change the course of history") Ask: How does Jess's attitude change at the end of the story? Why? Have students use evidence from the text to support their answer.

> If . . . students have difficulty understanding why Jess and Layla's attitudes change toward rewriting history,
>
> then . . . direct students to pp. 54–55. Ask students to find evidence of Layla's attitude toward bringing the astronomers into space.

EXTEND Have students write an opinion paragraph about whether they agree with Layla and Jess's decision to try not to change the course of history. Encourage students to use evidence from the text in their paragraphs.

EXPRESS Explain that the text begins in the present, moves to three separate time periods in the past, and returns to present time. Explain that students should look for clues in the text to orient themselves in time. Direct students to pp. 30–34. Ask: How do the illustrations on these pages suggest an earlier time period? (Galileo's clothing, including a nightcap and nightshirt; the wooden telescope) Ask: What evidence in the text points to an earlier time period? (Galileo says that "girls don't study astronomy," and calls the van a "horse" with "very bright eyes;" Galileo says that "Copernicus has been dead for almost a hundred years")

EXTEND Have students extend the dialogue between Galileo, Jess, and Layla on the bottom of p. 32. Ask students to consider the types of questions Galileo would have about life in Jess and Layla's time and what questions they would have for him. Encourage students to write at least four lines of dialogue.

MORE SUPPORT

ENGLISH LANGUAGE LEARNERS

Provide students with sentence frames to write a paragraph about Layla and Jess's decision. For example: I agree with Jess and Layla's decision to ___because ___. I think it is important to ___.

STRUGGLING READERS

Have students create a chart to analyze Jess and Layla's decisions. Have students use one column to write evidence that expresses Layla's or Jess's opinion about changing history; in the next column, have students interpret the evidence.

EXPRESS Talk about Sentences and Words

Display and read aloud the following sentences from *Jess and Layla's Astronomical Assignment*.

> Layla **flashed** Jess a smile and then **jammed** her thumb down hard on the button. There was a powerful flash of pure white light, and suddenly the astronomers stopped arguing and **grabbed** their seat belts as the van **rocketed** upward.

Point out the bolded words in the passage. Provide more general replacements for the bolded words such as *gave, pressed, held,* and *moved*. Have students discuss the differences between using the bolded words and the replacement words. Point out that word choice can make a passage more interesting, as well as allow for more specific descriptions of actions. Ask: How do the verbs the writer chose help to set a tone? (the verbs set an urgent and fast-paced tone)

TEAM TALK   In pairs, have students read several pages of the text and list precise, descriptive verbs. Have students discuss the impact of word choice on the tone of the story.

EXTEND Have students write one paragraph of Jess and Layla's homework assignment, describing the interaction between astronomers in the text. Students should make verbs as precise and descriptive as possible, working with a partner to edit for specific word choice. Encourage students to use new vocabulary words.

EXPRESS Have students reread Chapter 4. In small groups, have students make a list of the facts about Earth and the Solar System that are revealed through the journey.

If . . . students have difficulty finding information in the text,

then . . . guide them to look for information about categories such as Earth's shape, the moon's surface, Jupiter's surface, and the planets' orbits.

EXTEND Ask students to imagine they are Aristotle or Anaximander just returning from the group's journey in space. Have students write a two-paragraph journal entry explaining what they have learned and how it changed their theories about Earth and the Solar System. In pairs, have students read their paragraphs aloud.

ACCELERATED LEARNERS

Have students choose an astronomer and conduct research to learn more about the technology or sources he used to develop his theories. Ask students to write one paragraph explaining how the astronomer reached his conclusions.

Unlock the Text

QUALITATIVE MEASURES

Levels of Meaning	informational text about how the universe was formed and scientists' predictions for the future; sequence of events in the formation of the universe; similarities and differences among the four types of galaxies
Structure	chapters; headings; text features such as photos, diagrams, captions, labels, and sidebars; sequence of events
Language Conventionality and Clarity	many scientific terms, most defined in context; multiple-meaning words
Knowledge Demands	broad knowledge of the universe; how to use text features; scientific theories

Prepare to Read

LEVELS OF MEANING

Our Mysterious Universe delves into scientific theories about how the universe may have been formed and describes the galaxies, stars, solar systems, and black holes within it. It also discusses Earth's place in the universe and theories about the changes to the universe that could take place in the future.

STRUCTURE

PREVIEW Have students review the text features (headings, photos, diagrams, captions, labels, and sidebars) and how they help readers locate information. Ask: How is the text divided? (into sections with

MORE SUPPORT

ENGLISH LANGUAGE LEARNERS

Have students create a running list of multiple-meaning words from the text. For each word, have them write definitions and draw illustrations. Instruct students to use this list while reading to help decide which definition fits best with the text.

STRUGGLING READERS

The multitude of text features can be distracting for students when they are trying to decipher the text. Demonstrate how to read the text features in order to enrich, rather than distract from, the meaning of the text by doing a think aloud.

headings and subheadings) What is the difference between a photograph and a diagram? (A diagram explains or demonstrates a complex idea, while a photo shows what an object looks like.) What type of information do sidebars usually contain? (additional details and facts that help readers understand main ideas in a text)

LANGUAGE CONVENTIONALITY AND CLARITY

PREVIEW VOCABULARY Use the Preview and Review Vocabulary Routine in Part 3 to assess what students know about the following words: *unpredictable, accumulated, regularity, catalog, revolutionary, churning, luminous, disturbances, emitted, interacted, primitive, destination, hypothesis,* and *theory.*

DOMAIN-SPECIFIC VOCABULARY Use the Vocabulary Activities in Part 3 to teach domain-specific vocabulary words, such as *celestial, constellation, terrestrial, debris, galaxy, subatomic particles,* and *dark matter.*

MULTIPLE-MEANING WORDS Help students expand their understanding of multiple-meaning words by sharing sentences, definitions, and pictures that demonstrate a word's various meanings. For example, contrast *objects,* as in "things," with *objects,* as in "protests." Emphasize the different pronunciations and have students use the words in sentences. Use the Analyze Multiple-Meaning Words Routine in Part 3 for additional support.

COGNATES Use the list of Spanish cognates at the beginning of this module to guide your Spanish-speaking students as they read the selection.

KNOWLEDGE DEMANDS

ACTIVATE BACKGROUND KNOWLEDGE Have students preview the images throughout the book to help them remember information they might have learned in the past. Have students tell what they know about what a solar system is, what objects exist in our solar system, and other instances when they've heard the words *universe* or *solar system.* Use the Quick Write and Share Routine in Part 3 for students to record their responses.

Model an exemplar response. Say: I have seen a television show about the universe. On the show, they discussed our solar system. I know that our solar system includes the sun; eight planets that orbit the sun, including Earth; and the moons of each planet. It also includes objects like asteroids and comets.

Interact with Text

To help students understand the relationships between celestial events, break down the steps that occurred in the formation of the solar system and list them in order. First, reread the text that describes the process, and then say: The first event is that the sun formed in the center of a spinning cloud of gas and dust. Ask students what they think comes next.

After completing the ordered list as a class, assign pairs an important event from the selection and have them make a new list to record the steps that led to the important event.

> If . . . students have difficulty ordering events,
>
> then . . . help them identify sequence words and phrases, such as *first, then, after,* and *because of.*

STRUCTURE

Our Mysterious Universe includes several text features that provide additional details or visual representations of the processes described in the text. Demonstrate how to use the text features by reading p. 9 aloud as students follow along in their books. Then read the sidebar. Show how the sidebar gives more details about the subject discussed in the text. Also point out that the diagram on pp. 8–9 reinforces this main idea by showing a sequential image of how the solar system formed.

After the demonstration, assign students a different two-page spread. Have them work in pairs and write a few sentences describing how two of the text features support information in the text.

MORE SUPPORT

ENGLISH LANGUAGE LEARNERS

Provide more exposure to sequence words by having students work independently to write down words in the text that tell when an event happens. Afterward, have them share the words they found with a partner.

STRUGGLING READERS

Remind students that words in boldfaced type are ones the author considers important. If they are unsure of the meaning of a word in boldfaced type, they can refer to the glossary in the back of the book for a definition.

LANGUAGE CONVENTIONALITY AND CLARITY

As you read, monitor students' understanding of definitions of important vocabulary terms.

If . . . students have difficulty recalling definitions of important vocabulary terms,

then . . . use the Act Out or Draw Meaning Routine in Part 3.

Assign each student two vocabulary words from the text. After completing the graphic organizers, have students get into groups of four and place all their graphic organizers in a pile. Students should take turns choosing a graphic organizer from the pile. After acting out one of the words, the remaining students should try to guess the word and its definition. The first person to correctly guess the word and give the correct definition gets to choose next.

KNOWLEDGE DEMANDS

Students may have difficulty understanding many of the scientific theories, hypotheses, and details listed in the text. Use the Monitor Understanding: Listening Skills Log in Part 3 to demonstrate for students how to take notes.

For example, read aloud "The Life Cycle of Stars" on pp. 16–17. As you read, have students take notes about the stars using the Listening Skills Log. Then, allow students to share their notes with a partner and work together to create a summary of what was read.

If . . . students have difficulty following along with text that is read aloud,

then . . . have students follow along in their books using their finger to point to the words as they are read aloud.

Express and Extend

EXPRESS Have pairs of students work together to discuss *Our Mysterious Universe.* Then have them write a paragraph that compares and contrasts two of the four different types of galaxies.

> If . . . students have difficulty organizing information into similarities and differences,
>
> then . . . have them use a T-chart to plan their paragraph.

EXTEND Divide students into four groups. Assign each group a type of galaxy (elliptical, spiral, barred spiral, or irregular). Provide students access to reference materials or the Internet to research one of the types of galaxies in further detail. Have them create a class presentation that includes appropriate text, images, and diagrams.

EXPRESS Review several of the sidebars in the text with students. Point out how each expands on a fact or detail from the main body of the text. Then have groups expand on their presentations above by writing a sidebar with additional information about the type of galaxy they researched or something associated with it. Have groups present their research to the class.

EXTEND Have students independently write a report about the formation of the solar system. Encourage them to refer to the list of sequential steps they created earlier in the unit. Tell them to include at least one sidebar or graph with their report.

ENGLISH LANGUAGE LEARNERS

Students may need help with their reports. Have them first describe each section of their galaxy diagram. Then have them create sentences based on their description. Finally, have students edit their sentences to include only the most important details about each part of their diagram.

STRUGGLING READERS

Help students compare and contrast galaxies by guiding them to focus on one galaxy at a time. Provide sentence frames such as: One type of galaxy is ___. The shape of this galaxy is ___. One other unique feature of this galaxy is ___.

MORE SUPPORT

EXPRESS Talk about Sentences and Words

Display the following sentence from *Our Mysterious Universe*. Read it aloud with students.

> The inner and outer planets are separated by the asteroid belt, a band of many millions of smaller objects called asteroids (or minor planets) that orbit the Sun.

Ask: What is an asteroid belt? (a band of many millions of smaller objects called asteroids) What is an asteroid? (a minor planet that orbits the sun) What does the word *separated* tell you about the location of the asteroid belt in relation to the inner and outer planets? (The asteroid belt is in between the inner planets and the outer planets.)

TEAM TALK Have partners view the diagram on the bottom of pp. 10–11 and then discuss how the context clues provided in the sentence are further supported in the diagram.

EXTEND Have students use the context clues to break the sentence into two or three sentences that define *asteroid* and *asteroid belt.* A possible response might be: An asteroid is a minor planet. An asteroid belt is a band of many millions of asteroids that orbit the sun.

EXPRESS Have small groups create skits about what they learned about the universe. Tell them to refer to the graphic organizers they completed during this unit and to create visual aids or props to help the presentation.

EXTEND Have students work independently to create their own hypothesis about the future of the universe based on the information provided in the text and their own research. Tell students to write a short report that explains their theory. Remind students to include charts, diagrams, illustrations, headings, and sidebars, as needed.

ACCELERATED LEARNERS

Have students choose a particular theory or hypothesis that was most interesting to them, such as the Big Bang Theory. Assist them in choosing an online or library resource to learn more about the theory or hypothesis. Then, have them write a paragraph in which they evaluate whether the additional resource was helpful in understanding the theory or hypothesis.

Unlock the Text

QUALITATIVE MEASURES

A Black Hole Is NOT a
Hole, pp. 29–55

Levels of Meaning	exploring black holes—their formation, qualities, and the history of their discovery; hypothetical scenario to stimulate readers' imaginations
Structure	section headings and subheadings; art and photos with captions; dates given for historical events; speech bubbles
Language Conventionality and Clarity	domain-specific vocabulary; context clues; descriptive adjectives and verbs; gerunds
Knowledge Demands	basic astronomy facts; black holes and how they form in space

Prepare to Read

LEVELS OF MEANING

In *A Black Hole Is NOT a Hole,* readers explore the science of black holes: their formation, their qualities, and the history of their discovery and exploration.

STRUCTURE

PREVIEW Have students review the title page, illustrations, headings, and subheadings throughout the book and ask: How is the book divided? (into sections separated by headings) What are the smaller headings used for? (They mark smaller, specific sections of the text.) Why might the author include illustrations of black holes? (to help readers understand what the text will be about) Why do some of the pictures have writing next to them? (These are captions that explain the pictures.)

MORE SUPPORT

ENGLISH LANGUAGE LEARNERS

When students come across a new word they don't know, ask them if they can identify a word part or stem that is familiar. Ask them to use their knowledge of word parts to try and identify the new word's definition.

STRUGGLING READERS

Boldfaced headings give hints about what kind of information will come in each section. Point out that using the Main Idea and Details Graphic Organizer in Part 3 for each heading can be a useful tool to break apart the text. Have students add details to the graphic organizers as they read.

LANGUAGE CONVENTIONALITY AND CLARITY

PREVIEW VOCABULARY Use the Preview and Review Vocabulary Routine in Part 3 to assess what students know about the following words: *quadrillion, symmetric, singularity, nucleus, atom,* and *event horizon.*

DOMAIN-SPECIFIC VOCABULARY Use the Vocabulary Activities in Part 3 to preteach critical, domain-specific vocabulary words, such as *asteroid, galaxy, supernova, quasar,* and *constellation*.

COGNATES Use the list of Spanish cognates at the beginning of this module to guide your Spanish-speaking students as they read the selection.

KNOWLEDGE DEMANDS

ACTIVATE BACKGROUND KNOWLEDGE Ask students to share what they know about astronomy and black holes. Use the Quick Write and Share Routine in Part 3. Have students look at pictures throughout the selection to help them remember information they might have learned in the past. Ask: What is a black hole? (It is something that looks like a hole in space.) Why do you think the title of the selection states that it is not actually a hole? (It just looks like a hole, but is not an actual hole in space.)

Have students begin the KWLH Chart Graphic Organizer in Part 3 about the topic of astronomy and black holes. Have students record information in the *What Do I Know?* and *What Do I Want to Learn?* sections of the graphic organizer. After students finish reading the selection, have them return to this graphic organizer and complete the *What Did I Learn?* and *How Did I Learn It?* sections.

Interact with Text

LEVELS OF MEANING

The author describes a black hole by comparing it to a whirlpool. After reading pp. 32–35, make sure students first understand what a whirlpool is. They may have seen whirlpools on television, or in their sinks, toilets, or bathtubs. Then, together with students, complete a Venn diagram with information from the text to compare whirlpools and black holes. Write *Whirlpool* in the left circle, *Black Hole* in the right circle, and *Both* in the center area. Have students suggest information to write in each portion of the diagram to indicate what is unique to each and what both have in common.

Remind students to create other similar diagrams or charts whenever they need to compare information.

STRUCTURE

Have students reread pp. 45–48 of the selection. Use the Time Line Routine and Graphic Organizer in Part 3 to help them organize and clarify the historical events, scientific discoveries, and dates mentioned in that section. Have students work together to decide which events are the most important and why.

If . . . students have difficulty identifying key events,

then . . . provide a list of important events in learning about black holes in random order. Have students use the list to complete their time lines.

ENGLISH LANGUAGE LEARNERS

To provide students with additional practice using context clues, have students write unfamiliar words from the text. Say sentences aloud using these words and including a context clue to help infer the meaning. Have students draw pictures of what they think the word means.

STRUGGLING READERS

Help students match some of the illustrations in the selection to the vocabulary words they illustrate. For example, the illustration on p. 36 shows a black hole and gas clouds. Help students draw and label the part of the picture that is a black hole and the parts that are gas clouds. Seeing visuals of difficult vocabulary will aid students' understanding.

LANGUAGE CONVENTIONALITY AND CLARITY

To help students understand domain-specific and advanced vocabulary, have them work with a partner to find context clues that will help them understand a word's meaning. Then have students use a dictionary or online reference to find and record the word's definition in a vocabulary notebook. Remind students to use this strategy any time they encounter an unknown word.

If . . . students have difficulty using context clues to define words,

then . . . practice using context clues as a class.

As they read, have students record unfamiliar words in a notebook. Have them share their words with the class. Have students read the sentences from the selection in which the words appear. As a class, discuss the meanings of these words by using context clues or other evidence from the text.

KNOWLEDGE DEMANDS

Have students reread p. 43 of the selection to help them understand how a star ends before sometimes turning into a black hole. Use the Description: Sensory Details Routine and Graphic Organizer in Part 3. For example, notice that the writer uses sound words to explain what it might sound like to hear a star collapsing in on itself (*CRASH! BOOM! WHOOOOOOSH!*). For sense of touch, the author mentions intense heat, the *whooooosh* of wind as it breezes by, a hard bump, and a comparison to slamming against a cliff wall. For sense of sight, *giant surges of light* are described in the text and *surges of motion* are described in the caption.

As applicable while reading, have students return to the KWLH chart graphic organizer from the Activate Background Knowledge activity and fill in information they learned about black holes in the *What Did I Learn?* section. For example, they can now fill in information about how a star ends before becoming a black hole; how black holes are similar to whirlpools, though not exactly the same; and how gravity is the source of a black hole's super pulling strength.

Express and Extend

LEVELS OF MEANING

EXPRESS The selection ends with a section that includes the author imagining what it might be like if a person were able to visit a black hole, based on what scientists know to be true about black holes. Have students identify descriptive or imaginative language that makes this section different from the other sections of this selection.

> If . . . students have difficulty identifying descriptive language,
>
> then . . . point out that the author uses made-up words, such as *spaghettification,* that do not really exist. Then have them work with a partner to decode the made-up words.

EXTEND Have students rewrite the section using their own made-up or imaginative descriptive language.

STRUCTURE

EXPRESS Point out the humorous asides in speech bubbles throughout the selection. Since the bubbles don't give any extra information, have students discuss whether they think the bubbles should be there. Have them tell why or why not.

EXTEND Have students write a small speech bubble to go on a page of the selection that does not currently have one. Their speech bubble should make a humorous comment that relates to the information discussed.

ENGLISH LANGUAGE LEARNERS

The text includes many made-up or fun descriptive terms, such as *spinners, lumpies,* and *smoothies*. Discuss with students why the author might make up these terms and what they mean.

STRUGGLING READERS

The figurative language in the story may be challenging. Explain that words do not have a literal meaning in some expressions, such as *fiery furnace*. Use the Analyze Idioms and Expressions Routine in Part 3 to guide students' understanding.

EXPRESS Talk about Sentences and Words

Display the sentence below and read it aloud with students. Then ask the questions below.

Now blazing, flaring, spewing, and spouting, the new star is a fiery furnace.

Ask: What does this sentence describe? **(the birth of a new star)** What kind of colorful language does the narrator use to describe the event? **(descriptive verbs, metaphor of a fiery furnace)** Why does the author use the word *furnace* to describe the new star? **(A star and a furnace are both fiery and hot.)**

TEAM TALK **Ask:** Among the four gerunds in the first part of the sentence (*blazing, flaring, spewing,* and *spouting*), which two are synonyms for each other? **(One matching pair is *blazing* and *flaring*, and the other matching pair is *spewing* and *spouting*.)**

If . . . students need more support understanding the meaning of the sentence,

then . . . have them use dictionaries to look up the meanings of the four verbs and draw pictures of what those actions look like.

EXTEND Have students research a planet other than Earth on the Internet. Have them come up with a list of adjectives that describe the planet or verbs that describe how the planet moves in the solar system.

EXPRESS Have small groups discuss what they learned about black holes and how they could learn more information about them. Have students refer back to their KWLH chart graphic organizer and compare their graphic organizer with a partner's graphic organizer. Give students an opportunity to add information to their graphic organizers after they review them with a partner.

EXTEND Have students write a one-page summary about black holes—how they form, what they are, and how they act in space. Students' KWLH chart graphic organizers should provide an outline for this assignment.

ACCELERATED LEARNERS

Have students write about something new and exciting in the universe that they would want to study if they were astronomers. Have them tell why they are interested in this topic. Then, have them write a persuasive letter to convince scientists that they should study their idea or topic.

Exploring New Worlds

TEXT SET

ANCHOR TEXT
Explorers: Triumphs and Troubles

SUPPORTING TEXT
Pedro's Journal

SUPPORTING TEXT
Secrets of the Canyon Cave

TEXT SET

ANCHOR TEXT
Beyond the Horizon

SUPPORTING TEXT
Explorers of North America

SUPPORTING TEXT
New Beginnings

Cognates

Cognates are words that have similar spellings and meanings in two or more languages. Many words in English and Spanish share Greek or Latin roots, and many words in English came from French, which is closely connected to Spanish (and to Portuguese, Italian, and Romanian). Because of this, many literary, content, and academic process words in English (e.g., *gracious/gracioso; volcano/volcán; compare/comparar*) have recognizable Spanish cognates.

Making the connection to cognates permits students who are native Spanish speakers to understand the strong foundation they have in academic and literary English. These links between English and Spanish are also useful for native speakers of English and other languages because they help uncover basic underlying features of our language.

ANCHOR TEXT Explorers: Triumphs and Troubles

ENGLISH	SPANISH	ENGLISH	SPANISH
adventurer	aventurero	line	línea
attacked	atacó	millions	millones
bandits	bandidos	mutiny	motín
battles	batallas	mythical	mítico
camels	camellos	nobles	nobles
catastrophe	catástrofe	occupied	ocupó
companions	compañeros	officer	oficial
conflict	conflicto	patriot	patriota
conquistador	conquistador	permission	permiso
continent	continente	population	población
disaster	desastre	prisoner	prisionero
empire	imperio	reason	razón
existed	existió	reparations	reparaciones
expedition	expedición	result	resultado
experience	experiencia	rich	rico
explorer	explorador	rival	rival
force	fuerza	route	ruta
hero	héroe	soldiers	soldados
history	historia	tactic	táctica
indigenous	indígena	temples	templos
information	información	territory	territorio
inspired	inspiró	treasure	tesoro
invaders	invasores	triumph	triunfo
leader	líder	unusual	inusual

SUPPORTING TEXT Pedro's Journal

ENGLISH	SPANISH	ENGLISH	SPANISH
abandon	abandonar	impatient	impacientes
arrogant	arrogante	interpreter	intérprete
ceremony	ceremonia	island	isla
convince	convencer	jungle	jungla
double	doblar	native	nativo
escape	escapar	palaces	palacios
fame	fama	palm	palma
horizon	horizonte	solemn	solemne

SUPPORTING TEXT Secrets of the Canyon Cave

ENGLISH	SPANISH	ENGLISH	SPANISH
anticipation	anticipación	interconnected	interconectados
canyon	cañón	nebula	nebulosa
companion	compañero	officials	oficiales
contented	contento	phenomena	fenómenos
humidity	humedad	photo	foto
instructions	instrucciones	scientific	científica

These lists contain many, but not all, Spanish cognates from these selections.

Unlock the Text

QUALITATIVE MEASURES

Levels of Meaning	informational text about explorers and their journeys; theme of exploration and its positive and negative effects
Structure	multiple text features and graphics; contrasting viewpoints; cause and effect
Language Conventionality and Clarity	informal writing style; author's viewpoint; domain-specific and academic vocabulary
Knowledge Demands	summarize events; understanding motivation; understanding actions and their effects

Explorers:
Triumphs and Troubles

WRITTEN BY PAUL MASON

Prepare to Read

LEVELS OF MEANING

Say: Learning about history can be more than just learning about the facts, or what happened. People have different opinions about events and people from the past. *Explorers: Triumphs and Troubles* tells the stories of explorers from the past and their successes and failures. While exploration led to many discoveries, explorers' actions had lasting effects on local people.

STRUCTURE

PREVIEW Have students review the Table of Contents and then study the pages of one chapter to analyze the text structure. Ask: How is the text divided overall? (into sections organized by location; within each location section, there are subheadings) Ask: What features, in addition to the main text, do you notice on each page? (illustrations, maps, a "Journey Fact File," photographs, captions, and boxes with thumbs up and thumbs down icons) Ask: How is the main text on each page organized? (The main text is set in boxes with headings.)

ENGLISH LANGUAGE LEARNERS

As they read, have students group proper nouns by category to help them understand the relationships between individuals and places. For example, have students write and group explorers' names, locations, and names of local people.

STRUGGLING READERS

Students may be overwhelmed by the layout of text and graphics on the page. Encourage students to focus on one element at a time as they read, beginning with the main text and then returning to the page to study visuals and supplementary text boxes.

LANGUAGE CONVENTIONALITY AND CLARITY

PREVIEW VOCABULARY Use the Preview and Review Vocabulary Routine in Part 3 to assess what students know about the following words: *ruthless, limitless, fierce, heroic, bold, legendary, brilliant, venomous,* and *mythical.*

COGNATES Use the list of Spanish cognates at the beginning of this module to guide your Spanish-speaking students as they read the selection.

DOMAIN-SPECIFIC VOCABULARY Use the Vocabulary Activities in Part 3 to pre-teach the following domain-specific vocabulary: *continent, mountain passes, rain forest, downstream, bay, mangrove,* and *swamps.* Explain that students can use these words to compare and discuss the different locations explorers encountered.

KNOWLEDGE DEMANDS

ACTIVATE BACKGROUND KNOWLEDGE Explain that often, explorers discovered land that was new to them, but people were living on the land long before the explorers arrived. Ask: What do you know about exploration? Can you name any explorers from the past? After students generate a list, ask: What are some positive things about exploration? Generate a list on the board. Then ask: What might be some negative things about exploration? Students may discuss the hardships explorers encountered on a journey, and conflict between explorers and people already living on the land.

STRUGGLING READERS

Students may struggle with the quick transitions between different explorers and journeys in the text. Before students move on to a new section, have them write a sticky note summarizing the explorers and the journey discussed in the section. Have students place the sticky note summary at the beginning of that section.

MORE SUPPORT

Interact with Text

LEVELS OF MEANING

As you read *Explorers: Triumphs and Troubles,* help students distinguish between facts and opinions about events in history. Explain that learning to tell the difference between fact and opinion will help students form their own ideas and opinions about events and people from the past.

> If . . . students have difficulty distinguishing fact from opinion,
>
> then . . . guide students to use text structure to help sort facts from opinions. Explain that the *Triumph…* and *…or Trouble?* text boxes express opinions. Have students identify words from these boxes that signify opinion.

Remind students that facts about history include information about what happened, who was involved, and when something happened. They include information that everyone can agree on. Opinions can be different from person to person; not everyone agrees that an opinion is true.

STRUCTURE

Students may struggle to make connections between multiple, separate text boxes on a page. Encourage students to look at subheadings, or the headings of each individual text box, and determine how they fit together.

> If . . . students have difficulty forming connections between text boxes,
>
> then . . . have students focus on pp. 4–5. Ask students to write out the subheadings *Looking for Land?, Route Finding, Hunting for Wealth,* and *Fame and Glory.* Point out that all of these answer the question *Why explore?*

Explain that, in this case, the separate text boxes give reasons or evidence that support a main idea in the text. In other sections, the subheadings help summarize the information in each box.

ENGLISH LANGUAGE LEARNERS

To check comprehension, have students frequently summarize information in their own words. After reading each text box, have students turn to a partner and summarize the events. Encourage students to avoid reading from the text to summarize.

STRUGGLING READERS

To help students distinguish fact from opinion, guide them to identify specific words in the text that indicate bias. For example, point out the words *badly behaved, bold, great, ruthless,* and *cruel* on pp. 14–15. Have students discuss why these words indicate opinion.

LANGUAGE CONVENTIONALITY AND CLARITY

Help students analyze the author's word choice and sentence structure to understand his informal writing style. Point out that while the author writes facts about history, his writing incorporates his own style and opinions.

If . . . students have difficulty finding examples of the author's informal style,

then . . . guide students to analyze specific sentences from the text.

For example, point out the phrases *became obsessed with* and *wanted to get their hands on it* on p. 16. Explain that the writer uses more conversational language to tell a story about the explorers.

Have students point out examples of other conversational language the writer uses, including idioms and expressions. Explain that the author's use of contractions such as *weren't* (p. 12) also indicates a more informal, conversational tone.

KNOWLEDGE DEMANDS

Explain that explorers had different motivations for beginning their journeys. Check students' understanding of each explorer's reasons behind his actions. Have students generate a list of each of the main explorers in the text: Marco Polo, Francis Younghusband, Hernán Cortés, Francisco de Orellana, Robert Scott, the First Fleet, and Robert Burke. Remind students that motivation is why someone does something. Have students write motivations next to each individual's name and compare lists with a partner. Explain that people often have more than one reason, or motivation, behind their actions.

ENGLISH LANGUAGE LEARNERS

Have students practice reading aloud and acting out events in the text to aid comprehension. In groups, have students alternate reading sections of the text aloud and acting out summaries of the events in the text. Encourage students to incorporate dialogue as they recreate events from the text.

MORE SUPPORT

Express and Extend

EXPRESS Explain that students can use both facts and opinions in the text to build arguments about explorers and situations. Have students practice finding facts and evidence to support a statement about an explorer from the text. Encourage students to take a stance supporting or criticizing an explorer, and to list evidence from the text to support their viewpoint.

> **If . . .** students have difficulty finding facts and evidence to support an argument,
>
> **then . . .** point out that students can use the *Triumph…* and *…or Trouble?* boxes to help them choose an argument. Then, encourage students to find evidence from the main text to support their view.

EXTEND In pairs, have students present their arguments and evidence about explorers in the text. Have partners choose the strongest evidence from their peer's argument and explain why it is effective.

EXPRESS Check students' understanding of the chronology of events within the main text of each section. As students read, have them list main events from the text. Remind students that they should list important, general ideas rather than smaller details. Have students use their lists to create a short timeline of events for each section in the text. Remind students to incorporate exact dates from the text when possible. Have students refer to their timelines as they return to sections of the text.

EXTEND Have students use their timelines to individually give a summary of a section of text aloud in a small group. Explain that students should use their timelines as a reference to summarize the events in a section, rather than only read the facts directly.

ENGLISH LANGUAGE LEARNERS

If students struggle to find main ideas in the text, remind them to look at headings that break up the main text. Explain that these headings usually summarize the main ideas in the following text.

STRUGGLING READERS

Help students structure their arguments about explorers. Provide sentence frames such as I think ___was ___. Remind students that their argument should include an opinion word, or an adjective that describes an explorer. Then ask students to list three reasons why they chose that adjective, citing specific examples from the text.

EXPRESS Talk about Sentences and Words

Display and read aloud the following sentences from *Explorers: Triumphs and Troubles.*

> The Eora people had lived on the land for centuries and respected the land, taking only what they needed and managing it well. The British fenced off large areas of the Eora people's land, which prevented them from crossing it.

Point out that the author uses specific words that suggest a viewpoint, or attitude, toward the Eora and British people's actions. Point out the words and phrases *for centuries, respected,* and *managing it well.* Then point to the phrases *fenced off* and *prevented them from crossing it.* Ask students to consider the connotations of each set of phrases. **Ask:** Who do you think the author feels had a right to the land? (The Eora; the words the author uses to describe their actions are more positive.)

TEAM TALK Have students reread the *Triumph…* and *…or Trouble* fact boxes. For each explorer, have students decide which fact box has stronger evidence and discuss their reasoning with a partner.

EXTEND Have students write an opinion paragraph stating whether the author takes the side of the explorers, of the people with whom the explorers came into conflict, or is neutral. Ask students to cite evidence from the text at least twice in their paragraphs.

KNOWLEDGE DEMANDS

EXPRESS Check students' understanding of explorers' actions and the effects they had on native people. For each section of the text, have students discuss what explorers did and how each action affected the people who already lived on the land.

If . . . students have difficulty discussing effects of explorers' actions,

then . . . have them use a two-column chart. Ask students to generate a list of explorers' actions from each section of the text. Next to each action, have students write the effect, if any, the action had on local people.

EXTEND Have students choose one pair from their list, and write one paragraph from the perspective of a native person about the event. Encourage students to use evidence from the text to explain how the event affected them and how they responded to it.

ACCELERATED LEARNERS

Have students choose an explorer from the text and decide whether the individual should be considered a hero. Encourage students to supplement evidence from the text with additional research to write two paragraphs supporting their argument.

Unlock the Text

QUALITATIVE MEASURES

Levels of Meaning	narrative that fictionalizes true events; first-person point of view; character development
Structure	chronological sequence of journal entries; cause-and-effect relationships; illustrations
Language Conventionality and Clarity	multiple-meaning words; descriptive language; figurative language
Knowledge Demands	general knowledge of Christopher Columbus and his exploration of the New World

Pedro's Journal,
pp. 66–90

Prepare to Read

LEVELS OF MEANING

Pedro's Journal is a fictional retelling of Christopher Columbus's voyage to the New World. The narrator's point of view, that of a young ship's boy, allows the reader to see Christopher Columbus in a different light.

STRUCTURE

PREVIEW Read the title of the text aloud, including the subtitle. Have students preview the text. Ask: How is the text divided? (into chapterlike sections, often called "entries" in a journal or diary) What do you notice about the titles of each journal entry? What information is provided? (The titles are dates that provide the month and day.) What do the illustrations tell you about what might happen in the story? (A boy leaves on a ship; the ship's crew is upset about something; the people on the ship meet people on land.)

ENGLISH LANGUAGE LEARNERS

Have students practice asking and answering questions about the text with a partner, using the starter words *who, what, when, where,* and *how.* Ask students to phrase the questions in their home language first before practicing the words in English.

STRUGGLING READERS

Have students preview the text and create a list of unfamiliar words. For each word, have students recall strategies from previously learned routines and activities to determine the definition. Have students use this list while reading to confirm their definitions with the text.

PREVIEW VOCABULARY Use the Preview and Review Vocabulary Routine in Part 3 to assess what students know about the following words: *roster*, *sandbar*, *fleet*, *helmsman*, *leagues*, *assent*, *horizon*, *mutiny, dugouts, overboard*, *interpreter*, *arrogant*, and *cowardly*.

MULTIPLE-MEANING WORDS Use the Analyze Multiple-Meaning Words Routine in Part 3 to help students understand the multiple meanings of each of these words: *suspect*, *favors*, *log*, *leagues*, *watch/watches*, *froze*, *scrambled*, and *stern*.

COGNATES Use the list of Spanish cognates at the beginning of this module to guide your Spanish-speaking students as they read the text.

ACTIVATE BACKGROUND KNOWLEDGE Use the Quick Write and Share Routine in Part 3 to activate background knowledge about Christopher Columbus and his exploration. Ask: Have you heard of Christopher Columbus? What do you know about him? What did he accomplish? After students have written responses to the above questions, have them share their responses with a partner. Then, have partners share their ideas with the whole class.

Interact with Text

LEVELS OF MEANING

As students read, periodically stop to assess their ability to identify facts and opinions by asking them to differentiate between the narrator's recorded facts about the voyage and the narrator's personal observations and opinions about the voyage. Assign students a section of the text to reread, and have them create a two-column chart with the headings *Fact* and *Opinion,* on which to list their examples. Remind students to include page numbers in their notes. Have students share the reasoning for their responses.

> If . . . students are struggling to distinguish between facts and opinions,
>
> then . . . provide an example for students by modeling a think aloud.

Say: It is a fact that the *Santa Maria* led the way into the sheltered bay because this information can be proved. Other witnesses could verify that this actually happened. Pedro's prediction that no one will get much sleep that night is an opinion. It is a prediction, or speculation, made by Pedro. It is his belief or feeling, so it is an opinion.

STRUCTURE

To help students keep track of the story's important events, use the Time Line Routine and Graphic Organizer in Part 3. After reading a journal entry, have students write the date on the space provided under the time line. On the vertical line, have them record two important events from that entry. Afterwards, assess students' understanding of important events by circulating around the room while they discuss, in small groups, why the events they chose are the most important. Clarify any misunderstandings as a class.

MORE SUPPORT

ENGLISH LANGUAGE LEARNERS

Help students interpret the vivid descriptive language in the text by having pairs of students act out parts of the text that use this language. Seeing others act out descriptive words will give students mental images of events in the text.

STRUGGLING READERS

If students mistake interesting details for important events, guide them to be more discriminating by asking: Would the story be different if (insert detail) weren't included? What impact does this event have on the events that come next? Why do you think the author chose to include this event?

LANGUAGE CONVENTIONALITY AND CLARITY

Students may need help understanding descriptive language. At descriptive points in the text, such as when the narrator describes how the boat moves in the sea, what the new land looks like, or what the natives look like, use the Description: Sensory Details Routine and Graphic Organizer in Part 3. After reading through the description once as a class, have students reread with a partner and fill out the graphic organizer to record which descriptions relate to seeing, hearing, touching, smelling, or tasting. Have students use their graphic organizers as an aid to illustrating the scene being described. When they have completed their illustrations, have students present them to the class. When presenting, students should explain how the text influenced their drawing.

KNOWLEDGE DEMANDS

Have students reread the portions of text that describe Pedro and those that describe Christopher Columbus. Then provide students with the Venn Diagram Graphic Organizer in Part 3 with the labels *Pedro* and *Christopher Columbus.* Have students list characteristics of each character in their respective circles before writing the similarities in the center. Afterward, have students decide whether Pedro and Christopher Columbus are more alike or more different. Remind students to refer to the text in their explanations.

If . . . students struggle to identify characteristics of the two characters,

then . . . provide a bank of phrases that describe the two characters. Students can then choose whether the phrase describes Pedro only, describes Christopher Columbus only, or describes both Pedro and Christopher Columbus. They can then record the phrase in the correct part of the Venn diagram.

STRUGGLING READERS

When describing characters, direct students to avoid overused words such as *good, bad, happy,* and *sad.* Create a word wall to illustrate shades of meaning. Work together to think of increasingly vivid words such as *glad, joyful, thrilled,* and *ecstatic.* Encourage students to use these words in their writing and discussions.

Express and Extend

LEVELS OF MEANING

EXPRESS Provide students with the Venn Diagram Graphic Organizer in Part 3 and have them compare how Pedro feels about the Captain at the end of his first entry with how Pedro feels about the Captain at the end of his entry on October 16th. Afterward, ask: Have Pedro's feelings about the Captain changed? Why or why not? Remind students to use evidence from the text in their responses.

If . . . students have difficulty recognizing how Pedro feels about the Captain,

then . . . think aloud about the first entry and record your findings on a displayed Venn diagram. As you think aloud, make sure to point out sentences that demonstrate Pedro's feelings, such as "...Captain already favors me and has called upon me to write and to copy certain of his writings." Say: It says here that the Captain favors Pedro. This means the Captain likes Pedro and uses him a lot. I'm sure Pedro likes the Captain too, because he seems eager to please the Captain.

EXTEND Have students infer emotions based on a character's actions. Instruct them to reread the last paragraph on p. 79 to the end of the entry. Then ask: Why would Pedro's mother lower her eyes? Students should write a paragraph in response to this question and include at least one example from the text to support their response.

STRUCTURE

EXPRESS Use the Cause and Effect Routine and Graphic Organizer in Part 3 to help students record the impact of important events in the selection. Have pairs of students pick three important events from the text and write them in the *Cause* boxes. Then have them reread the text to identify their effects.

If . . . students have difficulty selecting three important events,

then . . . give them five events to choose from, some that are important and others that are simply interesting details. Have them choose three from your list. Before they continue, assess their choices by asking them to explain to you why they chose the three they did.

EXTEND Have students look at their *Effect* boxes, and ask: Based on the effects of the journey, do you think it was worthwhile? Students' responses should be in paragraph form and refer to evidence from the text.

MORE SUPPORT

ENGLISH LANGUAGE LEARNERS

Use the Express Opinions Routine in Part 3 to help students give their point of view. For extra support, provide sentence frames: I think ___. I believe ___. I agree/disagree with ___ because ___.

STRUGGLING READERS

Understanding emotion words in text may be difficult for some students. Help them process these words by reading aloud a sentence from the text that conveys a character's emotion. Ask: Based on this sentence, how do you think (character's name) feels? How do you know?

EXPRESS Talk about Sentences and Words

Display this sentence, which includes examples of figurative language from *Pedro's Journal,* and read it aloud.

> The air was thick with mutiny and betrayal, until finally everything came to a dead stop.

Ask: What does the word *mutiny* mean? (The crew of a ship takes charge and gets rid of the captain.) How can the air be *thick with mutiny*? (*Thick* means that something is "layered on or heavy." So this means the crew was thinking about mutiny so much that they felt like the thought of mutiny surrounded them.) What does the phrase *until finally* imply? (It means that whatever comes after this phrase had taken a while to occur.) What does the phrase *dead stop* mean? (It means that everything came to a sudden, complete stop.)

TEAM TALK Have students rewrite the sentence, replacing the phrases *thick with betrayal and mutiny* and *dead stop*. Remind students not to change the meaning of the sentence. For example, the sentence might be rewritten as follows: There were uncomfortable feelings about betrayal and mutiny among the crew, until suddenly everything completely stopped.

EXTEND Assign students other examples of figurative language from the text and have them rewrite the sentences to be literal. After students have rewritten their sentence, ask: Which version do you think is better and why? Have students record their responses and share them with the class.

EXPRESS Use the Web Routine and Graphic Organizer in Part 3 to help students record important details from Columbus's expedition. Instruct students to write *Columbus and His Expedition* in the center circle. In the outer circles, have students record important details about Christopher Columbus and the expedition. Place students in pairs to discuss the details they chose and to discuss any differences in their graphic organizers.

EXTEND Have students conduct research to verify whether the details on their lists are historically accurate. For details that are not accurate, ask students to use the Draw Conclusions Graphic Organizer in Part 3 and then discuss why the author might have made that decision.

ACCELERATED LEARNERS

Hold a debate between two teams of students in which one supports the idea that exploration had a positive impact on the world and the other supports the idea that exploration had a negative impact on the world. Have students use evidence from the text, as well as additional research. Monitor the debate so that everyone has at least one turn to speak and that no one is cut off.

MORE SUPPORT

Unlock the Text

QUALITATIVE MEASURES

Levels of Meaning	fictional story referencing Native American artifacts; solving problems; third-person narrative text
Structure	chronological plot that builds to a climax; illustrations; conflict and resolution
Language Conventionality and Clarity	figurative language; detailed descriptions; words in italics; domain-specific vocabulary
Knowledge Demands	cave dwellings; Gooseneck State Park

Secrets of the Canyon
Cave, pp. 91–100

Prepare to Read

LEVELS OF MEANING

One level of meaning in "Secrets of the Canyon Cave" is the unexpected discovery of Native American artifacts during a scavenger hunt. Another level of meaning is pursuing a challenge despite previous failure.

STRUCTURE

PREVIEW Have students preview the illustrations of "Secrets of the Canyon Cave." Ask: Will the story be fiction or nonfiction? How do you know? (It looks like fiction because I see a lot of dialogue and illustrations of children exploring by themselves, and I don't see any photos.) Based on the pictures, what do you think the story is about? (a boy and girl who are lost in a canyon or a cave) Who do you think made the drawings in the cave? (people who lived a long time ago)

ENGLISH LANGUAGE LEARNERS

Discuss the title of the story with students. Define *canyon* and *cave,* using pictures if available. Then discuss the meaning of the word *secret,* and brainstorm how a cave could have a secret. Have students look for the secret as they read the text.

STRUGGLING READERS

Tell students that they might read about a topic that they've heard of but don't know much about. Discuss strategies they can use to learn about the topic as they read, such as reviewing pictures, having class discussions, or using graphic organizers to record new information.

LANGUAGE CONVENTIONALITY AND CLARITY

PREVIEW VOCABULARY Use the Preview and Review Vocabulary Routine in Part 3 to assess what students know about the following words: *ranger*, *scavenger hunt*, *squiggly*, *entrenched*, *meander*, *cringed*, *geological*, *smirked*, *ventured,* and *crevices.* Help students find these words in the story and use context clues or a dictionary to write a brief definition for each word.

DOMAIN-SPECIFIC VOCABULARY Use the Vocabulary Activities in Part 3 with the following domain-specific terms: *Anasazi, Pueblo Indians, cliff dwellings, cave paintings, Four Corners, North Star,* and *Polaris.*

COGNATES Use the list of Spanish cognates at the beginning of this module to guide your Spanish-speaking students as they read the text.

KNOWLEDGE DEMANDS

ACTIVATE BACKGROUND KNOWLEDGE Use the Quick Write and Share Routine in Part 3 to assess students' background knowledge about caves and cave dwellings. Have students look at the illustrations throughout the book to help them remember information they might have learned in the past. Ask: What is a cave dwelling? Who might live in it? What might it look like? Where would one be located?

Interact with Text

LEVELS OF MEANING

Help students document the story's major conflicts. Remind students that there are three major points of conflict in "Secrets of the Canyon Cave": Derrick Sweeney (the bully who always wins); choosing a path to take for the scavenger hunt; and the storm clouds, which force the main characters into the dwelling. Provide students with a two-column chart with columns labeled *Conflict* and *Solution*. Have students write one of the above conflicts in the *Conflict* column and then record the way Brandon (or Brandon and Ría) chooses to resolve it in the *Solution* column. Then have students discuss each conflict and solution using the following question: Why did the character choose to resolve the conflict in this way?

STRUCTURE

After Ranger Merker starts the scavenger hunt, the action of the plot begins to rise to the climactic point of the story. Tell students: The climax of a story is the most exciting point. It is the part of the story that all the action leads up to. After students have read a large portion of the text, have them work in pairs to decide whether the climax of the story has been reached. Use the Story Prediction Routine and Graphic Organizer in Part 3 to help pairs record their ideas and any text clues they think are relevant.

If . . . students have difficulty understanding the concept of a climax in a story,

then . . . ask students if it feels like something more exciting is still going to happen as they are reading. If they answer "yes," then the climax has not yet been reached. If they answer "no," ask what they think the climax of the story was.

ENGLISH LANGUAGE LEARNERS

Help students sort through descriptive language in multiple readings. On the first reading, have students identify verbs they don't understand. After defining them, do another read so that students can focus on nouns they don't understand.

STRUGGLING READERS

Students may not have much background knowledge about cave dwellings and may not understand how caves could serve as homes for people. Give students additional information about the topic by bringing illustrations or photos to class that show actual cave dwellings.

MORE SUPPORT

LANGUAGE CONVENTIONALITY AND CLARITY

As students read, they should notice that some of the words are in italics. Help students understand the purpose of italicized text.

Read aloud the second paragraph of the story, putting emphasis on the italicized words. After reading, ask: Which character do these italicized words relate to, and how do you know? (The words relate to Brandon. We know it's him because the text says "thought Brandon.") Are these words being said aloud? (No, Brandon is thinking them, so no one can hear them.) If no one can hear Brandon's thoughts, why did the author write them? (to let the reader learn more about Brandon)

Have students look for additional examples of italicized text. Point out that, in some cases, the italics are used to emphasize a word. Have students practice reading these sentences aloud with a partner, emphasizing the italicized text. Have partners discuss why the author chose to italicize these particular words, and how the meaning of the sentence would differ if italics had not been used.

Students may also find the text that is italicized to show that it is the text contained in a text message. Discuss with students why the author chose to use italics in this example.

KNOWLEDGE DEMANDS

Students may need help to understand why a cave was a good place for desert natives to live—and for Brandon and Ría to stay in.

After reading the portion of text that describes Brandon and Ría's initial reactions to the cave dwelling, use the Web Routine and Graphic Organizer in Part 3 to help students record reasons. Have them label the middle circle *Reasons for Cave Dwelling.* In the surrounding circles, have them record reasons the cave is a good shelter. Students should use examples from the text when filling in their graphic organizers.

MORE SUPPORT

Express and Extend

LEVELS OF MEANING

EXPRESS Help students recall the differences between narrative and expository text. Remind them that narratives tell a story and expository texts explain something. Ask: What type of text is "Secrets of the Canyon Cave"? How do you know? (narrative; it tells a story) Is the story told in the first or the third person? How do you know? (third person; it uses *he/she*, not *I*) What do the pronouns tell you? (The story isn't told by Brandon. A narrator, rather than a character in the story, is telling a story about Brandon.)

EXTEND Have students read another short text with a similar topic or theme of discovery, either historical or modern day. Have students compare and contrast the two texts and discuss how related themes appear across literary works. Use the Story Comparison Routine and Graphic Organizer in Part 3 to help students record their thoughts on the two stories.

STRUCTURE

EXPRESS Use the Sequence of Events Routine and Graphic Organizer in Part 3 to show the chronological sequence of events in the plot. As students complete the graphic organizer, remind them to include the resolution as the final event. Then provide time for students to use their graphic organizer to retell the story to a partner.

If . . . students have a hard time sequencing the events,

then . . . provide students with the following sentence frames: First, Brandon and Ría ___. Next, they ___. Then, ___. Finally, they ___.

EXTEND Point out that the Sequence of Events Graphic Organizer is a basic form of a more detailed plot diagram. Draw a plot diagram that includes Exposition (characters, setting, situation), Conflict (problem), Rising Action, Climax/Falling Action, and Resolution. Complete the organizer as a group. Have partners compare the plot diagram to their sequence of events graphic organizers. Ask: Which graphic organizer provides more information? Which is easier to understand? Which one do you prefer to use? Why?

MORE SUPPORT

ENGLISH LANGUAGE LEARNERS

Help students distinguish between first-person and third-person points of view by sharing sentences from *Pedro's Journal* and "Secrets of the Canyon Cave." Point out the different ways pronouns are used and what that reveals about who is telling the story.

STRUGGLING READERS

To help students sequence the events, write *exposition, conflict, rising action, climax, falling action,* and *resolution* on index cards. Write the corresponding events from the text on another set of cards. Have students match the event to the corresponding element of the plot. Then have students put the events in order.

LANGUAGE CONVENTIONALITY AND CLARITY

EXPRESS Talk about Sentences and Words

Display the following sentences from "Secrets of the Canyon Cave." Read them aloud with students.

> Spikes of cool air and a strong wave of humidity hit them. The burning sun disappeared behind massive dark clouds.

Ask: What would "spikes of cool air" feel like? (A spike is sharp, so "spikes of cool air" would feel sudden and maybe unpleasant.) How can humidity be like a wave? (An ocean wave rolls into the shore, so the humidity must have rolled into the area.) What might a "burning sun" feel like? (The word *burning* suggests something that is intensely hot, so the sun might be so hot that Brandon feels like it is burning him.)

TEAM TALK Have students rewrite the sentences, describing the same event, but using literal language. Have students discuss whether figurative language or literal language is more effective and why.

EXTEND Have pairs reread another section of the text and look for language that appeals to the senses. Provide students with the Three-Column Chart Graphic Organizer in Part 3. As they read, have them record sensory words and phrases in the first column of the graphic organizer. In the second column, have them indicate the sense to which the words appeal. After reading, have the pairs explain the meaning of the descriptive language and write their explanations in the third column.

KNOWLEDGE DEMANDS

EXPRESS Have students research the setting of the story, Gooseneck State Park, and create a travel brochure for prospective visitors. Remind students to use details from the text, such as *entrenched meanders, sandstone cliffs, cottontails, prairie dogs, blackbrush,* and *snakeweed* to guide their creation of the brochure. Provide students with sample travel brochures if necessary.

EXTEND Challenge students to analyze the details from their research and the experience of Brandon and Ría to formulate an opinion about whether Brandon and Ría should have kept the paintings and ancient artifacts a secret. Remind students to include reasons with details from the text in their writing. Use the Opinion Writing Routine and Graphic Organizer in Part 3 to guide students' writing as needed.

ACCELERATED LEARNERS

Ask students to consider how the story would have changed if Brandon had been partnered with Derrick Sweeney, his archenemy. Have students rewrite a shorter version of the story using this conflict. Ask students to share their stories with the class.

MORE SUPPORT

Cognates

Cognates are words that have similar spellings and meanings in two or more languages. Many words in English and Spanish share Greek or Latin roots, and many words in English came from French, which is closely connected to Spanish (and to Portuguese, Italian, and Romanian). Because of this, many literary, content, and academic process words in English (e.g., *gracious/gracioso; volcano/volcán; compare/comparar*) have recognizable Spanish cognates.

Making the connection to cognates permits students who are native Spanish speakers to understand the strong foundation they have in academic and literary English. These links between English and Spanish are also useful for native speakers of English and other languages because they help uncover basic underlying features of our language.

ANCHOR TEXT **Beyond the Horizon**

ENGLISH	SPANISH	ENGLISH	SPANISH
accident	accidente	impatient	impaciente
animals	animales	language	lengua
anxious	ansioso	market	mercado
arms	armas	medicine	medicina
authority	autoridad	moment	momento
barbarous	bárbaro	north	norte
captain	capitán	ocean	océano
channel	canal	paper	papel
coast	costa	person	persona
companion	compañero	port	puerto
company	compañía	precaution	precaución
confusion	confusión	probably	probablemente
corrected	corrigió	protect	proteger
curious	curioso	pyramids	pirámides
descended	descendió	rations	raciones
described	describió	reins	riendas
different	diferente	revelation	revelación
distance	distancia	routes	rutas
explained	explicó	sacks	sacos
expression	expresión	silence	silencio
families	familias	tomb	tumba
fort	fuerte	treaty	tratado
fortune	fortuna	unrecognizable	irreconocible
fruits	frutas	vegetables	vegetales
horizon	horizonte	voice	voz

SUPPORTING TEXT Explorers of North America

ENGLISH	SPANISH		ENGLISH	SPANISH
astronomy	astronomía		mythical	mítica
botanist	botánica		native	nativas
camp	acampar		navigation	navegación
canal	canal		ocean	océano
canoe	canoa		palace	palacio
classify	clasificar		personal	personal
continent	continente		plants	planta
convinced	convencido		President	presidente
desert	desierto		rebel	rebelarse
diamond	diamante		replica	réplica
emperor	emperador		salt	sal
except	excepto		secretary	secretario
famous	famoso		territory	territorio
interpreter	intérprete		thermometers	termómetros
medal	medalla		trap	atrapar
mineral	mineral			

SUPPORTING TEXT New Beginnings

ENGLISH	SPANISH		ENGLISH	SPANISH
action	acción		immediately	inmediatamente
ceremony	ceremonia		inspire	inspirar
civilization	civilización		leader	líder
colony	colonia		mystery	misterio
continue	continuar		native	nativos
decision	decisión		opportunity	oportunidad
difference	diferencia		organize	organizar
fortune	fortuna		prepare	preparar
group	grupo			

These lists contain many, but not all, Spanish
cognates from these selections.

Unlock the Text

WRITTEN BY PAUL B. MASON
ILLUSTRATED BY LYDIA SANCHEZ

Beyond the Horizon

QUALITATIVE MEASURES

Levels of Meaning	fictional narrative about a girl who uses a disguise to board her father's ship to India on a journey to set up a trading post; character motivation and cause and effect; compare and contrast characters' attitudes
Structure	chapters and section breaks; chronological text structure; varied pace of events
Language Conventionality and Clarity	figurative and descriptive language; challenging academic and domain-specific vocabulary; varied sentence length; dialect
Knowledge Demands	understanding about colonial India and trading posts; knowledge of timeline of events

Prepare to Read

LEVELS OF MEANING

Beyond the Horizon tells the story of a girl named Sarah who disguises herself as a boy to make the journey to India on her father's ship. Sarah and her father's worlds collide when explorers and local villagers come into conflict, challenging ideas about exploration and settlement.

STRUCTURE

PREVIEW Have students preview the text's organization and illustrations. Ask: Based on the illustrations, what do you think the text is about? (a journey by ship; experiences in a village in a foreign country; conflict between explorers and villagers) Ask: How is the story divided? (into four chapters) Explain that chapters are further divided into smaller scenes. Point out that students can distinguish scenes by looking for small breaks in the text, where the setting changes, or where the text

MORE SUPPORT

ENGLISH LANGUAGE LEARNERS

If students are distracted by difficult pronunciations and new vocabulary, have them do multiple readings. In the first reading, have students focus on pronunciation as they read aloud. In the second reading, have students focus on meaning.

STRUGGLING READERS

Have students track new characters as they are introduced. Next to each new character, have students list his or her characteristics, relationships with other characters, and any quotations from the text that help describe the character's attitudes and beliefs.

involves a different set of characters. Explain that while the text switches between Sarah's experiences and her father's experiences, it is generally told from Sarah's perspective.

LANGUAGE CONVENTIONALITY AND CLARITY

PREVIEW VOCABULARY Use the Preview and Review Vocabulary Routine in Part 3 to assess what students know about the following words: *wondrous, barbarous, pondered, pungent, anguish, tethered, lilting, imploring,* and *grudgingly.*

COGNATES Use the list of Spanish cognates at the beginning of this module to guide your Spanish-speaking students as they read the selection.

DOMAIN-SPECIFIC VOCABULARY Use the Vocabulary Activities in Part 3 to pre-teach the following domain-specific vocabulary: *breeches, tunic, doublet, galley, gunwales,* and *weigh anchor.* Explain that students can use these words to talk about Sarah's journey at sea.

KNOWLEDGE DEMANDS

ACTIVATE BACKGROUND KNOWLEDGE Help students place the text in historical context. Explain that *Beyond the Horizon* takes place in the early 1600s, in the age of colonialism. Say: In the early 1600s, the British traveled to India hoping to set up trading posts. They wanted to establish trade in new territory to gain wealth. To do this, the British had to control new land in India. In the story, the land in India that the British want is already occupied by local people. As they read, ask students to write down details from the text that help explain why Captain Booth and his men are traveling to India.

STRUGGLING READERS

Have students create word webs to make associations with new vocabulary words from the text. In the center, have students write the new vocabulary word. In smaller circles, have students write simpler synonyms for the word and illustrations that help them remember the word's meaning.

Interact with Text

Students can use cause and effect relationships to understand characters' motivation. Say: A character's motivation is the reason he or she does something. It answers the question *why?* Have students keep track of reasons behind characters' actions as they read *Beyond the Horizon.*

If . . . students have difficulty using cause and effect to understand character motivation,

then . . . have students create a chart with two columns. In the first column, have students write *Character Action;* in the second, have students write the question *Why?*

Model filling in the chart by pointing to events associated with Sarah's decision to join her father's ship. Ask: Why does Sarah decide to follow her father? (She feels that staying would be "withering away till there was nothing left of her." She was very unhappy without her father.) Ask: Why does Sarah disguise herself as a boy? (She does not want her father to know she is on the ship; she needs to be "unrecognizable." Her father says "'India is no place for a girl.'")

Have students discuss why the writer divided the text into four chapters. Ask students to look at the end of each chapter and the beginning of the next. Ask: Why does it make sense to have a break in the text at this point? What changes between the two chapters? Students should explain that chapters indicate changes in time, location, and characters involved in scenes.

If . . . students have difficulty explaining chapter breaks,

then . . . focus on the break between Chapter 3 and Chapter 4. Read the last paragraph of Chapter 3 aloud and the first paragraph of Chapter 4. Model explaining the writer's choice to divide the text.

Ask: What happens at the end of Chapter 3? (Sarah cries after finding out that her father's ship has left.) Ask: What happens at the beginning of Chapter 4? (Captain Booth and his crew reach land.) Explain that the writer divided the text with a chapter so he could more naturally jump between events involving Sarah and those involving her father and his crew.

ENGLISH LANGUAGE LEARNERS

Have students practice explaining characters' motivation by working in pairs to ask questions about why events in the text happened. Have students read their two-column charts to ask a partner why a character did something. Give partners frames to use for responses such as: Sarah decided to___ because ___.

STRUGGLING READERS

Point out the multiple names associated with characters in the story. For example, *Booth, Captain Booth,* and *Sarah's father* all refer to the same person. Sarah is referred to as *Sarah, Sam,* and *the cook's boy.*

Students may have difficulty with challenging descriptive vocabulary and figurative language in the text.

If . . . students have difficulty understanding descriptive and figurative language,

then . . . discuss and analyze each example on a case-by-case basis.

For example, point to the phrases *heaving thoroughfare* and *pulsing mass of people and animals* on p. 30. Ask students to define *heaving* and *pulsing* in context. Explain that the word *heaving* implies that the road was very crowded, and *pulsing* describes the steady, rhythmic movement of the people in the street. Ask: How do these words help set the scene? (They describe a very crowded, overwhelming atmosphere.)

Repeat the model above for the phrases the *house became a tomb* (p. 8) and *buildings looming over them like cliffs* (p. 26).

KNOWLEDGE DEMANDS

Although the text follows a chronological order, its rhythm varies. Point out that in certain places in the text, time passes quickly from one passage to the next, and in others it moves more slowly. Have students create a timeline of events beginning with Sarah's arrival on the ship. Encourage students to use cues from the text to mark important events on the timeline and indicate weeks, months, and years between events. Encourage students to look for time cues in the text such as *month after month passed* (p. 16) and *the next day* (p. 37).

ENGLISH LANGUAGE LEARNERS

Help students understand expressions and idioms used in the text. Explain that students will not hear many of the expressions in everyday speech today. Point out phrases such as *taken a fancy to* and *come hither* in Sarah's conversation with the cook on pp. 12–14.

MORE SUPPORT

Express and Extend

EXPRESS Have students compare and contrast characters' attitudes toward the villagers. Say: Captain Booth, Lieutenant Armitage, and Sarah have different opinions and attitudes toward the local people in India. These attitudes develop and change throughout the story.

> If . . . students have difficulty defining characters' attitudes,
>
> then . . . model using evidence from the text to build support for a character's attitude.

Point to Lieutenant Armitage's answer to Captain Booth's question on p. 36: "A village or two, perchance, it matters not. Peasants can be persuaded to leave." Explain that Lieutenant Armitage does not care about the villagers already living on the land; he does not mind forcing them out.

EXTEND Have students imagine they are Captain Booth. Ask students to write a paragraph explaining why they told Lieutenant Armitage not to advance on the villagers. Have students use evidence from the text to support their writing.

STRUCTURE

EXPRESS Students may be confused by the jumps in chronology and abrupt transitions between section breaks and chapters. Check students' orientation to chronology and location at the beginning of each new chapter. Ask students to fill in the gaps between the two chapters. For example, ask: What must have happened between page 10 and page 12? (Sarah arrived at the ship and talked to the bosun about working on the ship.)

EXTEND Have students write two paragraphs to fill in the chronological gap between Chapter 2 and Chapter 3. Encourage students to use Priya's explanation of events on p. 40 to help them with events, and to fill in details using their imagination.

MORE SUPPORT

ENGLISH LANGUAGE LEARNERS

Students may be overwhelmed by longer writing assignments. Have students first create an outline of ideas and short phrases to include. Then, have students add connecting words and phrases to form a paragraph.

STRUGGLING READERS

Have students use a Venn diagram graphic organizer to more easily compare and contrast characters' attitudes toward the villagers. Have students create circles for Sarah, Lieutenant Armitage, and Captain Booth. Remind students that characters may have conflicting attitudes and that attitudes may change over time.

EXPRESS Talk about Sentences and Words

Display and read aloud the following sentences from *Beyond the Horizon.*

> Then over the hill women came running from the direction of the ships, crying out in an anxious stream of words, their water jugs abandoned. Something was coming.

Point out that the passage uses varied sentence structure to set a tone of suspense and urgency. Ask: What is the effect of the long sentence in the passage? (It builds tension, showing chaos and a flurry of activity.) Ask: What is the effect of the short sentence? (It is straight to the point, and builds suspense; something is coming, but the villagers do not know exactly what to expect.)

TEAM TALK Have partners reread the scene on pp. 54–55, noting sentence length. In pairs, have students discuss the strongest uses of varied sentence length and explain why each is effective at building suspense or creating a mood.

EXTEND Have students scan the text to find another instance where the writer varies sentence length and structure. For example, students may point to the long sentences used to describe the scene on p. 30. Ask students to write a paragraph describing the effect of the sentence structure on mood or tone.

EXPRESS Explain that much of the dialogue is written in a dialect, or way of speaking, that may sound unfamiliar to students. Point out that the writer chooses words to make the dialogue sound more natural and realistic for that time period.

If . . . students have difficulty determining what the characters are saying,

then . . . have them read aloud dialogue between characters and work with a partner to reword or define unfamiliar words and phrases.

EXTEND In small groups, have students choose the conversation between the cook and Sarah on pp. 12–13 or the conversation between Sarah and her father on pp. 4–7. Have students first act out the dialogue as it is written; then, have groups work to rewrite dialogue to use more familiar, modern phrases. Have students discuss the differences between the two versions of dialogue and their effects on the story.

ACCELERATED LEARNERS

Have students consider Priya's perspective and how she might have felt about Sarah's appearance in the village and the later arrival of Captain Booth and his ship. Ask students to write two paragraphs from Priya's point of view describing the events of Chapter 4.

Unlock the Text

QUALITATIVE MEASURES

Levels of Meaning	brief expository history of explorers and their explorations to the Americas
Structure	brief summaries of informational topics; sidebars and illustrations with captions; chapters with subsections
Language Conventionality and Clarity	parenthetical pronunciation of difficult words; multiple-meaning words; simple and compound sentences
Knowledge Demands	early explorers of North America; world geography and exploration; reasons for exploration

Prepare to Read

LEVELS OF MEANING

Explorers of North America is an informational text about people who explored North America. It provides specific facts and details about explorers—including Lewis and Clark, Christopher Columbus, Henry Hudson, Hernán Cortés, and Francisco Coronado—and their voyages.

STRUCTURE

PREVIEW Display the book's cover and have students read the title and then scan the pages. Ask: What do you notice about the pages of the text? (There are a lot of text features such as headings, subheadings, illustrations, captions, sidebars, and callouts.) What do the titles of chapters 2, 3, and 4 tell you about the topics that will be discussed? (The topics seem to be about what the explorers were searching for.)

ENGLISH LANGUAGE LEARNERS

To enrich students' understanding of the vocabulary, have them place these words into two logical categories: *settlement*, *colony*, *territory*, *emperor*, *governor*, and *ruler*. Have students decide how the words in each category relate to one another.

STRUGGLING READERS

Provide students with a photocopy of the Important Words section before they start reading the text. Have students keep the photocopy available as they read to avoid the distraction of flipping back and forth between the words and the text.

LANGUAGE CONVENTIONALITY AND CLARITY

PREVIEW VOCABULARY Use the Preview and Review Vocabulary Routine in Part 3 to assess what students know about the following words: *navigation*, *coast*, *ruins*, *goods*, *mythical*, *emperor*, *governor*, *ruler*, *colony*, *settlement*, *territory*, *interpreter*, *botanist*, *rain forest*, and *species*.

MULTIPLE-MEANING WORDS Use the Analyze Multiple-Meaning Words Routine in Part 3 with the following words: *ruins*, *capital*, *ruler*, *mouth*, *trap*, and *gorge*.

COGNATES Use the list of Spanish cognates at the beginning of this module to guide your Spanish-speaking students as they read the text.

KNOWLEDGE DEMANDS

ACTIVATE BACKGROUND KNOWLEDGE Use the Quick Write and Share Routine in Part 3 to activate background knowledge about the people who explored North America. Ask: Who is responsible for discovering America? What did the first explorers of America find? What are some of the issues that occurred during their explorations?

As a class, discuss what students know about some of the explorers featured in the text, including Christopher Columbus, Lewis and Clark, Leif Erikson, Hernán Cortés, Francisco Coronado, Henry Hudson, James Cook, Jacques Cartier, and any other explorers featured in the book. Students should recall some details about one or more of them from previous readings.

ENGLISH LANGUAGE LEARNERS

Have students create a running list of multiple-meaning words from the text. For each word, have students write the definitions and draw illustrations. Tell them to use this list while reading to determine which definition fits best with the text.

STRUGGLING READERS

When discussing new vocabulary, include practice with pronunciation. Writing words on the board with stress marks will reinforce students' understanding of correct pronunciation. Demonstrate pronunciation by saying the word aloud, and have students repeat after you.

MORE SUPPORT

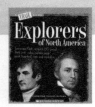

Interact with Text

Enrich students' understanding of various explorers by having them compare and contrast their explorations.

After reading the first two chapters, use the Three-Column Chart Routine and Graphic Organizer in Part 3 to help students compare and contrast Christopher Columbus's exploration with Cortés's exploration. Have students label and fill out the following within the three columns: *Explorers' Goals, Interactions with Natives,* and *Accomplishments.* Afterward, have students use the information from their three-column charts to write a few sentences comparing and contrasting the explorers.

> **If . . .** students have difficulty comparing and contrasting details about the two explorers,
>
> **then . . .** use the Retell or Summarize Routine and Graphic Organizer in Part 3 to help students identify and record specific details. Students should complete one for the section discussing Christopher Columbus's exploration and another for Cortés's exploration.

STRUCTURE

Use the Main Idea and Details Routine and Graphic Organizer in Part 3 to help students find the main idea that links all of the subsections in each chapter.

Model this activity by rereading Chapter 2 with students and thinking aloud, showing how you found the main idea of the chapter: The title of the chapter is "A Trade Route to Asia," so I know this chapter will likely be about explorers who wanted to find a way to Asia. Pages 10 and 11 give details about why finding a better route to Asia was so important to European traders. The rest of the chapter discusses the explorers who tried to find a sea route to Asia. I think the main idea of the chapter is finding a sea route from Europe to Asia. After modeling, have students complete a Main Idea and Details Graphic Organizer for the next chapter.

MORE SUPPORT

ENGLISH LANGUAGE LEARNERS

Students may need help reading the parenthetical pronunciations of words. Help students by pulling examples from the text and saying them aloud. Then have students repeat them for practice.

STRUGGLING READERS

Have students choose one graphic organizer to keep the main ideas from each chapter in order and understandable. Allow them to choose from any previously used organizers from class. This will help students become more autonomous and responsible for their own learning.

LANGUAGE CONVENTIONALITY AND CLARITY

Help students understand the purpose of the pronunciations in parentheses. When you come to words accompanied by parenthetical pronunciations, stop and ask students: Why did the author put this here? (to help readers sound out new or confusing words) Demonstrate how to pronounce each one by reading aloud a sentence that has a parenthetical pronunciation. Then ask: What do you do when the letters in parentheses are uppercase? (You give them emphasis, as an accented syllable.)

KNOWLEDGE DEMANDS

Help students document the events of a particular exploration, including preparations for the voyage. Use the Time Line Routine and Graphic Organizer in Part 3 to help students put the events of the exploration in order, based on information from the text. For example, if a student documents Lewis and Clark's exploration, the first event might be "received permission from President Thomas Jefferson." The next event might be "gathered the Corps of Discovery to go on the voyage." The third event might be "collected information about people and animals that lived in the new land."

If . . . students struggle to order events,

then . . . encourage them to draw the exploration as a series of drawings or a comic strip, with the drawings showing the events from beginning to end. They can later add captions describing what is happening in the pictures.

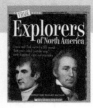

Express and Extend

LEVELS OF MEANING

EXPRESS After finishing the "Modern Explorers" chapter, have students compare and contrast the modern explorers with those from the Age of Exploration. Ask: What kinds of things do modern explorers search for? What kinds of things did previous explorers search for? What did past explorers need to do before being able to start their journey? Do modern explorers need to do all of the same things?

If . . . students have trouble remembering what previous explorers did,

then . . . have them use the graphic organizers they created previously during the unit to summarize information about past explorers.

EXTEND Based on what they've learned about both types of explorers, ask students: Would you rather be a modern explorer or a past explorer? Have students write a paragraph response in which they explain the type of explorer they would rather be and why. Make sure students use at least one example from the text in their response.

STRUCTURE

EXPRESS Assign students a two-page spread, such as pp. 22–23 or pp. 34–35, that contains pictures, captions, and enlarged orange text. Provide students with the Three-Column Chart Graphic Organizer in Part 3 with the headings *Pictures, Captions,* and *Enlarged Text,* and have them reread their assigned pages. Then, in the appropriate column, have students write how each text feature supports the text or another text feature.

EXTEND Have students select one text feature from their two-page spread (or from another part of the book) that they feel does not support the text. In a paragraph response, have them explain why they think the text feature does not support the text on the page and what they would replace it with to make it more useful to readers.

MORE SUPPORT

ENGLISH LANGUAGE LEARNERS

Remind students that captions explain the importance of a photo or illustration, and may provide additional information beyond what is in the main text. Ensure students are reading the captions by asking them the purpose of the pictures after reading a spread.

STRUGGLING READERS

If students have difficulty identifying the most important events or details, help by providing them three choices. When a student has chosen one, have them explain why it is the best option and why the others are less important.

LANGUAGE CONVENTIONALITY AND CLARITY

EXPRESS Talk about Sentences and Words

Display the following sentences from *Explorers of North America*. Read them aloud with students.

> He was hoping the river would bring him to the Pacific Ocean. It did not. But Cartier saw many animals along the river. Later, French fur traders would come to trap some of these animals.

Ask: Why does the third sentence start with the word *but*? (to show another perspective of an idea; This sentence shows the positive side of Cartier's travel down the river.) What does the word *later* mean? (What follows occurred after Cartier's exploration.) In this sentence, is *trap* being used as a noun or a verb? How do you know? (It is a verb. It suggests an action is taking place.)

TEAM TALK Have students rewrite the last two sentences, combining them into one complete sentence.

> If . . . students have difficulty combining the sentences,
> then . . . use the Simple and Compound Sentences Activity in Part 3 to review these sentence formats with students.

EXTEND Have students find other examples of adjacent simple sentences in the text, and instruct them to combine the sentences into one compound sentence. For additional practice, students can also look for examples of a compound sentence, and try to break it down into two simple sentences.

KNOWLEDGE DEMANDS

EXPRESS Each chapter lists reasons behind the explorations. Have students revisit a chapter of their choosing and list reasons the explorers kept searching. Have students share their lists with the class.

EXTEND Ask students to write about one of the explorations discussed in chapters 2, 3, or 4. Using evidence from the text as support, have students state an opinion about the importance of the exploration.

ACCELERATED LEARNERS

Have students reread the section on Lewis and Clark and complete the KWLH Chart Graphic Organizer in Part 3 from Lewis and Clark's perspective. Since specifics about what Lewis and Clark actually learned aren't covered in the text, provide students with grade-appropriate resources to help them complete the *What Did I Learn?* and *How Did I Learn It?* columns of the chart.

MORE SUPPORT

Unlock the Text

QUALITATIVE MEASURES

Levels of Meaning	colonists' daring decision to start a new life in the New World; the effects of colonists' interactions with Native Americans; enduring hardships
Structure	densely packed information clarified with illustrations, captions, maps, and sidebars; section headings
Language Conventionality and Clarity	unfamiliar vocabulary; suspenseful language
Knowledge Demands	colonial America—Jamestown; Native American life; problems faced by settlers; survival in the wilderness

ReadyGEN 5
Text Collection

New Beginnings, pp. 101–119

Prepare to Read

LEVELS OF MEANING

One level of meaning in *New Beginnings* is the daring and difficult choice English colonists made to travel to a new land to start a new life. The second level of meaning is based on the colonists' interactions with Native Americans, who were initially friendly but eventually became hostile, and how the colony was almost destroyed by starvation.

STRUCTURE

PREVIEW Have students preview the title, section titles, maps, and pictures. Ask: Based on the title and section titles, what do you think the book is about? (how the first colony was settled and a history of what happened there) Look at the map on the opening page. What does it show you? (the text's setting) Look at the pictures. What information do they

ENGLISH LANGUAGE LEARNERS

Have students look at the illustrations. Ask partners to ask and answer questions about people or places in the text's illustrations. Provide question starters such as: Who is _____? Where is _____? What is _____?

STRUGGLING READERS

Have students create a glossary to keep a running list of definitions for unfamiliar words. As students encounter new words, have them record the word, use context clues to determine a definition, and draw a small illustration.

show you about the text or the setting? (Based on the clothes, the events take place a long time ago. There might also be conflicts in the colony because we see people with guns, and there are headings such as "Massacre.")

LANGUAGE CONVENTIONALITY AND CLARITY

PREVIEW VOCABULARY Use the Preview and Review Vocabulary Routine in Part 3 to assess what students know about the following words: *settlers* (or *settlement*), *colonists* (or *colony*), *warriors* (or *war*), *riches*, *opportunity*, *raids*, *invaders*, *indentured servant*, and *massacre.*

COGNATES Use the list of Spanish cognates at the beginning of this module to guide your Spanish-speaking students as they read the text.

KNOWLEDGE DEMANDS

ACTIVATE BACKGROUND KNOWLEDGE Prompt students to share what they already know about early America. Tell students that they can look at illustrations and maps throughout the text to help them remember information they might have learned in the past. Use the Web Routine and Graphic Organizer in Part 3 to help students organize their information. Have them write the term *Early America* in the center of the web. Ask students to recall information they know about early America and fill in the outer circles of the web. Ask guiding questions, such as: Where did the colonists travel from? Whom did they encounter when they came to what is now America? How did the colonists get food? What problems or challenges did they face?

Interact with Text

LEVELS OF MEANING

The English settlers endured many hardships as they began to build their new community. Discuss with students the impact the Native Americans had on the colonists as you read the sections titled "The Colonists and the Native Americans" and "The First Months." Use the Cause and Effect Routine and Graphic Organizer in Part 3 to help students record information from the text about what went wrong for the settlers and how the Native Americans provided help. **Ask:** What did the Native Americans have that the settlers needed? What did the settlers have that the Native Americans wanted?

STRUCTURE

After the first reading of the text, have students form small groups and take turns summarizing the sections of the text. Remind them to focus only on key details. One student will record the summaries in notes or a few sentences, using their own words.

If . . . students have difficulty summarizing important information from the text,

then . . . remind them that headings usually provide clues to the information contained in the section that follows. Tell students to recall strategies previously used for summarizing information.

When groups finish discussing a section of text, use the Main Idea and Details Routine and Graphic Organizer in Part 3. The heading from the text should go in the *Main Idea* box. In the *Details* boxes, have students work independently to choose the three most important details or events discussed in that section. Have students share the information they recorded to see whether classmates recorded different details in their graphic organizers.

MORE SUPPORT

ENGLISH LANGUAGE LEARNERS

If students need help summarizing text, provide sentence frames to guide them in choosing important information and putting it into their own words: The main idea of this section is ___. One important idea in this section is ___.

STRUGGLING READERS

To help students understand problems that arose for settlers, lead a discussion on the topic. **Ask:** What kinds of problems might arise when people are new to an area? What are some ways people can solve problems?

LANGUAGE CONVENTIONALITY AND CLARITY

Lead a discussion about the author's word choices throughout the selection. Have students discuss whether the language is interesting and easy to understand. Begin a discussion by analyzing an excerpt from the selection. Display the following excerpt and read it aloud with students.

> Relations between the Indians and the settlers were always uneasy. To the Powhatan, the colonists were invaders. The English thought they were bringing civilization to the Indians. They believed that the English way of life was the best way.

Discuss the meaning of this excerpt. Ask: What does the word *uneasy* mean in the context of the first sentence? ("uncomfortable or troublesome") What words would you use to describe an invader? (*stranger, trespasser, intruder*) What does the phrase *bringing civilization* mean? (showing the Powhatan how to live as proper English do) Based on what you read in the text, how would you describe the "English way of life"? (a society that includes a class system, a government, and a desire to earn riches)

KNOWLEDGE DEMANDS

Before reading the section "A New Beginning," provide students with the Three-Column Chart Graphic Organizer in Part 3 to record information about the problems the settlers faced. Label the first column *Land,* the second *Meeting Natives,* and the third *Leadership.* Under each heading, have students record examples from the text as they read of the problems concerning land, meeting the natives, or leadership.

If . . . students struggle to identify conflicts,

then . . . direct students to particular paragraphs or sections that illustrate examples of conflicts. Have them reread the text, decide which category it falls under, and record the example in the chart.

MORE SUPPORT

Express and Extend

LEVELS OF MEANING

EXPRESS Have students reread the two questions that begin the section titled "Introduction." Tell students to answer these questions using information from the text. Afterward, have them share their answers with the class.

EXTEND Have students write an opinion stating whether they think the colonists made the right choice based on the information gathered from their reading. Remind students to provide reasons and cite evidence from the text to support their opinions. Use the Opinion Writing Routine and Graphic Organizer in Part 3 to guide students' writing as needed.

STRUCTURE

EXPRESS Point out that the author uses text features such as sidebars, maps, illustrations, and quotations from famous people. Ask: What types of text features do you think work best in an informational text? How do the text features from this selection help you understand the text?

> If . . . students have difficulty recalling the purpose of specific text features,
>
> then . . . review the purpose of the text feature and ask: How does this text feature help convey the author's purpose?

EXTEND Have small groups analyze the text features used in the text. Have each group select the three text features that they believe are the most helpful. Then, have them work together to write an explanation of why these were the most helpful to them.

ENGLISH LANGUAGE LEARNERS

Some events in this text are suspenseful. Students might struggle with this concept. Review the meaning of *suspense*. Then act out suspenseful situations. For example, model opening a door, not knowing what is behind it. Discuss how suspense affects readers.

STRUGGLING READERS

To help students express their opinions about text features, use the Express Opinions Routine in Part 3. Provide sentence frames such as: The text feature that works best is ___ because ____. I think ___ is the most helpful because ___.

MORE SUPPORT

LANGUAGE CONVENTIONALITY AND CLARITY

EXPRESS Talk about Sentences and Words

Display and read aloud the following sentences from *New Beginnings*.

> Peace seemed to rule the day. Then in March 1622, the Powhatan chief led a group to Jamestown.

Ask: What does the author mean by "Peace seemed to rule the day"? (When someone rules, he or she guides others. So if peace rules the day, then peace is the mood that guides the people in Jamestown.) What does the word *seemed* imply? (that things weren't as peaceful as people thought) What does the phrase "Then in March 1622" tell us? (Something happened that month that proved everything wasn't peaceful.)

TEAM TALK Have students rewrite the above sentences so that the suspenseful language is removed. This will require them to replace the word *seemed* and the phrase "Then in March 1622."

EXTEND Have students look for other places in the text where the language creates suspense. Have them find two examples and then ask: Why did the author use suspenseful language? Have students create a one-paragraph response to the question. Remind students to use a graphic organizer to organize their ideas prior to writing.

KNOWLEDGE DEMANDS

EXPRESS Have students work in small groups to find details in the text that explain how the settlers managed to survive and how the settlement eventually became successful.

> If . . . students have difficulty discussing their findings in a small group setting,
>
> then . . . use the Prepare for Discussions Routine in Part 3 to ensure students understand the procedure for collaborative discussions.

EXTEND Have students write a list of five rules or guidelines the settlers should have followed in order to avoid some of the issues they encountered. Afterward, have students write a few sentences explaining what might have happened if the settlers had followed those rules.

ACCELERATED LEARNERS

Have students reread the sections that discuss John Rolfe's interactions with the Powhatan people and the Powhatan chief. Based on what they read, have students create a script of what the peaceful interaction between John Rolfe and the chief might have been like.

MORE SUPPORT

Unlock the Writing

Part 2 **Unlock the Writing**

Scaffolded Lessons for the
Performance-Based Assessments

Unlock the Task: Write a Short Story

Distribute copies of the task found on p. 196 of the Teacher's Guide. Read the task together. Have students identify key words or phrases to highlight in the task. Discuss why each word or phrase might be important. When students agree that the word or phrase is important, have them highlight it.

> Write a short story about a character who cares about his or her surroundings. Describe the actions the character takes to show his or her understanding of the environment.

Remind students of the questions they should be able to answer to show they understand a task. Have students look at the words and phrases they highlighted to help them answer the questions below. You may wish to provide this as a handout for students to complete individually. Scan the group to determine who needs more support and who is ready to work independently.

- **What type of writing is this?** (narrative)
- **What will the text of my writing look like?** (a short story)
- **What will my story be about?** (a character cares about his or her environment)
- **Where will my ideas come from?** (They can be real or imaginary.)
- **What do I need to include in my story?** (a clear beginning, middle, and end; transitional words; dialogue and description)

Have students restate the task in their own words. Check for possible misunderstandings or missing elements.

ENGLISH LANGUAGE LEARNERS

If . . . students are unsure what the words *surroundings* and *environment* mean

then . . . review the meaning of the words with them. Work with students to generate a list of possible environments for their stories. Encourage students to choose an environment that they understand well so that they can include descriptive details in the story.

STRUGGLING WRITERS

If . . . students have difficulty rewording the task,

then . . . have students go back and examine the key words they highlighted and say one sentence about each word or phrase. Example: I need to write a short story. It needs to be about a character whose actions show an understanding of the environment.

Other students might move on to gathering ideas with independence.

Prepare to Write

DETERMINE FOCUS

Once students clearly understand the task, have them review the selection *Night of the Spadefoot Toads*. Discuss who the narrator of the story is, what problem or situation is established in the story, and what techniques the author uses to help the reader get to know the story characters. Explain to students that their narrative should have the same elements.

Have students identify the situation that will be the focus of their story and who their main character will be. Point out that they can use a graphic organizer to organize ideas they want to include. For example, they might want to organize their main ideas into groups to answer questions like the following: What is the story situation? Who is my main character? How does my character feel about the situation? What actions does my character take?

GATHER IDEAS

Now have students begin gathering details for their short story. Tell students they first need to establish the situation for their story. Then they should determine how their character will respond to the situation and show an understanding of the environment. Have students keep in mind that writers develop a character with details about the character's traits—what the character does and says. A character's motivation is often revealed through his or her words, thoughts, feelings, and actions. Suggest that students create a web for each part of their story: character, setting, problem/situation, character's reactions, and resolution. Students can then record their ideas in each web.

Remind students that dialogue is often used in a narrative to develop the characters. Students should think about using dialogue in their stories. Explain that dialogue in a narrative should be natural and free-flowing. If students become stuck when writing dialogue, have them listen to conversations between two people. What emotions did the speakers share? Did they seem to hear what the other person was saying or was the conversation one-sided? Tell students to read aloud dialogue as they create it to be sure it is something their characters would say. It is their job to make the reader believe the character would respond the way he or she does in the story.

ACCELERATED WRITERS

If . . . students have already established the situation and details they will use to develop their characters,

then . . . have students reflect on the theme and resolution of their short story. Remind them that the theme is the author's message about life, and it is often a statement about one of the text topics. Have students answer questions, such as: What will the main topic of my story be? What life lesson do I want the reader to think about after reading my story? Will my resolution support the theme? Have students evaluate their character development plan and assess how their characters relate to the theme of their story.

MONITOR AND SUPPORT

Encourage students to talk through the situation and the character they plan to develop to help them clarify their ideas. Students may benefit from modeling these prewriting conversations or reviewing some questions the writer might ask his or her partner.

Questions a Writer Might Ask

- What situation will I establish?
- Who is my main character?
- How will my character feel about the situation?
- How will the situation relate to the character's understanding of the environment?
- What will be the sequence of events?
- What action will my character take to resolve the situation?
- What narrative techniques, such as dialogue and description, should I use?
- How will my conclusion resolve the situation?
- Is there anything I should add?
- Is there anything I should leave out?

Have students also formulate questions of their own.

Have students think about the feedback they received when talking through the task with a partner. Remind them that using that feedback to organize their short story will save them time and effort when writing and editing.

Remind students that a short story must be told from a narrator's point of view. Point out that the narrator will help establish the situation and develop the characters in the story by providing details. Have students consider whether a first-person narrator or a third-person narrator would tell the most engaging story.

ENGLISH LANGUAGE LEARNERS

If . . . students have difficulty understanding the difference between first-person point of view and third-person point of view,

then . . . review with them which pronouns are used with first-person narratives (*I, we, me, my, mine, us, our, ours*) and which are used with third-person narratives (*he, she, it, him, her, his, hers, it, its*). Read short excerpts from sample narratives and have students identify whether they are first-person or third-person narratives and tell how they know.

STRUGGLING WRITERS

If . . . students have difficulty developing characters that are convincing,

then . . . remind students to use dialogue to help develop their characters. Dialogue helps the reader learn more about the characters and what their motivations are. Have students think about how a character's conversations in the story reveal what he or she cares about.

Write

Work with students to create a chart that describes the elements of a short story. Remind them that narrative writing should include an established situation, a narrator, well-developed characters, and events that flow naturally and at a logical pace. Also remind students that a narrative has a conclusion that resolves the situation in a manner consistent with the character development in the story. Work with students to provide examples for the chart.

Element	Definition	Example
Title	• Catches readers' attention • Gives a quick idea of the situation or theme	It's in the Bag Don't Trash It, 3 R It
Beginning	• Establishes the situation and introduces the narrator or main character	Molly clenched her fists and scurried past the overflowing lunchroom trash cans.
Middle	• Includes events that unfold naturally • Uses narrative techniques, such as dialogue and description, to develop events and characters • Uses transitional words and phrases to connect the events	The smell of rotten bananas and stale peanut butter was sickening. Molly stood before the student council and said, "We have to do something about this! We have to make it a school goal—no more lunchroom trash." Molly and her friends painted cans green for recycled items and brown for compost items. Then, they made posters with the motto Reduce, Reuse, Recycle.
End	• Provides a conclusion that follows the narrated events or situation	But best of all, every student got a canvas lunch bag with his or her name on it. Now, when Molly leaves the lunchroom, she feels like clapping.

ENGLISH LANGUAGE LEARNERS

If . . . students have difficulty writing dialogue,

then . . . write a simple conversation, such as: *Mary said, "Hi! How are you?" Will replied, "Today, I am tired."* Point out each speech tag, the comma after the phrase, and the use of quotation marks. Repeat with other conversations or samples from the texts. Explain to students that when their characters speak, the dialogue should follow this format.

STRUGGLING WRITERS

If . . . students have difficulty writing a convincing conclusion to their story,

then . . . remind them that the conclusion must flow from the events in the story. Have students talk about the situation they established in their story. Discuss the character and the actions the character took to resolve the situation. Does the conclusion demonstrate the character's concern for the environment? If not, have students revisit their story and make adjustments as needed to create a character that shows concern for the environment.

Look Closely

LOOK AT CONVENTIONS

SENTENCES Remind students that they have worked recently on using linking verbs, helping verbs, and action verbs. Explain that a linking verb connects the subject to another word or words that describe or rename the subject. A helping verb tells when an action happened and is part of the verb phrase. And an action verb shows action. Have students review their writing for the accurate use of linking, helping, and action verbs.

PRONOUNS Remind students that all pronouns take the place of, or refer to, a noun. The noun that is replaced by a pronoun is the antecedent of the pronoun. Pronouns should agree with their antecedents in number and gender. Have students review their story for the proper use of pronouns.

PRINCIPAL PARTS OF VERBS Remind students that a regular verb has four principal parts: the present, present participle, past, and past participle. Tell students that the present participle is formed by adding -ing to the present form of the verb. The past and past participle are formed by adding -d or -ed to the present form of the verb. Point out that irregular verbs do not follow the regular pattern. Have students review their story for the proper use of verbs.

LOOK AT CRAFT

SENTENCES Have students check that their sentences work together within each paragraph to support the situation that the main character must resolve. Remind them that, in a narrative, the details provide character development and should flow logically. Tell students to review their work to be sure the details help develop the main character and show that he or she cares about the environment.

DIALOGUE Remind students that authors often use dialogue in narratives to help readers get to know the characters, their experiences, and their responses to situations. Review the rules for punctuating dialogue. Have students read the dialogue in their narratives to confirm that it helps develop the characters and to check for proper punctuation.

ENGLISH LANGUAGE LEARNERS
If . . . students have difficulty using the correct verb form of irregular verbs,

then . . . create a four-column chart with these heads: Present, Past, Present Participle, and Past Participle. Write both regular verbs, such as *walk, walked, am walking,* and *was walking,* and irregular verbs, such as *grow, grew, am growing,* and *have grown,* on note cards. Have students select a card and use the verb in a sentence. Then have students tell which column of the chart the verb belongs in.

STRUGGLING WRITERS
If . . . students have difficulty revising their work,

then . . . give students particular areas to focus on for their revision, such as sequence of events, description, or dialogue. Have students reread their story, looking specifically for each focus area and making adjustments as needed to improve their story.

Name _____

Title _____

Write a Short Story
Writing Checklist

❏ Did I establish a situation clearly?

❏ Did I develop a believable character who cares about the environment?

❏ Did my events unfold naturally in a logical sequence?

❏ Did I provide descriptive details that develop events and characters?

Example: _____

_____

❏ Did I include dialogue that develops events and characters?

Example: _____

_____

❏ Did I use pronouns that agree with their antecedents? Example: _____

_____

❏ Did I use verbs properly? Example: _____

_____

❏ Did I include a strong conclusion?

❏ Did I review my work for correct capitalization, punctuation, and spelling?

❏ Did I find online images of the environment I chose and embed them in my story?

Unlock the Task: Write About Environments

Distribute copies of the task found on p. 396 of the Teacher's Guide. Read the task together. Have students identify key words or phrases to highlight within the task. Discuss why each word or phrase might be important. When students agree that the word or phrase is important, have them highlight it.

> You will write an informative essay that describes one of the environments you read about in the selections. Use facts, definitions, and details from the texts to support your ideas.

ANSWER QUESTIONS ABOUT THE TASK

Remind students of the questions they should be able to answer to show they understand a task. Have students look at the words and phrases they highlighted to help them answer the questions below. You may wish to provide this as a handout for students to complete individually. Scan the group to determine who needs more support and who is ready to work independently.

- **What type of writing is this?** (informative/explanatory)
- **What will the text of my writing look like?** (an informative essay)
- **What texts can I reference?** (*Washed Up!, Rain Forest Food Chains, Pale Male,* library resources, online resources)
- **What information should I include?** (a description of one of the environments you read about in the texts)
- **What do I need to include?** (an introduction that includes an observation, facts, specific vocabulary and definitions, visuals, a summary or conclusion)

RESTATE THE TASK

Have students restate the task in their own words. Check for possible misunderstandings or missing elements.

ENGLISH LANGUAGE LEARNERS

If . . . students are not sure how to make an observation about an environment,

then . . . remind them that an observation is a statement about something that one sees or notes. Explain that although students probably have not seen the environments from the texts in person, they have read about them. Point out that students should use what they have learned from these texts to make their own observation about the environment.

STRUGGLING WRITERS

If . . . students have difficulty rewording the task,

then . . . ask students to go back and examine the key words they highlighted and say one sentence about each phrase. Example: I need to write an informative essay. It needs to be about one of the environments I read about.

Other students might be ready to gather ideas independently.

Prepare to Write

Once students clearly understand the writing task, have them review the selections *Washed Up!, Rain Forest Food Chains,* and *Pale Male.* Have students make an observation about one of the environments presented in the texts. Explain that their observation should support an overall description of the environment they chose. Suggest that students use sticky notes to mark pages that they want to return to for ideas.

Remind students that they need to support their descriptions with facts and details from the texts. They should also focus on how living things interact with each other in the environment. Remind students that they should also think about how to include visuals, such as graphs and charts, to support their main idea.

GATHER IDEAS

Now have students put together the facts and details for their informative essay. Have them answer these questions as they conduct their research: What is unique about the environment you chose? What plants and animals live in the environment? How do living things interact within the environment? Students can write notes on note cards or use a web or main idea graphic organizer to record ideas. Remind students that their essay should include only those details that support their main idea.

Tell students that they should explain in their introductory paragraph the purpose of their writing so that readers understand their point of view. Then, students need to select the facts and details that will help the reader understand their main idea about the environment they chose. Explain that some of the facts and details might be best presented in direct quotations from knowledgeable sources. Help students determine which information would be best presented as a visual. Remind them that headings help organize their information for the reader, and domain-specific vocabulary terms with definitions help inform the reader.

ACCELERATED WRITERS

If . . . students are trying to provide too much information,

then . . . remind them that the purpose of an informative essay is to explain a topic. Point out that their essay should not include lots of details on the general subject but only those details that support the topic of the essay. Have students reread their notes and delete any information that does not support the topic. Also have them think about headings they might use to help organize the information for the reader.

Have students talk through their informative essay ideas with a partner to get feedback and to help them clarify their ideas. Students may benefit from modeling these prewriting conversations or reviewing some questions the writer might ask a listener.

Questions a Writer Might Ask

- What features in the environment will I focus on?
- What facts and details best support my ideas?
- What information is most interesting?
- What information is most important?
- Where will my information come from?
- What facts can I explain using a visual, such as a graph or a chart?
- Which domain-specific words should I clarify?
- Is there anything I can add?
- Is there anything I should leave out?
- How will my conclusion support my main idea?

Have students also formulate questions of their own.

Have students think about the feedback they received when talking through the topic with a partner. Remind them that using that feedback to organize their essay will save them time and effort when writing and rewriting.

Remind students that an informative essay does not provide every fact or detail about the topic. Instead, it provides facts, details, and domain-specific vocabulary about one focused idea. Have students group similar facts and details together. Once students have grouped the information, have them rate their details from 1 to 5 to decide which are the most necessary to understanding the essay's main idea (5) and which are the least necessary (1).

ENGLISH LANGUAGE LEARNERS

If . . . students have difficulty quoting directly from sources,

then . . . remind them that when they include a direct quote from a source, they must record the quote word for word. They must enclose the quote in quotation marks, and they must give credit to whoever spoke the words. Review examples of direct quotes from texts students are familiar with, and discuss how they enhance the text.

STRUGGLING WRITERS

If . . . students have difficulty synthesizing information from multiple sources,

then . . . have students start with one source to find as many details as possible. After reading over the details, have them answer questions such as these: *What information is missing? What else do I want to find out? Where can I look?* Point out that they can fill in more information by using another source.

MONITOR AND SUPPORT

Write

Work with students to create a chart that describes the elements of an informative essay. Remind them that they should introduce their topic clearly and include facts, details, domain-specific vocabulary, and a graphic that supports the topic. They should use information from multiple sources, and they should link this information to create a smooth flow of ideas. Also remind students that their conclusion should summarize the main idea of the essay.

Element	Definition	Example
Title	• Catches readers' attention • Gives a quick idea of the topic	Rain Forests: Teeming with Life
Introduction	• Includes the topic of the essay	The warm and tropical climate in rain forests make them an ideal home to many different plants and animals.
Body	• Provides facts and concrete details to support the topic • Includes precise and domain-specific language associated with the topic • May include quotations • May include a chart or graph to provide information about the topic • Includes linking words and phrases to connect ideas	The rain forest biome includes many ecosystems. These ecosystems support a vast diversity of life. The plant layers of the rain forest include the canopy, the emergent layer, and the understory; each layer is home to different animals. The chart that follows shows how energy moves from one organism to another in a rain forest's food chain. Today, more than half of the Earth's original rain forests have been burned or cut down for timber.
Conclusion	• Summarizes the topic and leaves the reader with something to think about	Rain forests must be protected because they are home to a rich variety of plant and animal life.

ENGLISH LANGUAGE LEARNERS

If . . . students have difficulty identifying information that might be made into a graph or a chart,

then . . . have them look at sample graphs and charts to answer questions such as these: *What is the main point of the graphic? Is it easier to read this information in a graphic or in paragraph form? Why?* Point out that information comparing ideas or information that shows time can often be set in graphic form. Have students revisit their details to see which ones could be set as a graphic.

STRUGGLING WRITERS

If . . . students have difficulty writing their conclusion,

then . . . remind students that their conclusion should bring the main ideas of the essay together, it should draw conclusions, and it should offer insight. Have students answer questions such as these: *What is the main point of the essay? What should people remember after reading the essay? Why is the information in the essay important?*

Look Closely

SENTENCES Remind students that one use of verbs is to show time. Point out that verb tenses change to show the time each event in a sequence occurs. Have students review the use of verb tenses in their writing to be sure the proper tenses are used to show sequence.

ADJECTIVES AND LINKING VERBS Remind students that an adjective describes a person, a place, a thing, or an idea and that an adjective can come before the noun it describes or after a linking verb. Point out that a linking verb connects the subject of a sentence to more information about the subject. Have students review their use of adjectives and linking verbs.

DEGREES OF COMPARISON Explain that different forms of adjectives and adverbs can be used to make degrees of comparison. The positive degree is used to describe one thing. The comparative degree is used to compare two things. The superlative degree is used to compare three or more things (*funny, funnier, funniest*). Remind students that some comparisons are formed using the endings *-er* and *-est* or the words *more* and *most,* whereas some are formed irregularly, such as *bad, worse,* and *worst.* Have students review their writing for the proper use of comparisons.

SENTENCES Have students look closely to see that their sentences work together within the introductory paragraph and the concluding paragraph to support the main idea. Remind them that the introduction should present the main idea of the informative essay in a way that catches the reader's attention, such as with an amazing fact or statistic. The conclusion should wrap up the essay and possibly challenge the reader to take action.

VISUALS Remind students that visuals, such as bold-face headings, charts, graphs, images, or videos, can help get a point across in a memorable way and can help readers better understand information. Point out that too many visuals can be distracting. Have students review their use of visuals in their essay.

ENGLISH LANGUAGE LEARNERS

If . . . students have difficulty using the correct forms of comparative and superlative adjectives,

then . . . write *red, redder, reddest; bad, worse, worst* on note cards. Have students select a card and read the word. Use the word in a sentence, such as "This hat is redder than that cap." Then ask: What is being compared in my sentence? How many objects are being compared? Have students say a new sentence using the same word. Repeat with other examples of both regular and irregular comparative and superlative adjectives.

STRUGGLING WRITERS

If . . . students have difficulty using proper verb tense sequence,

then . . . remind students that verbs show time. Say: If the judges like the essay Rachel submitted yesterday, then she will win an award. Have students say which action tells about now, in the past, and in the future. Then say: The judges liked the essay Rachel wrote, and she won an award. Have students say when each action took place. Point out that in the first sentence, the events happened over time, but the events in the next sentence are in the past.

Name _____

Title _____

Write About Environments
Writing Checklist

❏ Did I introduce the topic for my informative essay clearly?

❏ Did I describe one of the environments from the texts?

❏ Did I explain how living things interact in the environment?

❏ Did I support my topic with facts and details?

❏ Did I use visuals, such as graphs or charts, to help the reader understand difficult information?

❏ Did I include a strong conclusion?

❏ Did I use precise and domain-specific vocabulary and definitions? Example: _____

_____

❏ Did I use verbs to show time sequence correctly? Example: _____

_____

❏ Did I use adjectives and linking verbs correctly? Example: _____

_____

❏ Did I use the comparative or superlative form of adjectives correctly?

Example: _____

_____

❏ Did I review my work for correct capitalization, punctuation, and spelling?

❏ Did I include images or videos from the Internet to support my description?

Unlock the Task: Write an Opinion Speech

BREAK APART THE TASK

Distribute copies of the task found on page 196 of the Teacher's Guide. Read the task together. Have students identify important key words or phrases to highlight in the task. Discuss why each word or phrase might be important.

> Choose an example of inequality or injustice either from the selections, your own life, or the world around you.
>
> Use your example of inequality or injustice to write an opinion speech with facts, details, and evidence from the texts as well as quotes, if possible. You can also use visuals or audio to help you make your point.

ANSWER QUESTIONS ABOUT THE TASK

Remind students of the questions they should be able to answer to show they understand a task. Remind students to look at the words and phrases they highlighted to help them answer the questions below. You may wish to provide this as a handout for students to complete individually. Scan the group to determine who needs more support and who is ready to work independently.

- **What type of writing is this?** (opinion)
- **What will the text of my writing look like?** (an opinion speech)
- **What texts should I reference?** (*The Road to Freedom, Operation Clean Sweep*, and *Cesar Chavez: Champion of Workers*)
- **What information should I give?** (an example of an injustice, my opinion about it, and reasons for changing it)
- **What do I need to include?** (facts, details, evidence from texts, quotes, visuals and/or audio to support my opinion)

RESTATE THE TASK

Have students restate the task in their own words. Check for possible misunderstandings or missing elements.

ENGLISH LANGUAGE LEARNERS

If . . . students have difficulty understanding what an inequality or an injustice is,

then . . . explain that an injustice is a situation in which something is not equal or not fair. Give an example: Only students wearing blue sweaters today can use the library. Have students give reasons why the situation is unfair. Explain that this example is extreme, but it illustrates the point. Then have students suggest other examples of injustices.

STRUGGLING WRITERS

If . . . students have difficulty understanding why they need to write a speech instead of just saying it,

then . . . point out that good speeches are usually written first. It is very difficult to speak to a group spontaneously or without notes. Explain that written text helps a speaker remember what he or she wants to say and make all the necessary points in a logical manner. Provide samples of speeches for students to read.

Prepare to Write

Once students clearly understand the task, have them review the selections *The Road to Freedom*, *Operation Clean Sweep,* and *Cesar Chavez: Champion of Workers*. Have students recall some of the inequalities they read about. Suggest that they mark pages they want to go back to later with sticky notes. Tell students to think about what makes the situation in each text an inequality or an injustice.

Then have students list the injustices they identified from texts or that they know about from other reading or their own experiences. Have them prioritize their lists and identify an inequality or injustice that they feel strongly about. If students have a hard time deciding which one to write about, ask them whether they have a stronger opinion about one than any other. Which do they find most interesting?

GATHER IDEAS

Students can then begin gathering facts and details for their speeches. Students might create note cards or use a web or other graphic organizer to record their ideas. Point out that they want the reader/listener to think about the injustice from their point of view. Remind students that they will be expressing an opinion and that not everyone in the audience will agree with their opinion. The objective of their speech is to convince readers/listeners that the opinion they are expressing is the right one. Therefore, students should be thinking about strong reasons they will include to support their opinion.

Suggest students keep the following questions in mind as they gather facts: *What opinion am I expressing? What facts and evidence do I need to support this opinion? Where can I find quotes from important people that will help support my opinion? What visuals can I create to help get my points across?* Have students gather facts to support their opinion and use a graphic organizer to organize their facts in a meaningful way.

ACCELERATED WRITERS

If . . . students want to use visuals to support their opinion,

then . . . remind students that visuals can help make important ideas clear. Point out that visuals may also serve to engage the audience. Have students review their use of visuals and their effectiveness by asking questions such as these: *Why did I choose to use these visuals? What key ideas do I want the visuals to illustrate? How will the visuals help my audience understand my point of view?* Tell students to adjust their visuals as needed if they do not actively support their point of view.

MONITOR AND SUPPORT

Have students talk through their opinion and supporting facts and details with a partner to help get their ideas organized. Students may benefit from modeling these prewriting conversations or reviewing some questions the writer might ask his or her partner.

Questions a Writer Might Ask

- What injustice have I chosen to write about?
- What is my opinion about it?
- What facts or evidence will I provide to support my opinion?
- What visuals will I include?
- How do these visuals support my opinion?
- What quotes do I plan to include?
- Is there anything I can add?
- Is there anything I should leave out?

Have students also formulate questions of their own.

GET ORGANIZED

Have students think about the feedback they received when talking through the task with a partner. Remind them that using that feedback to organize their speeches will save them time and effort when writing and editing.

Remind students that speeches are usually limited by time and should, therefore, provide only the most important and convincing facts, details, and evidence as support to help the audience understand the topic. As students organize their writing, suggest they group similar facts and details together. Tell students they will use linking words and phrases to connect these similar ideas.

ENGLISH LANGUAGE LEARNERS

If . . . students have difficulty transitioning from one idea to the next,

then . . . remind students that linking words and phrases can signal cause and effect, comparison and contrast, time order, location, or importance. Write words that signal transitions, such as *therefore*, *because*, *although*, *above all*, and *finally*, on note cards. Select a card and model using the word in a sentence. Have students name the transition word. Discuss the type of transition the word signals.

STRUGGLING WRITERS

If . . . students are having difficulty stating their opinion clearly,

then . . . remind students that phrases like *I believe* and *I think* let the audience know this statement is their opinion. Suggest that students also use descriptive language, such as *horrified* or *disgusted*, to help the audience know how they feel. Students might develop a list of descriptive words, such as *fair*, *unfair*, *best*, *worst*, *admirable*, and *flawed*, that express feelings about their topic.

MONITOR AND SUPPORT

Write

Work with students to create a chart that describes the elements of an opinion speech. Point out that their speech must clearly state their opinion of an injustice. It must include well-organized facts and details that support the opinion. It may include quotations and visuals to support the opinion. Also remind students that their speech must have a conclusion that restates the opinion.

Element	Definition	Example
Title	• Catches readers' attention • Gives a quick idea of the topic	The Digital Divide: Closing the Gap The Digital Divide: Unfair to All the Have Nots
Introduction or Lead	• States the opinion about the topic • Sets the tone	The Digital Divide is the gap between those who have access to technology and those who do not. We must find a way to close the Digital Divide gap.
Body	• Provides reasons, facts, and concrete details that support the opinion • May use visuals that support the opinion • May include quotations from people or other sources that support the opinion • Includes linking words and phrases to connect the opinion and the reasons	Technology is all around us. If you don't know how to use technology or don't have access to technology, then you are at an economic and a social disadvantage. The pie chart shows how income helps create the Digital Divide in the United States. According to Dr. Quin, "Those with a lower income have less access to technology, which is a problem."
Conclusion	• Restates or summarizes the opinion	Finally, reducing the Digital Divide is critical to ensure that all citizens have an equal opportunity to succeed.

ENGLISH LANGUAGE LEARNERS

If . . . students come from a culture in which it is considered impolite or argumentative to strongly state an opinion,

then . . . have students practice stating opinions about everyday topics by responding to questions such as the following: *Do you like bananas? Do you like science or social studies better?* After stating their opinion, have students give reasons for their opinion. Point out that they will use this model of stating an opinion and supporting it with reasons as they write their speech.

STRUGGLING WRITERS

If . . . students are having difficulty writing a conclusion,

then . . . have students answer questions such as the following: *How can I restate my opinion clearly and concisely? What do I want people to remember about my opinion?*

Look Closely

SENTENCES Remind students that they have worked recently on writing compound and complex sentences using coordinating and subordinating conjunctions to join clauses. Have students review their use of coordinating and subordinating conjunctions.

PREPOSITIONS AND PREPOSITIONAL PHRASES Focus attention on the use of prepositions and prepositional phrases to answer where (location) or when (time) questions. Remind students that a prepositional phrase contains a preposition and a noun. A prepositional phrase can also contain adjectives to describe the noun, but it never contains a verb. Have students find prepositional phrases in their writing and add adjectives to make the details in their prepositional phrases stronger.

GERUNDS AND PARTICIPLES Remind students that gerunds and participles are both formed using *-ing* but that a gerund functions as a noun and a participle functions as an adjective. For example, the word *running* in the sentence *She loves running* is a gerund (noun). It tells what she loves. The word *running* in the sentence *She has a pair of running shoes* is a participle (adjective). It describes *shoes*. Have students look for *-ing* words in their writing and determine whether the word is used correctly as a verb, gerund, or participle.

SENTENCES Remind students that their reasons must support their opinion in a logical manner. Have students review their work to be sure that the reasons and facts provide strong support and that they have used linking words and phrases to transition from one idea to the next.

VISUALS Remind students that speeches often include visuals. Writers use visuals to illustrate a point, to add depth to and emphasize key ideas, and to engage the audience. Point out that there are many different types of visuals: fine art images, photographs, charts, or graphs. Remind students that any visuals they use must support their opinion.

ENGLISH LANGUAGE LEARNERS
If . . . students have difficulty using the *-ing* form of words correctly,

then . . . write examples of gerunds and participles, such as *talking*, *writing*, *helping*, and *looking*, on note cards. Select a card and model using the word as a verb, as a gerund, and as a participle: He is helping Jack make posters. He likes helping others. He often lends a helping hand. Repeat by having students follow your model to use gerunds and participles in sentences.

STRUGGLING WRITERS
If . . . students have difficulty recognizing dependent clauses,

then . . . point out subordinating conjunctions that signal dependent clauses in text: *after*, *although*, *because*, *before*, *if*, *since*, *though*, *unless*, *when*, *while*. Model using a subordinating conjunction in a dependent clause: After Ed finished his homework. Point out that the clause has a subject and a verb but does not express a complete thought. Have students suggest another clause to complete the sentence.

Name _____

Title _____

Write an Opinion Speech
Writing Checklist

❏ Did I state my opinion clearly in the introduction?

❏ Did I state reasons for my opinion?

❏ Did I support my opinion with facts, details, and textual evidence?

❏ Did I present my reasons and facts in an organized and logical manner?

❏ Did I use linking words and phrases to connect my reasons and facts to my opinion?

❏ Did I include quotes to support my opinion?

❏ Did I use visuals to support my opinion?

❏ Did I use prepositions and prepositional phrases correctly? Example: _____

_____

❏ Did I use gerunds and participles correctly? Example: _____

_____

❏ Did I include a strong conclusion?

❏ Did I review my work for correct capitalization, punctuation, and spelling?

❏ (Optional) Did I include images or multimedia from the Internet to support my opinion?

Unlock the Task: Write About Courage

Distribute copies of the task found on page 396 of the Teacher's Guide. Read the task together. Have students identify key words or phrases to highlight in the task. Discuss why each word or phrase might be important. When students agree that the word or phrase is important, have them highlight it.

> Write a brief essay to explain the courage exhibited by one of the people in *Real-Life Superheroes*.

Remind students of the questions they should be able to answer to show they understand a task. Have students look at the words and phrases they highlighted to help them answer the questions below. You may wish to provide this as a handout for students to complete individually. Scan the group to determine who needs more support and who is ready to work independently.

- **What type of writing is this?** (informative/explanatory)
- **What will the text of my writing look like?** (an essay about acts of courage)
- **Which text should I reference?** *(Real-Life Superheroes)*
- **What information should I give?** (information about a courageous person)
- **What do I need to include?** (an introduction; details and text evidence describing a person's courage; graphics, visuals, or illustrations; a conclusion)

Have students restate the task in their own words. Check for possible misunderstandings or missing elements.

ENGLISH LANGUAGE LEARNERS

If . . . students don't understand what an act of courage is,

then . . . break the phrase into parts. Point out that an act is an action and that *courage* means "bravery" or "what's needed to do something difficult or dangerous." Give examples of an act of courage, such as soldiers going to war or stopping a friend from making fun of another friend. Discuss how these actions show courage.

STRUGGLING WRITERS

If . . . students have difficulty rewording the task,

then . . . have students go back and examine the key words and phrases they highlighted and say one sentence about each word or phrase. Example: *I need to explain someone's courageous actions.* Other students might be ready to gather ideas independently.

Prepare to Write

Once students clearly understand the task, have them review the selection *Real-Life Superheroes*. Have students look through the text to identify acts of courage. Have them take notes or place sticky notes to mark pages they'd like to use and go back to later. As they review these pages, have students think about what each individual overcame and how each act of courage was revealed.

Then have students list two or three individuals they think were most courageous and why. A two-column chart with the headings *Name* and *Why* might be helpful. Then have students review their lists and choose the person that they would like to write about. If they have trouble deciding, have them think about which person interests them the most. Remind students that the purpose of their essay is to help the reader understand what this person did and why it was courageous.

GATHER IDEAS

Have students begin putting together the facts and details for their essay. Remind them to group their ideas logically. Suggest students use a graphic organizer. For example, they might use a main idea graphic organizer to group main ideas and their supporting details or a cause-and-effect graphic organizer to show cause-and-effect relationships. Have students look for concrete details and quotations that will build readers' understanding of why this action is an act of courage. Encourage students to conduct research on the individual on their own. They can use sources from the library or the Internet, as well as the unit selection.

Point out that a well-organized essay will help readers better understand it. For example, as students gather information, they might create an outline. Explain that an outline helps identify possible headings, and headings are helpful in cueing a reader to what information will follow. Students should also think about visuals or graphics that will help their readers understand historical settings or events.

ACCELERATED WRITERS

If . . . students have identified domain-specific vocabulary that they plan to use in their essay,

then . . . remind them to be aware of their readers' background knowledge when using domain-specific vocabulary. Suggest that students define terms that their readers may not understand. Have students review the words they plan to use and add more details or definitions for the words as needed. They may wish to create a glossary or word chart as one of their visuals.

MONITOR AND SUPPORT

Have students talk through their plans and ideas for their essay with a partner. Explain that writers often seek help from others to clarify their ideas. Students may benefit from modeling these prewriting conversations or reviewing some questions the writer might ask his or her partner.

Questions a Writer Might Ask

- What act of courage will I write about, and who performed it?
- Why do I consider this an act of courage?
- What historical details should I include?
- What information is most interesting?
- What information is most important?
- What visuals would be helpful?
- What might be missing?
- Is there anything that I should leave out?

Have students also formulate questions of their own.

GET ORGANIZED

Have students think about the feedback they received from their partners. Remind them that using this feedback to organize their essay will save them time and effort when writing and editing.

Remind students that they want their essay to inform the reader about a worthy action and why that action is considered an act of courage. Tell students they may need to provide some historical background to help their readers understand the context of the act of courage they are writing about. Have students organize their information in a logical manner and use transitional words and phrases to connect ideas within paragraphs and from paragraph to paragraph. Have students refer to their notes, graphic organizers, and feedback from prewriting conversations as they begin to write their essays.

ENGLISH LANGUAGE LEARNERS

If . . . students have difficulty understanding the need for historical background information,

then . . . have them skim the text to answer questions such as the following: Does the event take place now or in the past? How do you know? Why is it important to know when the event takes place? Tell students the answers will help them understand the historical setting of the event. Explain that they may need to provide details about the historical setting in their essay.

STRUGGLING WRITERS

If . . . students are having difficulty organizing their ideas,

then . . . remind them that events are often organized based on time order or on cause and effect. Tell students they can also use a combination by including cause and effect elements within a time-order sequence. Have students review their facts to determine if a time-order sequence, cause and effect, or a combination would work best for their essay.

Write

Work with students to create a chart that describes the elements of an informative/ explanatory essay. Remind them that their introductory paragraph should clearly state the act of courage they plan to discuss, why it is an act of courage, and the person who performed it. Point out that the facts, details, quotations, vocabulary, and visuals included in the essay should support the main idea, and the conclusion should summarize or extend the main idea. Work with students to provide examples for the chart.

Element	Definition	Example
Title	• Catches readers' attention • Gives a quick idea of the topic	The Courageous Choice of Rosa Parks
Introduction or Lead	• Includes the main idea	In the United States in the mid-20th century, blacks and whites were often segregated in public places. In Montgomery, Alabama, black passengers on buses were even expected to give up their seats for white passengers. In 1955, Rosa Parks took a stand against this practice. She refused to give up her seat, which showed great courage.
Body	• Provides facts and concrete details to develop the main idea • May include precise language, domain-specific vocabulary, quotations, and visuals • Includes linking words and phrases to connect the ideas and present the information logically	Rosa Parks was arrested for her choice. She lost her job. She received threats. To show their support for Rosa Parks, many blacks boycotted the buses in Montgomery. A bus boycott is when people stop using buses. As a result of Rosa Parks's brave act, many other people began to protest racial segregation in the United States.
Conclusion	• Summarizes the main idea and leaves the reader with something to think about	When I read about life during segregation, I know it took an act of courage to challenge authority like Rosa Parks did. I don't know if I could have done that. Could you?

ENGLISH LANGUAGE LEARNERS

If . . . students have difficulty connecting the ideas in their essay,

then . . . remind them to use transitional words and phrases. Point out that words that indicate order of events include *first*, *then*, *later*, *finally*, *now*, and *so on*, whereas words that indicate cause and effect include *as a result*, *caused*, *therefore*, *because of*, and *due to*. Model using these words in sentences. Then have students use the same transitional words and phrases in sentences of their own.

STRUGGLING WRITERS

If . . . students have difficulty including visuals to get their points across,

then . . . remind students that headings or other text features can also be considered visuals. These can help clarify information in the essay. For example, show the text *Real-Life Superheroes* and discuss how the headings help the reader know what each section will be about.

Look Closely

SENTENCES Remind students that the subject and verb in a sentence must agree in number. Point out that this rule is true for common and proper nouns, collective nouns, special nouns, and indefinite pronouns. Have students review their writing to check for subject-verb agreement. Tell students to isolate the subject and verb so that they are not confused by interrupting phrases.

COMMAS Focus attention on the use of commas with items in a list, introductory elements, yes-and-no interjections, tag questions, quotations, and direct address. Remind students that direct address can be in the beginning, middle, or end of a sentence. Have students review the use of commas in their writing.

TITLES OF WORKS Remind students that titles of long works, such as book titles, movie titles, magazines, and TV shows, should be either underlined or set in italics. Point out that either underlining or italics is acceptable, but not both. Tell students that titles of short works, such as poems or magazine articles, are set in quotation marks. Have students check that they formatted titles of works correctly.

SENTENCES Have students look closely to see that their sentences work together within the introductory paragraph and the concluding paragraph to support the main idea. Remind them that sentence structure is the key to a well-written selection. Tell students to review their work for sentence fragments and run-on sentences and to correct any of these that they find.

QUOTATIONS Remind students that facts and details in their essay must support their main idea. Tell students that using direct quotations from the source material can add interest and meaning to an essay. Encourage students to include direct quotations if the source material includes firsthand accounts, sensory language, statistics, or particularly clear explanations. Have students review their essay to make sure they have punctuated direct quotations correctly and properly acknowledged the source of the quotation.

ENGLISH LANGUAGE LEARNERS

If . . . students have difficulty with subject-verb agreement when the subject and verb are interrupted,

then . . . write examples such as these: *The shelf of books is full. The bowls of fruit are on the table.* Model finding the subject and verb in each sentence *(shelf/is; bowls/are)*. Explain that the verb agrees in number with the subject, not with the object of the preposition that interrupts the subject and the verb. Repeat with other examples. Have students find the subject and verb.

STRUGGLING WRITERS

If . . . students have difficulty using commas properly,

then . . . write sample sentences such as these: *At dawn the sun rose. Yes I can go to the movies. No I don't have that book. I don't want any more do you? Swim Nel swim fast.* Model where to add commas in the sentences. Then, have students write their own sentences with commas for introductory phrases, yes-and-no interjections, tag questions, and direct address, using the corrected sentences as models.

Name _____

Title _____

Write About Courage
Writing Checklist

❑ Did I state the main idea of my essay clearly in the introduction?

❑ Did I make it clear whom I was writing about and what the act of courage was?

❑ Did I support my main idea with facts, details, and text evidence?

❑ Did I group related information logically?

❑ Did I use graphics or other visuals?

❑ Did I use precise and domain-specific vocabulary and definitions? Example:

_____

❑ Did I use linking words and phrases to connect my facts and details? Example:

_____

❑ Did I use subject-verb agreement correctly? Example: _____

_____

❑ Did I use commas correctly? Example: _____

_____

❑ Did I include a strong conclusion that leaves the reader with something to think about?

❑ Did I review my work for correct capitalization, punctuation, and spelling?

❑ (Optional) Did I use the Internet to find visuals to support my essay?

Unlock the Task: Write a Science Fiction Story

Distribute copies of the task found on page 196 of the Teacher's Guide. Read the task together. Tell students to identify and discuss some key words or phrases to highlight in the task.

> Using *George's Secret Key to the Universe* and "Mayday on Moon of Jupiter" as models, write a science fiction story. Include interesting characters experiencing and responding to unusual events. Describe a sequence of events that heightens and resolves tension and comes to a satisfying conclusion.

ANSWER QUESTIONS ABOUT THE TASK

Remind students of the questions they should be able to answer to show they understand a task. Have students look at the words and phrases they highlighted to help them answer the questions below. You may wish to provide this as a handout for students to complete individually. Scan the group to determine who needs more support and who is ready to work independently.

- **What type of writing is this?** (narrative)
- **What will the text of my writing look like?** (a science fiction story)
- **What texts should I reference?** (*George's Secret Key to the Universe* and "Mayday on Moon of Jupiter")
- **What information should I give?** (events that resolve tension in a satisfying ending)
- **What do I need to include?** (interesting characters, a sequence of events, narrative techniques, sensory details, a conclusion)

RESTATE THE TASK

Have students restate the task in their own words. Check for possible misunderstandings or missing elements.

ENGLISH LANGUAGE LEARNERS

If . . . students have difficulty understanding the vocabulary in the task,

then . . . review the meanings of *heightens, tension,* and *satisfying.* Discuss synonyms for each word with students. Then have students use each word in a sentence of their own. By familiarizing themselves with the words, students will be better able to understand the task.

STRUGGLING WRITERS

If . . . students have difficulty rewording the task,

then . . . have students make a list of story elements they should include, such as characters and a sequence of events. Point out that this information summarizes what students should include in their story.

Prepare to Write

DETERMINE FOCUS

Once students clearly understand the task, have them review *George's Secret Key to the Universe* and "Mayday on Moon of Jupiter." Tell students to record ideas of what they might want to include in their science fiction story. Some students may benefit from brainstorming ideas for a science fiction story and then selecting an idea that interests them from the group's ideas.

Have students prioritize their list of ideas to determine one or two that they think could be the focus of their science fiction story. Remind them that the idea they select should be based on science but that they will take the science idea and use it in a new, believable way in a made-up story. If students have difficulty thinking of ideas, remind them that science fiction is often about the future, advanced technology, or invented scientific developments or discoveries. Point out that it often includes elements of space travel, time travel, or an alternate world or universe and that the characters might come from another world or be humans with advanced abilities.

GATHER IDEAS

Have students put together ideas for their science fiction story. Suggest they identify the science fact(s) that their story will be based on, and then identify characters and settings that will encounter or use the science in a fictional way. Tell students to decide if their story will include an unusual environment, such as space or the deep sea, and if their characters will be humans or creatures from another world. Point out that dialogue can be used to help readers get to know the characters as well as develop the sequence of events. Suggest students use a graphic organizer to help them organize their information.

Remind students that in a science fiction story the information must have a scientific foundation, but the events and details around the scientific facts should be fictional. If students become stalled, have them think of ways the setting or the characters in the story can be used to change the story from science to science fiction.

ACCELERATED WRITERS

If . . . students have already established the characters for their story,

then . . . have them answer questions that will help them create more rounded characters, such as: How is your character feeling at this moment? Why? What would your character say in this situation? How does that reflect your character's personality? Help students understand that by providing more detail, using concrete words and phrases, and including vivid sensory details and dialogue, they can develop characters that are more interesting for the reader. Suggest they revisit their story plan and add details to help develop their characters.

MONITOR AND SUPPORT

Encourage students to talk through their science fiction story with a partner to help them clarify their ideas. Students may benefit from modeling these prewriting conversations or reviewing some questions the writer might ask his or her partner.

Questions a Writer Might Ask

- Where will my story take place?
- Who are the characters in my story?
- What science is behind my story?
- What will the sequence of events in my story be?
- Where can I add dialogue and character description?
- What events or details should I add?
- How should I end my story?

Encourage students to also formulate questions of their own.

GET ORGANIZED

Have students think about the feedback they received when talking through the topic with a partner. Remind them that using that feedback to organize their story will save them time and effort when writing and editing.

Have students group together information about their story elements, such as their characters, setting, and situation, before writing their science fiction story. Suggest they add details as needed to enhance each element. Explain that creating background on each of these elements will help them write their story. Tell students that they can include an illustration or photograph that adds meaning to their story.

ENGLISH LANGUAGE LEARNERS

If . . . students have difficulty pacing the events in their science fiction story,

then . . . provide a list of transition words, such as *before*, *first*, *next*, *then*, and *in addition to*. Have students place the transition words in time or sequence order. Then have students name the events in their story in time order. Show students how using the transition words can help events flow more naturally.

STRUGGLING WRITERS

If . . . students are having difficulty thinking of an illustration or photograph to include,

then . . . have them write down key words about each element of their story, such as their main character, the setting, or an exciting event. Suggest they use the key words associated with one element to help them draw an illustration or find a photograph to accompany their story. Remind students that the illustration or photograph should have a purpose and should help increase readers' understanding of the story.

Write

Work with students to create a chart that describes the elements of their science fiction story. Remind them that their science fiction story should have some element of science associated with it. Also remind students that their story should have a clear beginning, middle, and end. Work with students to provide examples for the chart.

Element	Definition	Example
Title	• Catches readers' attention • Gives a quick idea of the situation or theme	Strong Suit! Suit Up for Strength
Beginning	• Introduces characters and situation • Provides some science on which the story is based	Liam has a muscle disorder that makes it hard for him to walk. Equipment, such as braces, helps, but could he create a suit that would let him wear his muscles on the outside?
Middle	• Provides details about the characters, setting, and events • Manages event flow using transitions • Includes a visual to provide more detail • May include dialogue	Liam wants to run and jump and play like other kids. Then he thinks, "What if I could make an exoskeleton like a grasshopper? Maybe then I could hop, too." Illustration shows a hard shell with movable joints.
End	• Provides a satisfying conclusion that follows the story's events or situation	Liam's exoskeleton was a big hit. Soon several other people with muscle disorders bought the suit. It was a success!

MONITOR AND SUPPORT

ENGLISH LANGUAGE LEARNERS

If . . . students have difficulty writing events that heighten and then resolve tension,

then . . . suggest that they start by writing a problem and a solution to the problem. Then encourage them to think of details that will make the problem seem even worse and create tension. Explain that the more details they include about the problem and how the problem affects the character, the more satisfying the solution will be for readers.

STRUGGLING WRITERS

If . . . students are having difficulty writing their story,

then . . . tell them to name the key elements of a fiction story. Then ask questions about one of the elements, such as: Was the character engaging? Do you understand what the character was thinking and feeling? Do you understand why the character acted the way he or she acted? Was the character development effective, or is more detail needed? Encourage students to use their answers to these questions to improve their writing.

Look Closely

SENTENCES Remind students that they have worked recently on using pronouns in their sentences, including personal pronouns, possessive pronouns, relative pronouns, intensive pronouns, indefinite pronouns, and pronoun/antecedent agreement. Have students review their writing to locate examples of pronoun use. Using examples from the text, show students how pronouns are used correctly. Encourage students to add variety to their writing by using pronouns.

PRINCIPAL PARTS OF VERBS (REGULAR AND IRREGULAR) Focus attention on the four principal parts of a regular verb: present, present participle, past, and past participle. Remind students that some verbs are irregular and that these verbs do not follow the same pattern as regular verbs. Encourage students to review their stories for proper verb use.

LINKING VERBS Remind students that linking verbs connect the subject of a sentence to a word or words that describe the subject. Linking verbs do not show action. Encourage students to review their stories for linking verbs and to be sure they can identify the subject and the word or words that the linking verb connects to the subject.

SENTENCES Have students check that their sentences work together within each paragraph to support the main ideas. Remind them that they want the events to unfold naturally in their science fiction story. Tell students to review their work for transition words that help move the story along, build suspense, and provide order to the story.

DEVELOP CONFLICT Remind students how writers use conflict to help build suspense or create a dramatic turning point. Encourage students to review their story to be sure that they included science fiction elements in their narrative's conflict. Point out that their character's actions to resolve the conflict must fit the character they have developed.

ENGLISH LANGUAGE LEARNERS

If . . . students have difficulty identifying the difference between linking verbs and helping verbs,

then . . . help students make two lists showing both. Linking verb examples include: *is, are, were, become, feel, look,* and *seem.* Helping verb examples include: *has, is, was, do, can,* and *will.* Use one of the words in a sentence, and have students say if it is a linking verb or a helping verb. If it is a linking verb, have students name the words that are linked. If it is a helping verb, have students name the word it helps.

STRUGGLING WRITERS

If . . . students are having difficulty staying motivated,

then . . . have students draw their story. Encourage them to show the characters, the conflict, and how the character resolves the conflict in their drawings. Then, have students use their drawings to write their story. Remind students to add details, use transition words, and create dialogue to help enhance their story.

Name _____

Title _____

Write a Science Fiction Story
Writing Checklist

❏ Did I create a believable character?

❏ Did I use scientific facts in a new and believable way in my story?

❏ Did I use transition words and pacing to help create tension in the story?

❏ Did I use dialogue effectively to develop a character or the conflict? Example:

_____

❏ Did I include a satisfying conclusion to the story?

❏ Did I use pronouns correctly? Example: _____

_____

❏ Did I use linking verbs and helping verbs correctly? Example: _____

_____

❏ Did I use the correct verb tense in each sentence? Example: _____

_____

❏ Did I review the story for correct capitalization, punctuation, and spelling?

❏ Did I use the Internet to do research or find images to include in the story?

Unlock the Task: Write a Science Journal Article

Distribute copies of the task found on p. 396 of the Teacher's Guide. Read the task together. Have students identify key words or phrases to highlight in the task. Discuss why each word or phrase might be important. When students agree that the word or phrase is important, have them highlight it.

> Write a science journal article on a piece of new and exciting information about the universe. First, conduct research to find a suitable topic for your article. Then use several sources to build knowledge and investigate different aspects of your chosen topic. Use this research to create your journal article.

Remind students of the questions they should be able to answer to show they understand a task. Have students look at the words and phrases they highlighted to help them answer the questions below. You may wish to provide this as a handout for students to complete individually. Scan the group to determine who needs more support and who is ready to work independently.

- **What type of writing is this?** (informative/explanatory)
- **What will the text of my writing look like?** (a science journal article)
- **What texts should I reference?** (*Jess and Layla's Astronomical Assignment, Our Mysterious Universe, A Black Hole Is NOT a Hole,* and resource books I select)
- **What information should I give?** (a clear explanation of a topic about the universe)
- **What do I need to include?** (facts, definitions, details, domain-specific vocabulary, formatting, illustrations a conclusion)

Have students restate the task in their own words. Check for possible misunderstandings or missing elements.

ENGLISH LANGUAGE LEARNERS

If . . . students don't understand what it means to investigate different aspects of a topic,

then . . . explain that investigating a topic is the same as researching it. Students should choose a topic about the universe that they want to learn more about. Tell students that they will use a variety of sources to learn facts and details about their topic. Through their research, they will build knowledge. Through their writing, they will share that knowledge.

STRUGGLING WRITERS

If . . . students have difficulty understanding what kinds of topics are suitable for this task,

then . . . provide a variety of science-related books and magazines, and have students page through the selections. Remind them that while there may be information in these books or magazines about ecosystems and Earth sciences, they should be looking for topics that relate to the universe. Then ask: Which topic are you most excited about? Why? Would that be a good topic to research further and write about?

Prepare to Write

Once students clearly understand the task, have them review the selections *Jess and Layla's Astronomical Assignment, Our Mysterious Universe, A Black Hole Is NOT a Hole,* and any other science-related materials you have gathered. Have students record ideas of topics they might want to write about for a science journal article. Encourage students to share their ideas with the class. Suggest students enhance their list by adding new topics that interest them as they hear others mention them.

Tell students to prioritize their list, limiting it to one or two ideas that they think might be the focus of their science journal article. Remind them that this should be the idea about which they think they will find the most information to share. If students have difficulty choosing between two topics, have them make a list of what they know and what they want to know about each topic. They can use this list to determine which topic interests them the most. Some students might prefer to write about a topic they are familiar with, while others might prefer to learn about an unfamiliar or a less familiar topic.

Have students put together ideas for their science journal article. Be sure students understand they will need to introduce their topic clearly and then support the topic with facts, definitions, concrete details, quotations, illustrations, and other information related to the topic. Remind students that when gathering facts about their topic, they should be careful to decide whether the fact is one that will be cited with a source—in which case it should be copied carefully word for word—or whether the fact is information that should be summarized and not copied exactly. Suggest students use a two-column chart to keep track of facts and their associated sources. Students should also include domain-specific language in their article. Explain that readers appreciate definitions for terms that might not be familiar.

ACCELERATED WRITERS

If . . . students have more domain-specific language than is appropriate for their science journal article,

then . . . have them review the vocabulary used in their article. Remind students that a science journal must be tightly focused to keep the readers' interest. However, an article with too many domain-specific vocabulary words can be hard for some readers to follow. Point out that domain-specific vocabulary should be used only if it helps the reader understand the topic. Suggest that students review their domain-specific vocabulary to ensure each term will help the reader better understand the topic. Have them replace or delete any words that aren't needed.

MONITOR AND SUPPORT

Encourage students to talk through their science journal article with a partner to help them clarify their ideas. Students may benefit from modeling these prewriting conversations or reviewing some questions the writer might ask his or her partner.

Questions a Writer Might Ask

- What science topic will I write about?
- What facts, details, and quotations will I use to explain the topic?
- What domain-specific language will I use?
- How will I help the reader understand any unfamiliar words?
- What illustrations might help the reader understand the topic better?
- What details or other information might be helpful to add?
- What unnecessary details or information should be deleted?
- How will my conclusion summarize the topic?

Encourage students to also formulate questions of their own.

GET ORGANIZED

Tell students to think about the feedback they received when talking through the topic with a partner. Remind them that using that feedback to organize their science journal article will save them time and effort when writing and rewriting.

Have students review the facts and details they have gathered about their topic. Remind students that writers find supporting details through research. Point out that effective research should include information from multiple perspectives to help readers understand the topic better. As students organize their information, encourage them to do additional research if more information is needed to present their topic clearly.

ENGLISH LANGUAGE LEARNERS

If . . . students have difficulty with domain-specific vocabulary,

then . . . have them write the domain-specific words on note cards. Help them find pictures that illustrate each word. For example, if they are writing about stars, they might want to find pictures to help explain these terms: *luminous, constellations, core, rotations,* and *orbit.* Suggest students use the illustrations in their scientific journal article.

STRUGGLING WRITERS

If . . . students are having difficulty linking ideas,

then . . . suggest they use a graphic organizer to help them see relationships. For example, if students are writing about the moon, they might use a cause-and-effect graphic organizer to help them understand the scientific facts. Their graphic organizer might include *Causes: gravity and revolution; Effects: tides and phases.*

MONITOR AND SUPPORT

Write

Work with students to create a chart that describes the elements of a science journal article. Remind them that they must introduce their topic clearly and support it with facts, use precise language, provide illustrations, and link the ideas. Also remind students that they should include a conclusion that summarizes the topic. Work with students to provide examples for the chart.

Element	Definition	Example
Title	• Catches readers' attention • Gives a quick idea of the topic	You Are What You Eat! Genetically Modified Food
Introduction	• Introduces the topic clearly • Provides a general observation and focus	There are both benefits and drawbacks to using genetically modified foods.
Body	• Includes facts and details about the topic • Includes domain-specific vocabulary to help readers understand the topic • Includes visuals to help explain the facts • May include quotations from people involved or source material	Genetically modified (GM) foods are produced through genetic engineering. The DNA of the organism is changed. GM foods can be grown in conditions that do not support non-genetically modified foods. Dr. Sam, an opponent of GM foods, says, "GM foods pose environmental and economic concerns." The illustration compares an ear of corn that is genetically modified with one that is not.
Conclusion	• Gives readers a short summary • Gives suggestions for next steps	For now, GM foods are here to stay, but more research needs to be done to ensure the safety of all who use GM foods.

MONITOR AND SUPPORT

ENGLISH LANGUAGE LEARNERS

If . . . students are having difficulty writing a concluding statement,

then . . . remind them that the concluding statement can summarize the article topic. Ask questions, such as: What do you want the reader to remember about this topic? Why did you write about this topic? What is the most important idea in your article? Is there some action you want the reader to take after reading your article? Have students use the answers to these questions to write their conclusion.

STRUGGLING WRITERS

If . . . students have difficulty including visuals to help get their points across,

then . . . remind students that visuals not only can be illustrations and charts but also the way the text is formatted. Remind students that text features, such as headings and sections, can help clarify information in the article. Discuss how the headings in the text *Our Mysterious Universe* help the reader know what the section will be about. Have students review their articles to determine where section headings might help organize ideas.

Look Closely

SENTENCES Remind students that they have worked recently on the proper use of verb tense in their sentences. Use examples from the texts to show students how verb tense can be used to convey time, such as past, present, or future, and to convey sequence. Have students add consistency to their writing by using proper verb tense.

LINKING VERBS AND SUBJECT COMPLEMENTS Focus attention on the use of linking verbs and subject complements. Remind students that a linking verb serves as a bridge between a subject and its complement, which can be a noun, a pronoun, or an adjective. For example, in the sentence *Erosion is destructive*, point out that *is* links the subject *Erosion* with the complement *destructive*. Encourage students to review their scientific research articles for places where they could include linking verbs and subject complements to add descriptive detail.

MODAL AUXILIARIES Remind students that they have worked on modal auxiliaries, and their writing should show what they learned. Point out that modal auxiliaries are helping verbs that add meaning to a verb. Remind students that modal auxiliaries *might* and *may* relate the main verb to probability, while *must* and *ought to* relate the main verb to a sense of obligation. Have students review their scientific journal article for the use of modal auxiliaries.

SENTENCES Remind students that, in a science journal article, the topic is clearly presented first. Tell students to review their work to be sure the facts support their topic and that the ideas are linked using transitional words or phrases.

INCORPORATE VISUALS AND MULTIMEDIA Remind students that visuals and other multimedia elements can help the reader understand a topic or scientific concept. Have students review their use of visuals and multimedia to be sure they add meaning to the article. Have them add or revise captions to make the meaning of the visual clear and to show how it relates to the text. Point out good examples of visuals from the texts as models whenever possible.

ENGLISH LANGUAGE LEARNERS

If . . . students have difficulty forming regular verb tenses,

then . . . create a three-column chart with the labels *Past, Present,* and *Future*. Have students say a verb and tell if it conveys past, present, or future tense. Record their verb in the correct column. Then write the other forms of the verb. For example, write *eroded, erodes, will erode*. Help students identify the pattern used to form regular verb tenses, adding *-d* or *-ed* for past tense, *-s* for present tense, and *will* for future tense.

STRUGGLING WRITERS

If . . . students have difficulty with modal auxiliaries,

then . . . write *might, must, may,* and *ought to* on note cards and give one to each student. Say: I ___ go to the dentist this afternoon. Have students complete the sentence using the word on their card—for instance, "I must go to the dentist this afternoon." Talk about how the meaning of the sentence changes depending on which word is used to complete the sentence. Repeat with other sentences.

MONITOR AND SUPPORT

Name _____

Title _____

Write a Science Journal Article
Writing Checklist

❑ Did I clearly state the topic?

❑ Did I support the topic with facts, definitions, details, and quotations?

❑ Did I use several sources to gather my facts? Name them.

_____

❑ Did I use domain-specific vocabulary accurately? Examples:

_____

❑ Did I provide definitions for words that might be unfamiliar to the reader?

❑ Did I link ideas together using words, phrases, and clauses?

❑ Did I use correct verb tenses in each sentence? Example: _____

_____

❑ Did I use visuals and multimedia to make the facts clearer? Example: _____

_____

❑ Did I include a strong conclusion?

❑ Did I review my work for correct capitalization, punctuation, and spelling?

❑ Did I embed images or video that I found online into my article?

Unlock the Task: Write About Explorations

Distribute copies of the task found on page 196 of the Teacher's Guide. Read the task together. Have students identify and highlight key words or phrases in the task. Discuss why each word or phrase might be important.

> Write an opinion essay stating whether the positive or negative aspects of exploration had a greater effect on societies. Support your opinion with reasons and evidence from the anchor and supporting texts.

ANSWER QUESTIONS ABOUT THE TASK

Remind students of the questions they should be able to answer to show they understand a task. Have them look at the words and phrases they highlighted in the prompt to help them answer the questions below.

- **What type of writing is this?** (opinion)
- **What will the text of my writing look like?** (paragraphs with a list of sources)
- **What texts should I reference?** (*Explorers: Triumphs and Troubles, Pedro's Journal,* and "Secrets of the Canyon Cave")
- **What information should I give?** (my opinion about whether the positive or negative aspects of exploration had a greater effect on societies; reasons and information from the texts to support my point of view)
- **What do I need to include?** (opinion statement; logically ordered reasons supported by facts and details; linking words, phrases, and clauses; concluding statement; list of sources referenced)

RESTATE THE TASK

Have students restate the task in their own words. Check for possible misunderstandings or missing elements.

ENGLISH LANGUAGE LEARNERS

If . . . students have difficulty forming an opinion about exploration,

then . . . point out that their opinion will be based on what they learned about exploration in the selections. Ask questions about exploration to help them state their point of view, such as: What evidence tells you about whether exploration had a positive or negative effect on societies?

STRUGGLING WRITERS

If . . . students have difficulty understanding how to express their opinion,

then . . . point out that when they express their opinion they are expressing a point of view. Remind students that an opinion should be supported by facts and details. Have students state their opinion on a topic, such as a favorite sports team or movie, and then have students provide facts to support their ideas. Explain that they will use a similar approach when they write their opinion essay about exploration.

Prepare to Write

Once students clearly understand the task, have them review the selections *Explorers: Triumphs and Troubles, Pedro's Journal,* and "Secrets of the Canyon Cave." Tell students to record the positive and negative aspects of exploration presented in the texts. Some students may benefit from paging through the texts to help them remember how exploration affected societies.

After reviewing the texts, have students form an opinion about whether the positive or negative aspects of exploration had a greater effect on societies.

GATHER IDEAS

Have students gather ideas for their opinion essay. Remind them that they will need to state their opinion clearly at the start of their writing so that the reader understands the purpose of the piece. Remind students that the reader may not agree with their opinion, but the reader should get to know the positive or negative aspects of exploration better as a result of reading their opinion piece.

Remind students that they will need facts and details to support their point of view. Explain that the facts and details should be grouped logically and that the writing should flow smoothly from one idea to the next so that the reader can easily follow the argument.

ACCELERATED WRITERS

If . . . students can easily state their opinion and reasons for their opinion,

then . . . have them review their writing to determine how they can enhance their writing with stronger reasons or more convincing language. Encourage students to revise their use of language to sway the reader to agree with their opinion. Suggest that students add more descriptive language to their reasons in an effort to cause the reader to align with their opinion.

MONITOR AND SUPPORT

Encourage students to talk through their notes for their opinion essay with a partner to help them clarify their ideas. Students may benefit from modeling these prewriting conversations or reviewing some questions the writer might ask his or her partner.

Questions a Writer Might Ask

- Which aspects of exploration will I write about?
- What is my opinion about how exploration affected societies?
- What are some facts I will include about exploration?
- Do the facts support my opinion?
- How should I group my facts and details?
- What sources did I use in gathering research?
- Is there any information missing that would be helpful to include?
- How does my conclusion support my opinion?

Encourage students to also formulate questions of their own.

Have students think about the feedback they received when talking through the topic with a partner. Remind them that using this feedback to organize their opinion piece will save them time and effort when writing and editing.

Remind students to include only facts and details that support their opinion and to use transitions to help the reader understand the flow of the writing. Remind them to include a conclusion that summarizes their writing.

ENGLISH LANGUAGE LEARNERS

If . . . students have difficulty using transition words,

then . . . provide a list of transition words, such as *specifically*, *consequently*, and *therefore*, and explain how they are used. Point out how the word *specifically* connects a particular example to a general statement. Repeat with other examples, using a transition word such as *therefore* to connect an effect or result to its cause.

STRUGGLING WRITERS

If . . . students are having difficulty remembering their facts and details,

then . . . have them flip through their source books and place sticky notes next to a fact or detail that supports their opinion. Have students create a note card for each fact by writing key words and phrases about each fact (and the page number where the fact can be found) on the note card. Have students organize the note cards by grouping like facts together and then placing the groups in a logical order.

Write

Work with students to create a chart that describes the elements of their opinion essay. Remind them that their opinion should be supported by facts and details. Also remind students that an opinion piece has a concluding statement that summarizes the writer's opinion. Work with students to provide examples for the chart.

Element	Definition	Example
Title	• Catches readers' attention • Gives a quick idea of the topic	The Dark Side of Exploration
Introduction	• Includes your opinion about exploration • Provides some reasons to support your opinion	I believe the negative aspects of exploration had a greater effect on societies than the positive aspects did. Explorers often were violent and spread diseases to those people whose land they took over.
Body	• Provides facts and details to support your opinion • Manages the flow of ideas using transitions	In the 16th century, Spanish conquistador Francisco de Orellana brought European diseases to the Americas, which killed many native people. In 1903, British explorer Francis Younghusband led an expedition to Tibet. It became an invasion in which British soldiers killed hundreds of Tibetans.
Conclusion	• Gives readers a short summary that restates your opinion and provides support for that view	Even though exploration led to many exciting discoveries of new lands and cultures, violence and disease negatively affected societies and overshadowed the positive side of exploration.

MONITOR AND SUPPORT

ENGLISH LANGUAGE LEARNERS

If . . . students have difficulty stating their opinion,

then . . . explain that certain phrases help the reader know that an idea is the writer's opinion. Remind students that phrases like *in my opinion*, *I believe*, *I think*, and *as I see it* all signal to the reader that the information that follows is an opinion, or the writer's point of view. Have students practice using these phrases to state an opinion, such as about a favorite book or a favorite meal.

STRUGGLING WRITERS

If . . . students are having difficulty writing the conclusion,

then . . . remind them that the conclusion can be a restatement of their opinion given in their introduction, and that it can provide the key details that support their opinions. Have students reread their introductory paragraph, and then rephrase that paragraph for their conclusion. Tell students to start with the main reasons that support their opinion, and then use a transition word or phrase such as *consequently*, before stating their opinion again.

Look Closely

SENTENCES Remind students that they have worked recently on using subordinating conjunctions. Point out examples from the texts that demonstrate the correct use of subordinating conjunctions. Have students add variety to their writing by using subordinating conjunctions where applicable.

PREPOSITIONAL PHRASES Remind students that in a prepositional phrase, the phrase begins with a preposition and ends with a noun or a pronoun or multiple nouns or pronouns. Point out that a prepositional phrase can include one or more adjectives, but it can never include a verb. Have students add details to at least one of their sentences by adding a prepositional phrase.

VERBALS Remind students that verbals are verb forms used as other parts of speech. Point out to students that they have been studying the following verbals: gerunds (such as *eating*, as in "I am thinking of eating that grasshopper"), participles (such as *eaten*, as in "Having eaten that grasshopper, I got sick"), and infinitives (such as *to eat*, as in "I have decided not to eat any more grasshoppers"). Have students revise at least one of their sentences to include one type of verbal.

SENTENCES Have students look closely to see that their sentences work together within each paragraph to support the main ideas. Remind them that the reasons should unfold logically in their opinion essay and their ideas should be linked. Tell students to review their work for transition words.

SYNTHESIZE RESEARCH Remind students that their opinion must be supported by the facts and details they gathered through research. Point out that once they have their facts and details, they must be able to synthesize, or combine, their research so that it makes sense to the readers. Have students review their opinion piece to find facts and details they combined from different sources. Point out that when they synthesize their research, they will combine the information using their own words.

ENGLISH LANGUAGE LEARNERS
If . . . students have difficulty using verbals,

then . . . write several verbs, such as *explore*, *sail*, and *write,* on note cards. Then create a three-column chart with the headings: Gerund, Participle, and Infinitive. Have students complete the chart by writing each verbal form for the verbs on the note cards, such as *exploring (exploring the cliffs)*, *explored (having explored the cliffs)*, and *to explore (to explore the cliffs)*. Then have students use the verbals in sentences.

STRUGGLING WRITERS
If . . . students are having difficulty synthesizing their research,

then . . . help them think of key words that support their opinion. Have students look through their notes and put facts that support their key words with each key word. Point out how all of the facts do not come from the same source. Explain to students that when they use their own words to combine the ideas with each key word, they are synthesizing their research.

MONITOR AND SUPPORT

215

Name _____

Title _____

Write About Explorations
Writing Checklist

❏ Did I clearly state my opinion?

❏ Did my introductory paragraph make my purpose clear?

❏ Did I provide logical reasons for my opinion?

❏ Did I support my opinion with facts and details?

❏ Did I use multiple sources to gather my evidence?

❏ Did I use transitions to link my opinion with reasons? Example:

_____

❏ Did I use verbals (gerunds, participles, and infinitives) correctly? Example: _____

_____

❏ Did I use prepositional phrases correctly? Example: _____

_____

❏ Did I use subordinating conjunctions correctly? Example: _____

_____

❏ Did I include a strong conclusion?

❏ Did I include a list of sources that I used?

❏ Did I review my writing for correct capitalization, punctuation, and spelling?

❏ (Optional) Did I use the Internet to locate multimedia to support my opinion?

Unlock the Task: Write an Opinion Essay

BREAK APART THE TASK

Distribute copies of the task found on page 396 of the Teacher's Guide. Have students read the task. Then have them name and discuss the important key words or phrases to highlight in the task.

> Use the information on pages 30–31 of *Explorers of North America* as well as what you have learned about explorations to write an opinion essay. Name five items you think would be the most important to bring on an exploration.

ANSWER QUESTIONS ABOUT THE TASK

Remind students of the questions they should be able to answer to show they understand a task. Have students look at the words and phrases they highlighted to help them answer the questions below.

- **What type of writing is this?** (opinion)
- **What will the text of my writing look like?** (an essay)
- **What texts should I reference?** (*Explorers of North America, Beyond the Horizon,* and *New Beginnings: Jamestown and the Virginia Colony.*)
- **What information should I give?** (an opinion; logically ordered reasons; facts and details to support my opinion)
- **What do I need to include?** (opinion statement; reasons supported by facts and details; linking words, phrases, and clauses; concluding statement)

RESTATE THE TASK

Have students restate the task in their own words. Check for possible misunderstandings or missing elements.

ENGLISH LANGUAGE LEARNERS

If . . . students have trouble understanding what it means to go on an exploration,

then . . . provide examples of explorations from history. What challenges did people face on explorations? What benefits did explorations provide to people?

STRUGGLING WRITERS

If . . . students have difficulty selecting the items they would bring,

then . . . look at *Explorers of North America* and discuss the explorations they have read about. Ask questions such as the following: If you went on an exploration, what items might make your trip easier? safer? more fun?

Prepare to Write

Once students clearly understand the task, have them review the selection *Explorers of North America*. Tell students to record ideas regarding items that would be helpful to bring on an exploration and why. Have students page through the text and think about the explorers and their expeditions. Then ask questions such as the following: What items were important for these explorers to have? What items might have made their explorations easier? Explain that answering these questions will help bring focus to their essay.

Remind students that the purpose of their essay is to share their opinion. Point out that their opinion should be supported with facts and presented in a logical manner. Tell students that it is important to know their audience, the people who will be reading their essay, so that they can write to that audience. Remind students that they must state their opinion clearly, so that there is no doubt about the point of view of the essay in the reader's mind.

Have students put together ideas for their essay on what items to bring on an exploration. Be sure students understand they will want to state their opinion clearly, and then support their opinion with facts and other information related to the exploration. Explain to students that, in addition to stating supporting facts, they should address opposing arguments to their opinion. Remind students that if they gather facts from multiple sources they need to keep track of the sources they use. Have students create a two-column chart to keep track of facts and their associated sources.

ACCELERATED WRITERS

If . . . students have more facts than needed to support their opinion,

then . . . remind students that they should focus on the five things that would be most helpful on an exploration. Have them make a list of all the supporting facts they found and then rank them in order of how helpful they would be on an exploration.

Have students talk through their opinion and supporting facts and details with a partner to help them clarify their ideas. Students may benefit from modeling these prewriting conversations or reviewing some questions the writer might ask his or her partner.

Questions a Writer Might Ask

- What is my opinion about five important items to bring on an exploration?
- What facts and details should I include to support my opinion?
- How can I link my reasons to create a logical structure?
- How can I address ideas that do not agree with mine?
- Is there any information missing that might be helpful?
- What is the most persuasive argument that I can make in support of my opinion?
- How will my conclusion summarize my opinion and reasons?

Encourage students to also formulate questions of their own.

GET ORGANIZED

Tell students to think about the feedback they received when talking through the task with a partner. Remind them that using this feedback to organize their essay will save them time and effort when writing and editing.

Remind students that writers support an opinion with facts and details. Point out that writers should evaluate their reasons and evidence to be sure that the information is effective in supporting their opinion. Have students review the facts and details they have gathered for their essay. Tell students to reword or remove facts and details that don't effectively support their opinion.

ENGLISH LANGUAGE LEARNERS

If . . . students have difficulty organizing their reasons and facts,

then . . . remind students that reasons and evidence can be organized using different structures, such as time order, cause and effect, or order of importance. Have students name one of their facts, and then ask: Does this fact relate to time order, cause and effect, or order of importance? Continue in this manner until students have created logical groupings for their reasons and facts.

STRUGGLING WRITERS

If . . . students are having difficulty stating facts to support their opinion,

then . . . have students state their opinion about an exploration and then ask questions to help students focus on key elements, such as the following: Why did you select this item for the exploration? How might it affect the explorers who use it?

Write

Work with students to create a chart that describes the elements of an opinion piece. Remind them that they must state their opinion clearly and support it with reasons and facts that are linked in a logical and convincing order. Also remind students that an opinion piece has a concluding statement that summarizes the writer's opinion. Work with students to provide examples for the chart.

Element	Definition	Example
Title	• Catches readers' attention • Gives a quick idea of the topic	What to Bring on an Exploration
Introduction	• Introduces the topic clearly • Provides a general observation and focus	Explorations can be both exciting and dangerous. It is important for explorers to have certain items with them to make their explorations easier and safer.
Body	• Provides details • Includes facts and concrete details about the topic • Includes domain-specific language to help the reader understand the topic	First, explorers would need plenty of food and water (including water purification tablets and matches to cook food). Second, explorers would need clothing appropriate for the weather. If the weather is cold, they would need warm wool clothing. If the weather is warm, they would need lightweight cotton clothing. Third, explorers would need mosquito nets to protect themselves from dangerous bug bites. Fourth, explorers would need a compass to help them navigate unfamiliar lands. Fifth, explorers should have paper and pencils to record observations.
Conclusion	• Gives readers a short summary	The five most important items for explorers to have are food and water, appropriate clothing, mosquito nets, a compass, and paper and pencils. These items keep explorers healthy and safe.

ENGLISH LANGUAGE LEARNERS

If . . . students are having a hard time organizing the ideas in their essay,

then . . . discuss that they should use an organizational structure that groups their ideas in a logical way. For example, they can arrange their items from most important to least important or least important to most important.

STRUGGLING WRITERS

If . . . students are having difficulty writing their opinion essay,

then . . . have students organize their writing into manageable pieces. For example, students can use the Opinion Writing Graphic Organizer in Part 3 to record their information and reasons in the boxes provided and ensure they have all components of their writing. If students need more compartmentalized support, have them use the Main Idea and Details Graphic Organizer in Part 3 to list their opinion in the Main Idea box and their supporting reasons in the Details boxes.

Look Closely

SENTENCES Remind students that they have worked recently on the proper use of subject-verb agreement in their sentences. Have students review their writing to locate examples of subject-verb agreement. Use examples from the texts to show students subject-verb agreement with compound subjects, with indefinite pronouns, with collective nouns, and with hard-to-find subjects.

PUNCTUATING ITEMS IN A SERIES Focus attention on the use of commas to separate items in a series. Remind students that when words, phrases, and clauses appear in a series in a sentence, they are often separated by commas. For example, point to the use of commas in the following statement: *Lewis took tools that included a telescope, thermometers, cloth to make tents, pliers, and handsaws.* Have students review their essay for the use of commas in a series.

COMMAS Remind students that they have studied the use of commas after introductory phrases, after *yes* or *no* at the start of a sentence, and before a tag question. Point out how a comma after an introductory phrase or the words *yes* or *no* reminds the reader to pause briefly. Have students review their essay for the use of commas, especially after introductory phrases, after *yes* or *no*, and before tag questions.

SENTENCES Tell students to look closely to see that their sentences work together within each paragraph to support the main ideas. Remind them that, in an opinion essay, the topic is presented clearly first. Tell students to review their work to be sure that the facts support their opinion and that the ideas are linked using transitional words or phrases.

ADDRESSING OPPOSING VIEWPOINTS Remind students that they should address opposing viewpoints in their opinion essay. Explain that by doing this they strengthen the argument for their opinion because the reader understands that they have considered many different options before stating their opinion about what to bring on an exploration. Have students review their essay to see if they have addressed opposing viewpoints.

ENGLISH LANGUAGE LEARNERS

If . . . students have difficulty with subject-verb agreement when using compound subjects,

then . . . write the following: *Maria and Rosa are friends. Neither Maria nor Rosa takes the bus. Coats or hats hang in the closet.* Remind students that subjects and verbs must agree. Point out that the subject *Maria and Rosa* is plural, so it uses the plural verb form *are.* Repeat with the other two examples. Then have students find examples of compound subjects in the texts and explain why the verb agrees in number.

STRUGGLING WRITERS

If . . . students have difficulty using commas in a series,

then . . . write the following without commas: *Clark came to the river got in the canoe crossed the river and lifted the canoe out of the water.* Read the sentence aloud without any pauses. Then ask students: How many actions did Clark do, or take? (Four) How do you know? (There are four verb phrases.) Work with students to identify the verbs in the series and to correctly punctuate the sentence in order to clarify its meaning. Repeat with other sentences.

Name _____

Title _____

Write an Opinion Essay
Writing Checklist

❑ Did I clearly state my opinion?

❑ Did I support my opinion with reasons and facts? Example:

_____

❑ Did I link my opinions logically?

❑ Did I address opposing arguments?

❑ Did I provide a persuasive argument?

❑ Did I use correct subject-verb agreement in each sentence? Example: _____

_____

❑ Did I use punctuation in a series correctly? Example: _____

_____

❑ Did I use commas after introductory phrases, *yes* or *no*, or tag questions appropriately?

Example: _____

_____

❑ Did I include a strong conclusion that helps persuade the reader?

❑ Did I review my work for correct capitalization, punctuation, and spelling?

❑ (Optional) Did I use the Internet to find images of the five items I identified in my essay?

Scaffolded Lessons for the Writing Types

Unlock Opinion Writing

Ask students if they can name any examples of opinion writing that they have read in class throughout the year. Remind them that opinion writing tells the thoughts or preferences of the writer and discusses something that he or she believes. Provide an example of opinion writing, and allow students to look through the text and identify the topic of the writing as well as the writer's opinion.

Explain to students that when they read opinion writing, they may or may not agree with the writer's position on the topic. The ideas may be based on the writer's feelings, personal experiences, or personal knowledge. The writer includes reasons and evidence to support the opinion he or she is writing about. To give students practice recognizing and stating opinions, ask questions such as "Should the school year be adjusted?" or "Which character changed the most during the story?" Explain that book reviews and movie reviews are examples of opinion writing because they give the writer's opinion about a topic.

UNDERSTAND TASK AND TONE

Explain that opinion writing often takes on an emotional tone, because the writer may have strong feelings about the topic and use strong or expressive words. Tell students that they will be asked to write their opinions as part of homework assignments or assessments. Explain that they will usually be provided with the topic to write about but that they will decide what their opinion about the topic is. Remind them that before they begin writing an opinion, they should carefully read the assignment and understand all of its parts. Explain that most school assignments should be written in a formal tone, because they will be read by you, their teacher. Explain that as they write, they should concentrate on using clear language and descriptive words that express their opinion logically.

REFOCUS ON THE WRITING TYPE

Throughout the year as students read or are asked to write opinion texts, remind them of the key features of this text type. Opinion writing

- introduces a topic and clearly states an opinion about the topic.
- makes a claim about the topic.
- gives reasons for the writer's opinion.
- provides evidence to support the writer's opinion.
- may offer a possible solution to a problem.

Introduce an Opinion

What Students Should KNOW	What Students Will DO
• Write a sentence that introduces a topic.	• Introduce a topic or text clearly.
• Write a sentence that states an opinion related to the topic. • Develop a paragraph that introduces a topic and states an opinion related to the topic.	• State an opinion.

MODEL AND PRACTICE

Help students focus on how to introduce a topic and state an opinion in a clear and concise way for the reader. Explain that they may often be asked to write an opinion about texts they have read, so ask them to focus on how they might introduce a book topic and form an opinion about a book they have read.

MODEL I just read the story "Little Red Riding Hood." I was asked to write my opinion about it. The first thing I should do is to introduce the topic clearly and then state my opinion. So, I should include the name of the story to make sure the reader is clear about what I am writing about. I can write, "I read Grimm's fairy tale 'Little Red Riding Hood.' I thought Red was a brave character." My introduction can be as simple as this, or it can be a longer paragraph, but it needs to introduce the topic and my opinion.

PRACTICE Have students work in small groups. Ask them to choose one of the fiction selections they read as part of their reading unit. Have them work together to decide what they thought of the story or passage. Have them think as a group about what kind of opinion could be developed about the passage. Encourage them to consider what they thought of the characters and plot, and not just whether they liked or disliked the story.

DEEPER PRACTICE Using the information from the group practice, have students work independently to write an introductory sentence or two to introduce their topic and opinion about the passage.

ENGLISH LANGUAGE LEARNERS

If . . . students have trouble stating their opinion about the passage,

then . . . help them focus on specific parts of the story. Ask questions such as "What did you think of the main character?" Then guide them to answer in a complete sentence by modeling a sentence frame: I thought the main character was ___.

STRUGGLING WRITERS

If . . . students have trouble summarizing their opinion in a sentence,

then . . . provide students with a word web graphic organizer and ask them to write ideas about their topic and opinion. They may use single words or short phrases to describe their topic and opinion. Then ask them to put these ideas into one or more clear sentences.

Organize Writing

What Students Should KNOW	What Students Will DO
• Identify organizational structures for writing. • Know and apply the organizational steps for an opinion essay.	• Create an organizational structure in which ideas are logically grouped to support the writer's purpose.

MODEL AND PRACTICE

Explain to students that once they understand their assignment and topic and have settled on their opinion about the topic, they must create an organizing structure for their writing. Explain that an organizational structure is like an outline. It lets the writer know what will be discussed and in what order.

MODEL When I think about writing an opinion essay about the book I read, I should first organize the essay before I begin writing. I already set up my introduction by mentioning the topic and my opinion. Now I must organize my paragraphs. In each paragraph I'll give another reason that explains my opinion of Red as a brave character, and I'll give evidence from the book to support each reason. I think this will be an easy way to organize my essay.

PRACTICE Provide students with an example of an opinion essay. Ask small groups to use markers to draw and label a diagram showing how the writing is organized, including what is being discussed in each paragraph. Ask students if they think this is the best way to organize the information or if they think the writer should have done it another way. Have students explain their answers.

DEEPER PRACTICE Ask students to make a bulleted list to summarize the opinion essay they just analyzed. Have them include a bullet and sentence to describe each paragraph in the essay.

ENGLISH LANGUAGE LEARNERS

If . . . students have trouble describing how opinion essays are organized,

then . . . draw a series of boxes to represent the paragraphs. Help students use sequence words to describe the paragraph boxes. For example: *First* we have the introduction. *Next* we explain one of the reasons. *After* that we have other reasons. *Finally* we have a conclusion.

STRUGGLING WRITERS

If . . . students have trouble summarizing paragraph ideas in a bulleted list,

then . . . invite them to underline important words or phrases from the paragraph and decide which ones are most important to include in the bulleted list. Then guide them to use those words in their summary. When they are finished, ask them to review the list and decide if they are satisfied with their summaries. Have students work in pairs or small groups to improve the summaries as needed.

Support an Opinion

What Students Should KNOW	What Students Will DO
• Support an opinion. • Distinguish between facts and details that do and do not support an opinion. • Determine a logical order in which to present the reasons, facts, and details that support one's opinion.	• Provide logically ordered reasons that are supported by facts and details.

MODEL AND PRACTICE

Explain that good opinion writing must provide reasons to explain and support the writer's opinion. Reasons need to relate to the topic and help explain the opinion. Opinion writing often uses facts and details to support an opinion. Give students an example of a book review to illustrate that details from the book or story must be cited to help support the writer's opinion.

MODEL When I write about Red as a brave character in "Little Red Riding Hood," I must use details from the story to help explain what I mean and why I feel that Red is brave. For instance, I will give the example of how she walks through the woods by herself without being afraid. I might cite some exact words from the story to make it even clearer. I must also pick only the details that support my opinion. So I wouldn't write that Red wanted to surprise her grandmother, because that does not show why she is brave. I organize my information in an order that makes sense. I'll give one reason and then provide evidence to support it. Then I'll give another reason with evidence to support it. I might save my strongest reason for last, or I could put it first to make a strong impact at the beginning.

PRACTICE Ask students to work in the same groups to continue discussing the story they have been analyzing. Have them refer to the story and cite three details that support their opinion. Have students organize the details in the order in which they think the details should be presented in an opinion essay.

DEEPER PRACTICE Have individual students use the list from the practice section above to write two paragraphs that provide reasons and evidence to support their opinion.

ENGLISH LANGUAGE LEARNERS

If . . . students have trouble expressing whether a detail does or does not support an opinion,

then . . . create two cards. Write *supports* on one and *does not support* on the other. Place the cards face down in front of the group. Choose a topic and opinion with the group. Take a card and model saying a sentence that either does or doesn't support the opinion, and then explain your thinking. Work through more samples of each type together.

STRUGGLING WRITERS

If . . . students have trouble organizing ideas into paragraphs,

then . . . remind students that each paragraph should be about a separate idea. Ask them to organize the details they choose to support their opinion, and then have students make them into a bulleted list. Explain that each bullet on their list should be discussed in its own paragraph.

MONITOR AND SUPPORT

Link Opinions and Reasons

What Students Should KNOW	What Students Will DO
• Identify and use linking words and phrases. • Identify and use linking words and phrases that connect opinions with reasons.	• Link opinion and reasons using words, phrases, and clauses (*consequently, specifically*).

MODEL AND PRACTICE

Explain to students that their writing will be clearer and more understandable to the reader if they use linking words and phrases to connect ideas. Make a list of linking words and phrases with students. Explain the meaning of each word and phrase and use each in a sample sentence. Then ask students to use the linking words and phrases in their own sentences to show that they understand their meaning.

MODEL Linking words help me connect my opinion and reasons. I use them to help me explain ideas. I can use them to talk about Red and her bravery. I might write, "Red is brave, *specifically* when she walks through the woods by herself." *Specifically* shows that I am giving an example. Or I can use the word *consequently,* which means that I am telling a result of what happens. "Red visits Grandmother all by herself. Consequently, she bravely saves Grandmother from the Wolf."

PRACTICE Have students use linking phrases to complete these sentences:

- I am a big fan of mysteries. ___ I have read all of the Hardy Boys books. (*Consequently*)
- I like reading novels, ___ ones about animal characters. (*specifically*)

DEEPER PRACTICE Have students write a short paragraph about a personal favorite book, using both of the linking words *consequently* and *specifically.* Invite volunteers to exchange papers and read each other's work aloud.

ENGLISH LANGUAGE LEARNERS

If . . . students have trouble differentiating *consequently* and *specifically,*

then . . . write each word and its definition on a separate index card and underline the base words *consequent* and *specific.* Review the definitions and base words with students. Then help students name synonyms, such as *therefore* for *consequently,* and *exactly* and *precisely* for *specifically.*

STRUGGLING WRITERS

If . . . students do not know when to use linking words or phrases,

then . . . have them work in pairs to identify linking words and phrases in sample writing. Ask questions about why the writer chose to use those words. Ask: What ideas is the word connecting? Why did the writer choose this word? How does the word improve the writing? Then guide students to choose at least two places in their own writing that could benefit from linking words or phrases.

Write a Conclusion

What Students Should KNOW	What Students Will DO
• Identify the components of a strong concluding sentence or paragraph. • Write a strong concluding sentence or paragraph that relates to the presented opinion.	• Provide a concluding statement or section related to the opinion presented.

MODEL AND PRACTICE

Explain to students that opinion writing should have a strong concluding statement or section. The conclusion should relate to the opinion that was presented and discussed. Tell students that the most common way to conclude an opinion essay is to restate or summarize the topic and opinion. Explain that a conclusion provides a definite ending point to an essay and does not introduce new ideas or concepts. Point out that a clincher can be used as part of a conclusion to make an impression on the reader. Have students look for examples of conclusions in texts they have read.

MODEL After giving my reasons and evidence, it's time to conclude my opinion essay. I will restate my opinion and use a clincher to impress the reader. I might write, "Grimm's fairy tale 'Little Red Riding Hood' is a good example of a story with a brave main character. Red needs to be brave, too, to face the dangers that Wolf brings to the story!"

PRACTICE Provide groups with a copy of three different opinion texts. Ask students to analyze the conclusion of each text and discuss it with their group. Then ask each group to choose the conclusion they think is strongest, and tell why.

DEEPER PRACTICE Ask each student to write a sample conclusion about the story or passage that his or her group has been discussing. Invite volunteers to share their conclusions with the class. Have the listeners identify any restatements, summaries, or clinchers in each conclusion.

ENGLISH LANGUAGE LEARNERS

If . . . students have trouble summarizing their topic and opinion,

then . . . have them work in pairs and ask questions about each others' stories. As they attempt to explain the opinion to their partner, invite them to use a sentence frame: I read the story ___. I thought ___.

STRUGGLING WRITERS

If . . . students write conclusions that are too abrupt or do not summarize their opinion,

then . . . give students copies of additional samples to analyze for their conclusions. Invite them to talk about what the writer did in the conclusion besides restate the opinion. Ask students how they could do something similar to improve their own ending. Then give students a chance to revise their conclusions.

MONITOR AND SUPPORT

Support for Extended Writing

Refer to this process when students are writing a longer passage that requires development and organization to produce an opinion text. Remind students of the importance of the revising and editing stages of the writing process. Explain that these steps help them make their writing strong and effective.

UNDERSTAND THE TASK Tell students to review their writing prompt or writing assignment carefully to be sure they understand what is being asked. Have them answer these questions: Do I understand what I am being asked to do? What topic will I be writing about? Do I know my opinion about this topic? How can I summarize this task in my own words? Should I cite information from another text to support my opinion? How many parts are there to this writing assignment?

BRAINSTORM Provide students with guidance and support to brainstorm ideas that will help form their opinion writing. Explain that, depending on the topic they are asked to write about, they may need to brainstorm possible opinions, or they may need to brainstrom reasons that could support their opinion.

PROVIDE REASONS Have students focus on the part of their writing in which they give reasons to support their opinion. Ask them to decide if their assignment requires that they find evidence to support their opinions. If so, encourage them to find facts or details from outside sources, such as books or online material. Explain that book reviews or movie reviews must include evidence from the book or movie. Explain that their assignment will indicate the types of facts and details they should cite. Assignments about books or nonfiction topics will require text evidence, while assignments about personal experiences may not. Encourage students to list several reasons, even though they may not use them all in their writing.

ORGANIZE INFORMATION Have students focus on the way they will organize their writing into distinct paragraphs. Invite them to use a graphic organizer or create a bulleted list or outline. Have them list the reasons and evidence that will support their opinion. Have them decide whether they will list reasons from least important to most important, or from most important to least important. Have students also think about their concluding statement or section and how they will approach writing it.

WRITE

Provide students with encouraging tips to guide them through their writing process. Some tips might include:

- Remind students that their draft should focus on organizing their opinion and reasons, and they should not worry about making everything perfect in their first attempt.

- Explain to students that they can organize their ideas in lists, notes, outlines, or graphic organizers, and refer to them repeatedly as they write their first draft.

- Tell students to give their honest opinion about the topic and express it confidently without concern about what others think.

- Encourage students to express their opinions and reasons with descriptive words, confident language, and logical reasoning.

- When students are finished, have them double check that they have answered all parts of the writing prompt or assignment, included the information in their notes, and cited or referenced any related texts included in the prompt.

REVISE AND EDIT

Guide students through the revising and editing process. Work with students to develop writing and peer review checklists to help them address important points to focus on in their revision. You may choose to reproduce the checklists on the following pages and work with students to add task-specific items to the lists. After revising, have students review one another's work to further strengthen their writing.

PUBLISH

Provide students with support in presenting their final version. Invite students to record their presentations and load them onto a class or school Web site. You might provide them time to enter their final drafts into a computer software program and add images that support the opinion pieces. Allow students to print their final drafts, if possible.

ACCELERATED WRITERS

If . . . students have trouble providing other students with positive feedback,

then . . . instruct them to focus on providing three positive comments before they give any negative comments about the student's work. Explain that they should not make the writer feel inferior or sensitive about his or her work. The feedback is meant to make the writer feel good about the prospect of improving his or her work.

Writer's Checklist

Name _____

Title _____

❑ Did I include a clear introduction that stated the topic and my opinion?

❑ Did I explain my opinion clearly so that the reader understands it?

❑ Did I give an important reason early on to support my opinion?

❑ Are my paragraphs organized in a sensible and logical order?

❑ Did I use facts and details to support my reasons if necessary?

❑ Did I cite evidence from texts if required?

❑ Did I use linking words and phrases to make ideas clear?

❑ Did I summarize my opinion and reasons in the concluding statement or section?

❑ Did I include a clincher in the conclusion to make an impression on the reader?

❑ Did I answer all parts of the prompt or address all parts of the writing assignment?

❑ Did I review my work for correct capitalization, punctuation, and spelling?

❑ _____

❑ _____

❑ _____

❑ _____

❑ _____

Peer Review Checklist

Name _____

Writer's Name _____

Title _____

❑ Does the introduction describe the topic and the writer's opinion about it?

❑ Is the writing clearly organized into paragraphs?

❑ Does the writer give several reasons to support his or her opinion?

❑ Does the writer cite evidence if required in the task?

❑ Does the writer use facts or details from different sources when necessary?

❑ Is the writing organized in a logical way that gives reasons?

❑ Does the writing include linking words or phrases to connect or clarify ideas?

❑ Does the writing have a strong concluding statement or section?

❑ Does the writing clearly address all parts of the prompt or assignment?

❑ _____

❑ _____

❑ _____

❑ _____

❑ _____

❑ _____

Unlock Informative/ Explanatory Writing

Ask students to look through the classroom library to find examples of informative/ explanatory texts. Explain that the purpose of informative/explanatory writing is to explain a topic and to help the reader gain content knowledge about the topic. Explain that the writer of the text researched facts and details to give the reader information about a specific topic, refraining from giving opinions about the topic. Allow students to look through the texts and decide what the topic of each text is.

Point out examples of content vocabulary used in various informative/explanatory texts, and explain that these words help clarify and explain the topic in greater detail. Show students examples of different text organizations, such as chronological, listing, compare and contrast, cause and effect, definition, order of importance, sequential, description, or topical. Explain that the topic of the text helps the writer decide which organization type is best.

UNDERSTAND TASK AND TONE

Have volunteers talk about informative/explanatory writing they have come across in their own experiences. Discuss how this type of writing is different from opinion or narrative writing, including in the tone or voice. Explain that the "voice" of informative/explanatory text matches the audience that the text is meant for. Magazines have a more informal voice than encyclopedias or textbooks. Show students examples of informative/explanatory writing prompts. Tell students that they will usually be provided with the topic they should write about and may need to cite other texts. Explain that before they begin writing, they must carefully read the assignment and understand all of its parts. They should also make sure they understand the purpose of their writing and who their audience is.

REFOCUS ON THE WRITING TYPE

Throughout the year as students read or are asked to write informative/explanatory texts, remind them of the key features of this text type. Informative/explanatory writing

- gives information accurately.
- explains a topic by describing the "how" or "why" behind a topic.
- includes facts and definitions.
- may include visuals to make information as clear as possible.
- may explain a process or the relationship between events or ideas.

Plan and Introduce a Topic

What Students Should KNOW	What Students Will DO
• Discriminate between clear and unclear introductions. • Identify and use introductory words and phrases. • Determine the focus for writing about a topic.	• Introduce a topic clearly; provide a general observation and focus.
• Categorize information and organize into paragraphs or sections.	• Group related information logically.

MODEL AND PRACTICE

Explain that the goal of an introduction is to let the reader know what the topic is and describe what the reader might expect to read about. A clear introduction is focused and might make a general observation about the topic. Point out that facts in an introduction are researched from other sources, such as books, magazines, or the Internet. Mention both print and online sources as ways in which students can research topics.

MODEL I'm going to write about stars in our solar system. I've read books about stars and how they are formed. I'll gather the facts into a graphic organizer to show what I want to say in each paragraph. After I've organized the information in a logical way, I'll write my introduction. I think I'll start with a general observation. I'll write, "On a clear night, you may have seen countless stars in the sky." This introduces the topic without too many facts or details. Then I'll think about how to arrange my facts.

PRACTICE Ask students to work in small groups to choose a specific animal to write about. Have them research the topic on the Internet, or using other resources, and write at least three facts about the animal. Have them use a graphic organizer to order facts in a logical way.

DEEPER PRACTICE Have students work individually, using the group's graphic organizer, to write an introduction to the topic. Ask them to start with a general observation about the topic without giving an opinion about the animal. Have students compare their work.

ENGLISH LANGUAGE LEARNERS

If . . . students have trouble forming a general observation about their topic,

then . . . ask questions about the animal students are writing about. Ask: What do people know about the animal? What is it like? Have students respond in full sentences.

STRUGGLING WRITERS

If . . . students have trouble summarizing information they gather from their research,

then . . . give pairs of students practice in summarizing. Provide them with informative/explanatory texts and point out specific paragraphs. Help students identify the most important information in those paragraphs. Then help them retell the important information in their own words. Next, have students summarize their research again.

Use Illustrations and Multimedia

What Students Should KNOW	What Students Will DO
• Identify how illustrations, headings, and multimedia are used in texts students read. • Determine what to include in an illustration and how information is best illustrated. • Determine how to use multimedia in a useful manner.	• Include formatting (e.g., headings), illustrations, and multimedia when useful to aid comprehension.

MODEL AND PRACTICE

Review an example of a nonfiction book or magazine with students. Point out examples of graphics, including photos, artwork, diagrams, and charts. Then point out any captions or labels that go with these graphics. Explain to students that a magazine, book, or textbook may include multimedia references about the topic, such as videos or websites. Point out to students that headings also help narrow a topic so that the reader understands it better.

MODEL My writing about stars could really benefit from a diagram of some constellations. I'll label each of the constellations and include captions to explain them. I can even show an illustration or diagram of different kinds of stars so that the reader can see a comparison. I might include headings to break up the text and a chart or graph so that the reader can visualize the facts.

PRACTICE Provide groups with examples of various graphics and multimedia in informative/explanatory texts. Ask each student in the group to choose one graphic to show the rest of the class and describe how it helps them better understand the text.

DEEPER PRACTICE Have small groups list ways they can use graphics to help clarify their text about animals. Invite them to choose one of the graphics to make or print. Have them write a caption or labels to go with the graphic.

ENGLISH LANGUAGE LEARNERS

If . . . students have trouble explaining how graphics aid comprehension,

then . . . help students fold a piece of paper into four parts, and then ask them to write the name of a graphic in each box. Then have them draw an example of each graphic and write a sentence to tell what type of information the graphic provides. Next, discuss with students how that information might help a reader better understand a topic.

STRUGGLING WRITERS

If . . . students have difficulty writing a caption for their own graphic example,

then . . . have them review more examples of captions in nonfiction books. Explain that the caption tells what is in the graphic. Tell students that they can start writing their own caption by simply answering the question, "What does this graphic show?"

Develop a Topic

What Students Should KNOW	What Students Will DO
• Identify facts, definitions, concrete details, and quotations in texts students have read and how the facts help develop the topic. • Know how to state facts clearly to help develop a topic. • Identify important words to define. • Use proper conventions for including quotations when writing.	• Develop a topic with facts, definitions, concrete details, quotations, and other information and examples.

MODEL AND PRACTICE

Explain to students the importance of developing a topic. Explain that facts, definitions, and details help to make a topic clear and give a topic depth. Quotations and examples are also ways that can help to develop a topic.

MODEL When I write about stars, I must develop my topic with facts and define words the reader might not be familiar with, including *red giant, supernova,* and *black hole.* I might also include a quotation from an astronomer, but I must make sure that the quote helps explain my topic and that I use the correct conventions for writing the quote. I will try to develop all of these parts of my topic before I begin writing.

PRACTICE Provide each student with a different example of an informative/ explanatory text. Have them summarize for a partner how the author developed the topic. Invite them to list each technique, such as stating facts, defining terms, and providing quotes.

DEEPER PRACTICE Ask students to choose one of the details that they wanted to write about the animal they were researching. Have them focus on that one paragraph and include details, definitions, and quotations, if possible.

ENGLISH LANGUAGE LEARNERS

If . . . students have trouble including a definition in a text,

then . . . provide examples of words defined within a sentence. Have students read the sentence with the definition. Then have students place their finger over the definition and read the sentence without it. Discuss with students how the writer defined the word within the sentence and how the definition helps the reader. Model how a definition can be set off with commas. Then ask students to repeat the activity on their own.

STRUGGLING WRITERS

If . . . students have trouble using the proper conventions when writing quotations,

then . . . show them several examples. Work with students to make a checklist of these things to remember when writing a quotation: opening quote mark, capital letter, exact quotation from source, comma or other punctuation, and closing quote mark. Have students refer to the list as they write a quotation for their sample paragraph.

Use Linking Words

What Students Should KNOW	What Students Will DO
• Determine when linking words, phrases, and clauses are needed. • Determine the appropriate linking words, phrases, and clauses to use.	• Link ideas within and across categories of information using words, phrases, and clauses (*in contrast, especially*).
• Identify precise language and domain-specific vocabulary in texts students read. • Know the meaning of domain-specific vocabulary.	• Use precise language and domain-specific vocabulary.

MODEL AND PRACTICE

Discuss with students the importance of good word choices, including domain-specific words and linking words to connect ideas. Give examples of informative/explanatory texts that use precise language and domain-specific words. Tell them that linking words, phrases, or clauses, such as *in contrast* or *especially,* can help to clarify and connect ideas. Those ideas might be within a topic category or across different topic categories.

MODEL When I write about different kinds of stars, it helps to connect ideas with good linking words. I might write about red giants and include areas where people might *especially* find these types of stars. Then I can point out the differences between red giants and blue giants by using the linking phrase *in contrast.* The linking words and phrases help me to describe domain-specific words in greater detail, or link to other ideas altogether.

PRACTICE Provide students with samples of writing that includes the linking words and phrases *in contrast* and *especially.* Ask students to talk in a group about how they might use each word or phrase in a sentence of their own.

DEEPER PRACTICE Invite students to write another paragraph about their animal topic. Tell them that this paragraph should use precise language, domain-specific words, and linking words or phrases to connect ideas. Encourage students to underline examples of each.

MONITOR AND SUPPORT

ENGLISH LANGUAGE LEARNERS

If . . . students have trouble understanding the meanings of the linking words or phrases,

then . . . have them fold two index cards so that they stand up like a tent. Have them write *in contrast* on the outside of one card and *especially* on the outside of the other. Have students look up in a dictionary or online the meaning of *in contrast* and *especially.* Then help them to write a sentence inside the fold that uses the linking word or phrase correctly.

STRUGGLING WRITERS

If . . . students are not sure when to use each linking word or phrase,

then . . . provide them with practice by writing a sample paragraph that uses both *in contrast* and *especially.* Before giving the paragraph to students, switch the placement of the two words and ask them to determine what is wrong with the paragraph as it is written. Have them correct the paragraph by placing the linking words correctly.

Write a Conclusion

What Students Should KNOW	What Students Will DO
• Understand the goal of a concluding statement or section for informative/explanatory writing. • Identify the components of a strong conclusion. • Identify and use concluding words and phrases.	• Provide a concluding statement or section related to the information or explanation.

MODEL AND PRACTICE

Begin a discussion with students about the importance of having a good concluding statement or section in their writing. Explain that the concluding statement or section of informative/explanatory writing summarizes, or restates, the topic and the most important ideas about the topic. It does not include any new information but will sometimes provide the reader with a clincher, which is a statement that gives the reader something to think about.

MODEL At the end of my text, I will try to write a strong concluding statement or section. I will restate some of the most important ideas about the text, but I really want to leave the reader with a clincher, or something to think about. After summarizing the main idea I can write, "There are likely many more things for scientists to learn about stars. We can only hope to find out some of these things in our lifetime." This does not introduce new information, but it does give the reader something to think about.

PRACTICE Provide students with several examples of informative/explanatory texts. Ask student pairs to look for a clincher in the conclusion. Then have them come up with an additional clincher that the author could have used to conclude the text.

DEEPER PRACTICE Ask each student to write a sample conclusion for their text about the animal topic. Have students trade papers with a partner, and then ask them to provide feedback on one another's conclusions, noting strengths and areas that might need improvement.

ENGLISH LANGUAGE LEARNERS

If . . . students have trouble summarizing their topic for their concluding section,

then . . . ask them to review the rest of their writing and underline the three main things they want the reader to remember about their text. Guide students to name one or more of these ideas in a single sentence about their topic.

STRUGGLING WRITERS

If . . . students have trouble stating a clincher that could be used in their conclusion,

then . . . remind students about the general observation they made in their introduction. Explain that their clincher could relate back to that observation, or it could be another general observation they can make about their animal topic.

Support for Extended Writing

Refer to this process when students are writing a longer passage that requires development, organization, revision, and editing to produce an informative/ explanatory text.

UNDERSTAND THE TASK Tell students to review their writing prompt or writing assignment carefully to be sure they understand what is being asked. Have them answer these questions: What am I asked to write about? What do I already understand about this topic? What kind of research is needed about this topic? Do I need to cite or reference other texts? Where can I find good research information? How should I organize my ideas and paragraphs? How can I restate the task in my own words? How many parts are there to this writing assignment? How will I answer each part of the assignment?

RESEARCH Provide students with guidance and support to research the details of their writing topic. Have them first check the classroom library for reference material, and then have them visit the school library or computer lab. Explain that their research should be directed and focused on only their writing task. Have them preview the books they find about their topic before they check them out of the library so that students are sure the books will help them complete their assignment. Model how to save pages to refer to later without damaging the books or reference material. Have students use sticky notes instead of folding down the corners of pages, and explain that they should never write in library books, magazines, or other reference materials.

TAKE NOTES Model for students how to use their research to take notes about their topic. Explain that they must write down the title of the book, author, and page number on which they found each fact or detail. Explain that they must research and take notes about all parts of their writing prompt. Remind them that direct quotes must be copied word for word from the source material and that facts and dates must be exact. However, students should summarize the information and not use the author's exact words when taking notes about their topic.

ORGANIZE INFORMATION Ask students to choose the best organization form for their writing topic. Suggest that they choose from the following: compare-and-contrast, cause-and-effect, sequence, description, or problem-and-solution formats. Show students each type of graphic organizer, and discuss which would be most useful for explaining their topic.

WRITE

Provide students with encouraging tips to guide them through their writing process. Some tips might include:

- Remind students that they are writing a draft that should concentrate on the facts and details of the topic. They should not worry about making everything perfect in a draft.

- Remind students that illustrations, headings, and graphics can help to clarify their topic for the reader.

- If students have difficulty beginning to write their first draft, encourage them to look at their notes and write one sentence. Then ask them where that sentence would best fit into the whole text. Encourage them to take it one sentence at a time.

- Remind students that they should not provide their own opinion about the topic.

REVISE AND EDIT

Guide students through the revising and editing process. Work with students to develop writing checklists for details they might wish to address in their revision. Then work with students to develop a peer review checklist to help them review a partner's work to further strengthen their partner's writing and to help them think about their own writing. You may use the checklists on the following pages and add to them to include details specific to the assignment.

PUBLISH

Provide students with support in presenting their final version. You may wish to provide students with enough time to add illustrations, graphs, or tables to their final version and to bind the text and graphics into a booklet. Provide students with an area in the classroom where they can read each other's work.

ACCELERATED WRITERS

If . . . students have difficulty deciding how to focus their topic,

then . . . ask them to create a list of possible ways they can address the writing assignment with the topic they have been assigned. Then have them narrow their list to two of their favorite ideas. Ask them to make a list of pros and cons about each topic focus until they decide on the one that they think will best meet the assignment requirement and be most interesting to them to research and write about.

Writer's Checklist

Name _____

Title _____

❏ Did I include an effective introduction that presents the topic?

❏ Did I make a general observation in the introduction?

❏ Are my paragraphs organized clearly and in a logical way?

❏ Did I group related information?

❏ Did I use illustrations, headings, or other graphics to help make the topic clearer?

❏ Did I include definitions when necessary?

❏ Did I develop the topic with facts and details?

❏ Did I use concrete details, examples, or quotations?

❏ Did I cite or reference other texts as needed?

❏ Did I use linking words, phrases, or clauses to connect ideas?

❏ Is my concluding section clear and engaging?

❏ Did I include a clincher that creates an impression on the reader?

❏ Did I address all parts of the prompt or writing assignment?

❏ Did I review my work for correct capitalization, punctuation, and spelling?

❏ _____

❏ _____

Peer Review Checklist

Name _____

Writer's Name _____

Title _____

❏ Does the introduction describe what the text will be about?

❏ Does the introduction make a general observation about the topic?

❏ Is the writing clearly organized into paragraphs?

❏ Do illustrations, graphics, or multimedia help make the topic easier to understand?

❏ Does the writing include definitions, facts, and details?

❏ Does the writing include precise language and domain-specific vocabulary?

❏ Did the writer cite or reference other texts as needed?

❏ Does the writing have linking words, phrases, or clauses to connect ideas?

❏ Does the writing have a strong conclusion?

❏ Are all parts of the prompt or assignment addressed clearly in the writing?

❏ _____

❏ _____

❏ _____

❏ _____

❏ _____

❏ _____

Unlock Narrative Writing

Ask students to name a narrative text they have read as part of their reading assignments throughout the year. Remind them that it is an example of narrative writing because the writer tells about a real or imagined experience or event. Allow students to discuss and identify descriptive details they remember from the story and to recall the sequence of events.

Explain to students that the word *narrative* comes from the word *narrator*. Remind students that a narrator of a story is the person telling the story. Explain that the narrator may be a character in the story, or it may be an unseen voice or character who is describing the events. Ask students to work in small groups to come up with a list of examples of narrative stories they have read. Remind them that narratives can be set in the past, present, or future. As students list examples of narratives, ask them to tell whether the narrator is someone in the story or an unseen voice and where and when the story is set. Remind students that a narrative should tell a story. Differentiate narratives from other kinds of writing in which the writer's purpose is to give an opinion about a topic or to inform the reader about a topic. After students have successfully listed their own examples of narratives, present them with a mix of book genres, and ask them to identify the narratives.

UNDERSTAND TASK AND TONE

Show students examples of narrative writing prompts or assignments. Tell them that usually they will be provided with the narrative topic they will write about. Remind them that before they begin writing, they must carefully read the assignment and understand all of its parts. Remind students that they must understand the purpose of their writing and also who their audience is.

REFOCUS ON THE WRITING TYPE

Throughout the year as students read or are asked to write narrative texts, remind them of the key features of this text type. Narrative writing

- tells about a real or imagined experience or event.
- gives descriptive details about events or characters.
- includes a logical sequence of events.
- describes characters and events that the narrator may or may not be part of.
- may include dialogue to help tell a story or make it more interesting.

Establish a Situation

What Students Should KNOW	What Students Will DO
• Identify elements of setting and plot in narrative texts students read. • Determine and use the elements of setting and plot to establish a situation when writing a narrative.	• Orient the reader by establishing a situation.

MODEL AND PRACTICE

Explain that the first part of a narrative situates the reader into the story by establishing the general situation in which the story takes place. Explain that setting up the situation means establishing the setting and introducing the beginning of the plot. At the beginning of a narrative, the time and place the story happens should be established, as well as the setup, or exposition, of the story.

MODEL When I write a narrative, I must spend some time at the beginning thinking about the situation—I set up the time and place, as well as the start of the plot. I was asked to write a story about a day in the life of an animal. I will write about a stray cat that roams around a neighborhood. The setting will be the present time in an urban neighborhood. I will introduce details that show this in the beginning of the story. This will help the reader understand the situation and get involved right away.

PRACTICE Provide students with an example of a narrative text. Ask pairs of students to read the first two paragraphs and identify the situation, including the time and place the story occurs and any details they can gather so far about the plot, or story.

DEEPER PRACTICE Have students work individually to consider what they might write in a narrative about the day in the life of an animal. Have them list the details they would include to set up the situation, including the setting and the beginning of the story's plot. Invite students to use a graphic organizer or to write their ideas in a bulleted list.

ENGLISH LANGUAGE LEARNERS

If . . . students have trouble identifying the time and place of a story,

then . . . display a picture book and have students look at the photos for clues about the time and place of the story. Ask: *Where* does the story happen? *When* does the story happen? Invite students to respond using a sentence frame. For example: The story happens ___.

STRUGGLING WRITERS

If . . . students have trouble thinking of an idea to write about,

then . . . ask them to work with a partner and make a three-column chart. In the first column, they should brainstorm a list of animals. In the second column, they should brainstorm a list of places in which the story could take place. In the third column, they should brainstorm a list of times the story could take place. Then have each partner choose one item from each column to incorporate into his or her narrative.

Introduce Characters

What Students Should KNOW	What Students Will DO
• Identify the narrator and characters in texts students read. • Understand how writing to introduce the narrator and characters is helpful for the reader. • Identify ways that characters can help establish a situation.	• Orient the reader by introducing a narrator and/ or characters.

Begin a discussion about the narrator and characters in a story. Show students an example of a narrative they have read as a class. Ask them to name the characters in the story. Decide whether one of those characters was also the narrator of the story. Explain the role of the narrator as the storyteller. Tell students that if the narrator is also the main character of the story, it is written in first-person narration. A story with a narrator that is not a character in the story is written in third-person narration.

MODEL Part of getting ready to write a narrative is to decide who the narrator and characters are. If I write about a cat that roams a neighborhood, I must know who the narrator is. Should I make the narrator the cat? The cat is also the main character. This would be first-person narration. The cat would refer to herself as *I* or *me.* Or, should I make the narrator someone else who is not a character in the story? These are decisions that I should make before I start writing. I think I'll write the story as if the cat is telling the story. Some characters in the story will be another cat, a squirrel, and a rabbit.

PRACTICE Provide students with three examples of narrative writing. Invite small groups of students to examine the narratives to identify who the characters are and whether the narrator is one of the characters of the story. Ask students to identify the narrator of each story as a first-person or a third-person narrator.

DEEPER PRACTICE Ask students to work individually to list the characters and type of narration they would like to include in their own story idea about a day in the life of an animal. Then have students verbally describe their ideas to a partner.

ENGLISH LANGUAGE LEARNERS

If . . . students have trouble differentiating a character from a narrator,

then . . . read them a short story from the classroom library that is written in first-person narration. Have students list the characters in the story on paper. Say: Circle the name of the character who tells the story. Help students understand that the character they circled is also the narrator.

STRUGGLING WRITERS

If . . . students have difficulty differentiating first-person from third-person narration,

then . . . ask students to fold a piece of paper in half and label the left half *first-person* and the right half *third-person.* Provide students with examples of narratives that they can sort into each of the categories. Ask them to write the title of each story on the correct side of the paper. Then discuss with students why they sorted the narratives the way they did. Correct any misplaced narratives, and explain why they were misplaced.

Use Transitional Words and Phrases

What Students Should KNOW	What Students Will DO
• Retell events in the correct sequence from texts students read and describe how the events unfold naturally. • Determine how to organize a sequence of events.	• Organize an event sequence that unfolds naturally.
• Identify how transitional words and phrases help readers understand the sequence of events.	• Use a variety of transitional words and phrases to manage the sequence of events.

MODEL AND PRACTICE

Explain to students the importance of retelling events in the correct sequence so that they unfold naturally for the reader. Tell them that using transitional words and phrases can help make sequences of events clear and easier for the reader to follow.

MODEL Now that I know my story's setting and who the narrator and characters will be, it's time to organize events in a natural flow. My cat narrator and character, Nacho, will *first* wake up in her cat bed and *then* eat some breakfast. *Next* she will go outside and talk to her squirrel friend about a new cat in the neighborhood. *After that,* a rabbit will warn them that a storm is coming. *Finally,* the new cat will chase Nacho up a tree until the storm passes. I use transitional words and phrases to link all of these ideas together.

PRACTICE Provide students with a narrative that is new to them, or one they have already reviewed. Ask them to work in pairs to point out the events in the story and describe what is logical or sensible about the way the writer arranged the sequence of events. Have them list all transitional words or phrases on a separate sheet of paper.

DEEPER PRACTICE Ask students to write a paragraph about a day in the life of an animal. They should make sure events are arranged in a logical order and that they have used a variety of transitional words and phrases to connect the events in a logical sequence.

ENGLISH LANGUAGE LEARNERS

If . . . students have trouble using the correct transitions between events,

then . . . ask them to brainstorm a list of transition words or phrases. Remind students about the meaning of colors on traffic lights. Ask them to use a green pencil or marker to place a star next to the words or phrases that indicate a beginning event, such as *first* or *initially.* Have them place a yellow star next to the words or phrases that can be used in the middle of a sequence, such as *next* or *then.* Then have them place a red star next to the words or phrases that are used at the end of a sequence, such as *finally* or *in the end.*

STRUGGLING WRITERS

If . . . students have trouble expressing how they want to organize their story,

then . . . have them list each event they want to write about on separate index cards. Then have them put the index cards together in order to show the logical order of their events. Tell them that they can even remove events or add new ones to the lineup of cards.

MONITOR AND SUPPORT

Use Dialogue and Details

What Students Should KNOW	What Students Will DO
• Identify dialogue, descriptions, and pacing in texts students read. • Identify ways pacing can develop and move a narrative. • Use dialogue to develop experiences, events, and character responses to situations in a narrative.	• Use narrative techniques such as dialogue, description, and pacing to develop experiences and events or show the responses of characters to situations.
• Identify concrete words and phrases and sensory details in texts students read. • Improve sentences to make the descriptions more precise.	• Use concrete words and phrases and sensory details to convey experiences and events precisely.

MODEL AND PRACTICE

Discuss with students the importance of dialogue, descriptions, and sensory details to make narrative writing interesting to the reader. Review the senses and how each sense can be used to describe details. Explain that the details keep the reader's interest and convey experiences and events precisely.

MODEL My narrative would be boring if I wrote it in the same way I described my sequence of events. I need to add dialogue, descriptions, and sensory details to help make the story come alive for the reader and pace the story to develop it. The dialogue between Nacho and the squirrel is important and can give the story a flavor and develop the characters and experiences in the story.

PRACTICE Provide pairs of students with copies of a narrative that they can mark up, and have them find examples of narrative techniques, such as dialogue, descriptions, and sensory details. Ask them to underline and label each example.

DEEPER PRACTICE Have small groups take one event from the story you have described and write a paragraph using sensory details, dialogue, and descriptions. Challenge the groups to help the situation come to life for the readers.

ENGLISH LANGUAGE LEARNERS

If . . . students have trouble using details,

then . . . have students work with a partner. One partner looks at a simple picture and then describes it, while the other partner draws what is being described. Encourage students to use as many descriptive details as possible to assist the artist. Then have partners compare the drawing to the picture and discuss what details helped the artist and what additional details could have helped.

STRUGGLING WRITERS

If . . . students have trouble coming up with possible dialogue for characters,

then . . . ask students to fold a sheet of paper in half twice to make four boxes. Have them write four possible things that the cat and squirrel in the story might talk about. Invite groups of students to share or act out their ideas when they are finished so that they hear additional ideas from other students. Review how to punctuate dialogues using examples from familiar texts.

Write a Conclusion

What Students Should KNOW	What Students Will DO
• Explain how the conclusion follows from the narrated experiences or events in texts students read. • Identify the components of a strong conclusion.	• Provide a conclusion that follows from the narrated experiences or events.

MODEL AND PRACTICE

Explain to students that narrative writing should have a clear sense of closure, or a strong conclusion. Tell students that a conclusion should be straightforward and to the point, and it should summarize any moral, lesson, or theme that the story may have. Explain that a conclusion to a narrative should signal a definite end to the story, solve any story conflicts, and be memorable for the reader.

MODEL At the end of my story about Nacho, I'll have to solve her conflict of being chased up a tree and stuck there during a storm. I will have the squirrel and rabbit work to scare the other cat away so that Nacho can come down from the tree. My story can teach a lesson about the importance of friendship. I may even make a statement about Nacho's long day and how it ended well because of her neighborhood friends.

PRACTICE Provide students with several examples of short narrative texts. Ask students to read each conclusion and analyze them in small groups. Have students summarize how each narrative ends and tell which have a moral, or lesson, for the reader to learn. Ask them to identify what is strong about each of the conclusions.

DEEPER PRACTICE Ask students to write a concluding paragraph for their own narrative about a day in the life of an animal. Have them trade papers with a partner, and have the pairs provide each other with feedback.

ENGLISH LANGUAGE LEARNERS

If . . . students have trouble crafting a conclusion,

then . . . ask students to act out their story with a partner or small group. Have the group retell what happened at the end of the story. Write down some of the key words that are retold. Help students form these into a strong conclusion.

STRUGGLING WRITERS

If . . . students write a conclusion that does not provide closure for the narrative,

then . . . invite them to orally describe what they want the reader to understand about the story when he or she is finished reading it. Ask students if there is a moral or lesson that the reader should understand. Then provide feedback about how their conclusion can be revised to include this information.

Support for Extended Writing

Refer to this process when students are writing a longer passage that requires development, organization, revising, and editing to produce a narrative text.

UNDERSTAND THE TASK Tell students to review their writing prompt or writing assignment carefully to be sure they understand what is being asked. Have them answer these questions: What does the assignment ask me to do? What should my narrative be about? In what order should I write about the events or experiences? Am I the narrator, is one of the characters in this narrative the narrator, or both? Have I referenced any texts that are part of the assignment? How can I restate the task in my own words? How many parts are there to this writing assignment? Is there a lesson or moral I want the reader to learn?

BRAINSTORM Provide students with guidance and support to brainstorm the details of their narrative. Explain that brainstorming helps writers think of as many ideas as possible, even after they think they have found the idea they want to write about. Encourage students to brainstorm not only the topic but also the events that they will write about in their narrative. Then have students review their lists carefully and choose the strongest idea and events that would make the best narrative.

TAKE NOTES Explain to students the importance of taking notes about the narrator, characters, and sequence of events in their story. Model for them how to write down details about the story, including the story's setting and characters. Encourage them to refer back to the notes regularly as they write. Suggest that they use their notes as a checklist to see that they have covered everything they wanted to or written the story the way they intended to during their planning stage.

ORGANIZE INFORMATION Use a story map graphic organizer. Explain that the organizer has a box, or section, for each of the parts of their story—the beginning, middle, and end. Show students how to use the boxes to record the events of the plot. Explain that each box on the organizer can represent a paragraph or group of paragraphs in the narrative.

WRITE

Provide students with encouraging tips to guide them through their writing process. Some tips might include:

- Remind students that they are writing a draft, which is the time to concentrate on the organization and plot of their story, not the small details that make the writing perfect.
- Explain to students that planning ahead of time will make their actual writing task easier.
- Encourage students to think about writing one sentence at a time and to remember that they can move or change things later.
- Encourage students to think of details that can be added to help the reader imagine how things in the story look, smell, sound, taste, or feel.
- Ask students to think about what each character is like and what he or she might say or do in the story.
- Remind students to concentrate on an effective introduction and conclusion.

REVISE AND EDIT

Guide students through the revising and editing process. Work with students to develop writing checklists for details they might wish to address in their revision. Then work with students to develop a peer review checklist to help them review one another's work and further strengthen their writing. You may use the checklists on the following pages and add to them to include details specific to the assignment.

PUBLISH

Provide students with support in presenting their final version. You may want to give students time to illustrate their final work and perhaps share their stories with students in a younger grade. Set aside time for them to enter their stories into the computer, scan their illustrations to go with it, and upload them to a class or school website or blog.

ACCELERATED WRITERS

If . . . students have difficulty judging what needs improvement in their final draft,

then . . . provide them with additional examples of narratives to review. Ask them to compare their narratives to the examples to decide how they are alike and different. Ask students to write a reader's review of the sample narrative and explain what the writer could have done to improve his or her work. Then explain that even professional writers can stand to improve their work. Have students review their own work again to list some things that they might be able to improve in their narrative.

Writer's Checklist

Name _____

Title _____

❏ Did I include an effective introduction that presents the topic?

❏ Are my paragraphs organized clearly and correctly?

❏ Did I choose a real or imagined experience to write about?

❏ Did I establish the setting and situation of the narrative?

❏ Did I introduce the narrator and/or characters?

❏ Did I organize the events in a sequence that unfolds naturally?

❏ Did I develop the story with dialogue that shows thoughts and reactions?

❏ Did I develop the story with clear descriptions and sensory details?

❏ Did I use linking words and phrases to show a sequence of events?

❏ Did I provide a strong conclusion that describes a moral or gives a sense of closure?

❏ Did I address all parts of the prompt or writing assignment?

❏ Did I reference or cite any texts called for in the assignment?

❏ Did I review my work for correct capitalization, punctuation, and spelling?

❏ _____

❏ _____

❏ _____

Peer Review Checklist

Name _____

Writer's Name _____

Title _____

❑ Does the introduction describe what the narrative will be about?

❑ Does the introduction identify the narrator and some of the characters?

❑ Is the writing clearly organized into paragraphs?

❑ Is the setting described clearly?

❑ Does the writing organize events in a sequence that unfolds naturally?

❑ Does the writing include dialogue that describes characters' reactions?

❑ Does the writing include descriptions and sensory details?

❑ Does the writing have linking words that show a sequence of events?

❑ Does the writing have a strong conclusion that gives the reader a sense of closure?

❑ Are all parts of the prompt or assignment addressed clearly in the writing?

❑ _____

❑ _____

❑ _____

❑ _____

❑ _____

❑ _____

Routines and Activities

Part 3 Routines and Activities

Listening and Speaking Routines

Language Routines and Activities:
Vocabulary and Conventions

Noun Activities

Pronoun Activities

Verb Activities

Articles and Adjective Activities

Adverb Activities

Preposition and Conjunction Activities

Sentence Activities

Punctuation Activities

Word Study Activities

Vocabulary Activities and Games

Quick Write and Share

Use this routine to activate and build on students' prior knowledge before reading a selection.

PROCEDURE

1. Before reading a selection, pose a question to activate students' prior knowledge about a topic they will read about. Give students a few minutes to immediately jot down their ideas. Because this is a quick write, tell students that they do not need to worry about grammar or spelling.

2. Review class rules for discussion. Remind students of the proper methods for sharing ideas such as who goes first, what to do while someone else is speaking, and when it is okay to take your turn.

3. As a class, or in small groups or pairs, ask students to share their ideas with others in their group. Encourage students to make comments that contribute to the discussion and elaborate on the remarks of others. Again, remind them that each person should speak without interruption so that everyone has a chance to share. Walk around to assess the prior knowledge of each group and to clarify questions.

TEACHING TIPS

When creating questions for step one, make sure they are text specific and that answering them will help students unlock ideas in the text. For example, before starting a book on jungle frogs and their habitats, it would be appropriate to ask questions such as: *How might a jungle frog look or act differently than a frog in your backyard?* or *Why might a frog live in the jungle?* These questions are appropriate because they are specific to the text and ask students to recall information that will help them when reading. An inappropriate question would be *Do you like frogs?* because it is not text specific and responding to the question will not help students unlock ideas in the text.

- Additionally, it may benefit students to read a short excerpt or page relating to a key idea or topic in the text.

- This will help students gain confidence going into the text because it will ensure that everyone will have some foundational understanding of the text.

EXTEND

- Have one student from each group share ideas from their discussion with the class. Use student responses to create a class list or web of prior knowledge, and display the list/ web permanently in the classroom. This will act as a continual reminder to students of what they already know. As students acquire new knowledge, the information can be added to the list/web so they can see how their understanding is growing.

- After reading an excerpt relating to a key idea or topic of the text, have pairs discuss and write one or two questions about what they hope to learn as they read the rest of the text. Students may revisit their questions after reading to verify whether their initial questions have been answered. Identify questions that may need to be researched further, and help students locate sources to use.

Ask and Answer Questions

PURPOSE

Use this routine to build on students' use of asking and answering questions to better understand a text.

PROCEDURE

1. Use text that the class is currently reading. As a warm-up activity, review *how* and *wh-* questions, such as *Where does the princess live with the frogs? How do tarantulas shed their skin? What is a tall tale? Where are earthquakes most likely to happen? Why do glaciers melt?* Go around the class and have students take turns asking questions orally. (If students want to answer questions, give them the chance to do so.)

2. Choose a short passage, paragraph, or chapter from the text the class is currently reading. If the passage is short, you may want to read the text aloud as students follow along.

3. Model specific examples of questions relating to the selection, such as *Why are roots different shapes? Where do you find long, skinny roots? Which kind of root lives in water?* Invite students to think of their own questions to ask about the text.

4. If the class has completed reading the entire selection, you can have students ask questions based on the text as a whole, including questions about main idea, themes, or character development.

5. Hand out copies of the worksheet on the following page and direct students to the selection or passage. Explain that students should refer directly to the selection to ask and answer questions about it.

TEACHING TIPS

- Encourage students to ask themselves questions as they read on their own. For fiction, students might ask: *What is the problem in the story? What is the main character like? What is happening in the story now?* For informational text, students might ask: *What interesting facts did I learn so far? What else do I want to learn?* Answering these questions will help students understand and remember what they read.

- Students may ask questions to compare what they have just read to another text and look for similarities and differences between them. For example, in fiction, students may compare and contrast characters, events, or settings. For informational text, ask students to explain how authors use reasons and evidence to support their claims or opinions.

EXTEND

After completing Step B on the worksheet, ask students to share their most challenging questions with the class and have other students try to answer them. This will allow students to understand the text more fully and share what they already know. Encourage students to discuss ideas for further reading or research to find the answers to their questions and build overall knowledge about the topic.

Ask and Answer Questions

A. Read the text. On the first lines below, write three questions you think of as you read the text. The questions may be about details in the text, or they may be about ideas the text brings up.

1. Question: _____

_____

_____

_____

2. Question: _____

_____

_____

_____

3. Question: _____

_____

_____

_____

B. Exchange papers with a classmate. Read your classmate's questions in Step A. Write your responses to the questions below.

1. Response: _____

_____

_____

_____

2. Response: _____

_____

_____

_____

3. Response: _____

_____

_____

_____

Three-Column Chart

PURPOSE

Use this routine with the Three-Column Chart Graphic Organizer. This is a multipurpose organizer that works well for exploring and organizing ideas for three concepts, words, or ideas. It works well with many selections and can aid students in exploring or classifying ideas, story elements, genres, or vocabulary features. It can also help students recognize comparisons and contrasts, or chart ideas within and across texts.

PROCEDURE

1. Display the graphic organizer. Choose three headings and write them on the chart, such as three different vocabulary words.
2. Ask students for details or examples for each heading and record them on the chart. Details or examples should directly reference the text.
3. Point out that this chart helps students organize information and explore ideas in a new or different way.
4. Ask students for any comparisons, contrasts, or patterns they notice in the chart.

TEACHING TIPS

- Once you have explained how to use the organizer, students can complete the organizer independently, in pairs, or in small groups.
- Students can list facts, details, and ideas in their charts.
- Students can use the three-column chart to explore story characteristics or characteristics of genre.
- Students can use the chart to organize ideas they generate during brainstorming.
- Students can use the chart to organize synonyms, antonyms, and multiple-meaning words. Create a class chart to model using the chart for vocabulary study.

EXTEND

- Students can use the organizer to record key events or happenings that follow the *before*, *during*, and *after* format in a selection.
- Students can use the organizer to trace patterns among texts and compare a variety of selection elements, such as characters within or across selections, structures across selections, or themes across selections.
- After completing the class activity, have students use the chart in pairs or individually with another selection. Then, have them share their charts with the rest of the class.

Three-Column Chart

Venn Diagram

PURPOSE

Use this routine with the Venn Diagram Graphic Organizer. This graphic organizer works well in any situation that lends itself to comparing and contrasting. Students can use this organizer to record similarities and differences between places, ideas, characters, or other elements of fiction or nonfiction.

PROCEDURE

1. Start by comparing and contrasting something simple, such as plants and animals. Write the names of the two subjects you are comparing over the circles of the Venn diagram.

2. Point to where the circles overlap. Let students know that in this section you'll write similarities, or how the two things are alike. Ask how the two subjects are alike. Record students' responses. (Both plants and animals need water to survive.)

3. Point to an individual circle and let students know that, in this section, they will write details that describe only what is labeled at the top of the circle. Then ask how the two subjects are different and record students' responses. (Animals need shelter. Plants need soil.)

TEACHING TIPS

- Ask questions that lead students to share details for the diagram, such as: Where does the narrative take place? Find details from the text.

- Display sentence frames to guide students. Examples: These two things are alike because ___. These two things are different because ___.

- List words that signal comparing and contrasting, such as *alike*, *different*, and *but*. Students can point out those words and supporting examples in the text.

EXTEND

- Have students create Venn diagrams to compare characters in fictional texts.

- Have students use Venn diagrams to compare topics in informational texts, such as two types of government or two environments.

- Have students use Venn diagrams to compare themes and ideas between a fictional and nonfictional selection on the same topic. Have them cite explicitly from the texts to fill out their diagrams. Ask students: What was the author's message? Why was it told this way?

Venn Diagram

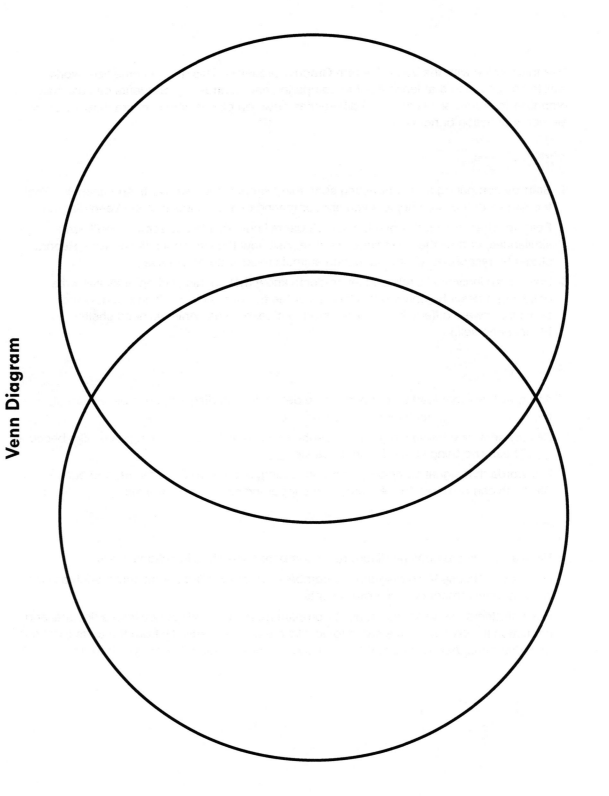

Web Graphic Organizer

PURPOSE

Use this routine with the Web Graphic Organizer to help students activate their background knowledge as they brainstorm related ideas, recognize concept relationships, or organize information. This organizer can also be used to highlight a central concept and connect it to related words, ideas, or details.

PROCEDURE

1. Display the graphic organizer. Write a central idea or topic in the middle of the web.
2. Ask students for ideas that are related to the central idea. Record those ideas in the circles attached to the middle circle.
3. You can add ideas related to the "subideas" in additional ovals.

TEACHING TIPS

- Once you have modeled how to use the organizer, have students complete the organizer independently, in pairs, or in small groups.
- Ask students to explain how the ideas on the web are related to the central ideas. Display sentence frames to help students talk about the web such as: The main idea is ___. One related idea is ___.
- Use this web to help students record and organize information such as main ideas and details, theme or topic, characters and their traits, and vocabulary words with their synonyms.
- As an aid to understanding what they've read, students may use this graphic organizer to record ideas and concepts across texts. For example, they may take notes about one topic from two separate texts. Recording main points and related details will help students classify ideas and examine the relationships between texts. Ask: What are the main ideas in these texts? What details support the main ideas? What kind of information does one text cover that the other does not?

EXTEND

- Have students use the web to record background knowledge about a topic. Use the webs to assess gaps in understanding as you plan instruction.
- After students create a web, have them write a paragraph telling how the concepts are connected.

Web

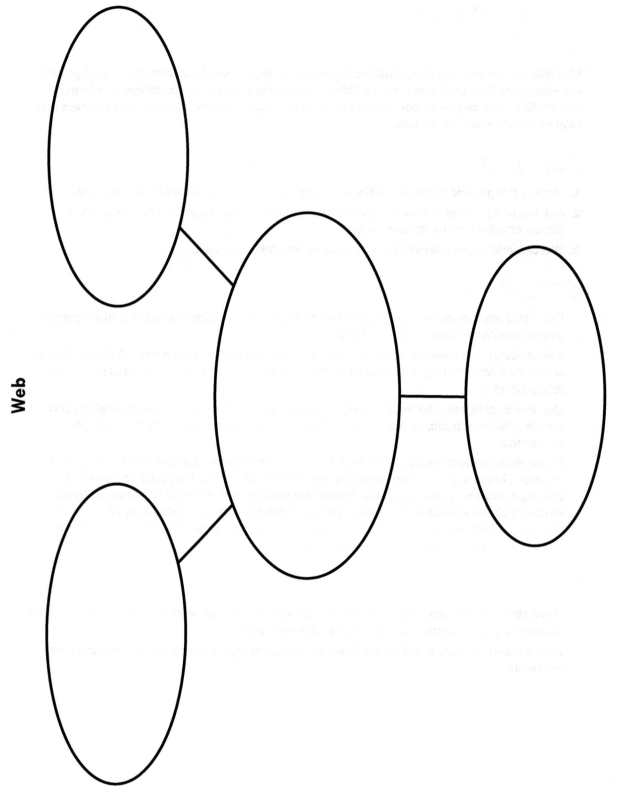

Story Map

PURPOSE

Use this routine with the Story Map Graphic Organizer. This organizer works well with any text that has a clear sequence of events. This graphic organizer can aid students in recording the sequence of events in a text.

PROCEDURE

1. Display the organizer. Write the title of the text on the graphic organizer.

2. As you read, record information about characters on the graphic organizer.

3. Read the text. Ask students where and when the story takes place. Record those details in the Setting section.

4. As you read, pause to record information about the sequence of events.

TEACHING TIPS

- Model talking about characters and setting: _____ is a person/animal in this story. This story takes place (in the future, in the past, today).

- Have students look for clue words for sequence. Have them make a list of clue words to display for reference.

- Students will likely need additional lines in some sections. Have them modify the organizer depending on the story.

EXTEND

- After completing this activity as a class exercise, have students use the graphic organizer in pairs, small groups, or independently.

- Students can draw events in the organizer and label those events.

- Help students think of words to describe characters or events. Make a list and have students add to it.

- Ask students to work in small groups to discuss the problem facing a main character and how he or she arrives at a solution. Ask students to think about character development. **Ask:** How does the character change as a result of overcoming the conflict or finding a solution to his or her problem? Does he or she learn a lesson? How do his or her actions contribute to the sequence of events?

Story Map

Title

_____

Characters

Who is in the story?

_____

Setting

Where does the story happen?

_____

When does the story happen?

_____

Events

What happens in the story?

_____

_____

_____

_____

_____

_____

_____

Story Prediction Chart

PURPOSE

Use this routine with the Story Prediction Chart Graphic Organizer. Students preview the text's title and illustrations and then predict what might happen in the text. This graphic organizer works well with any text in which the title and/or pictures suggest predictions about the events in a story. Consider using it for content-area texts as well.

PROCEDURE

1. Display the graphic organizer.

2. Preview the text with students. Read the title and lead a picture walk. Ask students what they think will happen in the text. Remind them to use what they know about the topic. Record their predictions in the graphic organizer in the first column.

3. Ask students how they figured out what would happen. Ask: Have you read a story like this before? What evidence from the pictures helped you figure out what would happen next? Record the clues they used in the graphic organizer in the second column.

4. After reading, look back at the predictions. Write what actually happened in the third column. Ask students if their predictions were different from what happened. Ask: Why do you think the story turned out differently than you predicted? Why might making predictions be a useful skill?

TEACHING TIPS

- Focus on clues in illustrations. What details in the illustrations help students make predictions?

- Provide sentence frames for predicting, such as: I think ___ will happen. I think this will happen because ___.

- Have students frame their predictions as answers to questions, such as *What will this character do or say next? What might happen next after this particular event? How might this story end?*

EXTEND

- After completing this activity as a class exercise, have students use the graphic organizer in pairs, small groups, or independently.

- Use the graphic organizer with content-area texts. Focus on the content, giving students a sentence frame to use: I think I will learn about ___ because ___.

Story Prediction Chart

Title

What might happen?	What clues do I have?	What did happen?

Story Comparison

PURPOSE

Use this routine with the Story Comparison Graphic Organizer. Students can use this graphic organizer to record how two texts are similar and different. This organizer works well with texts that have something in common. It is a great tool for comparing texts by the same author, about the same topic, or texts in the same genre.

PROCEDURE

1. Display the graphic organizer for students.

2. Choose two stories to compare. Write their titles on the graphic organizer.

3. Ask questions to elicit characters, setting, and plot events.

4. Record details on the graphic organizer.

TEACHING TIPS

- After you model how to use the graphic organizer, students can work on their graphic organizer with partners or in small groups. Guide students away from simply filling in the chart with names of characters or locations. Instead prompt them to think critically about what they are reading by asking questions, such as *In what way did these authors cover the same topic similarly? What choices did one make that the other did not?*

- Provide sentence frames for comparison and model how to use them, such as: The characters in this story are ___, but the characters in that story are ___.

- Invite students to use the graphic organizer to retell stories. Ask students to think about central themes, or authors' messages, in the texts being compared.

EXTEND

- Students can use this graphic organizer to compare a fictional story and a nonfiction text about the same topic.

- Have students use one half of the graphic organizer to plan the writing of their own stories. Ask volunteers to share their original stories with the rest of the class. You may wish to display the graphic organizer and lead a discussion in filling it out after two stories have been shared.

Story Comparison

Title A _____

_____

Title B _____

_____

Characters	Characters
Who is in the story?	**Who** is in the story?

Setting	Setting
Where and **when** does it happen?	**Where** and **when** does it happen?

Events	Events
What happens in the story?	**What** happens in the story?

KWLH Chart

PURPOSE

Use this routine with the KWLH Chart Graphic Organizer. Students can use what they know to explore prior knowledge about a text, set purposes for reading, and record what they learn and how they learned it as they read. This graphic organizer works well with expository texts.

PROCEDURE

1. Display the graphic organizer for students. Have volunteers read aloud the questions at the top of each column.

2. Before students begin reading, ask them for ideas to answer the first two questions of the KWLH chart: What Do I **K**now? What Do I **W**ant to Learn? Model recording responses on the graphic organizer. Explain that answering these questions sets objectives for reading and helps students focus on what they read.

3. Read the text together or have students read on their own.

4. After reading the text, model recording students' responses to the questions in the *L* and *H* columns: What Did I **L**earn? **H**ow Did I Learn It?

TEACHING TIPS

- After your modeling, students can complete the graphic organizer in pairs or small groups. Have students take turns reading parts of the chart aloud with their partner or within the group.

- Modify the graphic organizer, if necessary, by changing the headings into sentence frames: I know _____. I want to know _____. I learned _____. I learned it by _____.

EXTEND

- Use the graphic organizer as you read in various content areas, such as social studies and science. Post the organizers around the room. Students can add to them as they learn more about a topic over time.

- After reading, challenge students to identify information they wanted to learn that was not provided in the reading. Have them do research online or at the library to find that information.

- As an alternative, use the chart to catalog students' questions after presenting a scenario, such as *You have a recipe for making cookies, which yields 8. But you want to make enough for your whole class, so you want to increase the yield to 32. How would you go about making enough cookies?* Prompt students to fill out the columns. For example, under *W*, students may ask, *What is the plan? How can we ensure proper proportions of ingredients?* Under *L*, students may ask, *What about this process has been successful? What can be improved?*

GRAPHIC ORGANIZER

KWLH Chart

Topic _____

K now? What Do I	**W** ant to Learn? What Do I	**L** earn? What Did I	**H** ow Did I Learn It?

Main Idea and Details

PURPOSE

Use this routine with the Main Idea and Details Graphic Organizer. This graphic organizer works especially well with nonfiction selections that are organized around main ideas and details. Students recognize a main idea and distinguish between the main idea and the details. Use it with an entire selection, individual chapters, a section, or a paragraph in a selection.

PROCEDURE

1. Read the selection. Record the main idea in the top box. Define *main idea* as the most important idea.

2. Use a think aloud to model how to find a detail in the selection that supports, or tells more about, the main idea. For example, We found that the main idea of this paragraph is to tell why roots have different shapes. As I read, I will look for information that tells about different-shaped roots.

3. Have students supply additional details as you record them. Details should directly refer back to the text.

TEACHING TIPS

- Supply a sentence frame about main ideas, such as: The most important idea is ___.
  Supply a sentence frame about details, such as: One detail about this idea is ___.

- Model how to tell a supporting detail from a detail that is not a supporting detail. Let students know that some ideas are important to know and other ideas are interesting to know. Display part of a selection and model highlighting important ideas.

- Extend or add additional boxes if necessary to add more details.

EXTEND

- Have students use the organizer to record ideas for writing pieces of their own.

- As students become more independent, use the organizer in pairs or small groups to record important ideas and details from selections.

- Remind students that not every detail relates to the main idea. Also, not every main idea appears at the beginning of a sentence. Provide small groups with excerpts and ask them to record main ideas and details. Be sure they are able to discern which details to add that support the main idea.

Main Idea and Details

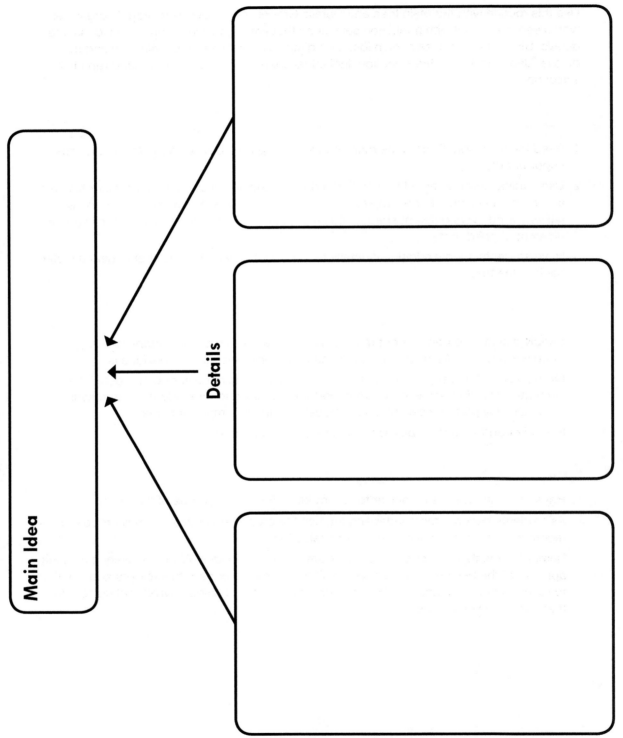

Main Idea

Details

Problem and Solution

PURPOSE

Use this routine with the Problem and Solution Graphic Organizer. This graphic organizer works well with any selection with clear problems and solutions. The organizer can aid students in identifying problems and solutions presented in fiction or nonfiction texts.

PROCEDURE

1. Ask students what they think a problem is, and record answers. Tell students that a problem is something that needs to be solved. Give an example of a problem from a selection.
2. Record it in the organizer in the Problem section.
3. Ask students what happens in the selection to fix the problem. Tell students that fixing a problem is the same as solving a problem.
4. Record their responses in the Solution section. Student responses should reference the text directly.

TEACHING TIPS

- Point out that not all solutions are "good." Sometimes the way a character solves a problem might result in an unhappy ending for the story. Lead a discussion that prompts students to think about how they might solve a problem better, and have them explain why their solution is better.

- Provide the following sentence frames to help students discuss problems and solutions: One problem in the text is ____. One way to solve it is ____.

- Explain that a text might have one main problem and also many smaller problems that get solved throughout the story. Point out examples of each of these types and have students record them on the organizer.

EXTEND

- Have students work individually or in pairs to brainstorm a problem in the school, classroom, or community. Tell them to write this problem in the first box and brainstorm solutions in the bottom section.

- After reading and identifying a selection's problems and solutions, have pairs review their graphic organizers and discuss alternative solutions to the problems in the text. How would they solve one of the problems differently? They may work together or independently to write a brief paragraph describing a different solution. In their paragraphs, they should explain why this choice is better than the one in the selection. Have volunteers share their ideas with the rest of the class.

Problem and Solution

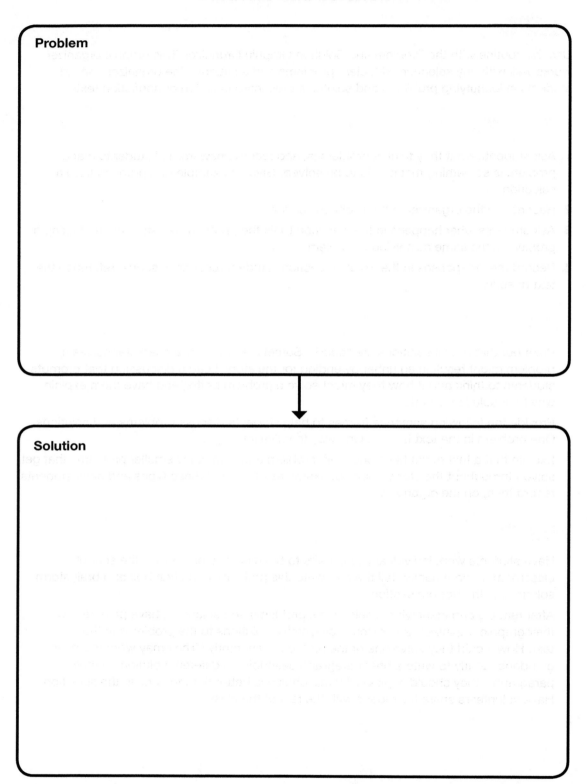

Problem

Solution

Cause and Effect

PURPOSE

Use this routine with the Cause and Effect Graphic Organizer. This graphic organizer works well with any fiction or nonfiction selection that has clear cause-and-effect relationships.

PROCEDURE

1. Discuss the meaning of the word *effect* with students. Explain that something that happens is an effect. Record an effect on the graphic organizer.
2. Then ask students: Why did it happen? Explain that the reason something happens is a cause. Record the cause on the graphic organizer.
3. Summarize: To find cause-and-effect relationships, let's look at one event that caused another event. For example, *I was late to school because I woke up late.* Ask students to identify the cause and effect in that situation. Prompt students to come up with more examples from the reading selection.

TEACHING TIPS

- It is usually easier to identify effects first, before the causes. Remind students to ask themselves, *What happened?* and *Why did it happen?* to identify causes and effects.
- List clue words that signal causes and effects, such as *because* and *so*. Remind students that not all causes and effects in selections have clue words.

EXTEND

- Students can write causes and effects from reading selections from science, math, or social studies classes. They could record, for example, causes of thunderstorms or events in history. Ask volunteers to share their work with the class.
- Once students are able to use this organizer, point out that, in some cases, there are many causes for one effect or many effects for one cause. Alter the organizer with students so they can use it with multiple causes and effects.
- If students need extra assistance, fill in either causes or effects before distributing the organizer.

Cause and Effect

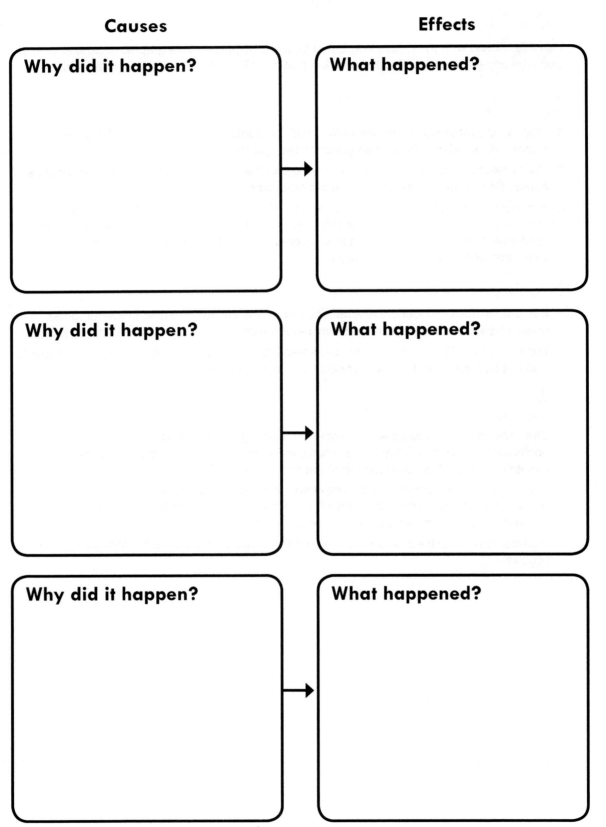

Causes

Effects

Why did it happen?

What happened?

Why did it happen?

What happened?

Why did it happen?

What happened?

Steps in a Process

Use this routine with the Steps in a Process Graphic Organizer. This organizer aids students in breaking down a process into simple steps or directions. This graphic organizer works well with any procedure that has relatively few steps. If students need more or fewer steps, help students redesign the organizer.

1. Read the text. It may be the whole selection or an individual chapter. Identify a process or procedure that takes place.
2. Display the graphic organizer. Write the title on the organizer, such as Solving the Case.
3. Ask students what the first step is. Record the first step in the organizer.
4. As a group, write the remaining steps in the organizer in order as students supply them.

- Once students can contribute to a group Steps in a Process Graphic Organizer, have them work in pairs or small groups to write the steps of a simple process, such as How to Make a Salad.

- Tell students to look for clue words such as *first*, *next*, and *later* to help them sequence the steps. Ask students to review their processes and check that each step is clear. They may ask themselves, *Is this process easy to follow? Which step might be broken down into two or three additional steps?*

- Students may illustrate the steps in the organizer and label them with words or phrases.

- Have students use the organizer to show steps in a recipe, a science project, or in another content area. Have volunteers share their work with the class and allow classmates to offer feedback on the procedures.

Steps in a Process

Process _____

```
┌─────────────────────────────────────────────┐
│ Step 1                                        │
│                                               │
│                                               │
│                                               │
└─────────────────────────────────────────────┘
                      │
                      ▼
┌─────────────────────────────────────────────┐
│ Step 2                                        │
│                                               │
│                                               │
│                                               │
└─────────────────────────────────────────────┘
                      │
                      ▼
┌─────────────────────────────────────────────┐
│ Step 3                                        │
│                                               │
│                                               │
│                                               │
└─────────────────────────────────────────────┘
```

Sequence of Events

Use this routine with the Sequence of Events Graphic Organizer. This graphic organizer works well with any fictional selection that has a clear series of events. It can help students understand the connection between the characters, setting, and events in the story. Use it with a selection or with individual chapters in a selection.

1. Display the organizer. Write the title of the selection or chapter on the organizer.
2. Read the text. Ask students where and when the story takes place. Record those details in the Setting section.
3. As you read, use a think aloud to model how to record information about the characters. *I noticed Drake talks about Nell. I wonder who Nell is and how Drake knows her. I will write her name in the left column under Characters. As I read, I will look for information about Nell and other characters I read about.*
4. Pause to record information about the sequence of events in the boxes under Character and Setting.

- Provide sentence frames for talking about characters and setting. Examples: ___ is a person/animal in this story. This story takes place in ___.
- Help students look for clue words for sequence. Make a list of clue words to display for students' reference, such as *first, next, then, finally.*
- Modify the organizer as needed to include more or fewer boxes or, for example, to focus on a single character and how each event affected that character.

- After completing this activity as a class exercise, have students use the chart in pairs, small groups, or independently with other selections.
- Help students think of words that describe the characters. Make a list and have students add to it as they read.
- After completing the chart, have students summarize, orally or in writing, information about the story from the graphic organizer.
- After reading a fictional selection, provide a list of its major events to small groups, leaving one event out. Have each group identify which event is missing. Ask students to discuss how the story changes if an event is missing.
- Have students write a short paragraph on a topic of their choice, or in response to a teacher-provided prompt. Ask them to list events in sequence. Remind them to use clue words that will signal first, next, and last.

Sequence of Events

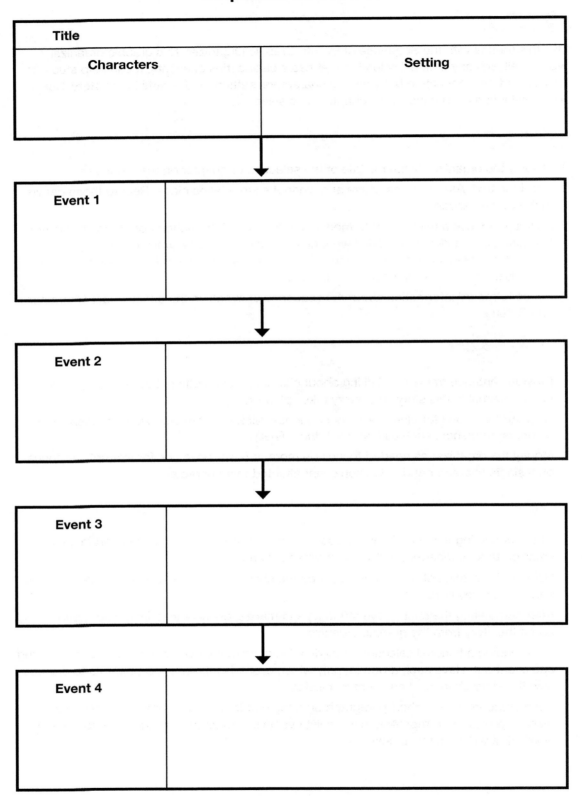

Title	
Characters	Setting

Event 1	

Event 2	

Event 3	

Event 4	

Time Line

Use this routine with the Time Line Graphic Organizer to organize events from fiction or nonfiction texts in sequential order. This organizer works well with any selection that presents events in sequential order. It can also help students organize events in order. It can be used with a selection, individual chapters, or a small section of a selection, depending on the complexity.

1. After reading a selection, ask students what happened first. Record the first event on the chart.
2. Continue asking students to name events in order, placing them on the continuum.
3. It may be helpful to list all of the events first, and then place them in order on the time line to ensure that all of the important events are included.
4. If there are specific dates or references to a specific time (for example *summer* or *January*), record those under the event.

- Remind students to look for clues in the text that will help them determine the order in which things happen. They might find dates or clue words such as *first*, *next*, *then*, and *last*.
- If students need extra support, write events from the text on sentence strips. Have students work in pairs or small groups to place the strips in order and then write the events on the time line.
- Some texts are not written in chronological order. For example, some fiction texts include flashbacks in the narrative that interrupt the sequential flow of events. Students can use the Time Line Graphic Organizer as they read to understand a complex text structure. Help them identify these occurrences and record them in the proper place on the continuum.

- Share time lines from social studies texts with students. Have them discuss what the time lines have in common. Identify those features.
- Have students read a biography of a historical figure such as the activist Cesar Chavez or the explorer Henry Hudson. Ask them to choose several key events in the person's life and plot them on a time line. Then have them compare and contrast what occurred then to the present day in a paragraph or two.

Time Line

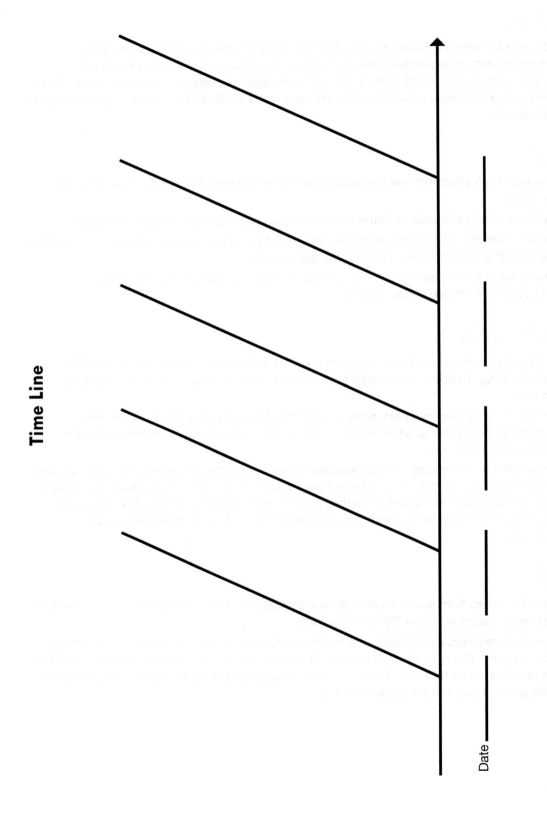

Date

Draw Conclusions

PURPOSE

Use this routine with the Draw Conclusions Graphic Organizer. Students preview the text and learn to draw conclusions from it. This graphic organizer works well with fiction and nonfiction texts.

PROCEDURE

1. Display the graphic organizer. Say: When you draw conclusions, you are getting at the meaning of a text. You are referring to information that is not clearly stated and forming a conclusion based on what you know and what you have read.

2. Preview the text with students. Read the title and ask students what they think will happen in the text. Remind them to use what they know about the topic to make educated guesses.

3. Present a section of the text to students. Ask them to analyze it and draw conclusions from it. Write their conclusions in the appropriate section of the graphic organizer.

4. Ask students to look for evidence to support their conclusions. Add their evidence to the appropriate section of the graphic organizer.

TEACHING TIPS

- Demonstrate how to use this graphic organizer to help students draw conclusions about fiction.

- Guide students to analyze informational texts and draw conclusions based on facts.

- Help students walk through the thought process of how to draw conclusions. Provide sentence frames, such as the following: I conclude that ___ because the text says ___ and I know that ___.

EXTEND

- Encourage students to think critically and compare and contrast their conclusions.

- Have volunteers debate their conclusions and support their positions with evidence from the text.

Draw Conclusions

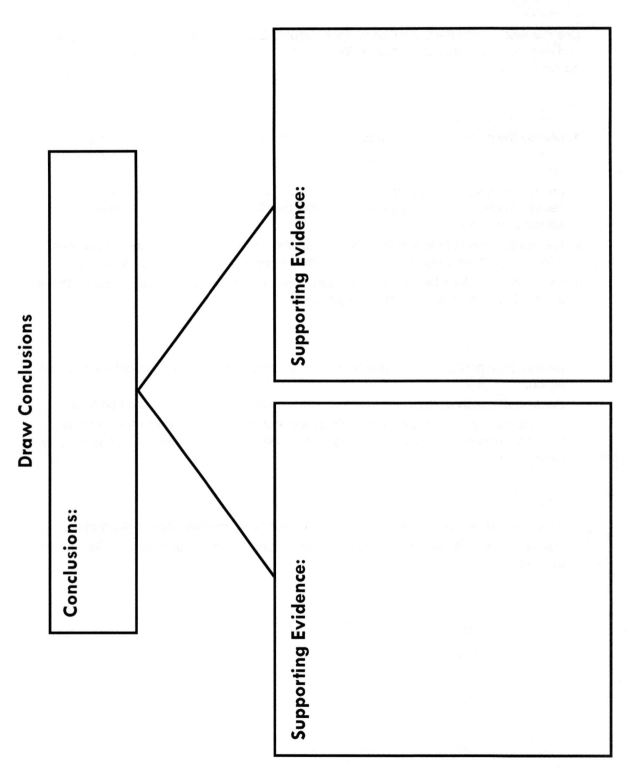

Conclusions:

Supporting Evidence:

Supporting Evidence:

Narrative Paragraph Writing

PURPOSE

Use this routine with the Narrative Paragraph Writing Graphic Organizer to help students plan and write a narrative paragraph or story or to add details to a description of a place or an event. (See also the Unlock Narrative Writing lesson in Part 2 of this handbook.)

PROCEDURE

1. Ask students: What is narrative writing? Say: It is a story told by a narrator.

2. Show examples of narrative writing that students have read recently. Say: Narrative writing may be fiction, such as a short story or folk tale, or nonfiction, such as a news story or biography. Ask students for additional examples of narrative writing they may already be familiar with.

3. Explain that a narrative paragraph usually describes one meaningful event or happening.

4. Distribute the graphic organizer. Review the parts of a paragraph with students: topic sentence, body, and closing sentence.

5. To demonstrate how to begin writing a narrative paragraph, provide story-starter sentence frames, such as the following: It was a dark and stormy night ____. We walked to the end of a long, crooked hall and pushed open the heavy door ____. When the phone rang in the middle of the night, ____.

6. Brainstorm ideas with the class about how the narrative might develop. Explain to students that they may include sensory details, or words and phrases that help a reader visualize what something may look, sound, smell, taste, or feel like, in their narrative paragraphs. Refer to the sentence frames and point out examples of sensory details. Write these ideas on the board. Work with students to choose the best ideas. Display the graphic organizer and model how to fill it in.

7. Repeat the process with the body and closing sentence.

8. Now ask students to write their own narrative paragraph using the graphic organizer. Provide them with several sentence frames to start. Or, students may think of their own sentence frames.

9. Invite students to read aloud their paragraphs to a partner or small group. Have the class identify examples of sensory details in volunteers' paragraphs.

TEACHING TIPS

- Make sure students understand the story starters. Supply an alternative sentence frame if needed.

- Remind students to pay attention to the self-monitoring questions in Step C on the graphic organizer.

EXTEND

Have students publish their paragraphs in a class booklet or on a class or school Web site. Check for proper grammar, capitalization, and spelling prior to publishing.

Narrative Paragraph Writing

A. Read the story starters. Choose one and brainstorm ideas for your paragraph. Write down these ideas on a separate sheet of paper.

B. Use your ideas to write sentences in the graphic organizer. Read the information in the left column, and write your ideas in the right column.

A **topic sentence** tells what the paragraph is about.	
The **body** of a paragraph gives information to help readers understand the narrative. Write three to five sentences here.	
In a narrative paragraph, the **closing sentence** tells the end of the narrative.	

C. Read your narrative paragraph. Ask yourself:

- Does the paragraph have a topic sentence that sets up the narrative?
- Do the sentences in the body of the paragraph tell the story?
- Does the closing sentence tell the end of the narrative?

D. Read aloud your narrative paragraph to a partner, small group, or the class.

Narrative Essay Writing

PURPOSE

Use this routine with the Narrative Essay Writing Graphic Organizer to help students plan and write a narrative essay. (See also the Unlock Narrative Writing lesson in Part 2 of this handbook.)

PROCEDURE

1. Remind students that narrative writing tells a story. Say: Narrative writing may be fiction, such as a short story or folk tale, or nonfiction, such as a news story or a biography. Explain that a narrative essay tells a story that has a point. The reader should gain insight or learn a lesson. The final paragraph should come to an important conclusion.

2. Distribute the graphic organizer. Go over the parts of an essay with students: beginning (introduction), middle (details), and end (conclusion).

3. Brainstorm ideas with the class about how the narrative might develop. Write these ideas on the board.

4. Model filling out the graphic organizer:

    - In the Subject box, fill in the name and a brief description of the situation or experience you are writing about.

    - In the Setting box, write when and where the experience takes place.

    - In the Beginning, Middle, and End boxes, describe the events of the experience in the order they occurred.

5. Now ask students to write their own narrative essays using the graphic organizer.

6. Invite student volunteers to read aloud their narrative paragraphs to a partner, small group, or the class. Ask students to identify the subject, setting, and where the narratives begin, where they are at midpoint, and where they end. Ask them also what the lesson or moral of the essay is.

TEACHING TIPS

- Use sentence frames to help students get started. For example: It was a dark and stormy night ____. We walked to the end of a long, crooked hall and pushed open the heavy door ____. The phone rang in the middle of the night ____.

- Students may also come up with their own sentence frames. Review them to ensure they are detailed enough to serve as a basis for their essays.

- Remind students that the order of events must flow logically and end in a manner that makes sense. Look for transitional words and phrases that will signal to readers where they are in the story and show the flow of the story from one part to the next. Students should also use a variety of descriptive details to highlight characters, places, or events. Finally, narratives may incorporate dialogue; check for the proper use of punctuation for what characters say. Remind students that their essays should teach readers something.

EXTEND

- Have students publish their narratives in a blog or on a class or school Web site.

- Have them create illustrations and post their work in the classroom.

Narrative Essay Writing

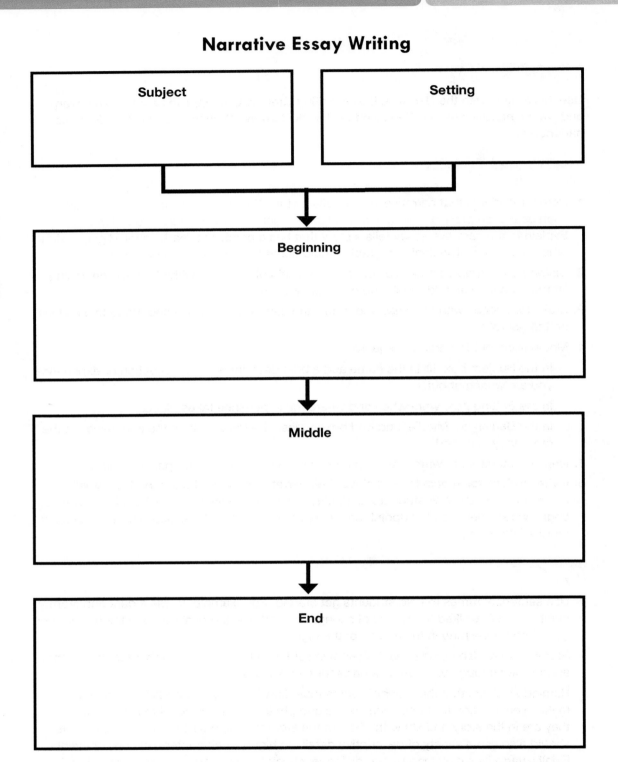

| Subject | Setting |

Beginning

Middle

End

Informative/Explanatory Writing

PURPOSE

Use this routine with the Informative/Explanatory Writing Graphic Organizer to help students plan and write an informative/explanatory piece of writing. (See also the Unlock Informative/Explanatory Writing lesson in Part 2 of this handbook.)

PROCEDURE

1. **Ask students:** What is informative/explanatory writing? **Say:** It explains a topic and clearly conveys ideas and information about the topic.

2. Show examples of informative/explanatory writing that students have read recently. **Say:** Informative/explanatory writing is factual, nonfiction writing. Newspaper articles, magazine articles, and textbooks are examples of informative/explanatory writing. What other examples of informative/explanatory writing can you think of?

3. Display the graphic organizer. Explain that the first step in creating an informative/explanatory piece of writing is to choose a topic. For example, if students choose to write about space exploration, they may ask questions such as *How do astronauts prepare to go on a space exploration? What does it take to become an astronaut?* The next step is to do some research and gather facts and information about the topic.

4. Then tell students that they will develop their topic and organize the information they have gathered. The topic is developed with facts, definitions, and details in the middle. They will write a draft and make sure they have a strong conclusion for their piece of writing.

5. Model how to complete the graphic organizer.

6. Now ask students to write their own informative/explanatory piece, using their graphic organizer.

TEACHING TIPS

- Have students use linking words and phrases (*because, therefore, since, for example*) to connect ideas within categories of information. Look for the use of precise language in students' writing.

- Have students refer to the checklist on the graphic organizer as they write.

EXTEND

- Have students publish their informative/explanatory essays with illustrations, photographs, and/or diagrams that support their writing.

- Invite volunteers to share their work with the rest of the class. Have students review the graphic organizer as they listen to check whether the essays meet the checklist criteria.

Informative/Explanatory Writing

Topic: _____

Facts About Topic

Conclusion

Use this checklist to remind yourself to

☐ introduce the topic.

☐ develop the topic with facts, definitions, and details.

☐ provide a concluding section.

Opinion Writing

PURPOSE

Use this routine with the Opinion Writing Graphic Organizer to help students plan and write an opinion piece, including formulating an opinion and identifying reasons that support the topic. (See also the Unlock Opinion Writing lesson in Part 2 of this handbook.)

PROCEDURE

1. Explain that an opinion is how a person feels or what a person believes about something. Say: An opinion cannot be proven true or false because it is not a fact. A fact can be proven to be true. Select two topics about which students can formulate an opinion. For example: *Should all elementary students learn a foreign language?* or *Should television be turned off for one night every week?* Use one topic to model instruction and the other for independent writing.

2. Explain that opinion writing involves the following steps:

   a. Students will first introduce the topic that they are writing about. This includes stating their opinion about the topic.

   b. Next, students will provide reasons that support their opinion.

   c. Finally, students will provide a concluding statement that revisits the topic and restates the opinion.

3. Display the graphic organizer and model filling it in. Begin by brainstorming some topic choices and making a decision about the best idea. Model writing a statement of opinion.

4. Next, fill in the reasons for the opinion. Remind students to provide strong reasons that support a point of view about the topic. The reasons should be based on facts. Remind students to keep in mind the reasons for their opinion as they write.

5. Finally, model writing an opinion piece using the information in the graphic organizer. Students should have several good supporting reasons for their opinion and a strong conclusion.

TEACHING TIP

Have students use linking words and phrases (*consequently, specifically*) to connect their reasons to their opinions.

EXTEND

- Have students publish their writing in a classroom book, or have them create a cartoon illustration and display them for the school to enjoy.

- Invite volunteers to share their work with the class. Encourage class discussion by allowing classmates to ask further questions or offer opposing opinions and reasons.

Opinion Writing

Topic: _____

Information About Topic

Opinion Statement: _____

Reasons For Opinion

Use this checklist to remind yourself to

☐ introduce the topic and your opinion.

☐ give reasons to support your opinion.

☐ provide a concluding statement that revisits the topic and restates the opinion.

Description: Sensory Details

PURPOSE

Use this routine with the Description: Sensory Details Graphic Organizer to help students break down and understand descriptive-rich passages. The organizer can also aid students in using sensory details to write their own description of a place or an event.

PROCEDURE

1. Because teaching sensory details has both a reading and writing component, find a paragraph that is rich in sensory details. Remove them one by one so that students can see what is lost in the description without them. Then put them back in so students can evaluate the role that sensory details play in making meaning.

2. Explain that writers use sensory details (sight, sound, smell, taste, and touch) when sharing important experiences. These sensory details also make the text more interesting to read because they create vivid images for the reader.

3. Display the graphic organizer. Choose a piece of text that contains examples of sensory details and read it aloud. Model how to fill in the chart with details from each sense that the author uses. Discuss how this makes writing more interesting for readers.

4. Use and display a new Sensory Details Graphic Organizer when assisting students in writing their own descriptive passages. As a class, choose a classroom object or an area of the classroom to describe. Ask questions, such as *What does it feel like? How does it smell? What colors, shapes, and features do you see? What are the sounds that it makes?*

5. Next, break students into five groups and give each group a sense. Students can work with their group or on their own to brainstorm words for their sense. For example, if your object is a dog and your sense is "touch," you would write down words like *furry, soft,* or *warm.*

6. Fill out the displayed organizer as a class. Go in order and have each group share their sensory words.

7. Use a think aloud to demonstrate how students can use the sensory words from the organizer to describe the object or place.

TEACHING TIPS

- The above activity works well as a guided collaborative writing activity.
- Use *I see, I hear, I feel, I smell,* and *I taste* as sentence starters.
- Display lists of vivid sensory words in the classroom for students to reference.

EXTEND

Have students work alone or in pairs and use the graphic organizer to write a description of an object or place. When they finish their descriptions, they can read them aloud and have others guess what is being described.

Description: Sensory Details

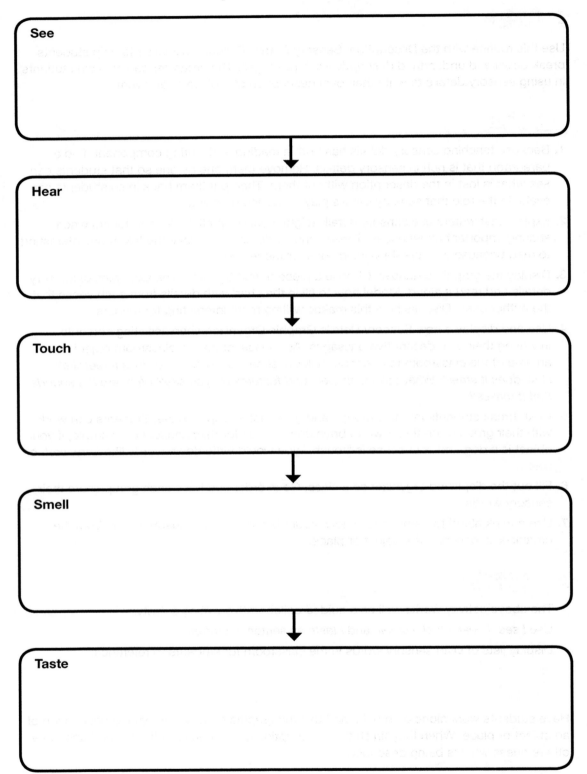

See

Hear

Touch

Smell

Taste

Retell or Summarize

PURPOSE

Use this routine with the Retell or Summarize Graphic Organizer.

PROCEDURE

1. **Model thinking aloud an example of summarizing:** I saw a movie yesterday. When my friends asked me about it, I didn't tell every detail from the beginning to the end. Instead, I told the most important ideas and events. This is called summarizing. I summarize things I see, things I read, and things I hear. When I summarize, I know that I have to sort out the most important details. A summary includes important ideas and events, not everything. Retelling is a little different. When you retell something, you listen to or read the message, and then say it in your own words to show you understand it.

2. **Ask students to listen carefully as you read a short passage aloud.** After you read, ask students to contribute to a summary of the passage. **Say:** A summary should answer the question, *What was it about?*

3. **Help frame their thinking as you list their ideas to create a summary.** Tell them they are only noting main ideas. Have pairs of students read the complete summary together.

4. **Then reread the passage.** Have pairs decide if the summary lists the most important details. **Ask:** What should be added or changed? What can be left out? Discuss and clarify answers. Repeat this process with another story to focus on retelling. Remind students that for both summarizing and retelling, they must use their own words.

TEACHING TIP

Students can use the sentence starters at the bottom of the graphic organizer to guide their writing.

EXTEND

Have students use the graphic organizer to list details from a written or spoken passage. In the box at the bottom, students can write their summaries. Encourage them to keep their summaries short and to the point. Ask them to read their summaries aloud to the class.

Retell or Summarize

Detail:	Detail:	Detail:

Summary:

Use the summary starters below if you need to.

In summary, . . .

The most important ideas are . . .

What we need to remember is . . .

Monitor Understanding: Listening Skills Log

PURPOSE

Use this routine with the Listening Skills Log to help students monitor their understanding and learn how to take helpful class notes.

PROCEDURE

1. Explain the purpose of the Listening Skills Log to students. Begin with questions, such as *Why is it important to listen?* or *Why is it important to take notes?*

2. Distribute the Listening Skills Log and model filling it out. Explain to students that good note-takers do not write down every word a speaker says. Instead, they listen for main ideas. Review the difference between a key idea and a detail.

3. Display the log you created in Step 2 as a model. Have students view the log while listening to the same media or audio selection. Afterward, discuss why you chose to write down what you did, and allow students to ask questions.

4. Read a text aloud, or present information using a form of media. When using media, preview the selection so you can pause after main ideas. This will allow students to practice listening for and writing down main ideas.

5. Have students compare their log entries in small groups prior to discussing them with the class. Encourage students to ask about any words they did not understand.

TEACHING TIPS

- Speak at a normal rate and enunciate clearly. Pause at appropriate places to allow students to process the information and ask clarifying questions, or seek further explanation. Prompt students to think critically about the text by giving example opinions or making connections to their own life experiences.

- If students have difficulty with a passage, pause to explain new words and concepts. As students become more proficient listeners, gradually increase the length and difficulty of the passages.

- Reread or replay the same text or media so students have multiple chances to catch main ideas. During each reread or replay, students should focus on a different portion of the speaking and listening sheet to hone their focus.

- Allow students to reread the selection to compare their Listening Skills Log to what was in the text. As they reread a selection, students can code parts of the text with self-stick notes to indicate: I understand / I need further explanation / I figured it out.

- If appropriate, post an essential question that students can refer to as they listen.

EXTEND

- Students can write a paragraph from their notes.

- After listening to a selection or read aloud and filling out the log, have students get in pairs and use classroom resources to find answers to their own questions, define unknown words, and clarify any misunderstandings. Pairs can present their findings to the class, and explain how they came to their answers.

Listening Skills Log

Topic	
Main Idea	
What did I learn?	
What was hard to understand?	
Questions I Have	
New Words	

Express Opinions

INTRODUCE

Use this routine to guide students in expressing opinions.

PROCEDURE

1. Explain to students that we express opinions to show what we think or believe about something. We cannot prove if an opinion is true or false. Say: If someone says, "It is raining outside," that's a fact. I can look outside and see rain falling. If someone says, "Rainy weather is the best weather," that's an opinion. That person may like rainy weather because it helps flowers grow. But others may not like rain. They have a different opinion.

2. Display the following opinion words and phrases:

I think	I disagree	best
I believe	I like	worst
my opinion is	I do not like	good
I agree	better	bad

Say: We use these words to give our opinions. These words tell what we think or believe. Model creating an opinion using one of the words or phrases.

3. Have students work with partners to state opinions about the text they are currently reading. Remind them that they need to refer directly to the text to show evidence that supports their opinion. Have them use the displayed opinion words and phrases. Provide the following sentence frames as needed: I like ___. I think ___. I believe ___. I do not like ___. My opinion is ___.

TEACHING TIP

Students may think of facts as true and opinions as false. Locate statements of opinions in the text that are supported by facts and discuss them with students. Point out that people trust opinions when they are supported with facts.

EXTEND

- For additional practice, have students elaborate by giving reasons for their opinions, referring directly to the text. Students can use the following sentence frames as needed: I like ___ because ___. Her opinion is ___ because ___. Have volunteers share their opinions and reasons with the class, reminding students to be respectful of others' opinions.

- Have students write a letter to the school editor expressing an opinion about the school such as a different lunch menu or a new sports team. Remind them that they should support their opinions with facts.

Prepare for Discussions

PURPOSE

Use this routine to help students prepare for and engage in collaborative one-on-one, group, and teacher-led discussions.

PROCEDURE

1. Ask: What does it mean to engage effectively in a range of collaborative discussions? (It means you can have a conversation with a partner, in a small group, or with the whole class. It also means that you communicate your ideas in a way that other people can understand.)

2. Ask: How can you communicate your ideas in a way that other people can understand? (by preparing for the discussion, including reading and understanding the text ahead of time; by asking questions before, during, and after the discussion to make sure you understand; by staying on topic; by building on others' ideas; by expressing your own ideas clearly; by linking comments made by different people in the discussion)

3. Review the rules of discussions on the worksheet on the following page.

4. Model a discussion with several student volunteers. Tell them that you are planning a party for a relative; list which of your family members you intend to invite to the party and what you will have to do to prepare for it. Ask students questions about how you should decorate for the party and what foods you should prepare for it. Reiterate what they say, and expand upon it.

5. Have students use the worksheet to rate themselves when they have a discussion with classmates.

TEACHING TIP

Set roles for class discussions, such as timekeeper, leader, note taker, and summarizer.

EXTEND

- Peruse a local newspaper for an article presenting a local controversy (a large department store opening next to a series of small businesses or a new traffic light proposal). Present this article to your students for discussion.

- Ask students to come up with topics for discussion. Have a few volunteers participate in the discussion, while the rest of the class listens. Have the listeners rate the discussion using the worksheet. Ask students to point out areas that the volunteers did well or could improve upon. Make sure that listeners offer helpful and respectful critiques.

Prepare for Discussions

Rate what you do during discussions with your classmates.

1 I need to practice this skill.

2 I do this sometimes.

3 I almost always do this.

I listen carefully to others when they speak.	1	2	3
I speak one at a time.	1	2	3
I talk about the topic when it is my turn.	1	2	3
I ask questions when I don't understand.	1	2	3
I come prepared.	1	2	3
I gain the floor respectfully.	1	2	3
I stay on topic.	1	2	3
I explain my own ideas.	1	2	3

What topics would you like to discuss with classmates?
List them here. Then **discuss!**

_____

_____

_____

_____

Understanding Media

Use this routine when watching a video or listening to an audio recording to help students understand the main idea.

PROCEDURE

1. Introduce a guiding question to help students focus while watching a video or listening to a recording.
2. Play the media once from beginning to ending. Then replay the media, pausing at critical points, such as when new information is taught. Ask questions to monitor students' comprehension.
3. Confirm that students understand what they have seen or heard by asking them to summarize each section.
4. Once students have watched or listened twice, have them answer the guiding question.
5. Replay the media a third time so that students can confirm their answers.

TEACHING TIPS

- Ask students to discuss any background knowledge they have about the guiding question.
- Have struggling speakers draw a picture that illustrates their background knowledge.
- If students are unable to summarize sections, watch or listen to each section again. Ask questions that will guide them to understand the main idea of the section.

EXTEND

Use the Three-Column Chart Graphic Organizer. Title one column What I Knew, the second What I Learned, and the last What I Want to Know. Have students fill in the columns using information that they already knew about the guiding question and information they learned while watching or listening. For questions still left unanswered, lead a class discussion to arrive at the answers. Help students find out more information about the subject by directing them to approved online and print resources.

Preview and Review Vocabulary

PURPOSE

Use this routine to assess what students know about words they will encounter in a reading selection. This activity also is a way to review the vocabulary from previous selections so that students internalize the words.

PROCEDURE

1. Select 12–14 words for vocabulary study. Use words from the vocabulary list in the Teacher's Guide and select the remaining words based on the needs of your students. Include 3–4 words from a previous selection in the list.

2. Display the words and read each one aloud to students. Have students write each word in a vocabulary notebook for later reference. Then have students read each word with you.

3. Ask students first to decide which words they think will be in the selection before joining a partner for the following step.

4. Have students explain to a partner why they chose each word and why they didn't choose others. Afterward, pairs can explain their choices to the class. Explaining why is a very important step, because students will use their understanding of the words to predict the content of the selection. These explanations also demonstrate what students know about a word. Sharing the explanations helps to provide more background to students who may not be familiar with the words.

OPTIONS FOR VARYING THIS ROUTINE Replace steps 3–4 with one of the following:
- Select words they want to know more about.
- Select words they don't know or don't understand.

EXTEND

- Have students create a word web relating the vocabulary terms to other words they know. These can be words with similar affixes, suffixes, sounds, or meanings.

- Before students read a fiction selection, choose 10 words from the text that exemplify the story's characters, setting, and problem. Have students sort the words into three categories: characters, setting, and problem. Then, work together as a class to create a 1–3 sentence prediction about the story. Make sure the prediction includes all of the words. The purpose is to have students use new words to practice making predictions, so it is okay if the predictions are "wrong."

- Have students discuss the words they are unfamiliar with in small groups. Guide them in making educated guesses to their meanings, referring to the selection for context. Once they have defined the words, have them work together to write new sentences using the words. Ask volunteers to share words, definitions, and new sentences with the class.

Act Out or Draw Meaning

PURPOSE

Use this routine with the Act Out or Draw Meaning Graphic Organizer to help students learn and remember new vocabulary.

PROCEDURE

1. Explain that one way to learn and remember new words is to draw or act out the meaning. Provide an example from something that students have recently read:

   I just read the word *fault* in a science text. A *fault* is a place in the earth where an earthquake takes place. To remember the word, I can draw a picture of a circle to show the earth and draw a line on it. I put arrows to show how the earth shifts at the fault line. (Display a picture.) I can also act out the meaning by rubbing my hands together to show what happens at a fault to make an earthquake.

2. Divide the class into small groups. Introduce words from the selection. Choose "picturable" words and give each group a word.

3. Have students work together to create a picture and/or demonstrate the meanings of the words. Say: Talk about what this word means. Then explain by drawing a picture of it or showing us what it means.

4. Have volunteers explain their drawings to the class. Clear up any misconceptions.

5. Ask: How did drawing the word or acting it out help you remember what it meant?

ASSESS Have students explain their drawings. Clear up any misconceptions about the words.

TEACHING TIPS

- Drawing a word aids understanding because it requires students to express ideas in a different format. If students doubt their artistic ability, reassure them that they will not be evaluated based on the way their drawings look, but rather on their ability to explain how their drawings help them understand new words.

- Note that while almost all words can be made into drawings and can serve as pictorial reminders as students read, not all words transfer well into actions. For example, action words such *dash* or *consume* lend themselves well to acting out but *telescope* and *experiment* do not.

EXTEND

- Play a guessing game with students. Distribute index cards with words that students have learned in class. Students can take turns drawing pictures or acting out word meanings for the class to guess. Then have students use the graphic organizer on the next page to create their own dictionary of pictures and gestures. Distribute copies of the drawing frames when students learn new words.

- Have students distinguish shades of meaning with words that describe the same general action, such as: *walk, stroll, prowl, march*. Have students in small groups create a list of words, and then expand them by adding synonyms.

Act Out or Draw Meaning

Word: _____

Drawing

This word means _____
_____.

Word: _____

Drawing

This word means _____
_____.

ROUTINE

Analyze Cognates

PURPOSE

Identifying cognates in texts is a useful strategy for expanding vocabulary, helping students understand more words in English, validating the home language, and making clear connections between the home language and the target language, English. Use this routine with the Personal Cognate Chart to help students who are literate in languages that have many cognates of English words, such as Spanish, Portuguese, French, and Italian.

PROCEDURE

1. Present a chart like the one below. Read the words with students, and note the similarities across various languages. Explain: When words look and mean the same in different languages, they are called cognates. Let's look at the word *demand* and its cognates. What other words can we add to this chart? Tell students that cognates can help them understand more words in English.

English	Spanish	French	Italian
demand	demanda	demande	domanda

2. Explain to students that cognates in different languages usually have the same origins. For example, the different words for *demand* are all based on the Greek word part *-mand,* which means "order." Explain that because many scientific words have Greek or Latin origins, they are often cognates.

3. Point out that sometimes words in different languages are "false friends," which means they look almost the same, but they don't mean the same thing. For example, the Spanish word *sopa* looks and sounds similar to the English word *soap*, but it means "soup." Ask students to give other examples of these false cognates, which are words that are not true cognates.Together, find an example of a word from a text that students think is a cognate and discuss their rationale.

4. Copy and distribute the Personal Cognate Chart. Have students look for English cognates of home-language words in an English text they are reading. Help them decide whether or not the words really are cognates.

5. Ask students to say or write five examples of cognate pairs in English and their home language, and one example of a "false friend." Ask: *How does knowing cognates help you understand the meaning of words?*

TEACHING TIPS

- Suggest that students consult resources such as bilingual dictionaries, other students, or the Internet (with your guidance) to find translations and word meanings.

- Students might make a class chart showing words such as *computer* in various languages.

- Ask students to pay attention to the context. If they believe they have identified a cognate, have them think of the meaning and check if it makes sense in context.

310 Part 3 • Routines and Activities

EXTEND

- Assist students in labeling and defining Latin and Greek roots of new words they encounter in classroom texts. Identifying and understanding the meaning of these roots will be a useful tool in helping students decode new words in the future, and it also allows them to make connections between words. Use the Personal Cognate Chart for this activity by relabeling the headings of each column. In column one write New Word, and have students write the word in English with its definition in the space provided. In column two write Latin and Greek Roots, and have students write the various Greek and Latin roots from the new word. In column three write Definition of Latin and Greek Roots, and have students define each of the Greek or Latin roots.

- To help students with identifying false cognates, present a list of words for students to define in their own words. Have pairs work together to make decisions about whether the cognates are true or false.

ENGLISH LANGUAGE LEARNERS

Cognates are words that share origins and appear in similar forms in different languages. For example, the English word *school* is of Greek origin and it is similar to the Spanish *escuela*, the French *école*, the Polish *szkoła*, and the German *schule*. For speakers of languages that share word origins with English, the study of cognates can be a powerful vocabulary-building tool.

Personal Cognate Chart

English Cognate	Cognate in Other Language	Meaning

Word Knowledge Strategy

PURPOSE

Model the following strategies to show students what to do when they come across a word they do not know. These strategies can be modeled through a think aloud or demonstrated explicitly through a mini lesson. The goal is that over the course of several units, students will become independent users of these strategies.

PROCEDURE

Begin with a question: *What do I do when I come to a word I don't know?*

- **Decode/Pronounce** Have students read the word aloud. Sometimes just hearing it will show them that they know it. Say it again and tap out the parts of the word as you say it. Check: *Does the word sound right?* If the answer is "no," go to the next step.

- **Word Structure** Look at the word parts, affixes, and roots. If students see a word part they know, have them underline it and define it. For example, *unknown*: *un-* means "not," so *unknown* means "not known or understood." This can also be done with compound words or word parts. For example, *know* means "to understand," so *knowledge* has to do with the ability to understand something. Check: *Does the word sound right?* If the answer is "no," go to the next step.

- **Related Words and Cognates** Is there another word that is similar in spelling and/or sound that can help? For example, if the unknown word is *medicate*, can knowing the meaning of the word *medicine* help students determine the meaning? If the answer is "no," go to the next step.

- **Context Clues** Read what comes before and after the word to find clues that will help students understand the meaning of the word. For fiction, think about the setting, characters, events, and actions taking place. For nonfiction, look for examples, explanations, and definitions within the text. Model a think aloud considering these elements. Check: *Does the word make sense?* If the answer is "no," go to the next step.

- **References** The final step is looking in a reference source such as a dictionary, glossary, or thesaurus. Remind students that words are listed in reference books in alphabetical order. Also discuss what to do if two words start with the same letter (*simulate* and *synthesize*).

TEACHING TIPS

- Remind students that there are times when they might know what a word means but that the meaning can change based on how it is used in a sentence. ("I am simply stumped" versus "The directions are written simply.")

- After students understand the word, have them use the new word in a sentence and record the new vocabulary word in a notebook.

- Have advanced students work with a partner to use new words in a linear graph to show where it would fit in relation to synonyms and antonyms. For example: *hot-warm-tepid-cool-icy.*

Multisyllabic Word Strategy

PURPOSE

Use this routine to help students understand and decode multisyllabic words that do not have prefixes, suffixes, or roots.

PROCEDURE

1. **Introduce the Strategy** Explain that word parts, or chunks, help us to read larger words. They can also help students learn to spell correctly.

   Display the word *rabbit*, for example.

2. **Connect to Sound-Spellings** Explain that the parts of a word are called syllables. Break the word into syllables.

   Say: *Rabbit* has two syllables: *rab* and *bit*.

3. **Model** Explain that syllables help us say and read words. Say each syllable as you run your hand from one syllable to the next. Then read the syllables together as you say the word. Then show students how they can use clapping to help identify syllables. Demonstrate by clapping once after saying each syllable.

4. **Read the Word** Read the syllables as you run your hand beneath them, and then read the syllables together as you say the word.

   Say: This is how I read this word. First I read each syllable, and then I read the syllables together: *rab/bit, rabbit.*

5. Display more examples. Have students read the syllables, and then read the word as you run your hand beneath the parts.

TEACHING TIP

If students have difficulty using sound-spellings and syllabication to read word parts, then read one part at a time as you cover the remaining parts.

EXTEND

Choose an excerpt from a selection that contains several multisyllabic words. Have volunteers read aloud to practice decoding and pronunciation.

Analyze Idioms and Expressions

PURPOSE

Idioms are phrases that have a figurative meaning such as *hit the road*. An expression is a group of words used as a unit, such as *wise guy*.

Because the meanings of idioms and expressions are not literal, students may need extra support to understand them. Students who speak other languages at home might have added difficulty, since there may not be a similar idiom in their own language they can relate it to. The best approach to teaching idioms and expressions is to discuss them in the context of a classroom text or in conversation. By exposing students to idioms and expressions, they will be better able to recognize and understand them when reading or listening to conversations and media.

PROCEDURE

1. Explain that idioms are phrases that communicate an idea or feeling that cannot be understood based on what they say. When I use an idiom, I don't exactly mean what the words say. For example, what do I mean when I say that Carl talked too much and he spilled the beans about the surprise party? Did he literally spill some beans? No, I mean to say that told the secret about the surprise party.

2. Ask students for other examples of idioms and expressions, or supply examples, such as *jumping down my throat, feeling under the weather,* or *bite the dust.*

3. Write them on the board and discuss what they might mean based on the context in which they were heard or read. Talk about why someone might be confused by a particular idiom. For example, *to sleep on it* can be confusing to understand because students might visualize someone sleeping on top of something.

4. Point out idioms and expressions in selections that students are reading or that you read aloud to them. Ask them to figure out the meanings. Clarify any misunderstandings and provide corrective feedback.

EXTEND

- Have volunteers practice using idioms and expressions in everyday conversation. Ask students to come up with a list, and then allow them to plan a dialogue and act out a brief skit using the idiom.

- Have pairs work together to write sentences using idioms and then explanations of what they mean. Ask volunteers to read their sentences to the class.

ROUTINE

Analyze Multiple-Meaning Words

PURPOSE

Use the Analyze Multiple-Meaning Words Routine to help students determine or clarify the meaning of words and phrases that have more than one meaning.

PROCEDURE

1. Explain that some words have more than one meaning. **Say:** Words like *leaves* have multiple meanings. *Leaves* can mean "the thin, flat, green parts of plants that grow from stems," but *leaves* can also mean "departs." When you come across a word in a text that has more than one meaning, how can you figure out which meaning is being used?

2. Present different strategies that students can use to determine or clarify the meaning of a word that has more than one meaning:

    a. Tell students that they can often use the context of the sentence to figure out what a word or phrase means. Using the context means looking at the other words in the sentence for clues. **Say:** If I told you that I jumped in a pile of leaves, you would know that I am talking about the thin, green parts of plants.

    b. If the text does not provide enough context to help students figure out the meaning of a word, tell them they can also use prefixes and suffixes that they do know to figure out the meaning of a word. For example, the prefix *un-* means "not" and the suffix *-able* means "can" or "able to."

    c. Another strategy is to use root words with which they are familiar. For example, *bio-* means "life."

    d. Finally, remind students that they can always use a dictionary or other reference tool if they need help finding the meaning of a word.

TEACHING TIPS

- To avoid too many interruptions while reading, have students use sticky notes to flag unknown words, especially those with multiple meanings, while they read.

- Point out that words may be used as different parts of speech. For example, *work* may be used as noun (We like doing our *work*) or as a verb (Our teachers *work* hard).

EXTEND

- Draw a two-column chart. Title one column Word and the other Meanings. Have students brainstorm additional multiple-meaning words and fill in the columns accordingly.

- Provide pairs with multiple-meaning words and have them write sentences using the words in two different contexts (for example, *button* as a noun and as a verb). Have volunteers share their work with the class.

Common Nouns

INTRODUCE Remind students that we have names for the things around us. A noun is a word that names something or somebody.

TEACH/MODEL Present the concept and provide examples of common nouns such as:

Person	Place	Animal	Thing
girl	country	dog	statue

PRACTICE Have pairs find more examples of common nouns to add to the chart. Fill out the chart with the class. Clarify questions students might have.

ASSESS Have students find other examples of nouns from new selections they are reading. Have them share their examples and explain why their choices are common nouns.

ENGLISH LANGUAGE LEARNERS

In languages such as Spanish and French, nouns have gender (masculine or feminine). You can point out that while some nouns in English refer to males or females (*boy, girl, uncle, aunt*), English nouns are not grouped by gender.

Proper Nouns

INTRODUCE Write a student's name on the board. Point out that everyone's name begins with a capital letter and that each of us has our own specific name. Explain that a proper noun is the specific name of a person, place, animal, or thing. Proper nouns all begin with capital letters. The word *city* is not a proper noun because it is not a specific place. *New York City* and *Chicago* are proper nouns because they are specific places. Likewise, the word *girl* is not a proper noun because many people are girls. However, *Sandra* is a proper noun because it is specific to a particular girl.

TEACH/MODEL Present the concept and provide examples:

- A proper noun names a specific person, place, animal, or thing.
- A proper noun begins with a capital letter.

Specific Person	Specific Place	Specific Animal	Specific Thing
Sandra	Africa	Fifi	Statue of Liberty

PRACTICE Model finding a proper noun in a text and recording it. Circle the capital letter. Have pairs work together to provide more examples to add to the chart.

ASSESS When students understand the concept, have them work independently to find examples from texts they read to add to the chart.

ENGLISH LANGUAGE LEARNERS

Students who are literate in non-alphabetic languages such as Chinese, Korean, and Japanese may not be familiar with capitalizing proper nouns and may need more practice.

Titles and Abbreviations

INTRODUCE Write the names of various school staff members on the board, including titles such as *Mr., Mrs., Ms.,* and *Dr.* Read the names aloud with students and underline the titles as you say them. Point out that these titles are abbreviations, or shortened forms of words.

TEACH/MODEL Present the concept and provide examples:

- Proper names may begin with a title such as *Mrs., Mr., Ms.,* or *Dr.*
- A title begins with a capital letter. If a title is an abbreviation it ends with a period.

Abbreviated Title	Example
Mr. (mister)	Mr. Garza
Ms. (miz)	Ms. Prince
Mrs. (missus)	Mrs. Dexter
Miss (miss)	Miss Wong
Dr. (doctor)	Dr. Marco

PRACTICE Have students expand the chart by adding adults they know. Next, have pairs find examples from a recent selection. Remind students that some titles such as *Senator, President,* and *Professor* are not abbreviated. Have them keep a running list of examples of the various titles they find in their reading.

ENGLISH LANGUAGE LEARNERS

- Explain that, in English, the title *Doctor* is used for both men and women.
- In some countries, the word *Teacher* is used as a title. Point out that in the United States teachers are addressed with a title such as *Mr., Ms., Mrs.,* or *Miss.*

Days, Months, and Holidays

INTRODUCE Ask students to name today's day and date. Write them on the board, and point out that the names of the day and month begin with capital letters.

TEACH/MODEL Present the concept and provide several examples:

- Days of the week, months of the year, and holidays begin with capital letters.

Days of the Week	Months of the Year		Holidays (Examples)
Sunday	January	July	New Year's Day
Monday	February	August	Labor Day
Tuesday	March	September	Thanksgiving
Wednesday	April	October	
Thursday	May	November	
Friday	June	December	
Saturday			

PRACTICE Students can write sentences featuring days of the week, months of the year, and holidays. Provide sentence starters such as: ____ is my favorite day of the week. The weather is often ____ during the month of ____. On ____, I celebrate by ____.

Singular and Plural Nouns

INTRODUCE Point to one book and say: book. Point to two books and say: books. Repeat with *(lunch)box* and *(lunch)boxes*. Have students name other singular and plural nouns as you point to them. Say: Some nouns name one thing. They are called singular nouns. Some nouns name more than one thing. They are called plural nouns. The word *plural* means "more than one."

TEACH/MODEL Present the concept and provide examples:

- Add *-s* to most nouns to form the plural.
- If the noun ends in *-ch, -sh, -s, -ss,* or *-x,* add *-es.*
- If the noun ends in a consonant + *y,* change the *y* to *i* and add *-es.*

Add *-s*	Add *-es*	Change *y* to *i* and Add *-es*
girl/girls	box/boxes	berry/berries

PRACTICE Have students make a three-column chart with the following headings: Add *-s*; Add *-es*; Change *y* to *i* and Add *-es.* Invite students to look through magazines to find nouns that fit each category.

Irregular Plural Nouns

INTRODUCE Write this sentence on the board: *The <u>children</u> brushed their <u>teeth</u>.* Ask a volunteer to name the singular of the underlined nouns *(child, tooth).* Tell students: Most nouns add *-s* or *-es* to form the plural. Some nouns form the plural in a special way. They are called irregular plural nouns.

TEACH/MODEL Present the concept and provide examples:

- Most nouns add *-s* or *-es: books, girls, boxes, brushes.*
- Irregular plural nouns have special forms. Here are some examples:

Irregular Plural Nouns			
child/children	foot/feet	life/lives	man/men
ox/oxen	tooth/teeth	leaf/leaves	woman/women

PRACTICE Have pairs create "singular noun" word cards: *child, tooth, leaf, foot, man.* Then have them create "irregular plural noun" cards, including incorrect forms: *childs, children, teeth, tooths, leafs, leaves, feet, feets, men, mans.* Have students place the "singular" and "plural" cards face down in two separate groups, then take turns drawing correct pairs.

Singular Possessive Nouns

INTRODUCE Display and read aloud these sentences, gesturing as appropriate: This is Maya. This is Maya's desk. **Explain:** The first sentence is about Maya. The second sentence says that Maya has something. To show that a person, place, or thing has or owns something, add an apostrophe (point to apostrophe) and the letter s. The word *Maya's* is called a singular possessive noun.

TEACH/MODEL Present the concept and provide examples:

- A singular possessive noun ends in *'s*.

Singular Nouns	Singular Possessive Nouns	Examples
Sam	Sam's	Sam's mom
friend	friend's	friend's house
class	class's	class's pet
child	child's	child's jacket

PRACTICE Have students place school supplies on their desks. Then have students point to and name a classmate's supplies, using a singular possessive noun. For example: *This is Lin's book. This is Lin's calculator.*

Plural Possessive Nouns

INTRODUCE Display and read aloud these sentences: All my friends have desks. These are my friends' desks. Encourage students to discuss the meaning of each sentence. Explain: To show that two or more people, places, or things have or own something, use a plural possessive noun.

TEACH/MODEL Present the concept and provide examples:

- If the plural noun ends in *-s*, *-es*, or *-ies*, add an apostrophe (') to make it possessive.
- If the plural noun does **not** end in *-s*, *-es*, or *-ies*, add *'s* to make it possessive.

Plural Nouns	Plural Possessive	Examples
friends	friends'	friends' houses
classes	classes'	classes' teachers
puppies	puppies'	puppies' tails
children	children's	children's jackets

PRACTICE Provide sentences such as the following and ask students to choose the correct plural possessive noun in each sentence: *This is the* (childrens', children's) *cake. These are my* (friends', friend's) *chairs. The* (lady's, ladies') *book club chooses a book.* Have students choose a plural possessive noun from the sentences and use it in their own sentence.

Possessive Pronouns

INTRODUCE Hold a book and say: This is my book. This book is mine. **Explain:** The words *my* and *mine* are possessive pronouns. They show that I have this book. Possessive pronouns show who or what has or owns something.

TEACH/MODEL Present the concept and provide examples from the current reading selection. Use *my, your, her, our,* and *their* before nouns. Use *mine, yours, hers, ours,* and *theirs* alone. *His* and *its* can be used before nouns and alone.

	Possessive Pronouns
Before Nouns	This is your pen. It is her doll.
Alone	The shoes are mine. The doll is hers.
Both	The pen is his. This is his home.

PRACTICE Have students look around the room and identify objects that belong to them or to someone else. Have them use each item in a sentence with a possessive pronoun and underline the possessive pronoun: Here is *my* pencil. This calculator is *yours*.

ENGLISH LANGUAGE LEARNERS

Students who speak Asian languages may try various forms for possessive pronouns *(the hat of her, you hat)* or may not always state the pronoun *(Mo Yun took off hat)*. Provide additional practice with possessive pronouns.

Subject Pronouns

INTRODUCE Point to yourself and say, I am a teacher. **Point to the students and say,** You are students. **Point to a boy and say,** He is a student. **Point to a girl and say,** She is a student. **Indicate everyone in the room and say,** We are at school. **Explain:** Pronouns such as *I, you, he, she, we,* and *they* are used in place of nouns or noun phrases, such as people's names. These pronouns are used for subjects of sentences. We do not say, "*Me* am a teacher" or "*Him* is a student."

TEACH/MODEL Present the concept and provide examples from the current reading selection. A subject pronoun is used as the subject of a sentence.

	Subject Pronouns
Singular	I, you, he, she, it
Plural	we, you, they

PRACTICE Say the following sentences, or choose examples from the text, and have students rephrase them using the correct subject pronoun: Ana sits in the third row. Max sits here. Ana and Max are cousins. The sandwich is the teacher's lunch.

ENGLISH LANGUAGE LEARNERS

In Spanish, unlike English, speakers may omit subject pronouns because Spanish verbs can indicate the subjects. Korean speakers may add a subject pronoun after the noun, reflecting a pattern in Korean, such as "Nathan, he is my brother."

Object Pronouns

INTRODUCE Display these sentences: *Give the book to me. Mom made us a snack. They talked with Tom and her.* Explain: Pronouns such as *me, you, him, her, us,* and *them* are used after verbs or after words such as *for, at, with,* or *to*. We do not say, "Give the book to I" or "Mom made we a snack."

TEACH/MODEL Present the concept and provide examples. An object pronoun is used in the predicate, after an action verb or preposition.

	Object Pronouns
Singular	me, you, him, her, it
Plural	us, you, them

PRACTICE Pose open-ended sentences, cueing object pronoun endings by gesturing to different people in the room: I will help ___ [gesture toward a girl]. Students should finish the sentence with the word *her*.

ENGLISH LANGUAGE LEARNERS

Spanish, Chinese, and Vietnamese speakers and other English learners may use subject pronouns as objects, for example, "Give the book to she." Additional practice in English will help clarify the different pronoun forms.

Indefinite Pronouns

INTRODUCE Display this sentence: *Someone wrote you a note.* Ask: Who is this someone? If we don't know, then we can use the indefinite pronoun *someone*. Other singular indefinite pronouns are: *anybody, everyone, everything, either,* and *each.* Some plural indefinite pronouns are: *few, several, both, others, many, all,* and *some.*

TEACH/MODEL Present the concept and provide examples from the current reading selection. Indefinite pronouns may not refer to specific nouns. Use the correct verb forms with singular indefinite pronouns and with plural indefinite pronouns.

	Indefinite Pronouns
Singular	Everyone is clapping. Somebody has sung very well.
Plural	Some are standing. Others are sitting.

PRACTICE Show students a picture of a concert. Have them describe it, using similar sentences: *Everyone is in the concert. Some are singers.* Give other examples using illustrations or pictures from the text or related to the text.

ENGLISH LANGUAGE LEARNERS

In some languages, the words *everyone* and *everybody* take a plural verb. Students may try using verbs such as "Everyone are" or "Everybody say."

Reflexive Pronouns

INTRODUCE Display these sentences: *I will write a note to myself. She will buy herself a snack.* Explain: *Myself* and *herself* are reflexive pronouns.

TEACH/MODEL Present the concept and provide examples. Reflexive pronouns reflect the action back on the subject, for example, *They gave themselves a chance to rest.*

	Reflexive Pronouns
Singular	himself, herself, myself, itself, yourself
Plural	ourselves, yourselves, themselves

PRACTICE Write these subject pronouns on index cards: *I, you, he, she, it, we, they.* Make another set with reflexive pronouns. Have students draw a card from the reflexive set and match it to its subject pronoun. Then, have them write a sentence with the words they chose.

ENGLISH LANGUAGE LEARNERS

Chinese speakers learning English may omit a second reference to one person in a sentence. Rather than "I enjoyed myself," a student may feel that "I enjoyed" is complete.

Pronouns and Antecedents

INTRODUCE Display and read aloud this sentence: <u>Sam</u> says <u>he</u> will go. **Explain:** In this sentence, the pronoun *he* replaces the name *Sam*. The sentence does not have to say, "Sam says Sam will go." *Sam,* the noun being replaced, is called the antecedent. A pronoun must agree in number and gender with the noun or noun phrase it replaces. Sam is one person, a boy. So we use the pronoun *he,* which is singular and masculine. The pronoun for a girl is feminine: *she.* Lisa says she will go.

TEACH/MODEL Present the concept and provide examples:

- A pronoun and its antecedent must agree in number and gender.

Pronouns and Antecedents
<u>Laura</u> knows what <u>she</u> wants.
<u>Ravi</u> and <u>Ben</u> called me when <u>they</u> got home.
<u>The parrot</u> repeats what <u>it</u> hears.

PRACTICE Display this sentence: *The cat eats what it likes.* Write the following on cards and distribute to students: *The girl; My brother; The children; The dog; she; he; they; it.* Invite students to use the cards to substitute antecedents and pronouns in the sentence.

Verbs in Present Tense

INTRODUCE Perform these actions as you narrate: I walk to the front of the room. I point to the board. Explain that the words *walk* and *point* are verbs. The tense of a verb tells when something happens. A verb in present tense, like *walk* or *point*, tells what happens now. To talk about one other person or thing, add -*s*: *He walks. She points.*

TEACH/MODEL Present the concept and provide examples from the text. Verbs in present tense tell what happens now.

	Verb	Example
I, you, we, they	see	I <u>see</u> my sister.
he, she, it	sees	She <u>sees</u> me.

PRACTICE Write these subjects on index cards: *The baby, The girls, Sam, my brother, I*. Write these verbs on another set: *work, sleep, run, jump,* and *play*. Have students draw a card from each set and create a sentence. You can also use characters, information, and verbs from the reading.

ENGLISH LANGUAGE LEARNERS

English verb endings differ from verb endings in languages such as Spanish and Polish, which use different endings for person and number. However, students may need practice adding -*s* or -*es* to present-tense verbs with third-person singular subjects.

Verbs in Past Tense

INTRODUCE Display these sentences: *I <u>walked</u> to the front of the room. I <u>pointed</u> to the board.* Explain: I did these things in the past. Many verbs in past tense end with -*ed*. If a verb ends in *e*, like *move*, drop the *e* and then add -*ed: moved*. If a verb has one syllable and ends with a vowel followed by a consonant, such as *shop*, double the consonant before adding -*ed: shopped*.

TEACH/MODEL Present the concept and provide specific examples from the current reading selection. Verbs in past tense tell what happened in the past.

	Verbs in Past Tense
Add -*ed*	He *jumped* over the chair.
Drop the Final *e* and Add -*ed*	I *moved* the chair.
Double the Consonant and Add -*ed*	He *slipped* on the rug.

PRACTICE Display a list of verbs: *walk, play, jump, call, move, push, listen,* and *watch*. Begin to tell a story: Yesterday, I walked to the park with my friend. Have students add to the story, using the verbs from the list in the past tense. Alternatively, use a list of verbs from the text.

ENGLISH LANGUAGE LEARNERS

In Chinese, Hmong, and Vietnamese, verbs do not change to show the tense. Adverbs or expressions of time indicate when an action has taken place. Explain that regular past-tense verbs in English always have an -*ed* ending.

Irregular Verbs

INTRODUCE Display these sentences: *I think about you. I write a note. I thought about you. I wrote a note.* **Explain:** Usually, you add *-ed* to a verb to form the past tense. But here, I didn't use *thinked* or *writed*. Some verbs are not regular verbs. They are called irregular verbs. An irregular verb has a different spelling in the past tense.

TEACH/MODEL Present the concept and provide specific examples from the current reading selection. Irregular verbs do not add *-ed* to form the past tense. Irregular verbs have different spellings in the past tense.

Irregular Verbs	Past Tense
write	I *wrote* a poem yesterday.
sing	I *sang* a song last night.
eat	I *ate* an apple earlier today.

PRACTICE Prepare index cards with irregular verbs. On one side, write the present tense. On the other side, write the past tense: *write/wrote; sing/sang; make/made; give/gave; eat/ate; have/had.* Have partners dictate sentences to each other using the words on both sides.

ENGLISH LANGUAGE LEARNERS

Many English learners need extra practice with the variety of irregular verbs that also feature unfamiliar phonics elements, such as *catch/caught, buy/bought,* and *can/could.*

Verbs in Future Tense

INTRODUCE Say: What will I do after school today? I will go home. I will eat a snack. I will read my e-mail. **Explain:** To talk about the future, we use verbs in the future tense. The future may be later today, next week, or even next year. **Write one of the statements and point out the word *will*.** Say: We use the helping verb *will* to form the future tense.

TEACH/MODEL Present the concept and provide examples from the current reading selection. Verbs in future tense tell what will happen in the future.

Verbs in Future Tense
I *will go* home.
I *will eat* a snack.
I *will do* my homework.

PRACTICE Have partners tell each other what they will do when they get home from school or at some point in the future. If students can pantomime the action, have them act out the verb. Then, have them write or say the complete sentence.

ENGLISH LANGUAGE LEARNERS

Spanish, Haitian Creole, and Hmong speakers may use present tense in places where English calls for future tense. Help students practice verbs in statements using the word *will*.

Principal Parts of Regular Verbs

INTRODUCE Display these sentences: *I talk to you. I am talking to you. I talked to you. I have talked to you many times.* Explain: A verb's tenses are made from four basic forms: present, present participle, past, and past participle. These are called the verb's principal parts. The present form is used in the first sentence. The second sentence uses the present participle form. The third sentence uses the past form, which is the *-ed* form of the regular verb. The fourth sentence uses the past participle.

TEACH/MODEL Present the concept and provide examples from the current reading selection. The four basic forms are called the principal parts. The present participle can use *am, is,* or *are* and the *-ing* form. The past participle uses *has, have,* or *had* and the *-ed* form.

	Principal Parts: Regular Verbs
Present	The baby *plays* all day.
Present Participle	The baby *is playing* now.
Past	You *helped* me yesterday.
Past Participle	You *have helped* me before.

PRACTICE Say and display these verbs: *jump, walk, talk, wave,* and *laugh.* Have students give the present participle of each verb with the subjects *I, you, she,* and *they.* Have them pantomime the actions and point to the corresponding subject.

ENGLISH LANGUAGE LEARNERS

Speakers of several languages, including Arabic, may find the English distinction between the past and present perfect tenses unfamiliar. Show contrasting examples, and explain how the sense of time differs.

Principal Parts of Irregular Verbs

INTRODUCE Display these sentences: *You grow every day. You are growing so much! You grew an inch last year. You have grown an inch every year.* Point out the past form and past participle. Irregular verbs change spelling in these forms.

TEACH/MODEL Present the concept and provide examples from the current reading selection. The principal parts of irregular verbs are the same four kinds as the principal parts of regular verbs. The *-ing* form is made the same way, such as *growing* or *going.* But irregular verbs do not use the *-ed* ending for the past and the past participle. For example, we do not say *growed;* we say *grew.* We do not say *have growed;* we say *have grown.*

PRACTICE Write the principal parts of *go, sing, take,* and *write* on index cards. Give each student a card. Students circulate to find others with principal parts of the same verb.

ENGLISH LANGUAGE LEARNERS

Spanish, like English, has irregular verbs (such as *ser,* which means "to be," and *ir,* "to go"). Challenge students who are literate in Spanish to identify irregular Spanish verbs, and see whether English verbs with the same meanings are irregular.

Helping Verbs

INTRODUCE Display these sentences: *I am planting seeds. They will grow fast. I have planted seeds before.* Explain: The underlined parts are called verb phrases. The main verbs—*planting, grow,* and *planted*—show action. The helping verbs—*am, will,* and *have*—tell more about the action. The helping verb *am* tells what I am doing now. *Will* tells what the seeds will do in the future. *Have* tells what I have done in the past.

TEACH/MODEL Present the concept and provide examples from the current reading selection. Helping verbs can tell the time of the action.

	Helping Verbs
Present	The dog *is* wagging his tail.
Past	He *was* barking last night.
Future	He *will* stay inside tonight.
Started in the Past	You *have* helped me before.

PRACTICE Have each student create three index cards labeled Present, Past, and Future. Say these sentences and have students hold up the corresponding card: *You were* playing basketball yesterday. *You are* listening to me now. *You will* go to the library later. Encourage students to say other sentences with helping verbs.

ENGLISH LANGUAGE LEARNERS

The uses of *have* and *had* as helping verbs may be familiar to Spanish-speaking students once they learn the English words. The Spanish verb *haber* is used similarly.

Linking Verbs

INTRODUCE Display these sentences: *I am tired. I feel sick. She seems sad. He is the leader. The car was new.* Explain: In these sentences, the underlined words are called linking verbs. They tell what the subject is or what the subject is like.

TEACH/MODEL Present the concept and provide examples. Linking verbs do not show actions. They tell what the subject is or what the subject is like.

Linking Verbs	Examples
is	Summer *is* here.
are	The days *are* longer.
feels	The sun *feels* warmer.

PRACTICE Have partners tell three nice things they observe about each other: *You seem happy. You are smart. You are funny.* Have them identify the linking verbs. Students can also find three sentences in a text that describe a character using linking verbs.

ENGLISH LANGUAGE LEARNERS

In languages such as Chinese and Korean, linking verbs often are not required: *she tired* or *they sad*. Help students practice English sentences with linking verbs. Vietnamese speakers may use the English verb *have* in place of *there are* or *is*, as in *Inside the box have a gift*. Help students practice with sentences using forms of *be*.

Troublesome Verbs *Lie/Lay, Sit/Set*

INTRODUCE Write and say: The boy lays his book on the table. Then, he lies down on his bed to take a nap. Explain that in the first sentence, the boy puts his book down on a table. In the second sentence, he goes to bed to rest. Write and say: Miguel sets the plates on the table. Then, he sits at the table. Show the difference between *set* and *sit* in these sentences by pantomiming the actions.

TEACH/MODEL Present the concept and provide examples from the text that the students are currently reading. Some verbs look similar or have similar meanings. Think of the meanings and the main parts of verbs. Tell students that the verbs *set* and *lay* usually take a direct object. Display the sentences: *She set her keys on the counter. He lays his wallet on the table.* Use the sentences to show students that a direct object (keys, wallet) is a noun or pronoun that receives the action of a verb (set, lays) or shows the result of the action.

Troublesome Verb	Past	Past Participle
lie: "rest" or "recline"	lay	(has, have, had) lain
lay: "put" or "place"	laid	(has, have, had) laid
sit: "sit down"	sat	(has, have, had) sat
set: "put something somewhere"	set	(has, have, had) set

PRACTICE In pairs, have students take turns creating sentences that include troublesome words. The partner accepts a correct example and offers a new example.

Troublesome Verbs *Leave/Let, Rise/Raise*

INTRODUCE Write and say: The girl will leave with her friends. Her mother let her go. Explain that first the girl is going away. Her mother allows, or permits, her to go. Write and say: The sun will rise every day. The children raise their hands in class. Use pantomime or pictures to discuss the differences between *rise* and *raise* in these sentences.

TEACH/MODEL Present the concept and provide examples from the students' reading. Some verbs look similar or have similar meanings. Think of the meanings and principal parts of the verbs to use them correctly.

PRACTICE Display several incomplete sentences, asking students to complete each sentence with a troublesome verb. For example: *The teacher ___ (let) the children go home. The children ___ (left) quickly.*

ENGLISH LANGUAGE LEARNERS

Have English learners study the meanings and principal parts of troublesome verbs. Then, provide additional examples of the verbs used correctly.

Contractions

INTRODUCE Display these sentences: _You're calling me. I'm far away. I can't hear you._ Explain: The underlined words are contractions. A contraction is a shortened form of two words. An apostrophe **(point to an apostrophe)** takes the place of one or more letters. Look at these contractions: _You_ and _are_ become _you're._ _I_ and _am_ become _I'm._ _Can_ and _not_ become _can't._

TEACH/MODEL Present the concept and provide examples:

- A contraction is a shortened form of two words.
- An apostrophe takes the place of a letter or letters that are removed when you write a contraction.

Two Words	Contractions
I and have	I've eaten breakfast.
should and not	You shouldn't run in the hall.
can and not	She can't come to my party.

PRACTICE Say the following sentences and have students rephrase them using contractions: You are hiding. I do not see you. I am going to find you. I could not stop looking. If necessary, help students learn the contractions for each of the sentences: _you're, don't, I'm,_ and _couldn't._

Negatives

INTRODUCE Display these sentences: _I never eat fish. I don't ever eat fish._ Explain: The underlined words are negatives. They mean "no" or "not." Contractions with _n't_ are negatives. In English, we use only one negative with one verb. _I don't never eat fish_ has a double negative. Take away one negative. **(See the first two examples.)**

TEACH/MODEL Present the concept and provide examples:

- Use only one negative with one verb.
- Use a positive verb in a sentence with _not._

Type of Word	Examples
negative word + verb	Nothing is on the table.
positive verb + _not_	I don't see anything there.
verb + negative word	They went nowhere.
positive verb + _not_	We didn't go anywhere.

PRACTICE Write these sentences on the board: _I can't never tell you. I won't say nothing. I don't want nobody to hear._ Invite students to come up and show how they would fix the double negative. Ask them to read the new sentence.

ENGLISH LANGUAGE LEARNERS

In Spanish, Haitian Creole, and some other languages, double negatives (similar to _We did not do nothing_) are correct. Tell students that standard English does not use double negatives.

Articles

INTRODUCE Say: I need a pencil. **Hold up a pencil and say:** Here is a pencil with an eraser. The pencil is yellow. **Show some pencils and say:** The pencils are new. **Explain that** a, an, and the **are called articles:** Articles are these words that come before nouns: a pencil, the paper, an ink pen. Use a or an before a singular noun. You can use the before singular nouns or plural nouns.

TEACH/MODEL Present the concept and provide several examples:

- A, an, and the are articles.
- Use a before a singular noun that begins with a consonant sound; use an before a singular noun that begins with a vowel sound.

Articles
I want <u>a</u> banana. Sue wants <u>an</u> apple.
<u>The</u> fruit salad was good. <u>The</u> girls ate it all.

PRACTICE Have students identify the articles in the following sentences.

1. Cali, Beth, and Ling found (an, a) rope in their garage.

2. (An, The) rope was six feet long.

3. Beth knew (a, an) song for jumping rope.

4. (The, A) girls jumped rope for (a, an) hour.

Adjectives: Size, What Kind, How Many

INTRODUCE Say: You know that nouns are words that name people, places, animals, or things—for example, girls and house. Adjectives are words that tell more about the nouns: small house, four girls, blue car, long hair. Which words are the adjectives? (**small, four, blue, long**)

TEACH/MODEL Present the concept and provide examples:

- An adjective tells more about a noun or pronoun.

	Adjectives
What Kind?	a <u>good</u> friend; The food is <u>spicy</u>.
How Many?	<u>two</u> men; <u>many</u> apples
Size	a <u>big</u> hat; The school was <u>small</u>.

PRACTICE Have students identify the adjectives in the following sentences: *My two brothers and I have a small garden. We have three plants. The plants have many tomatoes that are big and red. They are delicious!*

Adjectives: Comparative and Superlative

INTRODUCE Draw three long lines of different lengths on the board. Point to the different lines and say: This line is long. This line is longer. This line is the longest. Say: *Long* is an adjective. *Longer* compares two nouns, like two lines. To compare two nouns, add *-er* to most adjectives. *Longest* compares three or more nouns. To make a superlative adjective, add *-est* to most adjectives.

TEACH/MODEL Present the concept and provide examples:

- Many comparative adjectives end in *-er: faster, thinner, tinier.* Change the spelling of some adjectives, like *tiny,* when you add *-er.*
- Many longer adjectives use the word *more* instead of *-er: more exciting, more beautiful.*
- Many superlative adjectives end in *-est: brightest, loudest, tallest.* Use *most* with longer adjectives: *most beautiful.*
- Some adjectives have irregular forms such as *good, better, best.*

Comparative	Superlative
bigger; more important	fastest; most difficult

PRACTICE Have students choose the correct adjective to complete the following sentences: *The squirrel is* (smaller, smallest) *than the dog. Chico is the* (largest, larger) *of the three dogs. My bird is* (more beautiful, most beautiful) *than my friend's bird. The big dog should have a* (gooder, better) *name. My friend Buffy is the* (funniest, funnier) *person I know.*

Adjectives: Demonstrative

INTRODUCE Present three girls and three boys, with the boys farther away. Ask: Which students are girls? These students are girls. Those students are boys. Which girl is Audrey? This girl is Audrey. That boy is Oliver. *These, those, this,* and *that* are called demonstrative adjectives. They help you demonstrate, or show, which one or which ones. Use *this* and *these* when things are close. Use *that* and *those* when things are farther away.

TEACH/MODEL Present the concept and provide examples:

- Demonstrative adjectives: *this, that, these, those*

	Demonstrative Adjectives
Singular	This book is longer than that book.
Plural	These shoes are bigger than those shoes.

PRACTICE Have students choose the correct adjective to complete the following sentences: (These, This) *flowers are called poppies. Each spring,* (this, these) *field is full of poppies.* (That, Those) *tree on the hill looks like a person. People ride their bikes across* (those, this) *hills. Many people take pictures of* (this, these) *place.*

ADVERBS

Adverbs for *When, Where,* and *How*

INTRODUCE Say and act out this chant: Slowly I turn. Loudly I clap! I walk here and there. I end with a tap. **Say:** *Slowly, loudly, here,* and *there* are adverbs. They tell how, when, or where something happens.

TEACH/MODEL Present the concept and provide examples:

- Adverbs tell more about the actions of verbs.
- Adverbs that tell how something happens often end in *-ly.*

	Adverbs
When?	I <u>always</u> walk to school.
Where?	I like to walk <u>outside</u>.
How?	I walk <u>quickly</u>.

PRACTICE Write the following adverbs on slips of paper: *slowly, quickly, loudly, sleepily.* Display them. Have a volunteer choose one. Give a command, such as *Walk to the door.* The volunteer must walk in the manner of the adverb. The student who guesses the adverb takes the next turn.

ENGLISH LANGUAGE LEARNERS

Point out to Spanish speakers that the adverb suffix *-ly* is like the ending *-mente* in Spanish. Give examples with cognates such as *rapid/rápidamente.*

Comparative and Superlative Adverbs

INTRODUCE Say each sentence: I speak quietly. Katya speaks more quietly. Rob speaks most quietly. *More quietly* is a comparative adverb. It compares two actions: I speak, Katya speaks. *Most quietly* is a superlative adverb. It compares three or more actions. If an adverb does not end in *-ly,* add *-er,* or *-est* to compare.

TEACH/MODEL Present the concept and provide examples:

- A comparative adverb compares two actions.
- A superlative adverb compares three or more actions.
- Some adverbs are irregular: *well, better, best*

Comparative and Superlative Adverbs
Julia runs <u>fast</u>. Anil sings <u>beautifully</u>.
Pat runs <u>faster</u>. Kenji sings <u>more beautifully</u>.
Tere runs the <u>fastest</u>. Ivan sings <u>most beautifully</u>.

PRACTICE Display three pictures of athletes. Have students compare them using *well, better, best* or *fast, faster, fastest* with the verbs *run, play,* or *swim.*

Prepositions and Prepositional Phrases

INTRODUCE Stand behind a chair, and have students do the same. Say: Behind the chair. Have students repeat. Continue moving and speaking using the words *beside, around,* and *on* (sit). Explain: *Behind, beside, around,* and *on* are prepositions. *Behind the chair* and *on it* are prepositional phrases. *Behind* is a preposition, and *chair* is a noun. *On* is a preposition, and *it* is a pronoun.

TEACH/MODEL Present the concept and provide examples:

* A prepositional phrase can tell where, when, how, or which one.
* A prepositional phrase begins with a preposition (*above, across, at, behind, for, from, in, near, with,* and so on).
* A prepositional phrase ends with a noun or pronoun.

Preposition	around
Prepositional Phrase	around the chair

PRACTICE Model as you give students directions to follow: Walk to this side of the room. Walk across the room. Stand by a desk. Look under the desk. Have volunteers take turns giving directions that include prepositional phrases.

Conjunctions

INTRODUCE Use colored pens or markers to illustrate the following: I have a red pen and a green pen. The word *and* joins two similar things: two colors of pens. Do you like red or green better? The word *or* gives a choice: red or green. You can use the green pen, but don't use the red pen right now. The word *but* joins two different ideas: use and don't use. *And, or,* and *but* are called conjunctions.

TEACH/MODEL Present the concept and provide examples:

* A conjunction joins words, phrases, and sentences.

Related Ideas: Diego <u>and</u> I are friends.
Different Ideas: We live far apart, <u>but</u> we talk often.
Choice: We talk on the phone <u>or</u> we send e-mail.

PRACTICE Share these common phrases with conjunctions: *salt and pepper; thanks, but no thanks; stop-and-go traffic; left or right; boy or girl.* Invite students to say them while using gestures to help show the meanings.

ENGLISH LANGUAGE LEARNERS

Speakers of Chinese and some other languages may build sentences using two conjunctions where English typically uses one. For example: *Because the sun came up, so I could see the clock.* Help students practice English patterns.

PREPOSITIONS AND CONJUNCTIONS

Subjects and Predicates

INTRODUCE Display this sentence: _The girl walks to school._ Explain that _The girl_ is the subject of the sentence, or what the sentence is about. Explain that _walks to school_ is the predicate. A predicate tells something about the subject.

TEACH/MODEL Present the concept and provide examples:

- The subject of a sentence tells whom or what the sentence is about.

- The predicate of a sentence tells what the subject is or what the subject does.

Subject	Predicate
Sam	went to the store.
The students	write a paper.
The vegetables	are fresh.

PRACTICE Write these sentences onto strips of paper: _My friend rides a bike. My dog barks at cats. The fish smells good. The clown is funny._ Cut each strip into subject and predicate. Have students use the strips to form new sentences such as: _My friend is funny._

ENGLISH LANGUAGE LEARNERS

The typical English sequence of subject then predicate is not standard in some languages. For example, in Spanish the verb often appears before the subject, while in Korean and Hindi the verb typically appears at the end of a sentence.

Subject-Verb Agreement

INTRODUCE Display these sentences: _The <u>bird</u> <u>sings</u> a song. The <u>birds</u> <u>sing</u> a song._ Discuss the differences between the underlined parts: The first sentence has a singular subject: bird. The second sentence has a plural subject: birds. The subject and verb must agree.

TEACH/MODEL Present the general concept and provide examples:

- If the subject is singular, add _-s_ to the verb.

- If the subject is plural, do not add _-s_ to the verb.

Subject	Verb
man	dances
Mom	works
friends	play
both feet	hurt

PRACTICE Encourage students to scour the day's news headlines for examples of subject-verb agreement. For example: _Schools Close; Team Wins; Gas Prices Rise; Dog Saves Girl._

ENGLISH LANGUAGE LEARNERS

Students of various language backgrounds may add _-s_ to both the nouns and verbs in sentences: _The robots walks._ Point out that in English, verbs add _-s_ for singular nouns (A robot walks), not for verbs with plural nouns (The robots walk).

Word Order

INTRODUCE Display these sentences and read them aloud, gesturing: The bird flies. Flies the bird. **Ask:** What is the subject of the first sentence? **(The bird)** The second sentence does not sound right. The words are not in the right order to make a statement. In an English statement, the subject usually comes first. The predicate usually follows.

TEACH/MODEL Present the concept and provide examples:

* Sentences need to have words in the right order.

* In a statement, the subject usually comes first. The predicate usually follows.

In the Right Order:	Pablo is my friend.
Not in the Right Order:	Is friend my Pablo.

PRACTICE Say these groups of words: The food is good. Is good the food. My friend rides a bike. Rides a bike my friend. Plays the dog. The dog plays. **Have students say which sentences are in correct word order.**

ENGLISH LANGUAGE LEARNERS

Help students see that word order strongly affects meaning in English. *Lee thanked Tony* has a different meaning from *Tony thanked Lee.*

Complete Sentences and Sentence Fragments

INTRODUCE Write this sentence and fragment on the board: *Tom went to the library. Went to the library.* **Ask:** Who went to the library? **(Tom)** Which sentence tells you this? The first sentence tells a complete idea. It says who did something. The second set of words (*went to the library*) is called a sentence fragment. It does not tell a complete idea. It does not say who went to the library. How would you make this fragment a complete sentence? **(Add a subject.)**

TEACH/MODEL Present the concept and provide examples:

* A sentence tells a complete idea.

* A fragment is a piece of a sentence. It does not tell a complete idea.

Sentence	Ava eats her lunch.
Fragment	Her lunch in a bag.

PRACTICE Say these groups of words. Have students call out "sentence" or "fragment" after each one: My brother. We walk to school. We ride on the bus. In the car. After school. **Invite students to contribute other sentences.**

ENGLISH LANGUAGE LEARNERS

Spanish- and Chinese-speaking students may omit some pronouns as sentence subjects, because in their home languages the pronoun may be unnecessary. For example, the Spanish equivalent of *Am reading* is a complete sentence.

Types of Sentences: Statements

INTRODUCE Display these sentences: *I went to the library. My brother went, too. We both found good books.* **Say:** Let's look at these sentences. Each one starts with a capital letter and ends with a period. Each one tells something. A sentence that tells something is called a statement.

TEACH/MODEL Present the concept and provide examples:

- A sentence that tells something is called a statement.
- It begins with a capital letter and ends with a period.

Statements

I had a party yesterday.

All of my friends came to my house.

You ate pizza.

PRACTICE Write groups of words such as these on the board, including the mistakes: *my friends are funny. / They tell me jokes / I laugh every day* Have volunteers come up and fix the statements by adding correct punctuation and a capital letter at the beginning.

Types of Sentences: Questions

INTRODUCE Display these sentences: *What is your name? Where do you live? How old are you? Do you have any brothers?* **Ask:** How are these sentences different from statements? They each ask something, and they end with question marks. A sentence that asks something is called a question. **Model the difference in vocal intonation between these two sentences:** That is your dog. Is that your dog?

TEACH/MODEL Present the general concept and provide examples:

- A sentence that asks something is called a question.
- It starts with a capital letter and ends with a question mark.

Questions

How are you?

Did you go to Sam's party?

Does Ami like pizza?

PRACTICE Have pairs of students ask each other questions about what they did yesterday. For example: *What did we do in school yesterday? What is your favorite subject?*

ENGLISH LANGUAGE LEARNERS

Speakers of Chinese, Vietnamese, and other Asian languages often form questions by adding words to statements, comparable to *The food is hot, no?* or *You see or not see the bird?* Provide model English questions for students to understand and to follow the pattern.

Types of Sentences: Exclamations and Interjections

INTRODUCE Write and say in an excited voice: I am so happy! **Ask:** What feeling does that sentence express? (excitement; happiness) Whenever you say something with strong feeling, you are saying an exclamation. A written exclamation ends with an exclamation mark. **Next, write and say:** Hooray! **Explain:** This word also shows strong feeling and ends in an exclamation mark. However, it is not a complete sentence. It is called an interjection.

TEACH/MODEL Present the concept and provide examples:

- An exclamation is a sentence that shows strong feeling. It ends with an exclamation mark.

- An interjection is a word or group of words that shows strong feeling. It ends with an exclamation mark, but it is not a complete sentence.

Exclamation	I have a new baby brother!
Interjection	Wow!

PRACTICE Write these interjections on index cards: *Ouch! Wow! Oh, no! Hooray!* Display them. Have a volunteer secretly choose an interjection and pantomime a scene that would elicit that interjection. Whoever guesses correctly takes the next turn. Then have students share exclamations with the class.

ENGLISH LANGUAGE LEARNERS

Speakers of Russian, Polish, and other languages may need to practice correct word order in exclamations. Have students make and use sentence strips to correct exclamations, such as *We enjoy very much movies!*

Types of Sentences: Commands

INTRODUCE Give students various commands such as these: Please stand up. Walk to the front of the class. Say hello. Sit down. **Ask:** How are these sentences the same? (They told us to do something.) Sentences that tell someone to do something are called commands.

TEACH/MODEL Present the concept and provide examples:

- A command is a sentence that tells someone to do something.
- It begins with a capital letter and ends with a period.

Commands

Open the door. Turn on the light. Sweep the floor.

PRACTICE As a class, play the game "I Said So" in which a leader says command sentences, such as "Touch your nose," and the rest of the class follows.

ENGLISH LANGUAGE LEARNERS

Vietnamese speakers may recognize commands when they include an adverb or another clue word: *Go to school now. Take this to the office; go now.*

SENTENCES

Simple and Compound Sentences

INTRODUCE Display these sentences: *I went to Sal's house. We watched a movie.* Ask students to tell the subject and predicate (verb) of each sentence. Explain: A simple sentence has one subject and one predicate. But, we can join the two simple sentences this way: *I went to Sal's house, and we watched a movie.* The new sentence is called a compound sentence. The two simple sentences are joined with the word *and*. Now the sentence has two subjects and two predicates.

TEACH/MODEL Present the concept and provide examples from a reading selection:

- A simple sentence has one subject and one predicate.
- A compound sentence has two simple sentences joined by a comma and one of these words: *and*, *but*, or *or*.

Simple Sentences
- Lena is my sister. I love her.
- I like peanuts. They make me sick.
- You can walk to school. I can drive you.

Compound Sentences
- Lena is my sister, and I love her.
- I like peanuts, but they make me sick.
- You can walk to school, or I can drive you.

PRACTICE Provide several pairs of simple sentences from the current reading selection. Have students rewrite them as compound sentences.

ENGLISH LANGUAGE LEARNERS

Students may have difficulty distinguishing the clauses in a compound sentence in English. Give them additional practice finding the subject and verb within each independent clause.

Combining Sentences

INTRODUCE Display these sentences: *I ate a sandwich. I drank some milk.* Ask: What is the subject of both sentences? You can combine two sentences that have the same subject: *I ate a sandwich and drank some milk.* Display these sentences: *Max went to the beach. I went to the beach.* Ask: What is the predicate of both sentences? You can combine two sentences that have the same predicate: Max and I went to the beach.

TEACH/MODEL Present the concept and provide examples from the current reading selection:

- Combine two sentences that have the same subject.
- Combine two sentences that have the same predicate.

Same Subject
- Dan sat down. Dan did his homework.
- Dan sat down and did his homework.

Same Predicate
- Miguel walked to school. I walked to school.
- Miguel and I walked to school.

PRACTICE Make a set of sentence cards using sentences from the current reading selection. Include sentences with the same subject as well as sentences with the same predicate. Distribute the sentence cards to students. Have volunteers read their sentence. Ask the student with the same subject or predicate to raise his or her hand. Then have those two students combine their sentences.

Complex Sentences

INTRODUCE Review compound sentences. Then present these complex sentences: _When I run, I feel good. I feel good when I run._ Explain: This type of sentence is called a complex sentence. It has two parts, called clauses. The underlined part cannot stand alone as a sentence. If it comes first in the sentence, use a comma. The other part _(I feel good)_ can stand alone as a complete sentence.

TEACH/MODEL Present the concept and provide examples from a reading selection:

- A complex sentence contains two clauses.
- The two clauses are joined together with words such as _because, when, since, if,_ or _until._
- Example complex sentences: _When I grow up, I will be a teacher. I will be a teacher when I grow up._

PRACTICE Have students write sentences and tell whether they are complex: _My sister's name is Lupe._ (no) _Since she is little, I help her with homework._ (yes) _I also tie her shoes._ (no) _When I was little, my mom helped me._ (yes)

ENGLISH LANGUAGE LEARNERS

Functional words, such as _if, that, so,_ and _because_ are often used somewhat differently in English than their equivalents in other languages. Help students practice and understand usages of these words.

Independent and Dependent Clauses

INTRODUCE Present this complex sentence: _We cross the street when the light is green._ Explain: The underlined part of the sentence cannot stand alone as a sentence. It is a dependent clause. It depends on another part of the sentence. The other part _(we cross the street)_ can stand alone as a sentence. It is an independent clause.

TEACH/MODEL Present the concept and provide examples from a reading selection:

- A complex sentence is made of an independent clause and a dependent clause.
- The dependent clause cannot stand alone.
- The independent clause can stand alone.

Independent Clause	Dependent Clause
I am happy	because I passed the test.

PRACTICE Display the following dependent clauses, and have students add an independent clause to each to form complex sentences: _Since he was little, When I grow up, Because it was raining, If you help me._ Have students write the complex sentences.

ENGLISH LANGUAGE LEARNERS

Provide models of dependent clauses that begin with words such as _after, although, as, because, before, if, since, then, until, when,_ and _while._ These words may have uses that are unfamiliar to students of many language backgrounds.

PUNCTUATION

Commas: In a Series and in Direct Address

INTRODUCE Display this sentence: *My favorite colors are red, blue, and yellow.* Point out the commas. Say: Commas help you understand a sentence. They tell you when to pause, or rest. Put commas after items in a series of words such as *red, blue, and yellow.* Display these sentences: *Kim, may I use your pen? Yes, Lucas, you may.* Say: When we write a sentence in which a person is directly addressed by name, we use a comma.

TEACH/MODEL Present the concept and provide examples:

- Use commas to separate items in a series.
- Use commas with direct address.

Commas in a Series	I like baseball, basketball, and soccer. I play Monday, Wednesday, and Friday.
Commas in Direct Address	Lori, would you come here? Yes, Mom, I'm coming. I need your help, Lori.

PRACTICE On the board, write menu items such as *soup, salad, sandwich, milk, tea,* and *juice.* Have pairs play the roles of server and customer at a café. The server says, "May I take your order?" The customer names three items such as: "I want soup, salad, and milk." The server says and writes the order. Next, the customer says and writes a sentence thanking the server by name. Have pairs switch roles.

ENGLISH LANGUAGE LEARNERS

Some students may use commas where periods are used in the United States (1,5 for 1.5). Determine the meaning, and clarify the standard usage in American English.

Commas: With Appositives and Introductory Phrases

INTRODUCE Display these sentences: *Mr. Hays, <u>my teacher</u>, speaks Spanish. <u>Yes</u>, I know.* Explain: The underlined part of the first sentence is called an appositive. It is a noun phrase that describes another noun. Use a comma before and after an appositive. The underlined part of the second sentence is called an introductory word. Put a comma after an introductory word or phrase such as *well, no, oh,* and *in other words.*

TEACH/MODEL Present the concept and provide examples:

- Use a comma before and after an appositive.
- Use a comma after an introductory word or phrase.

Appositives	Mr. Simms, <u>my neighbor</u>, has a dog. The dog, <u>a poodle</u>, barks all night.
Introductory Words or Phrases	<u>Oh</u>, I am very sorry. <u>In other words</u>, you cannot sleep.

PRACTICE Write names and job titles of school staff, such as *Mrs. Olson, the bus driver.* Have students use this information to write sentences with appositives.

Quotation Marks

INTRODUCE Display and read aloud the following dialogue: "Do you have homework?" my mother asked. "Yes, I have to read a book," I said. "What is the name of the book?" my mother wanted to know. Point out the position of the quotation marks in the dialogue.

TEACH/MODEL Present the concept and provide examples:

- A quotation shows the exact words of a speaker.
- Quotation marks enclose a quotation.
- Use a comma to separate the speaker's exact words from the rest of the sentence. Don't add a comma when the quotation ends with a question mark or exclamation mark.
- Quotation marks are also used for poetry, titles, song titles, and story titles.

Quotation	Story Title
"Mr. Chung is my favorite teacher," said Joy.	"The Cat Has a Hat"

PRACTICE Display correct and incorrect examples of quotation marks used within a sentence. Write the sentences: *"He plays soccer"* (incorrect) *He said, "I am going to play soccer."* (correct) Offer several examples and ask students to identify correct and incorrect usage.

ENGLISH LANGUAGE LEARNERS

Help students use quotation marks in English by having them complete the following sentence frame in English and their home language: My favorite movie is "___." Model an answer as you make a gesture for quotation marks with your fingers when you say the name of the movie. Have students repeat.

Parentheses

INTRODUCE Write and say the following sentence: Jin has several pets (dog, bird, fish), but he is allergic to cats. **Ask:** What information is provided in the parentheses of this sentence? **Explain:** The information in the parentheses tells us more about Jin's pets.

TEACH/MODEL Present the concept and provide examples:

- Words in parentheses give an explanation or a comment in an already complete sentence.
- The information in parentheses is not necessary but adds detail to the sentence.

Sentence without Parentheses	Sentence with Parentheses
Some subjects are very hard for me.	Some subjects (especially math and science) are very hard for me.

PRACTICE Have students give extra details about a friend by completing the following sentence frame: My friend likes to do many things after school (such as ____).

ENGLISH LANGUAGE LEARNERS

The writing systems of students' home languages may have different conventions for parentheses. Have students practice finding parentheses in classroom texts.

Plurals and Possessives

INTRODUCE Write the following pair of sentences on the board, and ask students how they are different: *A chair and a table are in the room. Chairs and tables are in the room.* Students will probably notice that the nouns in the first sentence are in the singular form, whereas the nouns in the second sentence are in the plural form. Next, write these two sentences on the board, again asking students what they notice about them: *The pen of the teacher is red. The teacher's pen is red.* Say: Both sentences mean the same, but they use different ways to show possession, or ownership.

TEACH/MODEL Copy the following chart on the board and use it to teach students how to form plurals and possessives in English.

	Rules	Examples
Plurals	Add -*s* to the singular form of most nouns.	boys, girls, pens, balls, days
	Add -*es* to words that end with *sh, ch, x, s,* and *z*.	brushes, arches, boxes, classes, quizzes
	For words that end with a consonant and *y*, change the *y* to *i* before adding -*es*.	cities, stories, candies
Possessives with an Apostrophe	Add an apostrophe and *s* to most singular nouns.	Trina's idea, Kin's report, Carlos's dog
	Add an apostrophe to plural nouns that end in *s*.	the girls' uniforms, the boys' team

PRACTICE Have students take turns pointing to an object belonging to a classmate and then saying a sentence using both the name of the object and the classmate, such as "This is Marco's notebook." Have students write sentences about their classmates, using the possessive form.

Tell students to write pairs of sentences about a friend and a family member. The first sentence should introduce the person, and the second sentence should tell about something that person has or owns. Write this example on the board: *My friend's name is Samuel. Samuel's wheelchair can go fast.*

Verb Endings: -s, -ed, -ing

INTRODUCE Write these verbs on the board and read them aloud, slowly, for the class, asking students to pay close attention to the sound at the end of each word: *washes, cleans, writes, sleeps, fixes, plays, swims, talks.* Ask students if they noticed a difference in the way the final *-s* was pronounced in certain words. Confirm for them that *writes, sleeps,* and *talks* are pronounced with the sound of /s/ at the end, while *washes, cleans, fixes, plays,* and *swims* are pronounced with the ending sound of /z/. In a similar way, ask students to determine if the following words end with the sound of /d/ or /t/: *walked, enjoyed, liked, talked, played, measured.* Finally, have students practice saying the following gerunds aloud, modeling correct pronunciation as necessary: *playing, cleaning, jogging, talking, washing, swimming.*

TEACH/MODEL The following rules may help students know which pronunciation to use with words that end in *-s* and *-ed.* Remind students that these are general guidelines and that they should listen carefully to native speakers for further guidance.

For words that end in *-s,*

- use the sound of /s/ if the letter before it is *k, p,* or *t.*
- use the sound of /z/ if the letter before it is *b, g, m, n,* or a vowel.

Note: If a word ends in silent *e,* the sound of *-s* depends on the letter before the *e.*

For words that end in *-ed,*

- use the sound of /d/ if the letter before it is *b, l, m, n,* or a vowel.
- use the sound of /t/ if the letter before it is *ch, k, p, s, sh,* or *x.*

To make the *-ing* form of a verb,

- add *-ing* to the simple verb.
- double final *b, g, m, n,* or *p* before adding *-ing.*
- drop silent *e* before adding *-ing.*

PRACTICE Ask students to write *s, z, d,* or *t* after you have said the following verbs aloud, to indicate which sound they heard at the end of the word: *asks, plays, calls, runs, helps, walks, writes, sees, called, played, fixed, rubbed, helped, opened, walked, washed.* Then ask students to write the correct *-ing* form of each of the following verbs: *call, hope, play, run.* If needed, write the verbs on the board.

ENGLISH LANGUAGE LEARNERS

Some languages such as Chinese, Hmong, and Vietnamese do not use inflected endings to form verb tenses. Students may need help understanding that adding *-ed* to a verb indicates that the action happened in the past. Spelling changes in inflected verbs may also be difficult for English language learners to master. Provide students with extra practice as needed.

Compound Words

PURPOSE Compound words exist in many languages, including Spanish, Vietnamese, Haitian Creole, German, and Russian. Students may readily understand the concept of compound words but may need additional support determining how to break English compound words into their parts. The following activity provides practice with compound words.

INTRODUCE On two separate index cards, write two words that make up a compound word, such as the words *story* and *teller*. Ask students to define each word. If necessary, define *teller* as "a person who talks or tells something." Then, hold the cards side by side. Based on their previous definitions, ask students what *storyteller* means, and confirm that it means "a person who tells stories." Explain that the new word is a compound word. It is made up of two smaller words.

TEACH/MODEL Tell students: When you make a compound word, you put two words together to make a new word. Usually, there isn't any change to the spellings of the two smaller words. Use examples of compound words from a text, such as *snowbanks, heartberries, driftwood, lakeshore,* or *blueberry*. Discuss the meaning of each separate word, and then show how the words can be combined to create a new word. Point out that neither of the smaller words has a spelling change. The words are simply put together to create a new word. Ask students to share any other compound words that they know, and record their answers.

PRACTICE Give students note cards with small words that can be combined into compound words. Tell them to combine the small words to make logical compound words. Have students record the words they create. Conversely, students can take the compound word and draw a line to separate the two smaller words.

TEACHING TIP Providing visuals of the words can help students understand the meaning of compound words. Sometimes, the smaller words have different meanings from the compound word. Point these out to students.

ENGLISH LANGUAGE LEARNERS

There are compound words in Spanish. Examples include *abrelatas* (can opener) and *rascacielos* (skyscraper). Point these out to students to help them make connections.

Related Words

INTRODUCE On the board, write *breath, breathe,* and *breathless.* Ask students: What do these words have in common? Point out that they all have the word *breath* as the base. The endings on the other two words change their part of speech and meaning. *Breathe* is a verb and *breathless* is an adjective. Many other words are closely related in the same way. Tell students that they will expand their vocabularies if they try to learn new words in groups with other related words.

TEACH/MODEL Write the following chart on the board, asking students to provide additional examples for the second column. Once students are familiar with these examples, have them find words that are related to words from the text they are currently reading. Provide students with a list of base words from the current reading selection. Have students fill in a chart with the words that are related to each base word.

Base Word	Related Words
jewel	jeweler, jewelry
planet	planetary, planetarium
paint	painter, painting
act	action, actor, active
sign	signature
compute	computer, computation
horizon	horizontal
pot	potter, pottery
bank	banker, banking
heal	health, healthy
relate	relative, relationship
produce	product, production
please	pleasant, pleasure

EXTEND Ask students to find base words from the selection and make a chart listing the related words. Students can refer to and expand on these charts of word groups.

Homophones

INTRODUCE Tell students this joke in the form of a question and answer: What is black and white and read all over? A newspaper! Explain to students that the question seems to be asking about colors (black, white, and red), but there is a play on the word *red*. The color *red* sounds the same as *read,* a past-tense form of the verb *read*. Explain that this joke is based on a pair of homophones (*red* and *read*), two words that sound the same but are spelled differently and have completely different meanings.

TEACH/MODEL Write the following homophone pairs on the board: *pair, pear; flour, flower; made, maid; week, weak*. Explain the meaning of each word and point out the two different spellings. Model the pronunciation, emphasizing that the two words in each pair are pronounced in exactly the same way. Invite students to share any other homophones that they know. Spanish examples include *casa/caza* (house/hunt), *hola/ola* (hello/wave), and *ciento/siento* (one hundred/I feel).

PRACTICE Have students create a T-chart with the headings Same and Different. Write the following pairs of words on the board and have students read them aloud. Have them put a checkmark in the Same column, if the words sound the same. Have them put a checkmark in the Different column, if the words sound different. Write: *knew/new; flour/flower; meal/mail; tow/toe; hour/our; through/threw; sun/son; plate/played; best/beast; week/weak*. Invite volunteers to share their answers. Review the meanings of the words. Make corrections as necessary, and tell students to correct their own work as well.

Ask students to write three sentences that include a pair of homophones, such as: *Our English class is an hour long*. Encourage students to make simple jokes with the homophones; they can also write sentences that are fanciful or silly, as in: *On Monday, I was too weak to make it through the whole week*.

ENGLISH LANGUAGE LEARNERS

Homophones are also common in other languages, but English learners may not recognize that English homophone pairs have the same pronunciation despite their different spellings. They may need to learn to use their knowledge of word meaning to choose the correct spelling of homophones.

Prefixes: *un-, re-*

INTRODUCE Write these word pairs on the board: *happy, unhappy; safe, unsafe; lucky, unlucky*. Read the words aloud with students and discuss their meanings. Ask: What do you notice about these words? Guide students to see that each word pair is a set of opposites and that one word in each pair begins with *un-*. Circle the prefix *un-* in each word and say: This syllable, *un-*, is a prefix. A prefix is a word part that is added to the beginning of a word. Adding a prefix changes the meaning of a word. A new word is made.

TEACH/MODEL Present the prefixes *un-* and *re-*. Use these examples to explain how the prefixes can change the meanings of words.

Prefix	Meaning	Examples
un-	not	happy → unhappy safe → unsafe locked → unlocked
re-	again	tell → retell do → redo write → rewrite

PRACTICE Write the following word combinations on the board. Have students write a new word for each pair, using *un-* or *re-*: *read again; appear again; not believable; not familiar; heat again; not interested; not like; start again; use again; not kind*. Invite volunteers to write their new words on the board.

Have students write these prefixes and base words on cards: *un-, re-, afraid, lock, run, unite*. Have students use the cards in different combinations to make words that have prefixes. Have students show you a base word without a prefix, add a prefix, say the new word, and tell what it means.

ENGLISH LANGUAGE LEARNERS

Some English prefixes and suffixes have equivalent forms in the Romance languages. For example, the prefix *dis-* in English *(disapprove)* corresponds to the Spanish *des-* *(desaprobar)*, the French *des-* *(desaprouver)*, and the Haitian Creole *dis-* or *dez-* *(dezaprouve)*. Students who are literate in these languages may be able to transfer their understanding of prefixes and suffixes by using parallel examples in their home language and in English.

Prefixes: *im-, in-, mis-, over-*

INTRODUCE Write these word pairs on the board: *patient, impatient; polite, impolite; proper, improper; pure, impure*. Read the words aloud with students and discuss their meanings. Ask students what they notice about these words. Guide students to see that each word pair is a set of opposites and that one word in each pair begins with *im-*. Circle the prefix *im-* in each word and explain: This word part, *im-,* is a prefix. It usually changes the meaning of a word to its opposite.

TEACH/MODEL Present the prefixes *im-, in-, mis-,* and *over-*. Use these examples to explain how the prefixes can change the meanings of words.

Prefix	Meaning	Examples
im-	not	impatient, imperfect, impossible
in-	not	insecure, intolerant, indestructible
mis-	wrong	misunderstood, misbehave, mismatch
over-	beyond, more than	overcook, overpay, overweight

PRACTICE Have students write these prefixes and base words on index cards: *im-, in-, mis-, over-, correct, interpret, load, look, mature, take, use*. Tell students to combine the cards to make words with prefixes.

Circulate as the students work, asking them to show you a base word and a prefix that goes with it. Ask advanced students to tell you what the word means and to use it in an oral sentence.

ENGLISH LANGUAGE LEARNERS

Tell Spanish speakers that the Spanish prefixes *im-* and *in-* have similar meanings (*impaciente, intolerante*). The Spanish prefix *sobre-* is sometimes used like the English prefix *over- (sobrecarga)*.

Prefixes: *pre-, mid-, over-, out-, bi-*

INTRODUCE Write these word pairs on the board: *test, pretest; air, midair; time, overtime; run, outrun; monthly, bimonthly*. Read the words aloud with students and discuss their meanings. **Ask:** What do you notice about these words? Explain that the second word in each pair has a prefix that changes the meaning of the first word. Circle the prefix *pre-* and **say:** This syllable, *pre-*, is a prefix. A prefix is a word part that is added to the beginning of a word to change its meaning. When you add a prefix, a new word is made. The prefix *pre-* means "before." So, *prepay* means "to pay before."

TEACH/MODEL Present the prefixes *pre-, mid-, over-, out-,* and *bi-*. Using the chart below, explain how adding prefixes to base words changes the meaning of each word.

Prefix	Meaning	Examples
pre-	before	paid → prepaid view → preview
mid-	in the middle of	day → midday night → midnight
over-	more than normal, too much	grown → overgrown cooked → overcooked
out-	more, to a greater degree	side → outside run → outrun
bi-	two	cycle → bicycle

PRACTICE Have students write these prefixes and base words on index cards: *pre-, mid-, over-, out-, bi-, paid, air, time, field, weekly*. Have them use the cards in different combinations to make words with prefixes. As an additional challenge, have students show a base word without a prefix, add a prefix, say the new word, and tell what it means.

ENGLISH LANGUAGE LEARNERS

Point out to Spanish speakers that the prefix *mid-* is related in meaning to the Spanish word *medio*, which means "half" or "middle." Display cognates such as *midnight/medianoche* and *midday/mediodía* as examples.

WORD STUDY

Suffixes: *-ly, -ful, -less, -ness*

INTRODUCE Write the following words on the board: *careful, carefully, careless, carelessness.* Ask students what these words have in common and what makes them different from each other. Students should notice that all the words have the same base, *care.* But each successive word also has a different word part at the end. Explain that each of these word parts is a suffix. Say: A suffix is a word part that is added to the end of a word. Adding a suffix changes the meaning of a word.

TEACH/MODEL Present the suffixes *-ly, -ful, -less,* and *-ness.* Write the following chart on the board, asking students to provide additional examples for the last column.

Suffix	How and Why to Use It	Part of Speech	Examples
-ly	Add it to an adjective to tell how an action is done.	Adverb	quickly calmly completely
-ful	Add it to a noun to mean "full of" the noun.	Adjective	thoughtful colorful helpful
-less	Add it to a noun to mean "without" the noun.	Adjective	spotless joyless flawless
-ness	Add it to an adjective to describe a state of being.	Noun	darkness happiness carelessness peacefulness

PRACTICE Have students write these suffixes and base words on index cards: *-ly, -ful, -less, -ness, slow, quiet, good, fear, rude.* Tell students to combine the cards to make words with suffixes. Circulate as they work, asking students to show you a base word and a suffix that goes with it. Ask advanced students to tell you what the word means and to use it in an oral sentence.

Suffixes: *-tion, -sion, -able, -ible*

INTRODUCE Write the following words on the board: *perfection, decision, walkable, sensible.* Tell students that each of these words is made up of a base word and a suffix. Circle the suffix *-tion* in the first word and explain: This word part, *-tion,* is a suffix. Ask volunteers to find the suffixes in the other three words. Point out that the base word might need a spelling change before the suffix is added. The word *decide,* for example, drops the final *-de* before adding *-sion.* The reason for these spelling changes has to do with pronunciation, and the rules are hard to generalize, as there are many exceptions to the rules. Students will learn the different spellings with practice.

TEACH/MODEL Present the suffixes *-tion, -sion, -able,* and *-ible.* Explain that *-tion* and *-sion* have the same meaning, as do *-able* and *-ible.* Write the following chart on the board, asking students to provide additional examples for the last column. Spanish examples of these suffixes are *-ción (reacción), -sión (decisión), -able (confortable),* and *-ible (sensible).*

Suffix	How and Why to Use It	Part of Speech	Examples
-tion, -sion	Add it to a verb to describe an action or a state of being.	Noun	perfection imagination reaction decision admission confusion
-able, -ible	Add it to a verb to add the meaning "can be."	Adjective	workable comfortable dependable sensible reversible flexible

PRACTICE Have students write these suffixes and base words on index cards: *-tion, -sion, -able, -ible, sense, comfort, confuse, react.* Tell students to combine the cards to make words with suffixes. Circulate as they work, asking students to show you a base word and a suffix that goes with it. Ask advanced students to tell you what the word means and to use it in an oral sentence.

Suffixes: *-er, -or, -ess, -ist*

INTRODUCE Write the following words on the board: *swimmer, actor, hostess, tourist.* Tell students that each of these words is made up of a base word and a suffix. Remind students that a suffix is a word part added to the end of a word to change its meaning. Circle the suffix *-er* in the first word and explain: This word part, *-er*, is a suffix. Ask individuals to find suffixes in the other three words. Explain that the base word may require a spelling change before a suffix is added. For example, the word *swimmer* adds an *m* before the suffix. Point out that some spelling changes are related to pronunciation. Explain to students that they will become familiar with different spellings as they practice using the words.

TEACH/MODEL Present this chart to practice the suffixes *-er, -or, -ess,* and *-ist.* Ask students for additional examples of words with these suffixes.

Suffix	What It Means	Examples
-er -or	a person or thing that does something	teacher opener editor tutor
-ess	a female who does something as a job; a female	actress lioness
-ist	a person who has studied something or does something frequently or as a job	artist dentist

PRACTICE Have students write these suffixes and base words or word parts on index cards: *-er, -or, -ess, -ist, act, sell, host, dent, tour, teach, lion.* Have students use the cards in different combinations to make words that have suffixes. As an additional challenge, have students show a base word without a suffix, add a suffix, say the new word, and tell what it means.

Suffixes: *-y, -ish, -hood, -ment*

INTRODUCE Write the following words on the board: *rocky, foolish, parenthood, shipment.* Say each word aloud and tell students that each of these words is made up of a base word and a suffix. Remind students that a suffix is a word part that is added to the end of a word to change its meaning. Circle the suffix *-y* in *rocky* and explain: This word part, *-y,* is a suffix. The base word in *rocky* is *rock*. Ask students to find base words in the other three words. Have them tell you what each base word means.

TEACH/MODEL Present this chart to practice the suffixes *-y, -ish, -hood,* and *-ment.* Have students identify each base word and suffix in the examples. Ask students for additional examples of words with these suffixes.

Suffix	What It Means	Examples
-y	having the quality of	cloudy rainy thirsty
-ish	describing a nationality or language; somewhat	Spanish brownish foolish
-hood	a state or condition of	childhood fatherhood
-ment	a state, action, or quality	excitement movement

PRACTICE Have students write these suffixes and base words on index cards: *-y, -ish, -hood, -ment, smell, mother, excite, wind, green, false, ship.* Have students use the cards in different combinations to make words that have suffixes. As an additional challenge, have students show you a base word without a suffix, add a suffix, say the new word, and tell what it means.

Words with Greek Roots

INTRODUCE Write the following words on the board: *autograph, phonograph, photograph, paragraph.* Say them aloud, and then ask students what all these words have in common. Confirm for them that they all have the word part *graph*. Tell students that this word part comes from the Greek language. It means "written." Conclude by saying: Many other words in English have Greek roots, too. Learning these roots can help you learn more words.

TEACH/MODEL Write the following chart on the board, asking students to provide additional examples for the last column.

Greek Root	Meaning	Sample Words
biblio	book	bibliography
bio	life	biography
crac, crat	rule, govern	democrat
demos	people	democracy
geo	earth	geology
graph, gram	written, drawn, describe, record	photograph
log	idea, word, speech, study	biology
meter	measure	perimeter
phono	sound	symphony
scope	to see	telescope

Show students how different word parts can be combined. The root *bio,* for example, can be combined with *graph* to form *biography* (meaning "record of life"), and it can also be combined with *log* to form *biology* (meaning "study of life"). Knowing this, students can conclude that any word with the root *bio* has to do with life. Tell Spanish speakers that many Spanish words have these same Greek roots. Ask these students to provide translations for the sample words in the chart *(bibliografía, biografía, demócrata, democracia, geología, fotografía, biología, perímetro, sinfonía, telescopio).*

PRACTICE Write the following words on the board: *autobiography, phonology, geography,* and *telescope.* Ask students to copy these words and to write their definitions, based on what they've learned. When they've finished, have a volunteer write his or her answers on the board, and model corrections as necessary. You can collect students' work for later assessment.

Words with Latin Roots

INTRODUCE Write the following words on the board: *animal, animation, animated.* Ask students what all these words have in common. Confirm for them that they all have the word part *anima.* Tell students that this word part is from Latin, an ancient language that was originally spoken in Italy. *Anima* means "living." Conclude by saying: Many other words in English have Latin roots, too. Learning these roots can help you learn more words.

TEACH/MODEL Write the following chart on the board, asking students to provide additional examples for the last column. Tell Spanish speakers that Spanish comes from Latin, so these roots should be familiar.

Latin Root	Meaning	Sample Words
aqua	water	aquarium
aud	to hear	auditorium
cent	one hundred	century
cert	sure, to trust	certificate, certify
circ	around	circle
computar	to compute	computer, computation
dic, dict	to say, to speak	dictionary, dictate
fin	to end	finish
grad	step, degree	graduate
scrib	to write	scribble

PRACTICE Write the following words on the board: *certain, final, audition,* and *gradual.* Ask students to copy these words and to identify their Latin roots. To check comprehension, ask students to write a sentence with each of these words.

Syllable Patterns: V/CV and VC/V

INTRODUCE Write the word *lemon* on the board and draw or show a small picture of a lemon. Say: This is a lemon, lem/ən. How many vowel sounds do you hear in the word *lemon*? Say it with me, lem/ən, lemon. That's right, there are two vowel sounds. **Cover the letters *mon*.** Say: If the syllable ended after the *e*, I would pronounce the word with a long *e*: lē/mon. This does not make a word that I know. **Cover the letters *on*,** then say: I will try it with a short *e*, lem/ən. Now I pronounce the word *lemon*, and I recognize it. The short-vowel sound is correct. **Repeat with the words *broken* and *finish*, emphasizing the short- or long-vowel sound in the first syllable.**

TEACH/MODEL Write the word *pupil* on the board. Draw a line between the two syllables and tell students: When you hear a word with more than one vowel sound, divide it into parts. Explain that when there is one consonant between two vowels, it is important to figure out if the first vowel has a short or long sound in order to know where to divide the syllable.

Point out that because the first syllable in *pupil* has a long-vowel sound, it ends after the first vowel. Then write *finish* on the board. Draw a line between the *n* and the second *i*, then say: This word also has one consonant between two vowels. The first vowel sound in *finish* is short, so we know that the first syllable ends with a consonant. Say it with me: finish, fin/ish.

PRACTICE Write these words on the board: *music, lemon, frozen, tulip, broken, salad.* Clap as you read each word to emphasize the syllable break in the word. Then have students record the words. Say: I am going to read the words again. This time, circle each word with a long-vowel sound in the first syllable. Underline each word with a short-vowel sound in the first syllable. Review the answers as a class. (Circle: *broken, frozen, music, tulip;* Underline: *salad, lemon.*)

EXTEND Make word cards with these word parts: *bro, ken, si, lent, sev, en, fe, male, rap, id.* Give student pairs the pile of word cards. Have students put the various word parts together to create complete words. If necessary, list the words *broken, silent, seven, female,* and *rapid* on the board.

Syllable Patterns: CV/VC

INTRODUCE Write the word *violin* on the board and draw or show a small picture of a violin. Say: This is a violin, vī/ə/lin. How many vowel sounds do you hear in the word *violin*? Say it with me, vī/ə/lin, violin. That's right, there are three vowel sounds. Explain that if a word in English has three vowel sounds, it must also have three syllables. Repeat with the words *computer* and *calendar*, emphasizing vowel sounds and reviewing what students have learned about breaking words into syllables.

TEACH/MODEL Write the word *create* on the board. Draw a line between the first *e* and *a* and tell students: When you hear a word with more than one vowel sound, divide it into parts. Explain that when there are two vowels side-by-side, there is a syllable break between the two vowels.

Practice breaking multisyllabic words with the CV/VC syllable pattern into meaningful parts. Write the word *reorganize*. Read the word aloud, then point out the prefix *re-* and say: We know that the prefix *re-* is its own syllable and means "again." Then cover up the prefix so that only *organize* is visible. Say: *Organize* means "to put in order." We know that *organize* has three vowel sounds, so it has three syllables. Uncover the prefix, draw lines between the syllables, and blend the word. Have students repeat the word after you. Have them explain the meaning of *reorganize*. Repeat this exercise with the words *reunite, deactivate,* and *scientists*.

PRACTICE Make word cards with these word parts: *studi-, cre-, ide-, me-, pio-, immedi-, bi-, reli-.* Make another set of cards with these word parts: *-neer, -onic, -o, -ate, -dium, -ance, -a, -ate.* Divide the class into pairs. Give one student the first set of word parts. Give the second student the second set. Once students have pieced the words together, have them write out the words and draw lines between each syllable.

ENGLISH LANGUAGE LEARNERS

Speakers of monosyllabic languages such as Cantonese, Hmong, Khmer, Korean, and Vietnamese may pronounce a two-syllable word as two separate words. Have students practice saying multisyllabic words.

Syllable Patterns: VCCCV

INTRODUCE Write *dolphin* on the board and draw or show a small picture of a dolphin. Say: This is a dolphin, dol/fən. Point out that there are two vowel sounds in *dolphin*, and therefore two syllables. Say: How many consonants do you see between the vowels *o* and *i* in the word *dolphin*? Point to the *l, p,* and *h* as you say: That's right, there are three consonants between the vowels. Remind students that when two consonants, such as the *ph* in *dolphin*, make one sound, those letters stay together when you divide the word into syllables. Say: Now let's break the word *dolphin* into syllables: dol/fən, dolphin. Repeat with the words *explode* and *contract*, emphasizing vowel sounds.

TEACH/MODEL Write *surprise* on the board. Underline the three consonants between the vowels *u* and *i* and tell students: There are three consonants between two vowels in this word. Each vowel means that there is a syllable, so we know that there are two syllables in this pattern. Since it is hard to generalize where the syllable break comes in a word with the VCCCV syllable pattern, help students understand that they must look at each word separately to find its syllable breaks.

Practice breaking words with the VCCCV syllable pattern. Distribute several copies of a dictionary and point out how each word is divided into syllables. Write the word *complain* on the board. Ask: How many syllables does this word have? (two) What is the first syllable? (com) What is the second syllable? (plain) Repeat this exercise with the words *explore, sample, enclose,* and *hundred*.

PRACTICE Write the following words on the board: *address, district, substance, complete,* and *control*. Have students write the words on a piece of paper, showing the syllable divisions. Students should use what they know about dividing words into syllables. If they have difficulty with a word, they may use a dictionary to see how a word is divided into syllables.

ENGLISH LANGUAGE LEARNERS

Speakers of monosyllabic languages such as Cantonese, Hmong, Khmer, Korean, and Vietnamese may pronounce a two-syllable word as two separate words. Have students practice saying multisyllabic words.

Syllable Patterns: C + -le

INTRODUCE Draw or show a small picture of a candle. Say: This is a candle, kan/dl. How many syllables do you hear in the word *candle*? That's right, there are two syllables. Sound out and blend the following words with C + -le: *bubble, puddle, table*. Point out that the first syllable in each word carries more stress than the second syllable.

TEACH/MODEL Write *candle* on the board. Draw a line between the two syllables and tell students: When you hear a word with more than one vowel sound, divide it into parts. Cover the letters *can*. Say: If a word ends with -le, then the consonant before the -le is part of the last syllable. Show that in the word *candle*, the letter *d* comes right before the -le and is part of the second syllable. Now write *double* on the board. Draw a line between the *u* and the *b* and say: In the word *double*, the letter *b* comes before the -le and is part of the second syllable. Say it with me: double, dou/ble.

PRACTICE Display the following words for students, and have students record them on paper: *puddle, eagle, marble, middle, double, little, title, handle*. Ask students to write the two syllable parts that make up each word. For example, *mar + ble = marble*. If needed, write the following frame on the board for students to refer to: ___ + ___ = ___.

EXTEND Tell students: I will say some words. Put your thumb up if you hear a consonant with -le at the end of the word. Put your thumb down if you do not: *purple, bubble, puppy, people, softball, broken, noodle*. Then have students repeat the C + -le words back to you.

ENGLISH LANGUAGE LEARNERS

Many languages do not have the schwa /ə/ sound, so English learners may have difficulty pronouncing and spelling the unstressed syllable in words such as *table* and *apple*. Provide additional practice pronouncing these words.

PREPARE TO READ

Context Clue Caper

Display the vocabulary words for a particular selection. Explain that you will say each word aloud and use it in a sentence or two that provides effective context. Challenge students to be the first to explain, in their own words, what each word means based on its context clues. For example, for the word *reluctant,* you might provide a context sentence similar to the following: *At first, I was reluctant to drink the bluish-green vegetable smoothie my mom made for a snack.*

Vocabulary in a Flash

Write the vocabulary words for a selection or module on cards. Display each card. Ask students to indicate whether they have heard of the word. If some students have heard of the word, ask them to share the context in which they heard it or explain what they know about it. Once all ideas have been shared, challenge students to use the word in a sentence of their own.

Realia and Visuals

Write the vocabulary words for a selection or module on the board. Point to each in turn and provide a student-friendly definition. Then display items that evoke the words' meanings. For example, for the word *miniature,* you might show a tiny chair from a dollhouse and point out the difference between its size and the size of a classroom chair. Then ask students to name other miniature items.

INTERACT WITH TEXT

Situation Skits

Prepare a set of word cards by writing the vocabulary words from a particular selection, their meanings, examples of situations in which the words are used, and questions. For example, after writing on a card the word *gleeful* and its meaning ("so happy that you feel a little silly"), you might provide the following situation: *You just found out that school is closed because of a big snowstorm the night before. You jump up and down, hurry to put on your hat, coat, mittens, and boots, and then run outside to make snow angels.* Then you might write the following question: *When is the last time you felt gleeful? Describe the situation.* Form groups of students and give one card set to each group. Give the actors time to discuss the word and plan a brief skit, using the situation on the card. Before a skit is performed, have one member of the group write the word on the board and pronounce it. After the skit is performed, have another cast member ask the audience the meaning of the word and the question you prepared. The audience response can help you assess understanding and provide feedback.

Word Drawings

Assign each student a word from the reading selections that lends itself to a visual representation. Have students create drawings that evoke or convey the words' meanings. For example, to convey the word *shiver,* a student might write the word in shaky letters. Have students present and explain their drawings to the class. Display students' drawings around the room.

Dictionary Dash

Select words from the reading selections that have multiple meanings. Divide the class into groups and provide each group with a word and the selection and page number where it appears. Have students reread the sentence in the selection and use a dictionary to identify the correct definition of the word in this context. Then have them use the dictionary to identify another definition of the word. Challenge them to write a sentence that uses both meanings of the word correctly. For example, *I put a dash of salt on my boiled egg and then dash off to school!* Have groups read and explain their sentences to the class.

Word Sorts

Provide students with index cards on which vocabulary words are written, one word per card. Ask students to sort the words into categories you provide, such as Words That Show Action, Words That Name Things, Words That Connect to the Unit Theme, and so on. Or have students create the categories and explain the rationale behind their categories.

EXPRESS AND EXTEND

Card Games

Prepare a deck of 40 word cards, using the words students explored in a particular module or unit. Then prepare match cards for each word card, which might include a definition, a synonym, an antonym, a cloze sentence in which the word makes sense, a picture symbolizing the word's meaning, an English translation, or some other appropriate match. For example, a student might pair a word card labeled *desist* with a match card on which its definition appears: "to stop." Students can play a variety of games with these cards. For Fish, all the cards are dealt and players pick one card from the player on their left in turn, placing any pairs they make on the table. The first player to pair all cards wins. For Old Teacher (a variation of Old Maid), an extra card is prepared with a generic drawing of a teacher. The game is played like Fish, except the student who is left with this card is the "old teacher." In all card games, students must read their pairs aloud. Other players can challenge a student's pair, in which case a dictionary would be used to settle the dispute. Either the challenger or the player may get an extra turn, depending upon who is correct.

Memory Game

Prepare a maximum of 25 cards: 12 word cards with vocabulary words from the module; 12 match cards with definitions, synonyms, antonyms, pictures, and so on; and 1 wild card. Shuffle the cards and place them facedown in a 5 x 5 grid. Explain that, for each turn, a student will turn over and read two cards. If the cards are a match (for example, the word *immense* and a picture of an elephant), the student will take the cards. If they are not a match, the student will turn the cards back over and leave them in the same place. Play continues in turn until only a single card remains. Students may use the wild card only if they can provide an appropriate match. For example, if a student draws the elephant picture and the wild card, he can say the word *immense* aloud. This can be checked at the end of the game by looking at the remaining card, which should match the answer supplied earlier. The student with the most cards wins.

Bingo

Give students word cards with vocabulary words from a particular unit and ask them to arrange them in a 5 x 5 grid, placing a "free" card in a space of their choice. Assign one student to be the caller. Explain that the caller will select definitions from the definition pile and read them aloud. The players will then place markers on the words in their grids that match the definitions. The first student to mark an entire row, column, or diagonal wins the game. Have students check their work by reading the words and definitions aloud. Reshuffle the cards, ask students to reorganize their grids, and invite the winner of the game to be the caller for the next game.

Off Limits

Write vocabulary words from a module or unit on cards, along with three of the most common words, phrases, or concepts associated with each vocabulary word. Explain that these common synonyms or related words are considered "off-limits." For example, for the vocabulary word *nutritious*, clues listed as "off-limits" might be *food*, *eat*, and *healthy*. Divide the class into two teams. Explain that a player from Team A will have one minute to help Team A guess as many words as possible by giving any kinds of clues—as long as they are not on the "off-limits" list. A player from Team B will look over this player's shoulder to keep the player honest. Team A gains a point for every word correctly guessed based on the player's clues. If the player accidentally uses one of the "off-limits" clues, Team A loses a point. After one minute, points are totaled for Team A, and then Team B takes its turn. The team with the most points after a certain number of rounds wins.

Graphic Organizers

Give partners a list of words from a particular module. Explain that they will create a word web using at least 10 of these words. They can use any words from the list they like and design their webs in any way they like, but their webs should demonstrate their knowledge of the relationships between these 10 words. For example, they might connect two vocabulary words from the module that have similar meanings, such as *forlorn* or *melancholy*. In this case, explain that the line that connects these words on the web would be labeled "synonym." Or they might connect two words that have opposite meanings, such as *saunter* and *stroll*, and label the line connecting them "antonym." They might link two words that can be used to describe the same character in a text or two words that apply to the same scientific concept or topic. Encourage students to think in creative ways and make their webs as intricate as they can, with multiple connections between words. Invite them to present and explain their webs to the class when they have finished drawing and labeling.

Password

For this game, you as the teacher will play the game-show host, and two student players will play the contestants. Split the class into two teams, and have one member from each team come up and sit in chairs facing the class. Give the players one-word clues about a vocabulary word explored in the module or unit. For example, for the word *universe*, you might give clues such as *galaxies, planets, moons, stars,* and *infinite*. The first student to correctly guess the vocabulary word wins the round. If students have difficulty guessing the correct vocabulary word, give more obvious clues in the form of phrases, such as *even bigger than our solar system.*

Yes/No and True/False

Prepare a list of yes/no questions and true/false statements for the vocabulary words in a particular selection or module. For example, for the words *vital, burrow, extreme, spine,* and *disguise,* you might prepare the following questions or statements: Yes or no: Is sunlight vital to plants and animals? Yes or no: Is a rain shower an example of extreme weather? True or false: No plant or animal can have a disguise. True or false: Generally, animals that burrow are small in size. As in these examples, questions or statements should be designed so that answers require full knowledge of the words. Divide the class into two teams. Have one player from each team come up and sit in chairs in front of the class. Say each question or statement aloud, and the first student to correctly answer yes or no or true or false has 10 seconds to explain the answer. If the player successfully explains, that player's team gains a point. If the player answers incorrectly or cannot provide an adequate explanation within the time limit, that team loses a point. The team with the most points at the end wins the game.

Category Challenge

Have students draw a 5 x 5 grid and label each vertical row with a category: word; synonym/similar; antonym/different; example; and related word. Choose four challenging vocabulary words from a particular selection or module, and have students write the words in the first column. Give the players a designated time frame to fill in as many squares in each row as they can. For example, for the word *despise,* the remaining four columns might read: *dislike, adore, I despise bullying behavior; scorn.* At the end of the time limit, points are totaled: 5 points for every category square a player filled in that no other player has filled; 2 points for every category square that others have filled in, but with different words; and 1 point for every category square filled in where someone else has the same term.

Either/Or

Divide the class into two teams. Have the members of each team work together to create 10 either/or questions using the vocabulary words for a particular selection or module. For example, for the words *spine, vital,* and *nutrient,* students might create the following either/or questions: *Which animal has* spines *on its skin—a porcupine or a crocodile? If something is* vital, *is it very important or not important at all? When you hear the word* nutrient, *do you think of something that's bad for you or good for you?* Review student questions before the start of the game and provide feedback as necessary. Then have a player from Team A ask a player from Team B a question. If the player from Team B answers correctly and provides an adequate explanation for his or her response, Team B gets a point. If not, Team A gets a point. Make sure every member of each team participates. When Team A has asked all of its questions, the teams switch roles. The team with the most points at the end wins the game.

COGNATE ACTIVITIES

Cognate Sort

Create word/picture cards for words in English that have numerous cognates, such as *music, computer, park,* and *family.* Then create word cards with cognates for these words, such as *música, musique; computador, komputer; parque, parc; familia, famiglia.* Have students sort the cognates under the correct word/picture cards. Be sure to ask students if they know of other cognates you might add to the list. Afterward, conduct a discussion with students about what similarities and differences they notice between the words and how cognates can be helpful to them as they explore new languages.

Cognate Match

Make a list of words in English and their Spanish cognates, such as *bank, banco; university, universidad; museum, museo.* Give each student in the class either a word in English or a Spanish cognate. If there are an odd number of students, take one of the cards yourself. Challenge the students to move about the room until they find the person who has a match for their card. Then invite each matched pair to write the word and its Spanish cognate on the board and circle letters that are different. Repeat the activity with cognates from other languages.

Cognate Find

Create picture cards for words in English that have numerous cognates, such as *bank, train,* and *telephone.* Give pairs of students one of the picture cards and have them identify as many cognates for the word as they can, by either conducting research on the Internet or consulting multilingual speakers in the classroom or community. Have them share their findings with the class.

True or False?

Organize students in groups and give each group a different list of pairs between English words and true or false Spanish cognates for these words. Have students identify whether the words in each pair are true cognates or false cognates. For example, *class* and *clase* are true cognates, but *rope* and *ropa* are false cognates. Suggest that students consult multilingual speakers in their group or in other groups, use dictionaries, or conduct research on the Internet in order to identify whether each pair is true or false. Have groups share and explain their answers with the class. Repeat with cognates from other languages.

Unlock Language Learning

Part 4 Unlock Language Learning

Night of the Spadefoot Toads

BUILD BACKGROUND FOR *NIGHT OF THE SPADEFOOT TOADS*

Reproduce and distribute copies of *The Kinds of Life* student page on page 369. There are billions of living things on Earth. Each kind is a species. Read the first paragraph and bullet. How many species are there on Earth? *There are at least _____ species.* Have partners study the rest of the text and complete sentence frames such as *The Eastern spadefoot toad is _____ of _____ species of American spadefoot toads.*

TALK ABOUT SENTENCES

For students who need support in accessing key ideas and key language in *Night of the Spadefoot Toads,* use the Sentence Talk Routine on pages 437–438 to draw students' attention to the relationship between meaning and the words, phrases, and clauses in the text.

Lesson	Sentence(s) to Deconstruct
1	(p 9) Animals are living things and need to be treated carefully. They're not toys.
2	(p 31) He cradles the creature in both hands a moment longer, then slips it into his jacket pocket.
3	(p 45) His knee jiggles up and down as he thinks about it, and he presses his hand against his stomach, which is turning over and over like it has a life of its own.
4	(p 65) Mrs. Tibbets hands Ben a rake and a big plastic tarp and leads him around to a large flowerbed on the side of the house away from the garage.
5	(p 98) His only hope is to distract Mrs. Tibbets and pretend that he's just gotten here, then come back in a minute and make sure the snake hasn't gotten out.
6	(p 113) They're having a great time. Making noise in class is something no one ever lets them do.
7	(p 137) Those were just feel-good stories, nothing but make-believe.
8	(p 168) You need to do homework and play with friends and let grown-ups worry about problems like this.
9	(p 189) "You're new in Massachusetts, and it might be interesting for you to find out about your new environment."
10	(p 192) All of the things in the box seem like parts of his life from so long ago.
11	(p 217) Without a word, like they speak the same silent language, Mrs. Tibbets and Ben walk around the garage and head toward the woods.
17	(p 210) Even though it's small, it holds a thousand things.
18	(p 193) There's an awkward moment of silence, and Ben is glad he doesn't have to do anything but stand there and be a kid.

Use the Text-based Writing Routine on pages 439–440 to model how to speak and write about key ideas and details in *Night of the Spadefoot Toads.*

Lesson	Text-based Writing	Scaffolded Frames
1	By page 9, what attitude toward animals do Ben and Mrs. Tibbets share?	• Animals are _____. • Treat them _____ and not like _____.
2	On page 31, how does Ben treat the frog? Why?	• Ben holds _____. • Ben wonders _____.
3	On page 45, why does Ben feel "horrible and excited"?	• Ben is excited because _____. • Ben is worried that _____.
4	On page 65, why does Mrs. Tibbets lead Ben to the flowerbed?	• Ben is there to help _____. • Mrs. Tibbets wants Ben to _____.
5	On page 98, what does Ben hope for?	• Ben hopes Mrs. Tibbets will _____. • Ben hopes the snakes _____.
6	Based on page 113, what makes Mrs. Tibbets's class different and fun?	• Mrs. Tibbets tells the class to make _____. • Other teachers never _____.
7	Based on page 137, what are the problems Ben knows will be hard to fix?	• Mrs. Tibbets will probably lose her _____. • The toads don't have anywhere to _____.
8	On page 168, why does Ben's mother say, "This has got to stop"?	• Ben called _____. • Ben's mother thinks he should _____.
9	On page 189, what is significant about Mrs. Kutcher's suggestion to Ben?	• Mrs. Kutcher _____ a new topic. • Ben will get to _____.
10	On page 192, why isn't Ben as interested in the stuff anymore?	• Ben lives _____. He has new _____. • Ben's life today is _____.
11	What evidence on page 217 shows that Ben has changed since the novel began?	• Ben and _____ share _____. • Now Ben knows _____.
17	What details on page 210 show how special vernal pools are?	• The pools are _____. • They have _____.
18	What details on page 193 show a key problem in the story?	• Ben and Mrs. Tibbets want to _____. • Tabitha and Mrs. Garrett want to _____.

Use the Dig Deeper Vocabulary Routine on pages 435–436 to continue to develop conceptual understanding of the following adjectives: wry, baffled, deflated, sinister, murky, exasperated. Read aloud the following sentence from page 199: "Mrs. Tibbets blows a short, exasperated burst of air out of her mouth." Does *exasperated* describe an object or a feeling?

Unit 1 Module A

Name _____

The Kinds of Life

The world has plants, animals, bacteria—so many kinds of life! Each kind of living thing belongs to a *species*. A species is a group of living things with similar and unique qualities. Eastern spadefoot toads are one species.

• The world has at least 1,700,000 species (and those are just the species people know about). Every species is unique.

   • **1,371,428** species are **animals**. Most animals, such as insects, don't have backbones. Some animals do have backbones.

      • **66,178** species of animals have **backbones**. Amphibians, reptiles, birds, fish, and mammals have backbones.

         • **7,405** species are **amphibians**. Amphibians include frogs and toads; newts and salamanders; and caecilians, which look like earthworms or snakes.

            • **6,525** species are **frogs or toads**. They are grouped into 55 families.

               • **7** species belong to the **spadefoot toad** family. One group lives in Europe, and one group lives in the Americas.

                  • **3** species belong to the **American** group of spadefoot toads.

                     • **1** species is the **Eastern spadefoot toad**.

Give two facts about the Eastern spadefoot toad.

An Eastern spadefoot toad is one of _____ species of frogs or toads.

A frog or a toad is just one kind of _____.

Shells

BUILD BACKGROUND FOR *SHELLS*

Reproduce and distribute copies of the *Hermits, Crabs, and Shells* student page on page 371. Explain that to understand the characters and story events in "Shells," it helps to know the different meanings these words can have. Point to the dictionary entry for *hermit* and read it aloud. Help students define *hermit* in their own words. How do you think a hermit might feel about being around lots of people? Why? *A hermit might feel _____ about being around lots of people because _____.*

Next, read each definition of *crab* aloud. Help students understand the meaning of *bad-tempered*. Call on volunteers to give each definition in their own words. Why do you think a bad-tempered person might be called a crab? *A bad-tempered person might be called a crab because _____.*

Then have students work with a partner to discuss what else they learned about crabs.

TALK ABOUT SENTENCES

For students who need support in accessing key ideas and key language in "Shells," use the Sentence Talk Routine on pages 437–438 to draw students' attention to the relationship between meaning and the words, phrases, and clauses in the text.

Lesson	Sentence(s) to Deconstruct
12	(p 6) And though he denied it, he did hate Esther. She was so different from his mother and father.
13	(p 8) An attraction to a crab is something I cannot identify with.

SPEAK AND WRITE ABOUT THE TEXT

Use the Text-based Writing Routine on pages 439–440 to model how to speak and write about key ideas and details in "Shells."

Lesson	Text-based Writing	Scaffolded Frames
12	Based on the thoughts Michael has on page 6, what were his parents like?	• His parents were not _____. • Unlike _____, his parents were not _____. • Esther _____, which Michael's parents _____.
13	How do Esther's words on page 8 help explain her attitude toward Michael?	• Esther does not feel _____ to the crab. • However, she will let the crab _____.

Name _____

Hermits, Crabs, and Shells

HERMIT (n) a person who chooses to live alone. **Synonyms:** recluse, solitary, loner

CRAB 1. (n) an animal with an outer skeleton, five pairs of legs, and eyes on stalks.
      2. (n) a bad-tempered person. **Synonyms:** grouch, complainer

SHELL 1. (n) a hard protective outer case or covering. **Synonym:** armor
      2. (n) an attitude that hides one's feelings.
      3. (n) something hollow or empty.

WHAT IS A HERMIT CRAB?

Every crab has a skeleton on the outside of its body. When the crab grows, it climbs out of its skeleton, which has become too small. Then the crab grows another skeleton.

A hermit crab lives in a shell that another animal left behind. The shell protects the crab's soft belly. When a hermit crab gets too big for its shell, it has to find a larger shell.

A hermit crab is like a _____ because it lives _____.

A hermit crab can hide inside its _____.

Hatchet

Reproduce and distribute copies of the *Northern Canada* student page on page 373. Explain that to understand the story events in *Hatchet* it helps to know where the story takes place.

Identify Alaska and Hudson Bay on the map. Offering help as needed, have students take turns reading the first paragraph aloud. Elicit any prior knowledge students have about Alaska. How is Alaska different from our state? *Alaska is _____ than our state.* You can see that northern Canada is bigger than Alaska. Explain the concept of population density. Read the second paragraph aloud. Imagine that a person got lost in northern Canada. Why might it take a long time for someone to find and help that person? *Northern Canada is _____, and there are _____ people there.*

TALK ABOUT SENTENCES

For students who need support in accessing key ideas and key language in *Hatchet,* use the Sentence Talk Routine on pages 437–438 to draw students' attention to the relationship between meaning and the words, phrases, and clauses in the text.

Lesson	Sentence(s) to Deconstruct
15	(p 16) He couldn't leave them in, they had to come out, but just touching them made the pain more intense.
16	(p 22) He pulled and twisted bits off the trees, packing them in one hand while he picked them with the other, picking and gathering until he had a wad close to the size of a baseball.

SPEAK AND WRITE ABOUT THE TEXT

Use the Text-based Writing Routine on pages 439–440 to model how to speak and write about key ideas and details in *Hatchet.*

Lesson	Text-based Writing	Scaffolded Frames
15	On page 16, why is it so hard for Brian to remove the porcupine quills?	• The quills _____ his leg. • Just _____ them _____ more. • He _____ to touch them to _____ them out.
16	On page 22, what steps does Brian follow to gather birchbark for the fire?	• First, he _____ the bark off the trees. • As he _____ with one hand, he _____ them in the _____ hand. • He _____ and ____ into a _____.

Name _____

Northern Canada

Northern Canada is very big. It goes from the border with Alaska to the western shore of Hudson Bay. Some parts of northern Canada are farther north than Alaska. The climate is cold. In many areas, there are no people.

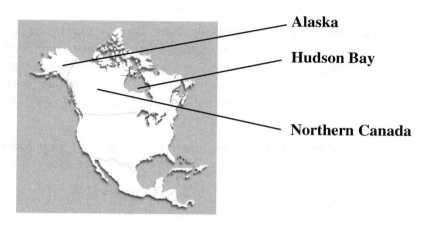

Alaska

Hudson Bay

Northern Canada

Northern Canada covers 1.35 million square miles. It has around 107,000 people. That means that for each person who lives there, there are about 11,536 square miles.

Describe northern Canada.
Northern Canada is as far north as the U.S. state of _____.
The weather can be _____ in northern Canada.
There are not many _____ in northern Canada.

Washed Up!

Reproduce and distribute copies of the *Three Environments on Earth* student page on page 376. Assess students' understanding of the word *environment*. Turn and talk to a partner about the meaning of *environment*. What are some examples of environments? Explain that to understand the story events in *Washed Up!*, it helps to be familiar with different kinds of natural environments.

If necessary, review how to read the chart. Read aloud the descriptions and features of each environment as students follow along. Discuss features that the environments have in common and ways in which they differ. Scaffold with sentence frames such as: *The rain forest and coastal mangrove both have _____. One feature of the rain forest that is different from the coastal mangrove is _____.*

Then have students work with a partner to report what they learned about each of the three environments.

TALK ABOUT SENTENCES

For students who need support in accessing key ideas and key language in *Washed Up!,* use the Sentence Talk Routine on pages 437–438 to draw students' attention to the relationship between meaning and the words, phrases, and clauses in the text.

Lesson	Sentence(s) to Deconstruct
1	(p 7) "Three unknown environments await these families, and three survival kits—one with a mosquito net, others with a length of rope."
2	(p 12) "It'll be OK, Papa!" lied Gabriela, as she surveyed the murky water, so shallow that the gnarled roots of the trees snaked above the waterline like the tangled hair of Medusa.
3	(p 23) There would be rising tides and hungry crocodiles, as well as the leeches and snakes that she hoped the palm fronds would protect them from.
4	(p 25) Didn't these primates of the Ethiopian highlands escape their windswept habitat by climbing down steep cliff faces at nightfall, roosting in ledges?
5	(p 31) They were walking in glum silence, slipping in the underbrush, getting scraped by thorns, when out of nowhere a sea breeze broke the stillness.
6	(p 38) Tall ferns fanned out, tangled vines wound their way around moss-clad tree trunks, drops of water nestled in the axils of leaves and trembled on leaf tips.
7	(p 47) Gabriela gave Shen plenty of coconut husks to build a fire with, and in return, Shen gave Gabriela a mosquito net to keep off the sand flies.
8	(p 56) "Who would have thought that three children could rewrite the very rules of survival? But they did, and they taught the grown-ups a thing or two about working together, pooling resources, and sharing knowledge."

Use the Text-based Writing Routine on pages 439–440 to model how to speak and write about key ideas and details in *Washed Up!*

Lesson	Text-based Writing	Scaffolded Frames
1	Based on page 7, why will living on the island be a challenge?	• The environments are _____. • Contestants need _____ to survive.
2	On page 12, how does the author describe the mangrove?	• The author describes the water as _____. • The author uses the words _____ and _____ to describe the roots. • The author compares _____ to _____.
3	Based on page 23, why can the mangrove swamp be dangerous?	• The water level in the swamp _____. • _____, _____, and _____ live in the swamp.
4	On page 25, how does Shen figure out how to survive the cold and wind?	• Shen thinks about _____. • He remembers that they _____ at nightfall to _____.
5	Describe the Walpoles' experience on page 31. What unexpected event happens?	• They were walking _____. • They were _____ and _____. • Suddenly, _____.
6	On page 38, what do the Lius see in the cloud forest they come across as they move downhill?	• The Lius see tall _____. • They also see _____ wound around _____. • There are drops of _____ on _____.
7	How did the events on page 47 affect Gabriela's and Shen's families?	• Gabriela gave Shen _____. • This meant that _____. • Shen gave Gabriela _____ so that _____.
8	What details on page 56 support the idea that cooperation is key to survival?	• The text says that "three children _____." • They did this by _____, _____, and _____.

Use the Dig Deeper Vocabulary Routine on pages 435–436 to continue to develop conceptual understanding of the following adjectives: ingenious, windswept, glum, murky, squelchy. Begin by reviewing what adjectives do in sentences. Display and read aloud the following sentences.

Shen had an idea.
Shen had a good idea.
Shen had an ingenious idea.

Explain the meaning of *ingenious*. Discuss the differences in the sentences. How are the sentences similar? How are they different? Point out how specific adjectives can change the meaning and tone of the sentence. Turn and talk to a partner about how the words *glum, murky,* and *squelchy* add to your understanding of the story.

Name _____

Three Environments on Earth

Earth has many different environments. The chart shows and tells about three of these environments.

	Environment	Description	Features
	mountain	A large piece of land that rises upward in the form of a peak	• The top is cold and has no trees, just areas of bare ground, rock, and small plants. • Forests often cover the lower sides of a mountain.
	rain forest	A thick forest with many kinds of plants and animals; found in a warm area that gets lots of rain	• There are four different layers. • Most plants and animals are found in the second layer from the top, which gets most of the sunlight. • The forest floor gets little sunlight. Many small insects live there.
	coastal mangrove	A swampy area near salt water that has many trees	• There are thick areas of trees and plants that can grow in salt water. • There are trees with large roots above the water. There are also dying plants and mud. • Many insects live there.

Share one fact you have learned about one of the environments.

The _____ is _____.

Rain Forest Food Chains

Reproduce and distribute copies of the *Rain Forest Producer Layers* student page on page 378. Explain that to understand the organisms and habitats described in *Rain Forest Food Chains,* it helps to know about the layers of plants in the rain forest.

Read aloud the descriptions of each layer. Have students count the layers in the rain forest. Which layer absorbs the most sunlight? *The _____ absorbs the most sunlight.* Have students work with a partner to discuss what they learned about each layer.

TALK ABOUT SENTENCES

For students who need support in accessing key ideas and key language in *Rain Forest Food Chains*, use the Sentence Talk Routine on pages 437–438 to draw students' attention to the relationship between meaning and the words, phrases, and clauses in the text.

Lesson	Sentence(s) to Deconstruct
9	(p 5) Energy flows from the food to the animal that eats it. For example, in the rain forest food chain to the left, the arrow leads from the figs to the sloth, from the sloth to the jaguar, and so on.
10	(p 12) Plants contain chlorophyll, a substance that makes them green. Chlorophyll is made of protein that helps plants trap sunlight to use in photosynthesis.
11	(p 24) Decomposers break down dead plant and animal matter. This frees up nutrients for the beginning of the food chain.
12	(p 35) Logging, farming, road building, and wars have led to widespread habitat loss.

SPEAK AND WRITE ABOUT THE TEXT

Use the Text-based Writing Routine on pages 439–440 to model how to speak and write about key ideas and details in *Rain Forest Food Chains*.

Lesson	Text-based Writing	Scaffolded Frames
9	On page 5, how do the diagram and text show how energy moves between organisms?	• The _____ in the diagram show _____. • Energy flows from _____ to _____ to _____ to _____.
10	What details on page 12 help you understand why plants are producers?	• Plants turn _____into _____ in the process of _____. • Chlorophyll _____.
11	Which domain-specific words on page 24 explain how important decomposers are in a food chain?	• _____ break down _____. • This frees up _____ for the beginning of _____.
12	Based on page 35, how do human activities lead to habitat loss in the rain forest?	• Habitats are destroyed by ___, ___, ___, and ___. • Land has been taken over by _____.

Name _____

Rain Forest Producer Layers

The producers, or plants, in the rain forest are divided into layers.

Emergent Layer: The top layer is called the *emergent layer*. It is made up of the tall treetops that stick out above the rest of the forest.

Canopy: Trees standing 75 to 100 feet tall form the *canopy*. The canopy absorbs about 80% of the sunlight that falls on the rain forest. Other plants grow on the trees. Toucans, parrots, and monkeys feed on leaves, fruits, and nuts in the canopy.

Understory: The *understory* is the layer of smaller plants, shrubs, and trees below the canopy. Tangled vines climb the trees. Colorful flowers in the understory attract birds and insects that eat pollen and nectar. There are many types of hummingbirds and butterflies in the understory.

Forest Floor: Because it receives so little light, only a few ferns, mosses, and herbs grow on the forest floor. Decaying leaves and plants cover the forest floor. They attract many insects, as well as rodents.

Share one fact you learned about the layers of the rain forest.

The _____ is _____.

Pale Male

Reproduce and distribute copies of the *Red-Tailed Hawks* student page on page 380. Explain that to better understand *Pale Male*, it helps to know more about red-tailed hawks.

Read aloud the information categories as students follow along. What do red-tailed hawks eat? *Red-tailed hawks eat _____.* Discuss the information in each category. Have students work with a partner to discuss what they learned about red-tailed hawks.

For students who need support in accessing key ideas and key language in *Pale Male*, use the Sentence Talk Routine on pages 437–438 to draw students' attention to the relationship between meaning and the words, phrases, and clauses in the text.

Lesson	Sentence(s) to Deconstruct
14	(p 36) By forcing sticks and branches between these spikes, the hawks made a nest that could withstand hurricane winds.
15	(p 44) In the wild their nest would have been in a tree with branches to hop down to until they got the hang of flying. The birders were worried.
16	(p 53) The Audubon Society and the U.S. Fish and Wildlife Service finally persuaded the owners to reinstall the anti-pigeon spikes and to construct an apron, or cradle, below the nest to catch the hawks' garbage.

Use the Text-based Writing Routine on pages 439–440 to model how to speak and write about key ideas and details in *Pale Male.*

Lesson	Text-based Writing	Scaffolded Frames
14	Based on page 36, what made Pale Male's nest strong?	• The sticks and branches _____. • The cornice _____. • Pale Male built the nest _____.
15	Based on page 44, what challenges did the fledglings face in their first flight in the city?	• In the wild, they would_____. • In the city, _____. • So, the first fledgling _____.
16	How do the picture on page 52 and the text on page 53 show how New Yorkers helped Pale Male and his mate?	• The picture shows that _____. • The protests _____. • When the workers replaced the spikes, they also _____.

Name _____

Red-Tailed Hawks

The red-tailed hawk is the most common species of hawk found in North America.

Measurements
Adult red-tailed hawks are 18–26 inches long. Females are longer than males. The hawk's wingspan is 45–52 inches, and they can weigh up to three pounds. The oldest known red-tailed hawk was nearly 29 years old.

Habitat
Red-tailed hawks are found across most of Northern America and into parts of northern Central America. They prefer open woodlands, such as grasslands, fields and pastures, and parks where they can easily use their excellent vision to spot their prey.

Mating Behavior
Once mated, red-tailed hawks often stay together until one dies. They work together to build nests up to three feet across out of dry sticks. They build their nests in tall trees, on cliff ledges, or on artificial structures such as window ledges.

Food
Red-tailed hawks prefer small mammals, such as rats, mice, rabbits, and ground squirrels. They also eat various birds and snakes. They can catch prey weighing up to five pounds!

What You May Not Know
Pale Male is a real hawk! He even has his own website with pictures of him, his mate, and his nest going back to 2002.

Share facts about red-tailed hawks.
A red-tailed hawk's wingspan can measure _____ .
Red-tailed hawks eat _____.

Name _____   Unit 1 Module A

Strike Zone

"Watch out!" shouted Ira as Darius and Kara ran into the garden. "Stop stepping on the plants!"

"I can't help it!" Darius and Kara said together as they stumbled around. It was the first nice day of spring, and everyone was outside. Ira, Darius, Kara, Chip, Lauren, and Ellie were getting ready for softball tryouts. It just felt *so* good to throw the ball and run around.

But Ira was too worried to join his friends. They were playing outside his house, where he'd helped his parents plant bulbs last fall. The tiny green plants were only visible if you knew where to look. Ira really did not want his friends to trample the plants. That's what would happen if they kept throwing the ball into the garden. Then he had an idea.

"Let's form teams of pitchers and catchers," Ira said. "We can make a home plate in the grass to represent the strike zone. The team that throws over home plate the most will win. How about it?"

Lauren nodded. "I need to practice pitching," she said.

Chip chimed in and exclaimed, "I want to practice catching, so this'll be cool!"

The group split into three teams. Ira made a home plate out of rocks. He set it in the grass so that good throws would stay away from the garden. That meant stray balls would not end up in the plants—and neither would his friends.

Every nice day for weeks, the group practiced throwing and catching through the strike zone. The plants in Ira's garden grew tall and strong. "They made it because of me," Ira thought to himself more than once.

Months later, at the end of the softball season, Lauren won a prize for throwing the most strikes of any pitcher in the league.

"Thanks for the strike zone," she whispered to Ira as she walked up to accept her trophy.

Name _____

The Rain Forest Environment

Tropical rain forests are one of Earth's most important environments. These forests are found around the world in areas just above and below the Equator. Here, the sun shines about 12 hours each day all year long. The steady climate and 80–400 inches of rain a year create a perfect environment for the growth of tall trees and thick vegetation. These are a few reasons rain forests are important.

1. Tropical rain forests are rich in *biodiversity*, or the variety of animal and plant life in a particular environment.
   - Tropical rain forests cover about 7% of Earth's surface but are home to about 50% of all living things on Earth.
   - There are more fish species in the Amazon rain forest river system than in the entire Atlantic Ocean.
   - Scientists estimate that there are thousands of undiscovered plant species in rain forests. Many rain forest plants are already used in medicines. Undiscovered species may hold the secrets to curing illnesses such as cancer.

2. Tropical rain forests help keep Earth's atmosphere in balance.
   - Rain forest vegetation produces about 20% of Earth's oxygen, which all animals need to survive.
   - At the same time, the vegetation absorbs huge amounts of carbon dioxide from the air. Too much carbon dioxide can lead to a gradual rise in Earth's temperature, known as *global warming*.

Today human activity, such as logging, mining, and clearing land for farms, roads, and cities, is reducing rain forests by more than 30 million acres a year. Some scientists predict that by the year 2060 there may be no rain forests left on Earth. Without the habitats provided by the rain forests, nearly half of the world's species of plants and animals may become extinct!

Many people are now working to save the rain forests. Rain forests may seem far from your everyday life, but everyone can contribute to the effort. Find out what you can do today to preserve this important environment for the future.

Performance-Based Assessment

Performance-Based Assessment
Unit 1 Module A

DISCUSS THE STUDENT MODEL

Reproduce and distribute copies of the student model on page 381. After completing the Prepare to Write activities on pages 176–177 in Unlock the Writing in Part 2, use the student model to illustrate the features of a narrative.

Note that "Strike Zone" appears to have many paragraphs. Show students that most of the paragraphs contain dialogue, and explain that some paragraphs begin when a new character is speaking. Who speaks first? _____ speaks first. Who speaks second? _____ and _____ speak second.

Read aloud the first three paragraphs. Ask: Who is the main character? Who are the other characters? After students name the characters, coach them to explain the situation Ira faces. Scaffold with a sentence frame: Ira wants to protect _____ from _____. Discuss the challenges Ira faces.

Continue reading the model aloud. Pause to have students tell you the sequence of events as they unfold. Help students identify transitional words and phrases such as so that, That meant, and Months later.

Unit 1 Module B

DISCUSS THE STUDENT MODEL

Reproduce and distribute copies of the student model on page 382. After completing the Prepare to Write activities on pages 182–183 in Unlock the Writing in Part 2, use the student model to illustrate the features of an informative essay.

Discuss the student model. Read aloud the first paragraph, and ask: How does the writer introduce the topic? The writer begins by _____.

Read aloud the second and third paragraphs. Ask: What facts and details does the writer include? The writer says that _____ and _____. How does the writer organize information about the same topic? The writer uses _____ to list different types of information. How does the writer introduce and use domain-specific words about the topic? The writer defines _____ and _____ and uses words such as _____, _____, and _____ to inform the reader.

Read aloud the last two paragraphs. Check to make sure students understand the purpose of a conclusion. Ask: How did the writer end the essay? (with a description of what human actions are doing to the rain forest and a call to action)

The Road to Freedom

Assess students' understanding of the term *slavery*. Reproduce and distribute copies of the *Slavery in the United States* student page on page 386. Explain that to understand the story events in *The Road to Freedom,* it helps to know the history of slavery in the United States.

Read aloud the events in order. Ask questions such as these: What year did slavery end in all northern states? *Slavery ended in all northern states in ____.* When did the Underground Railroad get its name? *The Underground Railroad got its name in _____.* Then have partners complete the Team Talk activity.

TALK ABOUT SENTENCES

For students who need support in accessing key ideas and key language in *The Road to Freedom,* use the Sentence Talk Routine on pages 437–438 to draw students' attention to the relationship between meaning and the words, phrases, and clauses in the text.

Lesson	Sentence(s) to Deconstruct
1	(p 4) "It's just talk is all, Mama," I said, hoping she didn't see my hand shaking while I stirred up supper, but she didn't stop fretting that night or the next nights either.
2	(pp 12–13) But when Mama crossed, all I could hear was the cracking until she stopped, frozen and scared.
3	(p 19) I held my breath and lay still as a possum, waiting.
4	(p 21) The rain poured in buckets from the sky and soaked through every inch of us.
5	(p 29) The space was so small we could hardly stand and as soon as we were down, she shut the door and pulled the rug and table on top, enclosing us in darkness.
6	(p 34) "You seen any runaways 'long this road?" the man asked. "A woman and her girl 'bout this high?"
7	(p 44) The barn doors creaked open and a small person, dressed in a heavy coat and hat, walked toward the ladder of the hayloft.
8	(p 46) It was no wonder she couldn't be caught by bounty hunters—she was always one step ahead.
9	(p 54) I didn't know what our new life in Canada would be, but I knew as I boarded that little rowboat that whatever it was, I was safe now from the auction block and we were together.
10	(p 55) An elaborate system of signals and codes, including references to the "drinking gourd" as a symbol of the Big Dipper constellation that points to the North Star, helped to keep the Underground Railroad's operations secret.

SPEAK AND WRITE ABOUT THE TEXT

Use the Text-based Writing Routine on pages 439–440 to model how to speak and write about key ideas and details in *The Road to Freedom.*

Lesson	Text-based Writing	Scaffolded Frames
1	On page 4, how do you know Emma and Mama are worried about being sold?	• The text says Emma is ____ as she stirs supper. • That shows she is _____. • Mama didn't stop _____ for days.
2	How does the author create suspense on pages 12 and 13 when describing Mama crossing the ice?	• When Mama crossed the ice, _____. • Mama stopped because she was _____. • It was suspenseful because _____.
3	On page 19, how does Emma react to the catchers and dogs?	• Emma knows that the catchers _____. • Emma reacts by _____ and _____.
4	How does Mama react to the rain on page 21? Why is this surprising?	• When it starts to rain, Mama _____. • This is surprising because _____. • But Mama reacts this way because _____.
5	On page 29, how is the hiding place in the Quaker woman's house described?	• The hiding space was _____. • It was under _____.
6	On page 34, what makes the wagon driver nervous?	• The wagon driver stops to talk to _____. • The driver is nervous because _____.
7	On page 44, how does the author describe Harriet when Emma first sees her?	• She is described as a _____. • Harriet is wearing _____.
8	On page 46, what does the author show about Harriet's character?	• Harriet teaches Mama and Emma _____. • Harriet changes her clothes to look like _____. • Harriet is good at avoiding bounty hunters because _____.
9	On page 54, what does Emma look forward to about Canada?	• In Canada, Emma will be safe from _____. • Emma and _____ won't be separated.
10	In the Epilogue, the author says that real events inspired the novel. What are some examples of real things mentioned in the story?	• Mama dreams about _____, which was a symbol for the Big Dipper. • Harriet teaches Emma and Mama to look for _____.

EXPAND UNDERSTANDING OF VOCABULARY

Use the Dig Deeper Vocabulary Routine on pages 435–436 to continue to develop conceptual understanding of the following verbs: grumbled, shivering, shuffling, tumbled, stuttered, hunched. Review what verbs do in sentences. Display and read aloud these sentences: *He said his name. He stuttered his name.* Explain that *said* and *stuttered* both express that the person was talking, but that *stuttered* also says how the person was talking. If needed, demonstrate *stuttered.* Turn and talk to a partner about why it is important to pay attention to verbs when you read.

Name _____

Slavery in the United States

Before the Civil War, millions of African Americans in the United States were enslaved, or owned by other people.

1619 — First enslaved people are brought to Virginia.

1777 — Vermont is the first state to stop, or abolish, slavery.

1804 — New Jersey abolishes slavery. No northern states allow slavery.

1807 — Traders are banned from selling people who have recently been brought to the United States from Africa as enslaved people. Selling enslaved people from one owner to another is still allowed.

1831 — The system for bringing enslaved people north to freedom is called the Underground Railroad.

1849 — Harriet Tubman escapes from slavery and begins helping other enslaved people escape.

1850 — The Fugitive Slave Law is passed and makes it harder for former enslaved people to hide in the North.

1861 — The American Civil War begins.

1863 — The Emancipation Proclamation ends slavery in the South.

1865 — The Thirteenth Amendment to the U.S. Constitution ends slavery in the United States.

Share facts about slavery in the United States.
The first _____ were brought to Virginia in 1619.
The Emancipation Proclamation ended slavery in _____.
The Thirteenth Amendment ended slavery in _____.

Operation Clean Sweep

Reproduce and distribute copies of the *Women's Suffrage* student page on page 388. Explain that to understand the story events in *Operation Clean Sweep,* it helps to know how women earned the right to vote in the United States. Introduce the word *suffrage* and explain that it means "the right to vote in an election." If needed, review the meanings of *vote, election,* and *amendment*.

Read aloud the information in the sequence chart. Have students discuss the order of events in the fight for women's suffrage. Scaffold with sentence frames such as *First, women _____. Then they _____. After _____, women _____.*

Then have students turn to a partner and explain how women earned the right to vote in the United States. Scaffold with sentence frames such as *Women started to fight for their rights when _____. Women got the right to vote when _____.*

TALK ABOUT SENTENCES

For students who need support in accessing key ideas and key language in *Operation Clean Sweep,* use the Sentence Talk Routine on pages 437–438 to draw students' attention to the relationship between meaning and the words, phrases, and clauses in the text.

Lesson	Sentence(s) to Deconstruct
12	(p 74) "I think it means Umatilla is going to get a clean sweep, but not by a broom."
13	(p 76) Those last ten minutes were the longest ten minutes of my life.
14	(p 77) If I didn't think we could give this town the improvements it deserves, I'd be the first to step down from office.

SPEAK AND WRITE ABOUT THE TEXT

Use the Text-based Writing Routine on pages 439–440 to model how to speak and write about key ideas and details in *Operation Clean Sweep.*

Lesson	Text-based Writing	Scaffolded Frames
12	On page 74, Cornelius explains the title of the book. What does this expression mean?	• Cornelius says that Umatilla _____. • This expression means _____.
13	On page 76, how does the author show Cornelius's feelings on election day?	• The author says that Cornelius _____. • These actions show he feels _____. • He feels this way because _____.
14	On page 77, what does Flora Sanwick say to the townspeople who think the election is a joke?	• Flora says _____. • She means _____. • After the election, she will _____.

Name _____

Women's Suffrage

Suffrage is the right to vote in an election. All women did not have the right to vote in the United States until 1920.

Sequence of Events in the Women's Suffrage Movement

Before the Civil War, women join the movement against slavery.

↓

Women begin to fight for their own rights in addition to rights for former enslaved people.

↓

Activists try to change state rules to allow women to vote. They succeed in 15 states by 1918.

↓

During World War I, most of the people in the United States think women should vote.

↓

In 1919, Congress passes an amendment to the U.S. Constitution that says women can vote.

↓

The states approve the amendment. Women have the same voting rights as men.

Share facts about how women got the right to vote.
Women started to fight for their rights when _____.
Women got the right to vote when _____.

Cesar Chavez: Champion of Workers

BUILD BACKGROUND FOR *CESAR CHAVEZ: CHAMPION OF WORKERS*

Reproduce and distribute copies of the *Migrant Workers* student page on page 390. Explain to students that this information will help them understand the events in *Cesar Chavez: Champion of Workers.*

Read aloud the introductory paragraphs and the first column of the chart. If necessary, review the meanings of *wages, conditions,* and *pesticides.* Then read aloud the information in the second column. Have students discuss what problems migrant workers faced. Finally, have partners carry out the Team Talk activity.

TALK ABOUT SENTENCES

For students who need support in accessing key ideas and key language in *Cesar Chavez: Champion of Workers,* use the Sentence Talk Routine on pages 437–438 to draw students' attention to the relationship between meaning and the words, phrases, and clauses in the text.

Lesson	Sentence(s) to Deconstruct
15	(p 84) After eighth grade, Chavez quit school to work in the fields full-time.
16	(p 92) The legislature passed the Agricultural Labor Relations Act, guaranteeing farmworkers the right to organize into unions.
17	(p 96) He helped make life better for thousands of farmworkers, but he never used violence to reach his goals.

SPEAK AND WRITE ABOUT THE TEXT

Use the Text-based Writing Routine on pages 439–440 to model how to speak and write about key ideas and details in *Cesar Chavez: Champion of Workers.*

Lesson	Text-based Writing	Scaffolded Frames
15	On page 84, what does the author reveal about Chavez's education?	• Chavez quit school after _____. • Chavez never went to _____. • Instead, Chavez had to _____.
16	On page 92, what victory did Chavez and the UFW achieve in 1975?	• In 1975, California's legislature passed _____. • Chavez and the UFW could now _____.
17	On page 96, how did Chavez reach his goals as leader of the union?	• Chavez's goals were _____. • He reached his goals by _____. • Chavez never used _____.

Name _____

Migrant Workers

A **migrant worker** is someone who moves from place to place to do work. Migrant workers often work on farms.

In the past, migrant farmworkers experienced many problems. The first column of the chart tells three areas in which migrant farmworkers experienced problems. The second column tells the exact problems that these workers experienced.

Area in which migrant farmworkers experienced problems	The problem
Farm wages	• Workers did not earn enough money to buy good food or have a house. • Owners could lower pay whenever they wanted.
Farm conditions	• Fields had no drinking water or bathrooms. • Days were long and made workers' backs hurt.
Pesticides **(chemicals used in farm work)**	• Some chemicals made farmworkers sick.

Share facts about the problems that migrant farmworkers experienced in the past.
One area in which migrant farmworkers experienced problems was _____.
One problem that migrant workers experienced in this area was _____.

Real-Life Superheroes

Reproduce and distribute copies of the *Jim Crow Laws* student page on page 393. Explain that to understand the story events in *Real-Life Superheroes* it helps to know about laws that discriminated against one group of people.

Review the information. Discuss each type of public place and public transportation. When did the Jim Crow laws begin? *The Jim Crow laws began _____.* What places did the Jim Crow laws apply to? *The Jim Crow laws applied to _____.* When did the Jim Crow laws end? *The Jim Crow laws ended _____.*

Then have students work with a partner to report what they learned about the discriminatory laws.

For students who need support in accessing key ideas and key language in *Real-Life Superheroes,* use the Sentence Talk Routine on pages 437–438 to draw students' attention to the relationship between meaning and the words, phrases, and clauses in the text.

Lesson	Sentence(s) to Deconstruct
1	(p 3) Emmeline Pankhurst was arrested several times as she campaigned to win the right for women to vote.
2	(p 10) Two years after Martin's Act was passed, Richard helped to form the Society for the Prevention of Cruelty to Animals (SPCA) to bring people who were cruel to animals to court.
3	(p 14) Thomas was so affected by the sight of these homeless children that he decided to set up a home where children would get food, shelter, and an education.
4	(p 16) Older children lived in children's homes until they were old enough to attend a workshop or an industrial school, where they learned a trade before going out to work.
5	(p 19) While he was in Palestine, Raoul met many Jews that had escaped from Germany, where Hitler's ruling Nazi party was making life very difficult for them.
6	(p 24) Despite his successes, Raoul began to fear that his life was in danger, and he started sleeping at a different house each night to avoid capture.
7	(p 28) Rosa and Raymond joined the National Association for the Advancement of Colored People (NAACP), a civil rights group that campaigned against discrimination based on the color of a person's skin.
17	(p 24) It is given to humanitarians who, like Raoul, have shown great bravery and determination in helping others.
18	(p 3) Some real-life superheroes will even risk going to prison in their efforts to make a change.

Use the Text-based Writing Routine on pages 439–440 to model how to speak and write about key ideas and details in *Real-Life Superheroes*.

Lesson	Text-based Writing	Scaffolded Frames
1	How do the image and caption on page 3 help you understand how difficult it was for women to win the right to vote?	• The image shows _____. • The caption describes _____. • Women who fought for the right to vote were often _____.
2	What role did the SPCA play in animal rights? Use details on page 10 to respond.	• The SPCA was the Society for _____. • It helped to _____.
3	Use the information on page 14 to explain what Thomas did for children.	• Some children slept on _____ or in _____. • They had to search for _____. • Thomas took action by _____.
4	On page 16, how did Thomas prepare older children for life after the children's homes?	• The older children attended _____. • They learned _____ so they could _____.
5	What did Raoul experience in Palestine? Use details from page 19 to respond.	• He met _____ who had escaped from _____. • This region was ruled by _____.
6	How did Raoul try to protect himself so he could continue helping others? Use an example from page 24.	• Raoul believed his life was _____. • To protect himself, he _____.
7	On page 28, how did Rosa Parks work for equal rights before the bus incident?	• Rosa joined a group called the _____. • This group worked to _____.
17	How is Raoul honored today? Use page 24 to respond.	• There is a _____ in his honor. • The Wallenberg Medal is given to _____.
18	What risks do real-life superheroes take for their work? Use the details on page 3 to respond.	• Real-life superheroes face _____. • They also face _____. • Some risk _____.

Use the Dig Deeper Vocabulary Routine on pages 435–436 to continue to develop conceptual understanding of the following nouns: welfare, cruelty, missionary, poverty, tragedy, persecution, authorities, discrimination. Review that nouns name a person, place, thing, or idea. Then help students identify what the nouns in the list name. Ask: Can you talk to a missionary? (yes) Can you talk to authorities? (yes) Can you talk to a tragedy? (no)

Explain that the nouns *missionary* and *authorities* are concrete because they name something you can see, hear, or touch. Explain that the other nouns in the list are abstract, or nouns that name a feeling or idea. Turn and talk to a partner about an abstract noun in the list. Explain how you know it's abstract.

Name _____

Unit 2 Module B

Jim Crow Laws

A few years after slavery ended in the United States in 1865, the South passed a set of laws to segregate, or separate, African Americans from whites.

The laws were called Jim Crow laws. "Jim Crow" was a name used to insult African Americans.

The laws required African Americans to stay separate from whites in public places. The laws even required African Americans to attend separate all-black schools. On buses and other public transportation, African Americans had to sit in an area separate from whites. The following lists identify places where African Americans had to stay separate from whites.

Public Places	Public Transportation
schools	buses
parks	trains
stores	streetcars
theaters	
restaurants	
water fountains	
apartments	
stores	
cemeteries	

The Jim Crow laws lasted for more than 70 years. Lawsuits during the 1950s civil rights movement helped to end the Jim Crow laws.

Share facts about the Jim Crow laws.
The Jim Crow laws separated _____.
African Americans and whites could not sit together on _____.

The Great Migration

Reproduce and distribute copies of *Struggles in the South, Opportunities in the North* student page on page 395. Review the timeline. Ask students to identify the events that occurred in various years. *In the year _____, _____.* Then have partners carry out the Team Talk activity.

TALK ABOUT SENTENCES

For students who need support in accessing key ideas and key language in *The Great Migration,* use the Sentence Talk Routine on pages 437–438 to draw students' attention to the relationship between meaning and the words, phrases, and clauses in the text.

Lesson	Sentence(s) to Deconstruct
8	(p 2) This is the story of an exodus of African-Americans who left their homes and farms in the South around the time of World War I and traveled to northern industrial cities in search of better lives.
9	(p 13) The flood of migrants northward left crops back home to dry and spoil.
10	(p 40) Longtime African-American residents living in the North did not welcome the newcomers from the South and often treated them with disdain.
11	(p 14) There was no justice for them in the courts, and their lives were often in danger.

SPEAK AND WRITE ABOUT THE TEXT

Use the Text-based Writing Routine on pages 439–440 to model how to speak and write about key ideas and details in *The Great Migration*.

Lesson	Text-based Writing	Scaffolded Frames
8	Based on page 2, when and why did African-Americans leave the South?	• They left around _____. • They went to the North because _____.
9	Based on page 13, what happened to the crops? Why?	• The crops _____. • This happened because _____.
10	Based on page 40, what was the relationship like between African-Americans who already lived in the North and the newcomers from the South?	• African-Americans who already lived in the North did not _____ the newcomers. • They often treated the newcomers _____.
11	How was life difficult for African-Americans living in the South? Use the details on page 14 to respond.	• The images show _____ and the text says _____. • Life was difficult for African-Americans living in the South because _____.

Name _____

Unit 2 Module B

Struggles in the South, Opportunities in the North

After slavery ended in 1865, African Americans in the South struggled to find jobs. The North provided many opportunities for African Americans. This led to many African Americans moving North.

1865 — Slavery in the United States ends.

1877 — The South passes laws to keep whites and blacks separate in schools and other public places.

1900 — Most African Americans live in the South.

1910 — The South goes through a 10-year depression, or period where many people don't have jobs or money.

1914 — World War I begins.

1915 — Thousands of new jobs are created in factories in the North.

1916 — African Americans begin moving north.

1917 — The United States enters World War I. More factory jobs are created to support the war. More jobs are available as Northerners leave to fight in the war.

1970 — By this year, 6 million African Americans have moved to the North.

Share facts about struggles in the South and opportunities in the North.
The South _____.
The North _____.

Angel Island

Reproduce and distribute copies of *The Gold Rush* student page on page 397. Review the text and web. Then have pairs complete the Team Talk activity.

TALK ABOUT SENTENCES

For students who need support in accessing key ideas and key language in *Angel Island*, use the Sentence Talk Routine on pages 437–438 to draw students' attention to the relationship between meaning and the words, phrases, and clauses in the text.

Lesson	Sentence(s) to Deconstruct
12	(p 101) For the next 30 years it served as the main point of entry for thousands of immigrants coming into the United States through the West Coast.
13	(p 103) Believing the stories they had heard about streets "paved with gold," the Chinese joined more than a half-million other people from around the world who flooded into the California mountains searching for gold.
14	(p 106) When riots began breaking out in several cities, the U.S. government passed laws to stop more Chinese from coming to the United States.
15	(p 110) As soon as immigrants arrived at Angel Island Immigration Station, they were separated into three groups: Whites, Japanese and other Asians, and Chinese.
16	(p 117) In 1922, even the U.S. commissioner general of immigration said that the buildings were dirty firetraps and not fit for humans.

SPEAK AND WRITE ABOUT THE TEXT

Use the Text-based Writing Routine on pages 439–440 to model how to speak and write about key ideas and details in *Angel Island*.

Lesson	Text-based Writing	Scaffolded Frames
12	What details on page 101 show how important Angel Island was?	• Angel Island was the main _____. • It was known as the _____.
13	How do the stories on page 103 help you understand why people moved to California?	• People told stories about _____. • The stories help me understand why so many people moved because _____.
14	Based on page 106, why did the U.S. government pass laws to limit immigration from China?	• Angry Americans destroyed _____. • The new laws kept _____.
15	On page 110, what happened when immigrants arrived at Angel Island?	• Immigrants were _____. • The groups were _____.
16	What was terrible about living in the immigration station? Use page 117 to answer.	• The buildings were _____ and not fit for for _____. • A main building was destroyed by _____.

Name _____

The Gold Rush

At the beginning of 1848, gold was discovered in northern California.

By the next year, about 80,000 people with dreams of becoming rich moved to California. Those who moved to California in search of gold in 1849 were called "Forty-niners." So much gold was found that 250,000 more people had moved to California by 1852.

Gold seekers were not just from the United States. They came from other countries too!

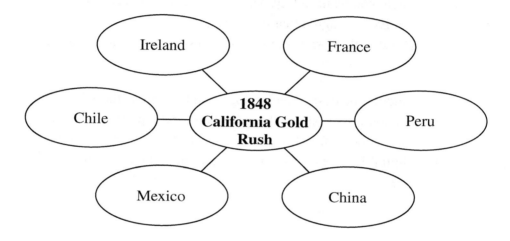

In 1849, $10 million worth of gold was mined, or dug up from the ground. That was a lot of money back then!

Share facts about the Gold Rush.
After gold was discovered in 1848, about _____ people moved to California by the following year.
Gold seekers mined about _____ worth of gold in 1849.

Name _____

The Digital Divide: Closing the Gap

Technology is all around us. The Digital Divide is the gap between those who have access to technology and those who do not. If you don't know how to use technology or don't have access to technology, then you are at an economic and a social disadvantage. We must find a way to close the Digital Divide.

Without access to technology such as the Internet or a smartphone, people have trouble finding out new information and applying for jobs. You can't search online for cheaper prices for products you want to buy. Many services, such as doing your taxes, are easier online. Experts agree that the Digital Divide is a problem. According to Dr. Quin, "Those with a lower income have less access to technology, which is a problem."

Some experts think reducing the cost of technology can help close the Digital Divide. Internet companies should have some cheaper plans, and laptops should be made less expensive. Services such as free Internet access at libraries helps too. In conclusion, reducing the Digital Divide is critical to ensure that all citizens have an equal opportunity to succeed.

Name _____

Taking on the Impossible

Many children lived on their own and in poverty in Victorian England. This issue seemed impossible to fix with so many people living in places such as the East End of London. Thomas John Barnardo witnessed the overcrowding and other effects of poverty while he was studying medicine. He decided that he would do whatever he could to make a difference in the lives of homeless children.

One of the first things Barnardo did was set up a home for boys in Stepney, London. He gave talks and made appeals in newspapers in order to raise money for this home. These actions took courage because Barnardo had to speak up for children who were usually forgotten or ignored by society.

In addition to providing a place to stay, children at Barnardo's home for boys could get meals and receive an education. In order to help as many children as possible, Barnardo decided that he would not refuse any children, even if the home was full. He put up a sign that said "No Destitute Child Ever Refused Admission." All of this care was hard work and the services required a lot of money. Barnardo continued to show courage by crusading for children's rights and collecting donations. He never stopped working to help the children. The following graph shows how many children Barnardo's charities helped.

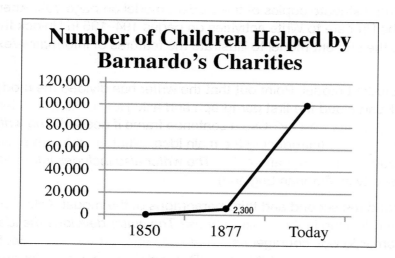

When I read about Barnardo, I know that it took a lot of courage to stand up for and care for children who had nowhere else to go. After seeing so many helpless children, most people would be overwhelmed by the problems and all the help these children needed. Barnardo showed courage because he took action in what most people would consider an impossible situation.

Performance-Based Assessment
Unit 2 Module A

Reproduce and distribute copies of the student model on page 398. After completing the Prepare to Write activities on pages 188–189 in Unlock the Writing in Part 2, use the student model to illustrate the features of an opinion speech.

Discuss the student model. Point out that the writer has divided the model into three parts or paragraphs. Read aloud the first paragraph and ask: How does the writer begin the opinion speech? Use a sentence frame if students need help answering. *The writer begins by clearly stating an _____.* (opinion) What is the writer's opinion? (that the Digital Divide must be closed because it creates an economic and a social disadvantage)

Read aloud the second paragraph. What does the writer include in this paragraph? If necessary, provide a frame for students to answer. *The writer gives _____ for the opinion.* (reasons) Point out that each reason is a fact about technology. Repeat this process for the last paragraph.

Unit 2 Module B

Reproduce and distribute copies of the student model on page 399. After completing the Prepare to Write activities on pages 194–195 in Unlock the Writing in Part 2, use the student model to illustrate the features of informative/explanatory writing.

Discuss the student model. Point out that the writer has divided the model into four paragraphs. Read aloud the first paragraph and ask: How does the writer begin the informative/explanatory essay? Use a sentence frame if needed. *The writer begins the essay by _____.* (introducing the main idea) What other information does the writer include in the first paragraph? *The writer also includes information about _____.* (poverty in Victorian England)

Next, read aloud the second and third paragraphs of the model. Ask: What idea does the writer develop in these paragraphs? *The writer develops the idea that _____.* (Barnardo was courageous) What facts support this idea? *Facts such as _____ and _____ support this idea.* (Barnardo's speaking up for homeless children; his efforts to raise money for these children)

Finally, read aloud the concluding paragraph. Ask: Why does the writer say that Barnardo is courageous? *The writer says that Barnardo is courageous because he _____.* (took action to improve a situation that most people thought was impossible)

George's Secret Key to the Universe

Reproduce and distribute copies of the *Biggest, Bigger, Big* student page on page 403. Tell students that this information will help them understand the story events in *George's Secret Key to the Universe.* Review the material and check comprehension with questions such as How long do blue giant stars last? What is the smallest class of star? Then have pairs do the Team Talk activity.

TALK ABOUT SENTENCES

For students who need support in accessing key ideas and key language in *George's Secret Key to the Universe,* use the Sentence Talk Routine on pages 437–438 to draw students' attention to the relationship between meaning and the words, phrases, and clauses in the text.

Lesson	Sentence(s) to Deconstruct
1	(pp 30–31) Eric walked back into the room with his shirt untucked, his hair standing on end, his glasses at a strange angle and a huge smile on his face.
2	(p 58) Dr. Reeper was standing right over him, staring down through his really smeared glasses.
3	(p 71) Wriggling free of his school sweater, which was hopelessly tangled in the spiky bush, he struggled out of the clinging branches.
4	(p 94) "Ah, the chill of outer space—how I long to feel it," he whispered, rubbing his hands together.
5	(p 119) But as they walked back, more and more little geysers of dust erupted around them, leaving a haze of smoke in the air.
6	(p 140) "Are you entering?" George asked, suddenly worried that Annie, with her interesting life, scientific know-how, and vivid imagination, would pull off a presentation that made his own sound about as exciting as cold rice pudding.
7	(p 158) "So, who wants to go first with the questions?" asked Dr. Reeper, excited to have an audience.
8	(p 181) Just as he was wondering whether to ring again, the door flew open and Eric's head popped out.
9	(p 206) The picture of the Milky Way zoomed inside the spiral very quickly, as if Cosmos was offended by George's lack of interest.
10	(p 242) Whatever Dr. Reeper's aim was, George felt sure it was a horrible one.
11	(p 269) George, Annie, and her mom fell silent and stared through the window, each willing Cosmos to get it right.
12	(p 294) He told me he wanted me to have his house, in case I ever needed somewhere to work on Cosmos.
15	(p 181) "Instead of considering all the evidence, I just applied some common sense—otherwise known as prejudice—and came up with a totally wrong answer."

Use the Text-based Writing Routine on pages 439–440 to model how to speak and write about key ideas and details in *George's Secret Key to the Universe*.

Lesson	Text-based Writing	Scaffolded Frames
1	On page 31, why is Eric smiling?	• Eric feels _____. • He found a _____ that he had _____.
2	On page 58, what do you learn about Dr. Reeper?	• Dr. Reeper is standing over _____. • He has on _____ and a jacket _____.
3	On page 71, why is George stuck? How does he free himself?	• George is stuck because _____. • He frees himself by _____.
4	Who are the bad characters in the story? How can you tell from Chapter 10?	• The characters of _____ and _____ are bad. • In Chapter 10, _____ is bad because _____ and _____ is bad because _____.
5	What is the main event in Chapter 13?	• George and Annie enter the _____. • They fly _____ Jupiter and its _____. • Then they get caught in an asteroid _____.
6	On page 140, what worries George?	• He worries that Annie will enter the _____. • If she does, George thinks Annie's _____ will be more _____ than his.
7	On page 158, why is Dr. Reeper excited?	• Dr. Reeper is excited to have an _____. • He wants to tell the boys about _____.
8	On page 181, how does Eric react to seeing George?	• Eric is _____ to see George. • Eric tells George to _____.
9	How does the picture on page 206 connect to the text?	• The picture shows _____ howling. • The text says "_____!" _____ George. • The picture _____ that George is _____.
10	What does George see and hear on pages 242–244 that confirms his opinion of Dr. Reeper?	• George sees Dr. Reeper and _____. • Dr. Reeper is _____ wildly. • He is also saying _____ and _____.
11	How do George, Annie, and Annie's mom feel about Cosmos in Chapter 29?	• They are _____ when they find Cosmos. • They want Cosmos to _____ so that Cosmos can _____.
12	Based on page 294, how did Eric end up living in the house next to George?	• The house belonged to _____. • He wanted Eric to _____ in case _____.
15	On page 181, why does Eric apologize to George?	• Eric thought _____. • Eric says _____.

Use the Dig Deeper Vocabulary Routine on pages 435–436 to continue to develop conceptual understanding of these adverbs: erratically, ominously, deliberately, defiantly, instinctively. Review how adverbs function in sentences. Choose an adverb from the list and use it in a sentence.

Name _____

Unit 3 Module A

Biggest, Bigger, Big

Use the following information to learn about the sizes of stars. The first star listed is the largest class of star. As the list goes down, the stars' sizes decrease.

Supergiant

When blue giant stars are at the end of their lives, they expand, or get larger. They then become supergiant stars. They run out of hydrogen to burn, and they begin burning helium.

Giant

Like supergiant stars, giant stars are stars that have expanded. Yellow stars eventually become giant stars. Our Sun will one day, many billions of years from now, become a giant star.

Blue Giant

An extremely bright class of stars, blue giants only last for about 10,000 to 100,000 years. When they die, they explode in a supernova. These explosions are very bright and spectacular.

Yellow

Yellow stars are medium-size stars, and they have a medium temperature. Our Sun is in this class. These stars usually live for about 10 billion years.

Red Dwarf

These are the smallest class of stars. They burn their fuel slowly, which means they can last for a very long time. But this also means they don't shine as brightly as other stars. These are the most common types of stars.

A _____ is the largest class of star.
A blue giant star is smaller than a _____ and larger than a _____.
Our Sun is a _____ star, but in many billions of years it will become a _____.

The Man Who Went to the Far Side of the Moon

Reproduce and distribute copies of the *Americans Go to Space* student page on page 405. Explain that fewer than 100 years ago, no one knew how to travel into space. People needed to invent rockets that could push objects out of Earth's atmosphere. Read aloud the introductory sentence and the first timeline. What were the first things that people sent into space? *They sent _____ into space, which each flew an _____ around Earth.* When did John Glenn fly an orbit around Earth? *John Glenn flew an orbit around Earth in _____.*

Read aloud the sentence about the moon and the second timeline. What did Americans send to the moon in 1962? *They sent a spacecraft that _____ the moon.* What did Americans do in 1966? *They sent a _____ that _____ and took _____.*

TALK ABOUT SENTENCES

For students who need support in accessing key ideas and key language in *The Man Who Went to the Far Side of the Moon,* use the Sentence Talk Routine on pages 437–438 to draw students' attention to the relationship between meaning and the words, phrases, and clauses in the text.

Lesson	Sentence(s) to Deconstruct
13	(p 6) As he looks toward the horizon, he can see that they have landed on a sphere: the horizon is a little bent since the moon is so small.
14	(p 13) During the trip itself they were so focused on their job that they didn't have time to think about what they have actually done.

SPEAK AND WRITE ABOUT THE TEXT

Use the Text-Based Writing Routine on pages 439–440 to model how to speak and write about key ideas and details in *The Man Who Went to the Far Side of the Moon.*

Lesson	Text-based Writing	Scaffolded Frames
13	On page 6, what feature of the moon helped Neil Armstrong know that the moon is smaller than Earth?	• Like Earth, the moon is a _____. • Unlike Earth's horizon, the moon's _____ appears _____. • Only a sphere _____ than _____ would have a _____.
14	On page 13, when do the astronauts realize what they have done? Why didn't they realize this before?	• The astronauts realize what they have done when _____. • Before, they were _____. • Because of that, they did not have time to _____.

Unit 3 Module A

Name _____

Americans Go to Space

Americans had to learn how to travel in outer space.

1958 Americans first sent objects into space, which each flew an orbit around Earth.

1961 One American (Alan Shepard) flew into space and came right back.

1962 Another American (John Glenn) flew an orbit around Earth.

Meanwhile, Americans tried to reach the moon.

1959 Americans sent a spacecraft that flew by the moon.

1962 Americans sent a spacecraft that hit the moon.

1966 Americans sent a spacecraft that landed on the moon and took pictures.

1968 Americans flew an orbit around the moon.

1969 Americans landed on the moon.

Eight years after the first American flew into space, Americans landed on the moon.

Share facts about Americans in space.
In 1961, Alan Shepard _____.
In _____, Americans flew an orbit around the moon.
Americans _____ in 1969.

Mayday on Moon of Jupiter

Reproduce and distribute copies of the *Help!* student page on page 407. Read the first paragraph aloud. Explain that pilots and ship captains around the world use a common language when they're in trouble. Point to SOS and tap the code out on a desk several times; be sure to pause after each SOS. Tell students that when telegraph operators hear this code, they know someone needs help.

Gesture to the three types of radio call, and read the descriptions one by one. The first level of distress call is saying the word *security* three times. The call means "be alert." What kind of conditions might cause a captain to send this message? *Dangerous _____ conditions could cause a captain to send this message.* If the danger is to a vehicle or if a person might get hurt, the captain calls "Pan-Pan" three times. The danger must be urgent, which means it calls for immediate action. "Mayday" is the strongest call for help. What must the danger be for a Mayday call? *The danger must be _____ and _____.* Grave means "very bad." *Imminent* means "about to happen." Which of these calls is the loudest, or strongest, call for help? _____ *is the strongest call for help.* Read the last two paragraphs. Ask: Why do people repeat the calls three times? Why shouldn't people say these calls as a joke?

TALK ABOUT SENTENCES

For students who need support in accessing key ideas and key language in "Mayday on Moon of Jupiter," use the Sentence Talk Routine on pages 437–438 to draw students' attention to the relationship between meaning and the words, phrases, and clauses in the text.

Lesson	Sentence(s) to Deconstruct
16	(p 24) Alicia gave him a look that made the guilty feeling in Justin's gut grow stronger.

SPEAK AND WRITE ABOUT THE TEXT

Use the Text-Based Writing Routine on pages 439–440 to model how to speak and write about key ideas and details in "Mayday on Moon of Jupiter."

Lesson	Text-based Writing	Scaffolded Frames
16	On page 24, why does Justin feel guilty? Use details from pages 23 and 24 to respond.	• Justin did not check the _____ kit before they left. • Justin feels bad that he did not make sure that the kit included _____ to eat in case of an emergency. • Justin knows that _____ is frustrated with him because of his poor planning.

Name _____

Unit 3 Module A

Help!

There are several ways to call for help from a ship, an airplane, or a spacecraft. Rescuers around the world know what these signals and calls mean.

SOS — a telegraph code, • • • – – – • • •, used when no one can speak

Security, Security, Security — a radio message about **safety** concerns or dangerous weather conditions; pronounced "si kyur ə tē," an English word meaning "freedom from danger"

Pan-Pan, Pan-Pan, Pan-Pan — a very **urgent** radio request for help when a ship, aircraft, other vehicle, or person is in danger; pronounced "pon-pon," from a French word meaning "breakdown"

Mayday, Mayday, Mayday — a radio request for immediate assistance due to **grave and imminent** danger; pronounced "mā dā," perhaps from French words meaning "come help me!"

When calling for help, a person says the word three times so everyone who hears the call knows that it is not a mistake.

Sending any of these messages as a joke is against the law!

Share facts about ways to call for help.
To tell other ships that dangerous weather is coming, say _____ three times.
Say _____ three times when there is urgent _____.
Saying _____ three times means that the danger is _____ and _____.

Jess and Layla's Astronomical Assignment

BUILD BACKGROUND FOR *JESS AND LAYLA'S ASTRONOMICAL ASSIGNMENT*

Reproduce and distribute copies of the *Our Solar System* student page on page 410. Explain that to understand the story events in *Jess and Layla's Astronomical Assignment,* it helps to know what makes up our solar system. Begin by confirming students' understanding of the phrase *solar system*. Then read aloud the diagram. If necessary, confirm students' understanding of *orbit* by asking a student to orbit around his or her desk or by demonstrating it yourself. Finally, have partners carry out the Team Talk activity.

TALK ABOUT SENTENCES

For students who need support in accessing key ideas and key language in *Jess and Layla's Astronomical Assignment,* use the Sentence Talk Routine on pages 437–438 to draw students' attention to the relationship between meaning and the words, phrases, and clauses in the text.

Lesson	Sentence(s) to Deconstruct
1	(p 6) "That's right, Jess," said Dr. Goggles, "and to understand astronomy, we must first look at history."
2	(p 12) Like Aristarchus, he believed that Earth revolved around the Sun; this theory is known as heliocentrism.
3	(p 20) The sky was suddenly filled with shining golden rain as twenty or more meteors fizzed, sparkled, and flew through the air, followed by a series of three flashes.
4	(p 22) As the girls hesitated, not sure what to do next, the van's passenger door swung open with a creak.
5	(p 28) "I suppose scientists do experiments," she said through her fingers, "and this is an experiment, right?"
6	(p 38) "You sound like squabbling schoolboys," said Jess.
7	(p 40) "I suggest that you are wrong because you are *clearly* wrong," said Copernicus loudly before adding, "or is your brain in your beard?"
8	(p 46) "Ha, I *told* you that Earth wasn't flat, Thales," crowed Anaximander, pressing his nose to the window while Thales stared out the window moodily, trying to hide that he was upset.
9	(p 53) "There *is* no music in the universe, you fool," snapped Copernicus.
10	(p 61) Layla grinned at the marble sculptures of Thales and Anaximander, and she wondered whether Pythagoras was still humming and whether Galileo's extra-clean telescope meant that he was making even bigger discoveries.
14	(p 12) A hundred years after Copernicus, an astronomer named Galileo tried to prove that Copernicus's ideas were correct, but Galileo was arrested in 1633 for suggesting that Earth wasn't at the center of the universe.

Use the Text-Based Writing Routine on pages 439–440 to model how to speak and write about key ideas and details in *Jess and Layla's Astronomical Assignment.*

Lesson	Text-based Writing	Scaffolded Frames
1	Look at pages 6 and 7. Why is the science class studying history?	• The science class is learning about _____. • Dr. Goggles says _____.
2	According to page 12, what is heliocentrism, and which scientists believed in it?	• Heliocentrism is _____. • _____ believed in heliocentrism. • Today we know that _____.
3	What event does the author describe on page 20?	• _____ appeared in the sky. • The author describes _____.
4	What details from page 22 help you know that the van is not an ordinary van anymore?	• The van _____. • When the girls go outside, they see ____.
5	On page 28, how does Jess justify Layla adjusting the knobs on the clock?	• Layla wants to _____. • Jess says ____.
6	On page 38, what do Galileo and Copernicus say when Layla tells them who they are going to meet?	• Copernicus says ____. • Galileo says _____.
7	On pages 40 and 41, how do the astronomers react to one another's ideas?	• The astronomers ____. • They act like _____.
8	On pages 46 and 47, how do the astronomers react to being proven wrong?	• Thales reacts by ____. • Anaximander reacts by ____.
9	On page 53, what do you learn about Copernicus?	• Copernicus _____ at Pythagoras. • That shows Copernicus is _____.
10	On page 61, what does Layla still wonder?	• Layla wonders if Pythagoras was ____. • She also wonders if Galileo _____.
14	On page 12, how do you know that some people thought the astronomers' ideas were dangerous?	• Galileo thought Copernicus was _____. • Galileo suggested the Earth was not _____. • In 1633, Galileo was _____.

Use the Dig Deeper Vocabulary Routine on pages 435–436 to continue to develop conceptual understanding of the following nominalized nouns: inspiration, astonishment, admirer. Explain that in English, verbs can be made into nouns using endings such as *-ation, -ment,* and *-er.* Display and read aloud the sentences *Copernicus inspired Galileo. He was an **inspiration** to Galileo.* The verb *inspire* was changed to the noun *inspiration* by adding the *-ation* suffix.

Name _____

Our Solar System

Our solar system is made up of the Sun and eight planets. These planets orbit, or move in an oval, around the Sun. Earth's orbit around the Sun takes one year.

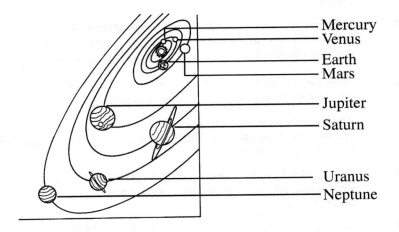

- Mercury
- Venus
- Earth
- Mars
- Jupiter
- Saturn
- Uranus
- Neptune

Share facts about the solar system.
Our solar system has _____.
The planets _____ the Sun.

Our Mysterious Universe

Reproduce and distribute copies of *The Scientific Process* student page on page 412. Review the material, asking questions to confirm students' understanding. Then have partners complete the Team Talk activity.

TALK ABOUT SENTENCES

For students who need support in accessing key ideas and key language in *Our Mysterious Universe,* use the Sentence Talk Routine on pages 437–438 to draw students' attention to the relationship between meaning and the words, phrases, and clauses in the text.

Lesson	Sentence(s) to Deconstruct
11	(p 8) Other scientists made observations that supported and further developed Copernicus's hypothesis.
12	(p 17) The mass of a star–the amount of matter it contains–determines its future.
13	(p 29) Using temperature-detecting radio telescopes and satellites, scientists have discovered a faint and constant hiss caused by background radiation spread throughout the universe.

SPEAK AND WRITE ABOUT THE TEXT

Use the Text-based Writing Routine on pages 439–440 to model how to speak and write about key ideas and details in *Our Mysterious Universe.*

Lesson	Text-based Writing	Scaffolded Frames
11	On page 8, what do you learn about Copernicus's idea of the universe?	• Copernicus thought _____. • Other scientists _____.
12	Based on page 17, how do scientists know what life cycle a star will follow?	• A star's life cycle is based on ____. • A star's life cycle includes _____. • At the end of its life, a star _____.
13	What evidence described on page 29 supports the Big Bang Theory?	• The Hubble Space Telescope looks at ____. • Scientists also use ____. • Scientists have heard ____.

Name _____

The Scientific Process

Scientists, including astronomers, follow a basic method called the scientific process when they conduct experiments.

Step 1: Make an Observation
The scientist begins by making an observation, or taking a careful look at something interesting in the world or universe.

Step 2: Ask a Question
The scientist then asks a question, such as "Why do the planets act the way I observed?"

Step 3: Make a Hypothesis
Next, the scientist makes a hypothesis to answer the question. A hypothesis is an idea that can be proven with experiments or more observations. For example, "The planets act the way I observed because of gravity."

Step 4: Test the Hypothesis
Now the scientist needs to conduct experiments or make more observations to see if his or her idea is correct.

Step 5: Analyze the Data
After conducting experiments, the scientist analyzes, or looks closely at, the information.

Step 6: Conclusion
The scientist finally comes to a conclusion. Was the hypothesis supported by the experiments? Then the idea might be called a theory and be used by other scientists. If not, then the scientist can make a new hypothesis and work to test that idea.

Share facts about the scientific process.
A hypothesis is _____.
To support a hypothesis, scientists _____.

A Black Hole Is NOT a Hole

Reproduce and distribute copies of the *Space Words* student page on page 414. Explain that to understand the information in *A Black Hole Is NOT a Hole* it helps to review some basic space terms. Read aloud each term and its definition. Confirm students' understanding by having students define each term in their own words. Scaffold using sentence frames such as *A galaxy is _____. It includes _____.* Then have partners carry out the Team Talk activity.

TALK ABOUT SENTENCES

For students who need support in accessing key ideas and key language in *A Black Hole Is NOT a Hole,* use the Sentence Talk Routine on pages 437–438 to draw students' attention to the relationship between meaning and the words, phrases, and clauses in the text.

Lesson	Sentence(s) to Deconstruct
15	(p 35) With a whirlpool, there's always a fast-enough fish—or a fast enough *something*—that moves so quickly it won't be pulled all the way into the center.
16	(p 46) Late into the night, Reber probed the sky with his new telescope, using it to locate the source of the mysterious radio energy.

SPEAK AND WRITE ABOUT THE TEXT

Use the Text-based Writing Routine on pages 439–440 to model how to speak and write about key ideas and details in *A Black Hole Is NOT a Hole*.

Lesson	Text-based Writing	Scaffolded Frames
15	According to page 35, in what way is a black hole not like a whirlpool?	• A whirlpool will _____. • A black hole will also _____. • But with a whirlpool, _____.
16	Look at pages 45 and 46. How did Reber discover "radio galaxies"?	• Reber noticed _____. • He wanted to _____. • He built a _____.

Name _____

Space Words

galaxy A galaxy is a large system containing billions of stars and planets. There are many galaxies in the universe. Our galaxy is called the Milky Way.

planet A planet is a large body that orbits a star. Planets can be rocky or made of gas. Earth is a planet.

solar system A solar system is a set of objects that orbit a star. These can include planets plus their moons, asteroids, comets, and many other objects.

Sun The Sun is the name for the star at the center of our solar system. The Sun is an average, or not special, star in the Milky Way.

universe The universe is all of space.

Share facts about space.
The Sun is different from a planet because _____.
Our solar system is different from a galaxy because _____.

Name _____

Junk Attack!

The mood in the command center was electric with worry. "It's coming right at us," whispered Gloria, the chief technician. She had rushed to the room when the crew told her that the Vac-U-Mag was malfunctioning in a very, very serious way.

Since the Space Junk Conference of 2110, Gloria and the Vac-U-Mag team had carried out their task supremely well. The team's job was to sweep up all the junk Earth had been leaving in space for 150 years. The team had deployed a tunnel of strong magnets that swept the trash methodically into a black hole. Discarded booster rockets, dead satellites, rickety rovers, and broken solar panels flowed past the space station at a stately pace—until now, that is.

"Magnet 54 is too strong!" gasped Rudolph as Gloria gazed out the window.

"Have you checked its log? Are you sure 54 is the one?" asked Gloria.

"Yes," Rudolph carefully replied. "An electrical disturbance, maybe from that short-circuited moon lander we saw go by this morning, has boosted magnet strength. As a result, 54 is bending the junk path toward us. All the junk from the Vac-U-Mag tunnel will hit us in less than an hour."

"Please save us, Gloria!" people murmured around the room.

Sharply, Gloria replied, "Why can't you think of something? This team is for solving problems, not whimpering!"

No one spoke, but the room became calmer. Brains were working. "I know," said Bart. "Let's reverse our own polarity and push the junk away!"

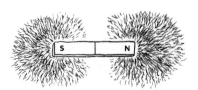
"Brilliant!" Gloria exclaimed. She ran to the wall and pulled a lever. The space station became a south pole instead of a north pole. The junk came close, but the reversed polarity sent it away. At last, the team had time to fix the Vac-U-Mag so it could start sweeping space once again.

Name _____

You Are What You Eat!
Genetically Modified Foods

Genetically modified (GM) plant foods are grown all around the United States today. There are both benefits and drawbacks to using GM foods.

Genetically modified organisms (GMOs) are used in GM foods. GMOs are produced through genetic engineering. Scientists change the DNA of the organism in a lab. Changing the DNA means that scientists can change the organism's features. Many scientists think genetic engineering can make plants better for farmers. For example, scientists can make plants that taste bad to bugs but not to people. That means bugs don't eat the plants before people can harvest them.

Corn is one example of a plant that may be genetically modified.

But not everyone is excited about GM foods. Some people say that we don't yet know enough about these plants. These people worry that the plants that taste bad to one bug might taste good to another. That would make new problems for farmers. Dr. Sam, an opponent of GM foods, says, "GM foods pose environmental and economic concerns."

For now, farmers are going to keep using GM foods. But more research needs to be done to make sure all GM foods are safe.

Performance-Based Assessment
Unit 3 Module A

Reproduce and distribute copies of the student model on page 415. After completing the Prepare to Write activities on pages 200–201 in Unlock the Writing in Part 2, use the student model to illustrate the features of a science-fiction narrative.

Read aloud the title and the first paragraph. Ask: Who are the characters? _____ *and the* _____ *are the characters.* (Gloria; Vac-U-Mag crew) Then read aloud the second paragraph. The writer has used concrete details to show how the dangerous situation has come about. What is the Vac-U-Mag used for? *The Vac-U-Mag is used to* _____ *space junk into* _____. (sweep, a black hole) Read aloud the dialogue in the next three paragraphs. The writer uses the transitional phrase *As a result* to help readers follow Rudolph's explanation.

Next, read aloud the sixth, seventh, and eighth paragraphs. Explain that they provide the turning point in the story. Gloria challenges the crew to find a solution. What do they do? *They decide to* _____ *the polarity of the* _____. (reverse, space station) Point out the illustration of the magnet. Explain that it reminds readers about the real science at work in the story. Finally, read aloud the last paragraph and ask: What is the story's conclusion? *The crew* _____ *the dangerous problem and then has time to* _____. (solves; repair the Vac-U-Mag)

Unit 3 Module B

Reproduce and distribute copies of the student model on page 416. After completing the Prepare to Write activities on pages 206–207 in Unlock the Writing in Part 2, use the student model to illustrate the features of a science report.

Point out that the writer has divided the model into four parts or paragraphs. Read aloud the first paragraph. Ask: How does the writer begin the science report? Use a sentence frame if students need help answering. *The writer begins by* _____. (introducing the topic) What is the topic of the report? (genetically modified foods) Read aloud the second and third paragraphs. What does the writer include in the second paragraph? *The writer includes* _____ *in the second paragraph.* (the benefits of GM foods) What does the writer include in the third paragraph? *The writer includes* _____ *in the third paragraph.* (the drawbacks of GM foods)

Read aloud the fourth paragraph of the model. How did the writer end the report? *The writer ended the report with* _____. (a call for more research)

Explorers: Triumphs and Troubles

Reproduce and distribute copies of *The Age of Discovery* student page on page 420. Explain that to understand the information in *Explorers: Triumphs and Troubles* it helps to know when in history these events happened. Confirm students' understanding of the words *explore* and *explorers*.

If necessary, review how to read a timeline. Then read each entry aloud as students follow along. Discuss who was involved and where each event happened. Scaffold with sentence frames such as *In ____, the explorer _____ went to _____.* Ask students if they know of other events that happened near those dates to establish more context.

Then have students work with a partner to report what they learned about explorers.

TALK ABOUT SENTENCES

For students who need support in accessing key ideas and key language in *Explorers: Triumphs and Troubles,* use the Sentence Talk Routine on pages 437–438 to draw students' attention to the relationship between meaning and the words, phrases, and clauses in the text.

Lesson	Sentence(s) to Deconstruct
1	(p 5) Between the 1400s and the 1800s, many explorers claimed to have discovered new lands, but these lands already had people living there.
2	(p 11) The British finally reached the Tibetan capital Lhasa on August 3, 1904, by which time all the Tibetan leaders had fled in fear.
3	(p 14) This was a normal tactic for conquistadors, who often captured local leaders and then forced them to rule as they wanted.
4	(p 17) Might the villagers have realized that a good way to make the Spanish go away was to tell them El Dorado was far away from their villages?
5	(p 23) However, the British also knew that there was no government, army, or police force, so they decided to claim the land as their own.
6	(p 27) After three months, the exhausted explorers reached Cooper's Creek— not even halfway to the north coast.
7	(p 30) Spain, for example, became Europe's richest nation because of the treasure from its territories in the Americas.
8	(p 31) Sometimes the explorers enslaved the local people, and the wealth they sent home was not theirs to take.
14	(p 31) Can we judge the triumphs and troubles of explorers based on things we know, but they did not?

Use the Text-based Writing Routine on pages 439–440 to model how to speak and write about key ideas and details in *Explorers: Triumphs and Troubles*.

Lesson	Text-based Writing	Scaffolded Frames
1	Based on page 5, why did explorers claim that they had reached new lands?	• Explorers claimed _____. • Those lands _____. • The people in those lands _____.
2	According to page 11, what was the result of Francis Younghusband's trip to Tibet?	• Younghusband reached _____. • He made officials _____. • Tibet had to _____ Britain for _____.
3	On page 14, what did Cortés do when Montezuma allowed him into Tenochtitlán?	• Cortés took Montezuma _____. • One of Cortés's men _____. • Then the conquistadors _____.
4	Based on page 17, why might the conquistadors have kept looking for El Dorado?	• The conquistadors _____. • Local people may have _____.
5	According to page 23, why did the British think they could claim Australia as their own?	• The British knew that people _____. • They also knew that _____. • So the British decided _____.
6	On page 27, how was Burke and Willis's expedition going when they reached Cooper's Creek?	• Burke and Willis were _____. • Cooper's Creek was _____. • The explorers needed to _____.
7	According to page 30, what were two triumphs of exploration?	• Exploration brought countries _____ from treasure such as _____. • It also allowed countries to _____.
8	Based on page 31, how did exploration affect indigenous peoples?	• Exploration took _____. • Native people got _____. • Some explorers _____.
14	Consider the question the author asks at the end of page 31. What things do we know now that explorers did not?	• Most explorers did not view their actions as _____. • Explorers did not know that _____.

Use the Dig Deeper Vocabulary Routine on pages 435–436 to continue to develop conceptual understanding of the following adjectives: legendary, ruthless, fierce, mythical, brilliant, heroic, venomous, traditional. Display and read aloud the following sentences: *He was smart. He was brilliant.*

Discuss the differences between the sentences. Explain that *smart* and *brilliant* are adjectives because they describe what something is like. In these sentences, *smart* and *brilliant* tell what the subject *he* was like. Turn and talk to a partner about why it is important to pay attention to adjectives when you read.

Name _____

The Age of Discovery

Europeans began to explore the world in the 1400s. They were curious about new lands and wanted to find new trade routes. The time was right, thanks to better ships and navigation technology. These European explorers went all around the world.

1275   Marco Polo reaches China.

1492   Christopher Columbus reaches North America (the Bahamas).

1519   Hernán Cortés arrives in Mexico and encounters the Aztec people.

1542   Spanish explorers looking for El Dorado reach the Amazon River.

1607   Jamestown, the first English colony in North America, is founded.

1788   A British fleet arrives in Australia to set up a colony.

1904   Francis Younghusband reaches Lhasa, Tibet.

1911   Roald Amundsen is the first man to reach the South Pole.

Share facts about explorers.

The earliest explorer mentioned on the timeline is _____.

Spanish explorers in search of El Dorado reached the _____ in _____.

In 1911, _____ was the first man to reach the _____.

Pedro's Journal

BUILD BACKGROUND FOR *PEDRO'S JOURNAL*

Reproduce and distribute copies of the *Christopher Columbus* student page on page 422. Review the text. Then have pairs complete the Team Talk activity.

TALK ABOUT SENTENCES

For students who need support in accessing key ideas and key language in *Pedro's Journal,* use the Sentence Talk Routine on pages 437–438 to draw students' attention to the relationship between meaning and the words, phrases, and clauses in the text.

Lesson	Sentence(s) to Deconstruct
9	(p 73) I've seen him go into white rages and then pace his small cabin saying his Hail Marys.
10	(p 76) Through the day, the day that was to have been our last day traveling westward, many things were seen floating in the water, things that stirred everyone's hopes and had the men once again scanning the horizon.
11	(p 82) Columbus tried to convince him of our good intentions through sign language and broken words and more gifts of glass beads and junk, and the man rowed back to some people on the shore.
12	(p 85) With a gentle smile on his face, he showed him the steel glistening in the sun, sliced clear through a leather strap the speechmaker bore around his neck, and the man's beads tumbled into the sand.
13	(p 90) Earlier, I was not able to sleep for the eerie noise the seaweed brings, the soft, enchanted swish against the hull, like a mother's hand soothing a baby's head, so I went above and found the Captain alone on deck, lit by the moon.

SPEAK AND WRITE ABOUT THE TEXT

Use the Text-based Writing Routine on pages 439–440 to model how to speak and write about key ideas and details in *Pedro's Journal.*

9	What do the details on page 73 tell you about Columbus?	• When Columbus gets mad, he _____. • Columbus motivates the men by _____.
10	On page 76, what stops the crew from turning around?	• The crew sees _____. • The crew believes _____.
11	On page 82, what does Columbus try to convince the captured man to believe?	• Columbus tries to convince the man _____. • Columbus does this through _____ and by giving the man _____.
12	On page 85, how does Columbus respond to the speechmaker's threat?	• Columbus shows the speechmaker _____. • Columbus slices _____. • This causes _____.
13	On page 90, how does the narrator meet Columbus?	• The narrator can't _____, so he _____. • He sees Columbus, who tells him _____.

Name _____

Christopher Columbus

Christopher Columbus was an Italian navigator. The king and queen of Spain, Ferdinand and Isabella, paid for his trips across the Atlantic Ocean. He was the first European since the Vikings to reach the Americas.

	First Voyage	Second Voyage	Third Voyage	Fourth Voyage
Date	August 3, 1492–March 15, 1493	September 25, 1493–June 11, 1496	May 30, 1498–October 1500	May 9, 1502–November 1504
Number of Ships	3	at least 17	6	4
New Places Visited	the Bahamas, Cuba, Haiti	Dominica, Jamaica	Trinidad, Venezuela	Martinique, Honduras, Nicaragua, Costa Rica, Panama

Share facts about Christopher Columbus.
Christopher Columbus went to the Americas _____.
Columbus visited _____.

Secrets of The Canyon Cave

Reproduce and distribute copies of *The Anasazi People* student page on page 424. Explain that to understand the story events in "Secrets of the Canyon Cave," it helps to know more about the Native Americans who lived in Utah. Remind students that the Anasazi people lived in the area many hundreds of years before European settlers came to the United States.

Read aloud the information as students follow along. Have students turn to a partner and discuss the Anasazi people. Scaffold with sentence frames such as *The Anasazi people lived in the states of _____. They made their homes in _____.*

Then have partners complete the Team Talk activity.

TALK ABOUT SENTENCES

For students who need support in accessing key ideas and key language in "Secrets of the Canyon Cave," use the Sentence Talk Routine on pages 437–438 to draw students' attention to the relationship between meaning and the words, phrases, and clauses in the text.

Lesson	Sentence(s) to Deconstruct
15	(p 93) Brandon would never consider a hike across pure desert *easy*, and he knew they'd find more items along his route.
16	(p 97) Soon, the clouds cleared away, and night unfurled over the canyon like a giant blanket of black velvet with silver glitter spilled all across it.

SPEAK AND WRITE ABOUT THE TEXT

Use the Text-based Writing Routine on pages 439–440 to model how to speak and write about key ideas and details in "Secrets of the Canyon Cave."

Lesson	Text-based Writing	Scaffolded Frames
15	Look at pages 92 and 93. When they start the scavenger hunt, how well do Brandon and Ría work together?	• Ría wants to _____. • Brandon says _____. • Brandon and Ría _____.
16	How is the night sky described on page 97? What feature of the night sky becomes important later in the story? Why?	• The night sky is like _____. • The _____ in the night sky become important later in the story because _____.

Name _____

The Anasazi People

- The Anasazi people are the ancient ancestors of today's Pueblo Native Americans. They lived in the states of Arizona, New Mexico, Colorado, and Utah.

- The Anasazi civilization thrived from A.D. 100 to 1600.

- Early on, the Anasazi lived in caves or houses dug into the ground. Later, the Anasazi built cliff dwellings right into the sides of mountains.

- The early Anasazi were nomadic, which means they moved from place to place. The caves they lived in were not permanent homes.

- The Anasazi didn't have calendars. They watched the sky, especially the sun and the moon.

- The Anasazi built structures that measured the locations of the sun and other bodies in the sky. Many of their later cities were organized based on the location of the sun.

Share facts about the Anasazi people.
The Anasazi civilization thrived from _____ to _____.
The early Anasazi were nomadic, which means they _____.
The Anasazi built structures that measured _____.

Beyond the Horizon

BUILD BACKGROUND FOR *BEYOND THE HORIZON*

Reproduce and distribute copies of the *Boys and Men, Girls and Women* student page on page 427. Explain that to understand the story events in *Beyond the Horizon* it helps to know what kinds of things boys and men were allowed to do long ago versus what girls and women were allowed to do.

Read aloud the introductory text as students follow along. Were boys and men or girls and women allowed to do more things? Why do you think so? *I think* _____ *were allowed to do more things because* _____.

Read aloud the list of things that boys and men were allowed to do. Act out each item in turn if necessary to help students understand each, or ask students to act them out. After each item, have students say *I would like to (sail on a boat)* or *I would not like to (sail on a boat)*. Encourage them to give reasons for their answers. Repeat with the things that girls and women were allowed to do. Then have students carry out the Team Talk activity.

TALK ABOUT SENTENCES

For students who need support in accessing key ideas and key language in *Beyond the Horizon*, use the Sentence Talk Routine on pages 437–438 to draw students' attention to the relationship between meaning and the words, phrases, and clauses in the text.

Lesson	Sentence(s) to Deconstruct
1	(p 8) Sarah knew then that she had to break free and follow her father or risk withering away till there was nothing left of her.
2	(p 15) Below decks it was damp and sticky, the stale air heavy with the breath of many men.
3	(p 26) Tom fled through the muddle of streets, Sarah close behind, the buildings looming over them like cliffs.
4	(p 39) The huts all had curved, thatched roofs, and the inside walls of each were smooth and straight.
5	(p 42) Dadi sat next to Sarah sifting rice in a flat basket, picking out the bad husks and throwing them to the chickens that clucked and fussed around them.
6	(p 55) Priya's father reached them, breathing hard, his eyes wild.
7	(p 64) Priya had been her rescuer, her companion, the girl who had given her the very clothes off her back.
8	(p 64) Sarah glanced at the ships in the distance, as if worried they would drift away with the current, and she'd be left behind once more.
14	(p 64) For the first time in a long time Sarah felt calm—India had turned out to be a revelation in so many ways.

Use the Text-based Writing Routine on pages 439–440 to model how to speak and write about key ideas and details in *Beyond the Horizon*.

Lesson	Text-based Writing	Scaffolded Frames
1	On page 8, what are the two choices Sarah is facing? Which choice do you think she will make? Why?	• Sarah can _____, or she can _____. • I think she will choose to _____. • I think she will make this choice because _____.
2	Based on the details on page 15, what was it like below decks?	• It was _____ and _____ below decks. • There was _____ air below decks. • This _____ air was caused by _____.
3	On page 26, what does Tom do? What does Sarah do as a result? What is the setting?	• Tom _____. • As a result, Sarah _____. • The setting of the scene is _____.
4	On page 39, what adjectives does the author use to describe the huts?	• The roofs of the huts are _____. • They are also _____. • The walls of the huts are _____.
5	On page 42, what was Dadi doing as Sarah rested nearby?	• First, Dadi _____. • Next, she _____, and then she _____.
6	On page 55, how is Priya's father described? Based on these details, how does he feel?	• Priya's father's was breathing _____. • His eyes were _____. • These details suggest that he feels _____.
7	On page 64, how does the author describe Priya's relationship with Sarah?	• Priya had been Sarah's _____. • She also had been Sarah's _____. • Priya was the girl who gave _____.
8	On page 64, what does Sarah do? How does she feel as she does this? Why?	• Sarah _____ at the distant _____. • As she does this, Sarah feels _____. • She feels this way because _____.
14	Based on the last line on page 64, how does Sarah feel? Why?	• Sarah feels _____. • She feels this way because _____.

Use the Dig Deeper Vocabulary Routine on pages 435–436 to continue to develop conceptual understanding of verbs and verb forms. Have students pay particular attention to the following verbs: pondered, tarry, weigh anchor, imploring, wager, wielding, tethered. Tell students that some of these verbs are in the present tense; they tell what is happening right now. Add that some are in the past tense; they tell what happened in the past. Add that the rest have a final *-ing* and are in the progressive tense, which usually goes with a helping verb like *is, are, was,* or *were.* Have students sort the words into the three categories. Then help them choose a word from each category and use the word in a sentence.

Name _____

Boys and Men, Girls and Women

Long ago, boys and men could do many kinds of things.

Girls and women were not allowed to do many of the things that boys and men could do.

Boys and men could…		
sail on a boat	fight in a battle	make tools
go on adventures	invent things	write music
open a store	make shoes	play sports
build houses	dig for gold	buy and sell things
Girls and women could…		
cook	clean	take care of children

Share ideas about some of the things that boys and men could do long ago.
Long ago, boys and men could _____.

Explorers of North America

Reproduce and distribute copies of the *Explorers Long Ago* student page on page 429. Review the material. Then have pairs complete the Team Talk activity.

TALK ABOUT SENTENCES

For students who need support in accessing key ideas and key language in *Explorers of North America,* use the Sentence Talk Routine on pages 437–438 to draw students' attention to the relationship between meaning and the words, phrases, and clauses in the text.

Lesson	Sentence(s) to Deconstruct
9	(p 9) He landed on the coast of what is now Canada in about the year 1000.
10	(p 11) The trip was thousands of miles long and could take years.
11	(p 18) He gave Cortés gifts of gold and let him stay in his palace.
12	(p 27) He was forced to turn back because the river became too narrow for his ship.
13	(p 36) But they learned valuable information about the plants, animals, people, and land in the new American territory.

SPEAK AND WRITE ABOUT THE TEXT

Use the Text-based Writing Routine on pages 439–440 to model how to speak and write about key ideas and details in *Explorers of North America.*

Lesson	Text-based Writing	Scaffolded Frames
9	According to page 9, where did Leif Erikson land, and when?	• He landed on what is now _____. • He landed in about _____.
10	On page 11, how far was the trip from Europe to Asia? How long could this trip take?	• The trip was _____ long. • This trip could take _____.
11	On page 18, what two things did Montezuma do for Spanish explorer Hernán Cortés?	• Montezuma _____. • He also _____.
12	On page 27, what was Hudson forced to do? Why?	• Hudson was forced to _____. • He had to do this because _____.
13	On page 36, what did the Corps of Discovery learn about during their explorations?	• They learned about _____ and _____. • They also learned about _____ and _____.

Name _____

Explorers Long Ago

What were explorers?	Explorers were people who went to new places.
Who were explorers?	Most explorers were men. Many explorers came from Europe. Later, many explorers came from the United States.
When did people explore?	Many people explored between about 1400 and 1900.
Where did people explore?	People explored all over the world. They explored the land and the oceans.
Why did people explore?	Some explorers wanted to learn about new places. Some were looking for gold or other valuable things.
How did people explore?	People used boats to explore. They also walked and traveled by horse.

Share ideas about explorers.

Explorers were _____.

Many people explored in the years between _____ and _____.

Some explorers wanted to _____, while others were _____.

New Beginnings

Reproduce and distribute copies of the *Colonists* student page on page 431. Explain that to understand the events in *New Beginnings* it helps to know what colonists are and what they do.

Read aloud the introductory sentence and the six steps. Emphasize that colonists set up a community in a place that is new to them, but that other people probably already live in that place. You may wish to connect this idea to *Beyond the Horizon*, in which the ship's captain and crew intend to set up a trading post on land that already belongs to another group of people. Have students read the six steps aloud, using time-order words such as *first, second, next,* and *last.* Then have partners carry out the Team Talk activity.

TALK ABOUT SENTENCES

For students who need support in accessing key ideas and key language in *New Beginnings,* use the Sentence Talk Routine on pages 437–438 to draw students' attention to the relationship between meaning and the words, phrases, and clauses in the text.

Lesson	Sentence(s) to Deconstruct
15	(p 107) They were often unable to hunt or fish because of the danger of attack by the Native Americans.
16	(p 118) Native Americans' arrows were no match for English guns, and many Indians were killed.

SPEAK AND WRITE ABOUT THE TEXT

Use the Text-based Writing Routine on pages 439–440 to model how to speak and write about key ideas and details in *New Beginnings*.

Lesson	Text-based Writing	Scaffolded Frames
15	Look at page 107. In the first few months, what were the colonists not able to do? Why?	• The colonists could not _____. • They also could not _____. • The reason was that _____.
16	Based on page 118, what were some differences between how colonists fought and how the Native Americans fought? Which group was more successful?	• Native Americans used _____ to fight. • Colonists used _____ to fight. • _____ were more successful because _____.

Name _____

Colonists

Colonists are people who travel to a new place and start a new community.

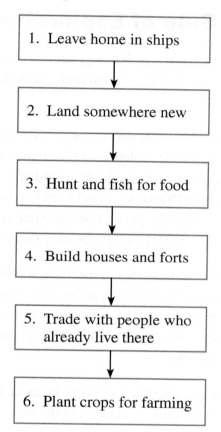

1. Leave home in ships

2. Land somewhere new

3. Hunt and fish for food

4. Build houses and forts

5. Trade with people who already live there

6. Plant crops for farming

TeamTalk

Use the following sentence frames to share facts about colonists.

Colonists are people who _____ .

Colonists _____ in the new place where they live.

Colonists also _____ in their new communities.

Name _____

The Dark Side of Exploration

I think the negative aspects of exploration had a greater effect on societies than the positive aspects did. Explorers often were violent and spread diseases to those people whose land they took over.

One reason why exploration had more negative impact than positive is because European explorers did not hesitate to use violence against native people. For example, in 1903, British explorer Francis Younghusband led an expedition to Tibet. It became an invasion in which British soldiers killed hundreds of Tibetans. Another example of this type of violence happened on the other side of the world. Hernán Cortés killed many Aztec people when he took over their capital.

Although violence was enough of a negative impact, exploration also led to the spread of disease. When European explorers arrived in North America, they brought new diseases with them. In the 16th century, troops led by Spanish conquistador Francisco de Orellana gave European diseases to the people of the Amazon, which killed many native people.

Exploration led to many exciting discoveries of new lands and cultures for Europeans, but violence and disease hurt the societies in the new lands. These negatives overshadowed the positive side of exploration.

Source: *Explorers: Triumphs and Troubles* by Paul Mason

Name _____

The Essential Exploration Packing List

On pages 30–31 of *Explorers of North America,* the author lists the items that Lewis and Clark bought for their travels. Since the land was new to them, Lewis and Clark had to be ready to handle any possible situation. Explorers like James Cook and even the colonists probably packed based on similar lists. Regardless of the journey, I think the five most important items for any explorer or colonist to pack are food and water, tents, weather-appropriate clothing, compasses and maps, and writing materials.

For any explorer, the first concern is staying physically healthy and safe while traveling. For this reason, the most important items to pack are food and water. The trails are unpredictable and unexplored, so explorers must have food and water to keep them going on their journey. The next important item is a tent or other shelter. A tent will give the explorer a dry, protected place to spend nights. The third important item is weather-appropriate clothing. Explorers will need to be dressed warmly if they are traveling in a cold place, or they will need more lightweight clothing if they are traveling in a warm climate.

In addition to items that keep them healthy and safe, explorers also need items that help them navigate and record what they find while on their journeys. For this reason, the next important items for an explorer to pack are compasses and maps. A compass and map will help the explorer find a way through the new land. Finally, the last important items are writing materials. Explorers can use these materials to record their observations and experiences to help future explorers.

Although there are many items that explorers could pack, the five most important items are food and water, tents, weather-appropriate clothing, compasses and maps, and writing materials. Food and water give the explorer the energy that he or she needs for the journey. Tents and clothing protect the explorer from the weather and land. Navigation and writing materials help the explorer travel and record what he or she sees. Without these essential items, explorers would be helpless as they traveled through the wilderness.

Performance-Based Assessment

Unit 4 Module A

Reproduce and distribute copies of the student model on page 432. After completing the Prepare to Write activities on pages 212–213 in Unlock the Writing in Part 2, use the student model to illustrate the features of an opinion essay.

Point out that the writer has divided the model into four paragraphs. Read aloud the first paragraph and ask: What is the writer's opinion in the essay? Use a sentence frame if students need help answering. *The writer's opinion is that _____.* (exploration had more negative than positive effects on societies)

Read aloud the second and third paragraphs. What reasons does the writer include to support the opinion introduced in the first paragraph? *The reasons the writer states to support the opinion are _____ and _____.* (European explorers used violence; they spread disease) Point out that the two reasons are details from *Explorers: Triumphs and Troubles,* which the writer lists as a source at the end of the essay. Ask students if they can think of any other details from the book that would support the writer's opinion. *I think another good detail is _____.*

Read aloud the last paragraph. How does the writer end the essay? *The writer ends the essay by _____.* (restating the opinion)

Unit 4 Module B

Reproduce and distribute copies of the student model on page 433. After completing the Prepare to Write activities on pages 218–219 in Unlock the Writing in Part 2, use the student model to illustrate the features of an opinion essay.

Point out that the writer has divided the model into four paragraphs. Read aloud the first paragraph and ask: What is the writer's opinion in the essay? Use a sentence frame if students need help answering. *The writer's opinion is that the most important items to pack are _____.* (food and water, tents, weather-appropriate clothing, compasses and maps, and writing materials)

Read aloud the second and third paragraphs. What types of items does the writer argue are important? *The writer argues that explorers need items that _____ and _____.* (keep them healthy and safe; help them navigate and record their journey) What reasons does the writer include for why each item is important to pack? *The writer says that _____ are important because they _____.* (Answers will vary; Sample answer: food and water; keep the explorer going).

Read aloud the last paragraph. Explain that the writer ends the essay by restating the opinion and summarizing main ideas from the essay.

Dig Deeper Vocabulary

PURPOSE

Use this routine to help students acquire a more in-depth understanding for select academic vocabulary. Through discussion using multimodal methods, students will unlock the meaning of vocabulary so they can use the words and learn elements of syntax.

PROCEDURE

1. Display the words listed in the Expand Understanding of Vocabulary section of the current Unit/Module Part 4 Unlock Language Learning lesson. Explain to students that these words appear in the text they are reading and that they are all similar in some way. For example, all words are verbs.

2. Model reading the words. Then have students practice reading the words aloud with you. Poll students about their familiarity with each word in order to gauge understanding.

3. Convey the meaning of the words using different modalities such as showing a picture from a magazine or the Internet, drawing a picture, acting out or gesturing, or using realia. Describe each word in context to guide students to associate the new words with familiar vocabulary. For example, show students what your face would look like if you were glum. *This is how my face would look if I felt glum.* Ask students to make a glum face. Then ask them how they think a person who is glum feels.

4. Have students turn and talk to a partner about the word. Then ask them to suggest sentences that show understanding of the new word. Use sentence frames as needed. For example: *I felt glum when _____.*

5. Review the concept of synonyms and provide a synonym for each listed word. Ask students if they can name any words that mean the same or almost the same thing as the target word. Provide a sentence frame such as: _____ *means almost the same as* glum. *(sad, down, blue, gloomy)*

435

6. Help students understand how different types of words function in a sentence. For example, share a sentence in which you signal out a specific kind of word or phrase using different colors to write each part of the sentence. Then explain the parts of the sentence and ask students to identify specific words or phrases in the sentence. Look at this example for using a describing word:

Jane was *glum* when she couldn't go on the picnic.

What person, place, or thing is being described? **(Jane)** What word describes Jane? *(glum)* The last part of the sentence gives more details about why Jane was glum. Why was Jane glum? **(she couldn't go on the picnic)**

TEACHING TIPS

- Have students use different modalities to figure out the meaning of words. Doing this aids their understanding, since they are using different formats to gain meaning.
- Have students write each vocabulary word on separate index cards and add a simple drawing or photograph from the Internet or a magazine that exemplifies the word on the back. Students can work in pairs to look at the picture and then name the word.

EXTEND

Have students create a word web relating the vocabulary words to other words they know. For example, words can be the same part of speech or have similar affixes, sounds, or meanings. Have students discuss how understanding word meanings helps them better understand the meaning of texts they read.

Sentence Talk

PURPOSE

Use this routine to deconstruct complex sentences from the texts that students are reading. Through instructional conversations students analyze key ideas, vocabulary, and sentence structures.

PROCEDURE

1. Identify a complex sentence from the current text. Recommended sentences can be found in the **Talk About Sentences** section of the Part 4 Unlock Language Learning lessons for each Unit/Module. Sentences should include key details or explain a key concept, important vocabulary, and phrases and clauses that merit attention. They may also include figurative language.

2. Decide how to break up the sentence for discussion, focusing on identifying meaning-based phrases and clauses. For example, you could break the sentence below into three parts.

   There would be rising tides and hungry crocodiles, as well as the leeches and snakes that she hoped the palm fronds would protect them from.

3. Display the sentence, writing each sentence part in a different color. Prepare conversation starters to focus children's attention on each sentence part. As you discuss each part of the sentence, record students' comments.

   • Why is the word *tides* an important word? Turn and talk to a partner about what you know about how water in the ocean moves.

   • What dangers does the author talk about? What would protect them from those dangers?

   • Suppose the author was telling about dangers a character would encounter in a desert setting. What words might replace *rising tides* and *palm fronds*?

4. Identify key words that may need to be defined in context or have structural significance.

   • What does the girl hope the palm fronds will do? Yes, she hopes the palm fronds will protect her. To *protect* means to "keep safe." The writer says, "There would be rising tides, hungry crocodiles" and "leeches and snakes." These are all things that can cause harm to the girl. The girl hopes that the palm fronds will keep her safe from these things.

   • Now let's read the entire sentence together. The word *protect* tells me that there are many dangers to overcome.

5. Initiate the activity with students by reading together the page or paragraph in which the sentence appears. Have students turn and talk to a partner about key ideas and details in the text.

6. Then draw attention to the color-coded sentence on display. Use the conversation starters you prepared to focus students' attention on each part of the sentence. Students should take an active role and should be speaking as much or more than you do in this conversation. Periodically, also have students turn and talk to a partner or a small group of peers. Record students' responses during the conversation and reread them at the end of the conversation.

7. Reread the entire sentence and have students discuss or write about what it means. Provide scaffolds as necessary.

   • There were dangers like _____, _____, _____, and _____.
   • She hoped that palm fronds would _____.
   • This means the girl is in _____.

TEACHING TIPS

• When recording students' comments, write each comment in the same color as the sentence part it refers to.

• Create and display a list of key words and phrases from the Sentence Talk Instructional conversations and encourage students to use the vocabulary when they speak and write about the text.

EXTEND

Have students discuss how understanding the meaning of the sentence helps them better understand the overall meaning of the text. Ask: What was the most important thing you learned? What will you keep in mind as you continue to read?

Text-Based Writing

PURPOSE

Use this routine to explore linguistic and rhetorical patterns and registers in writing. Model how to include evidence from text in a written response.

From the section of the text that was read closely that day, present students with a question for guided/shared writing. See the Text-Based Writing column in the Speak and Write About the Text section of the English Language Learners Support lesson for recommended questions.

PROCEDURE

1. Write the question on the board and read it aloud with students. For example: *On page 12, what is heliocentrism and which scientists believed in it?* Identify key words in the question and check understanding. Help students determine what the question is asking and what information they need to respond to it. The question asks about heliocentrism and scientist who believed in it. What does the text on page 12 suggest about heliocentrism? *Heliocentrism is the belief that Earth _____.* I can tell from the question that there were some scientists who did not believe that Earth revolved around the sun. How can we find out what heliocentrism is and who believes in it? *We can ____ the selection to find evidence in the text about _____.*

2. Locate and read aloud the sentence/sentences in the text that the question refers to. If appropriate, also read the text that comes before/after the sentence. Lead students in a discussion of the text, checking comprehension and explaining key vocabulary and concepts as needed.

   Why did some scientists believe in heliocentrism while others did not? *For a long time, people believed _____. It was a new idea to think of _____.* Which words show that heliocentrism was a new belief? *The words, "Galileo was _____."* Sometimes new ideas scare people. Heliocentrism was a new belief that Earth revolved around the sun. Copernicus and Galileo were the first to believe in heliocentrism.

3. Guide students to answer the question orally, using the scaffolded sentence frames as needed. Check that students use a rhetorical pattern appropriate to the question. For example, a question that asks *why* something occurred should elicit a response that identifies a cause and effect.

4. Restate the question for students: *On page 12, what is heliocentrism and which scientists believed in it?* Model writing a response, talking through the process as you write.

   Heliocentrism was a new belief that Earth revolved around the sun. Copernicus and Galileo were the first to believe in heliocentrism.

   I will start my sentences with a capital letter. The verb *revolved* tells what Earth does. **Where** does Earth revolve? Earth revolves around the sun. Now I will use text evidence to tell the meaning of heliocentrism. I will add those words to my second sentence. I will put the correct end punctuation at the end of both sentences.

5. Have students write their answers. For shared writing, have students work with a partner.

6. Give students the opportunity to share their writing with the group. Have students read their answers aloud or write them on the board. Check that students have used appropriate linguistic and rhetorical patterns and included text evidence as needed.

TEACHING TIPS

- Use graphic organizers, such as idea webs and cause/effect charts, to help students organize the text evidence needed to answer the questions.
- As you evaluate students' writing, identify sentences that can be expanded by adding details.
- Encourage students to write in complete sentences to reflect the more formal register of written English.

EXTEND

Ask a second question about the day's close read section and have students work with a partner or independently to discuss and write a response.

Clarify Key Details

PURPOSE

Use this routine to provide frames for conducting accountable conversations that require clarification.

PROCEDURE

1. **Explain:** Sometimes in a discussion, I don't understand what someone has said. Maybe the speaker talks very softly or uses words I have not heard before. Maybe the speaker needs to give key details to explain an idea. When this happens, I need to ask questions to help me understand what the speaker means. This is called clarifying.

2. Explain that sometimes others might have questions about what students say. Remind them that they should answer other students' questions and help them understand.

3. Remind students that when they ask questions in a group, they should be polite and not interrupt. Wait until the person finishes speaking. Then raise your hand or say, "excuse me." Wait for the person to look at you or say your name. Then you can ask your question.

4. Share the worksheet on the following page with students. Talk about situations in which they might use the questions. Model completing the sentence frames using a topic that is familiar to students.

5. Have students use the questions and frames in a discussion about a selection you have recently read.

TEACHING TIPS

- Have students role-play discussions in which they ask questions for clarification.
- Create a classroom poster listing useful clarifying questions for students to refer to as needed.

EXTEND

Have students think of more clarifying questions and add them to the worksheet. Have them practice asking the questions with a partner or in a group.

Clarifying Key Details

Look at the examples of questions.
Use them when you do not understand.

When you did not hear what the speaker said:
I did not hear you. What did you say?

When you do not understand what the speaker means:
You said _____. What does that mean?
I do not understand _____. Can you please explain?
Can you give me more details?

When someone says something you think is wrong:
I think you made a mistake. Can you show me in the book?

When you answer someone's question:
I said _____.
I mean _____.

Look at the picture.
Say questions the people can ask.

Clarifying Information

PURPOSE

Use this routine to provide frames for conducting accountable conversations that require elaboration.

PROCEDURE

1. **Explain:** Sometimes I need more information to understand what a speaker means. I can ask the speaker to explain his or her ideas. I can ask the speaker for more details and information. This is called elaborating.

2. **Point out that sometimes students might want to add ideas to a group discussion.** I can give more information, too. I can explain my ideas and give information from the text. I can give reasons for my opinions. I can give evidence to support my ideas.

3. **Remind students that when they add to a group discussion, they should be polite and not interrupt.** Wait until the person finishes speaking. Then raise your hand or say, "excuse me." Wait for the person to look at you or say your name. Then, you can speak.

4. **Share the worksheet on the following page with students. Talk about situations in which they might use the questions and statements. Model completing the sentence frames using a topic that is familiar to students.**

5. **Have students work with a partner to write an elaborating question and answer in the conversation at the bottom of the worksheet.**

TEACHING TIPS

- Have students role-play discussions in which they ask for more information and elaborate on their ideas.
- Create a classroom poster listing useful elaboration frames for students to refer to as needed.

EXTEND

Have students write another conversation between Pat and Jan, using the frames to ask for and give more information about another topic, such as a favorite story.

Clarifying Information

Look at the examples of questions and statements.
Use the questions when you need more information from the speaker.
Use the statements when you give more information.

When you want more information from the speaker:
I want to know more about _____.
Can you please explain _____?
Can you give me more information about _____?
What details support your idea?

When you want to give more information:
This makes me think _____.
Now I am wondering _____.
This reminds me of _____ because _____.
I believe this is true because _____.
I want to add to what [speaker's name] said about _____.

Pat and Dan are talking. Dan needs to ask for more information.
Pat needs to give more information. Write a question and an answer.
Pat: I think playing sports is important.
Dan: Why do you think _____?
Pat: _____.

Reach a Consensus

PURPOSE

Use this routine to provide frames for conducting accountable conversations that require achieving consensus.

PROCEDURE

1. **Explain:** Sometimes when I work with a group, my group has to decide something together. We all have to agree about something. This is called reaching consensus.

2. Explain that sometimes when they are in a group, students will need to **tell what they think.** When you tell others what you think, give reasons and evidence to explain your ideas and feelings.

3. Point out that all the members of the group should have a chance to tell what **they think.** When others tell what they think, listen carefully. If you need more information, ask clarifying and elaborating questions. **Remind students to use the frames they practiced on the other worksheets.**

4. Explain that group members may agree or disagree. When you have the same idea as someone else, you agree. When you have a different idea, or when you think the person is incorrect, you disagree. Say if you agree or disagree. Give reasons and evidence.

5. Remind students that it is important to be polite when they disagree. If you disagree, explain why in a friendly way.

6. Explain that to achieve consensus, most of the group members must agree. This is called reaching a consensus. When everyone agrees, you have a consensus. If some group members do not agree, you can vote. Count how many people agree and how many disagree.

7. Read the worksheet on the following page aloud to students. Talk about situations in which they might use the questions and statements. Model completing the sentence frames using a topic that is familiar to students.

TEACHING TIPS

- Have students role-play discussions in which they reach a consensus.
- Create a classroom poster listing useful consensus frames for students to refer to as needed.

EXTEND

Have students work with a group to choose the best activity for a rainy day. Remind them to use the frames on the worksheet to express ideas and agree or disagree. Encourage them to reach a consensus and present their conclusions.

Reach a Consensus

Look at the examples of questions and statements.
Use them when your group must decide something.

When you say what you think:
I think _____.
I believe _____

When you ask what others think:
What do you think, [name]?
Do you agree, [name]?

When you agree:
I agree with [name] because _____
I like what [name] said because _____.

When you disagree:
I disagree with _____ because _____.

When you both disagree and agree:
I think you are right about _____, but I do not agree that
_____.

When you want to reach a consensus:
Do we all agree that _____?
How many think that _____?
Raise your hand if you think _____.

Have a Discussion

PURPOSE

Use this routine to provide a frame for conducting accountable discussions.

PROCEDURE

1. **Explain:** Sometimes we talk about things in a group. Three or more people can be a group. When the people in the group talk about a topic, they are having a discussion.

2. **Point out that students can contribute to a good discussion.** How can you help the group have a good discussion? You can listen carefully to each speaker. When you listen, look at the speaker and pay attention.

3. **Explain that students should think before speaking, and stay on the topic.** Remember to explain your ideas. Ask questions if you need more information to understand a speaker's ideas.

4. Share the worksheet on the following page with students. Review the rules it lists. Have students use the worksheet to rate their behavior during group discussions.

5. Have students write the sentences at the bottom of the worksheet. Then, ask students to share their sentences with a partner.

TEACHING TIPS

- Have students role-play discussions in which they follow the rules listed on the worksheet.
- Model examples of nonverbal communication skills listeners can use, such as nodding and making eye contact.
- Create a classroom poster listing tips for successful group discussions for students to refer to as needed.

EXTEND

Have a group of volunteers model a discussion while the rest of the class listens.

Have listeners rate the group members' behavior during the discussion using the worksheet.

Have a Discussion

Rate what you do during a discussion with a group.

1 I need to practice this skill.
2 I do this sometimes.
3 I almost always do this.

I listen carefully.	1	2	3
I look at the speaker.	1	2	3
I am polite.	1	2	3
I explain and give evidence.	1	2	3
I ask for clarification.	1	2	3
I ask for elaboration.	1	2	3
I build on others' ideas.	1	2	3
I stay on the topic.	1	2	3
I think before speaking.	1	2	3

Write sentences that you can use in discussions during the situation below.
When you disagree with the speaker: _____
When you tell your ideas about a topic to the group: _____
When you ask for more information: _____

Scaffolded Reading/Writing Goals

UNIT 1: MODULE A

Reading Goal: Readers determine themes in literary texts by comparing and contrasting characters, settings, and events.

Emerging	Expanding	Bridging
Readers point out the character, setting, and events of a story an learn that they can be used to help determine theme.	Readers use visual aids such as graphic orgnaizers, photos, or illustrations to compare and contrast characters, settings, and events.	Readers correctly identify themes based on materials that compare and contrast characters, settings, and events in the texts.

Writing Goal: Writers use dialogue and details to develop challenging character experiences.

Emerging	Expanding	Bridging
Writers use sentence frames to write dialogue to develop challenging character experiences.	Writers select from a word bank details about characters and events, then collaborate to write dialogue to develop challenging character experiences.	Writers establish details about characters and events, then write dialogue developing challenging character experiences.

UNIT 1: MODULE B

Reading Goal: Readers explain the relationships between scientific concepts presented in texts.

Emerging	Expanding	Bridging
Readers combine diagrams with sentences to explain the relationships between scientific concepts presented in texts.	Using cloze sentences, readers explain the relationships between scientific concepts presented in texts.	Using learned words and phrases, readers explain the relationships between scientific concepts presented in texts.

Writing Goal: Writers examine a topic and convey ideas with facts, definitions, and details.

Emerging	Expanding	Bridging
Writers write informative sentences about a topic.	Writers write informative sentences about a topic, including relevant facts, definitions, and details.	Writers write an informative paragraph about a topic, including relevant facts, definitions, and details.

UNIT 2: MODULE A

Reading Goal: Readers quote accurately from a text when summarizing the events or the main ideas and details.

Emerging	Expanding	Bridging
Readers match relevant text evidence to an accurate summary of events or main ideas and details.	Readers identify relevant text evidence to select an accurate summary of events or main ideas and details.	Readers identify relevant text evidence when summarizing the events or main ideas and details.

Writing Goal: Writers state and support an opinion using evidence from a variety of sources.

Emerging	Expanding	Bridging
Writers make an opinion statement.	Writers make an opinion statement and gather relevant text evidence.	Writers make an opinion statement and support it using relevant text evidence from more than one source.

UNIT 2: MODULE B

Reading Goal: Readers explain the relationships between individuals and historical events based on information presented in texts.

Emerging	Expanding	Bridging
Readers select appropriate text evidence from a word bank to explain the relationships between individuals and historical events.	Readers select appropriate text evidence to complete sentence frames to explain the relationships between individuals and historical events.	Readers use appropriate text evidence to explain the relationships between individuals and historical events.

Writing Goal: Writers compose an informative text using linking words and phrases and specific vocabulary.

Emerging	Expanding	Bridging
Writers compose an informative sentence, incorporating specific vocabulary and appropriate linking words.	Writers compose an informative paragraph, incorporating specific vocabulary and appropriate linking words.	Writers compose an informative text incorporating specific vocabulary and appropriate linking words and phrases.

UNIT 3: MODULE A

Reading Goal: Readers use a text's chapters and sections to explain its structure.

Emerging	Expanding	Bridging
Readers identify chapters and sections in a text and use this information to complete a sentence frame about the text's structure.	Readers identify chapters and sections in a text and use this information to make a statement about the text's structure.	Readers describe the structure of a text, based on its chapters or sections.

Writing Goal: Writers create a narrative that is clearly developed and focused on the task, purpose, and audience.

Emerging	Expanding	Bridging
Writers plan a narrative, match examples of narrative techniques to literary terms, and use learned words and phrases to explain the narrative's task, purpose, and audience.	Writers work in pairs to plan a narrative, choose and give examples of techniques to develop the narrative, and write sentences explaining its task, purpose, and audience.	Writers plan a narrative, choose and give examples of techniques to develop the narrative, and write sentences explaining its task, purpose, and audience.

UNIT 3: MODULE B

Reading Goal: Readers determine the meanings of words and phrases to understand information in various texts.

Emerging	Expanding	Bridging
Readers use strategies and resources to determine the meanings of words and phrases to understand information in various texts.	Readers use strategies and resources to determine the meanings of words and phrases to understand information in various texts.	Readers use a variety of self-selected strategies and resources to determine the meanings of words and phrases.

Writing Goal: Writers use research and visuals to convey information effectively.

Emerging	Expanding	Bridging
Writers combine information from research and visuals effectively in informational writing, supported by sentence frames, note-taking guides, word banks, and image libraries.	Writers combine information from research and visuals effectively in informational writing, supported by sentence frames or note-taking guides.	Writers combine information from research and visuals effectively in informational writing.

UNIT 4: MODULE A

Reading Goal: Readers use details in texts to compare and contrast topics.

Emerging	Expanding	Bridging
Readers use graphic organizers or note-taking guides to understand topics in texts.	Readers use graphic organizers or note-taking guides to compare and contrast topics based on details in texts.	Readers compare and contrast topics based on details in texts.

Writing Goal: Writers compose opinion pieces on topics or texts, supporting a point of view with reasons and information and quoting accurately from text.

Emerging	Expanding	Bridging
Writers state a clear opinion and work with a partner to support the opinion.	Writers engage with topics or texts by stating a clear opinion and supporting the opinion.	Writers write an opinion piece and support their opinion with information from a text.

UNIT 4: MODULE B

Reading Goal: Readers identify multiple themes and ideas in various texts.

Emerging	Expanding	Bridging
Readers practice identifying themes in texts.	Readers use sentence frames to discuss different themes in various texts.	Readers use close reading and partner discussion to identify multiple themes and ideas in various texts.

Writing Goal: Writers understand that a conclusion summarizes the opinion presented.

Emerging	Expanding	Bridging
Writers accurately summarizes the opinion presented.	Writers use sentence frames to compose a conclusion that accurately summarizes the opinion presented.	Writers compose a conclusion that accurately summarizes the opinion presented.

450   Part 4 • English Language Learners Routines and Resources

Linguistic Contrastive Analysis Chart

	THE CONSONANTS OF ENGLISH			
IPA*	English	Spanish	Vietnamese	Cantonese
p	*pit* Aspirated at the start of a word or stressed syllable	*pato* (duck) Never aspirated	*pin* (battery)	*pʰa (to lie prone)* Always aspirated
b	*bit*	*barco* (boat) Substitute voiced bilabial fricative /ɑ/ in between vowels	*ba* (three) Implosive (air moves into the mouth during articulation)	**NO EQUIVALENT** Substitute /p/
m	*man*	*mundo* (world)	*mot* (one)	*ma* (mother)
w	*win*	*agua* (water)	**NO EQUIVALENT** Substitute word-initial /u/	*wa* (frog)
f	*fun*	*flor* (flower)	*ph*uʼoʼ*ng* (phoenix) Substitute sound made with both lips, rather than with the lower lip and the teeth like English /f/	*fa* (flower) Only occurs at the beginning of syllables
v	*very*	**NO EQUIVALENT** Learners can use correct sound	*Việt Nam* (Vietnam)	**NO EQUIVALENT** Substitute /f/
θ	*thing* Rare in other languages. When done correctly, the tongue will stick out between the teeth.	**NO EQUIVALENT** Learners can use correct sound	**NO EQUIVALENT** Substitute /tʰ/ or /f/	**NO EQUIVALENT** Substitute /tʰ/ or /f/
ð	*there* Rare in other languages. When done correctly, the tongue will stick out between the teeth.	*cada* (every) Sound exists in Spanish only between vowels; sometimes substitute voiceless θ.	**NO EQUIVALENT** Substitute /d/	**NO EQUIVALENT** Substitute /t/ or /f/
t	*time* Aspirated at the start of a word or stressed syllable English tongue-touch. Is a little farther back in the mouth than the other languages.	*tocar* (touch) Never aspirated	*tám* (eight) Distinguishes aspirated and non-aspirated	*tʰa (he/she)* Distinguishes aspirated and non-aspirated
d	*dime* English tongue-touch is a little farther back in the mouth than the other languages.	*dos* (two)	*Đōng* (Dong = unit of currency) Vietnamese /d/ is implosive (air moves into the mouth during articulation)	**NO EQUIVALENT** Substitute /t/
n	*name* English tongue-touch is a little farther back in the mouth than the other languages.	*nube* (cloud)	*nam* (south)	*na* (take)
s	*soy*	*seco* (dry)	*xem* (to see)	*sa* (sand) Substitute *sh*– sound before /u/ Difficult at ends of syllables and words
z	*zeal*	**NO EQUIVALENT** Learners can use correct sound	*rồi* (already) In northern dialect only Southern dialect, substitute /y/	**NO EQUIVALENT** Substitute /s/
ɾ	*butter* Written 't' and 'd' are pronounced with a quick tongue-tip tap.	*rana* (toad) Written as single *r* and thought of as an /r/ sound.	**NO EQUIVALENT** Substitute /t/	**NO EQUIVALENT** Substitute /t/
l	*loop* English tongue-touch is a little farther back in the mouth than the other languages. At the ends of syllables, the /l/ bunches up the back of the tongue, becoming velarized /ɫ/ or dark-l as in the word *ball*.	*libro* (book)	*cú lao* (island) /l/ does not occur at the ends of syllables	*lau* (angry) /l/ does not occur at the ends of syllables

* International Phonetic Alphabet

	THE CONSONANTS OF ENGLISH			
IPA*	**Hmong**	**Filipino**	**Korean**	**Mandarin**
p	***p**eb* (we/us/our) Distinguishes aspirated and non-aspirated	***p**aalam* (goodbye) Never aspirated	*pal* (sucking)	*pʰei* (cape) Always aspirated
b	**NO EQUIVALENT** Substitute /p/	***b**aka* (beef)	**NO EQUIVALENT** /b/ said between vowels Substitute /p/ elsewhere	**NO EQUIVALENT**
m	***m**us* (to go)	***m**abuti* (good)	***m**al* (horse)	***m**ei* (rose)
w	**NO EQUIVALENT** Substitute word-initial /**u**/	***w**alo (eight)*	*g**w**e* (box)	***w**en* (mosquito)
f	***f**aib* (to divide)	**NO EQUIVALENT** Substitute /p/	**NO EQUIVALENT** Substitute /p/	***f**a* (issue)
v	***V**aj* ('Vang' clan name)	**NO EQUIVALENT** Substitute /b/	**NO EQUIVALENT** Substitute /b/	**NO EQUIVALENT** Substitute /w/ or /f/
θ	**NO EQUIVALENT** Substitute /tʰ/ or /f/	**NO EQUIVALENT** Learners can use correct sound, but sometimes mispronounce voiced /ð/.	**NO EQUIVALENT** Substitute /t/	**NO EQUIVALENT** Substitute /t/ or /s/
ð	**NO EQUIVALENT** Substitute /d/	**NO EQUIVALENT** Learners can use correct sound	**NO EQUIVALENT** Substitute /d/	**NO EQUIVALENT** Substitute /t/ or /s/
t	***t**hem* (to pay) Distinguishes aspirated and non-aspirated	***t**akbo* (run) Never aspirated	***t**al* (daughter)	***t**a* (wet) Distinguishes aspirated and non-aspirated
d	***d**ev* (dog)	***d**eretso* (straight)	**NO EQUIVALENT** Substitute /d/ when said between vowels and /t/ elsewhere.	**NO EQUIVALENT** Substitute /t/
n	***n**oj* (to eat)	***n**aman* (too)	***n**al* (day)	***n**i* (you) May be confused with /l/
s	***x**a* (to send)	***s**ila* (they)	***s**al* (rice) Substitute *shi*– sound before /i/ and /z/ after a nasal consonant	***s**an (three)*
z	**NO EQUIVALENT** Learners can use correct sound	**NO EQUIVALENT** Learners can use correct sound	**NO EQUIVALENT** Learners can use correct sound	**NO EQUIVALENT** Substitute /ts/ or /tsʰ/
ɾ	**NO EQUIVALENT** Substitute /t/	***r**in/**d**in* (too) Variant of the /d/ sound	Only occurs between two vowels Considered an /l/ sound	**NO EQUIVALENT**
l	***l**os* (to come) /l/ does not occur at the ends of syllables	*sa**l**amat* (thank you)	*ba**l**am* (wind)	***l**an* (blue) Can be confused and substituted with /r/

* *International Phonetic Alphabet*

RESOURCES

IPA*	English	Spanish	Vietnamese	Cantonese
ɹ	*red* Rare sound in the world Includes lip-rounding	**NO EQUIVALENT** Substitute /r/ sound such as the tap /ɾ/ or the trilled /r/	**NO EQUIVALENT** Substitute /l/	**NO EQUIVALENT** Substitute /l/
ʃ	*sh*allow Often said with lip-rounding	**NO EQUIVALENT** Substitute /s/ or /tʃ/	*si*eu *th*ị (supermarket) Southern dialect only	**NO EQUIVALENT** Substitute /s/
ʒ	*vi*sion Rare sound in English	**NO EQUIVALENT** Substitute /z/ or /dʒ/	**NO EQUIVALENT** Substitute /s/	**NO EQUIVALENT** Substitute /s/
tʃ	*ch*irp	*ch*ico (boy)	*ch*ính *ph*ủ (government) Pronounced harder than English *ch*	**NO EQUIVALENT** Substitute /ts/
dʒ	*j*oy	**NO EQUIVALENT** Sometimes substituted with /ʃ/ sound Some dialects have this sound for the *ll* spelling as in *llamar*	**NO EQUIVALENT** Substitute /c/, the equivalent sound, but voiceless	**NO EQUIVALENT** Substitute /ts/ Only occurs at beginnings of syllables
j	*y*ou	*ci*elo (sky) Often substitute /dʒ/	*y*eu (to love)	*j*au (worry)
k	*k*ite Aspirated at the start of a word or stressed syllable	*c*asa (house) Never aspirated	*c*om (rice) Never aspirated	*kʰ*a (family) Distinguishes aspirated and non-aspirated
g	*g*oat	*g*ato (cat)	**NO EQUIVALENT** Substitute /k/	**NO EQUIVALENT** Substitute /k/
ŋ	*ki*ng	*ma*ng*o (mango)	*Ng*ūyen (proper last name)	*pha*ŋ (to cook)
h	*h*ope	*g*ente (people) Sometimes substitute sound with friction higher in the vocal tract as velar /x/ or uvular /χ/	*h*oa (flower)	*h*a (shrimp)

THE CONSONANTS OF ENGLISH

* International Phonetic Alphabet

THE CONSONANTS OF ENGLISH

IPA*	Hmong	Filipino	Korean	Mandarin
ɹ	NO EQUIVALENT Substitute /l/	NO EQUIVALENT Substitute the tap /ɾ/	NO EQUIVALENT Substitute the tap or /l/ confused with /l/	*ran* (caterpillar) Tongue tip curled further backward than for English /r/
ʃ	*sau* (to write)	*siya* (s/he)	Only occurs before /i/; Considered an /s/ sound	*shi* (wet)
ʒ	*zos* village)	NO EQUIVALENT Learners can use correct sound	NO EQUIVALENT	NO EQUIVALENT Substitute palatal affricate /tɕ/
tʃ	*cheb* (to sweep)	*tsa* (tea)	*cʰal* (kicking)	*cheng* (red)
dʒ	NO EQUIVALENT Substitute *ch* sound	*Dios* (God)	NO EQUIVALENT Substitute *ch* sound	NO EQUIVALENT Substitute /ts/
j	*Yaj* (Yang, clan name)	*tayo* (we)	*je:zan* (budget)	*yan* (eye)
k	*Koo* (Kong, clan name) Distinguishes aspirated and non-aspirated	*kalian* (when) Never aspirated	*kal* (spreading)	*ke* (nest) Distinguishes aspirated and non-aspirated
g	NO EQUIVALENT Substitute /k/	*gulay* (vegetable)	NO EQUIVALENT Substitute /k/ Learners use correct sound between two vowels	NO EQUIVALENT Substitute /k/
ŋ	*gus* (goose)	*angaw* (one million)	*baŋ* (room)	*tang* (gong) Sometimes add /k/ sound to the end
h	*hais* (to speak)	*hindi* (no)	*hal* (doing)	NO EQUIVALENT Substitute velar fricative /x/

International Phonetic Alphabet

THE VOWELS OF ENGLISH				
IPA*	English	Spanish	Vietnamese	Cantonese
i	*beat*	*hijo* (son)	*di* (to go)	*si* (silk)
ɪ	*bit* Rare in other languages Usually confused with /i/ (*meat* vs. *mit*)	**NO EQUIVALENT** Substitute /ē/	**NO EQUIVALENT** Substitute /ē/	*sik* (color) Only occurs before velars Substitute /ē/
e	*bait* End of vowel diphthongized—tongue moves up to /ē/ or short *e* position	*eco* (echo)	*kê* (millet)	*se* (to lend)
ɛ	*bet* Rare in other languages Learners may have difficulty distinguishing /ā/ and /e/ (short *e*): *pain* vs. *pen*	**NO EQUIVALENT** Substitute /ā/	**NO EQUIVALENT** Substitute /ā/	*seŋ* (sound) Only occurs before velars; difficult to distinguish from /ā/ in all positions
æ	*bat* Rare in other languages Learners may have trouble getting the tongue farther forward in the mouth	**NO EQUIVALENT** Substitute mid central /u/ (short *u*) or low front tense /o/ (short *o*)	*ghe* (boat)	**NO EQUIVALENT** Hard to distinguish between /æ/ and /ā/
u	*boot*	*uva* (grape)	*mua* (to buy)	*fu* (husband)
ʊ	*could* Rare in other languages Learners may have difficulty distinguishing the vowel sounds in *wooed* vs. *wood*	**NO EQUIVALENT** Substitute long *u*	**NO EQUIVALENT** Substitute long *u* (high back unrounded)	*suk* (uncle) Only occurs before velars Difficult to distinguish from long *u* in all positions
o	*boat* End of vowel diphthongized—tongue moves up to long *u* or ʊ position	*ojo* (eye)	*cô* (aunt)	*so* (comb)
ɔ	*law*	**NO EQUIVALENT** Substitute long *o* or short *o* Substituting long *o* will cause confusion (*low* vs. *law*); substituting short *o* will not	*cá* (fish)	*hok* (shell) Only occurs before velars Difficult to distinguish from long *o* in all positions
ɑ	*hot*	*mal* (bad)	*con* (child)	*sa* (sand)
ɑ ʊ	*house* Diphthong	*pauta*	*dao* (knife)	*sau* (basket)
ɔ ɪ	*boy* Diphthong	*hoy* (today)	*ròi* (already)	*soi* (grill)
ɑ ɪ	*bite* Diphthong	*baile* (dance)	*hai* (two)	*sai* (to waste)
ə	*about* Most common vowel in English; only in unstressed syllables Learners may have difficulty keeping it very short	**NO EQUIVALENT** Substitute short *u* or the full vowel from the word's spelling	*mua* (to buy)	**NO EQUIVALENT**
ʌ	*cut* Similar to schwa /ə/	**NO EQUIVALENT** Substitute short *o*	*giò'* (time)	*san* (new)
ɝ	*bird* Difficult articulation, unusual in the world but common in American English Learners must bunch the tongue and constrict the throat	**NO EQUIVALENT** Substitute short *u* or /er/ with trill	**NO EQUIVALENT** Substitute /ɨ/	*hæ* (boot)

* *International Phonetic Alphabet*

RESOURCES

		THE VOWELS OF ENGLISH		
IPA*	Hmong	Filipino	Korean	Mandarin
i	*ib* (one)	*ikaw* (you) This vowel is interchangeable with /ɪ/; hard for speakers to distinguish these	zɪːʃaŋ (market)	*ti* (ladder) Sometimes English /i/ can be produced shorter
ɪ	NO EQUIVALENT Substitute /ē/	*limampu* (fifty) This vowel is interchangeable with /ē/; hard for speakers to distinguish these	NO EQUIVALENT Substitute /ē/	NO EQUIVALENT
e	*tes* (hand)	*sero* (zero)	*be:da* (to cut)	*te* (nervous) Sometimes substitute English schwa /ə/
ɛ	NO EQUIVALENT Substitute /ā/	*sero* (zero) This vowel interchanges with /ā/ like *bait*; not difficult for speakers to learn	*thɛ:do* (attitude)	NO EQUIVALENT
æ	NO EQUIVALENT Substitute short *e*	NO EQUIVALENT Substitute short *o* as in *hot*	NO EQUIVALENT	NO EQUIVALENT Substitute /ə/ or short *u*
u	*kub* (hot or gold)	*tunay* (actual) This vowel interchanges with vowel in *could*; not difficult for speakers to learn	*zu:bag* (watermelon)	*lu* (hut) Sometimes English long *u* can be produced shorter
ʊ	NO EQUIVALENT Substitute a sound like long *e* (mid central with lips slightly rounded)	*gumawa* (act) This vowel interchanges with long *u* like *boot*; not difficult for speakers to learn	NO EQUIVALENT	NO EQUIVALENT
o	NO EQUIVALENT	*ubo* (cough)	*bo:zu* (salary)	*mo* (sword) This vowel is a little lower than English vowel
ɔ	*Yaj* (Yang clan name)	NO EQUIVALENT Spoken as short *o*, as in *hot*	NO EQUIVALENT	NO EQUIVALENT Substitute long *o*
ɑ	*mov* (cooked rice)	*talim* (blade)	*ma:l* (speech)	*ta* (he/she) Sometimes substitute back long *o* or *u*
ɑʊ	*plaub* (four)	*ikaw* (you)	NO EQUIVALENT	NO EQUIVALENT
ɔɪ	NO EQUIVALENT	*apoy* (fire)	NO EQUIVALENT	NO EQUIVALENT
ɑɪ	*qaib* (chicken)	*himatay* (faint)	NO EQUIVALENT	NO EQUIVALENT
ə	NO EQUIVALENT	NO EQUIVALENT Spoken as short *o*, as in *hot*	NO EQUIVALENT Difficult sound for learners	NO EQUIVALENT
ʌ	NO EQUIVALENT	NO EQUIVALENT Spoken as short *o*, as in *hot*	NO EQUIVALENT	NO EQUIVALENT
ɝ	NO EQUIVALENT Substitute diphthong /əɨ/	NO EQUIVALENT Spoken as many different vowels (depending on English spelling) plus tongue tap /ɾ/	NO EQUIVALENT	NO EQUIVALENT

* International Phonetic Alphabet

Acknowledgments

Photographs

Photo locators denoted as follows: Top (T), Center (C), Bottom (B), Left (L), Right (R), Background (Bkgd)

4 © Leland Bobbé/Corbis; **5(TL), 8, 10, 12** Peachtree Publishers; **5(BC), 34, 36, 38** Heinemann Library; **46** ©Ian Dagnall/Alamy; **47(BC), 76, 78, 80** HarperCollins Publishers; **88** Vadim Sadovski/Shutterstock; **89(TL), 92, 94, 96** Simon & Schuster; **89(BC), 118, 120, 122** Celebration Press; **130** Andrey Burmakin/Shutterstock; **131(BC), 160, 162, 164** Children's Press.